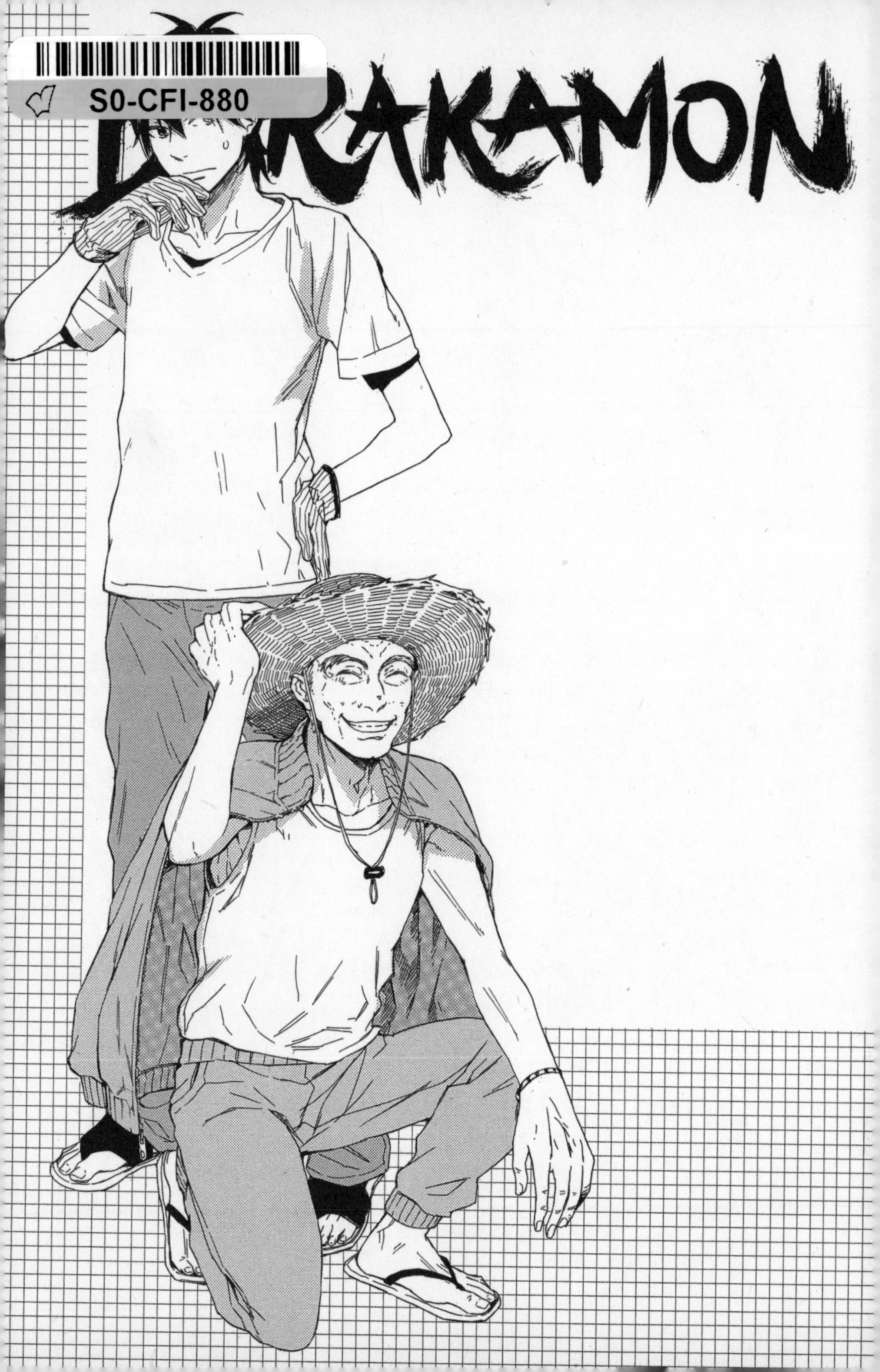
RAKAMON

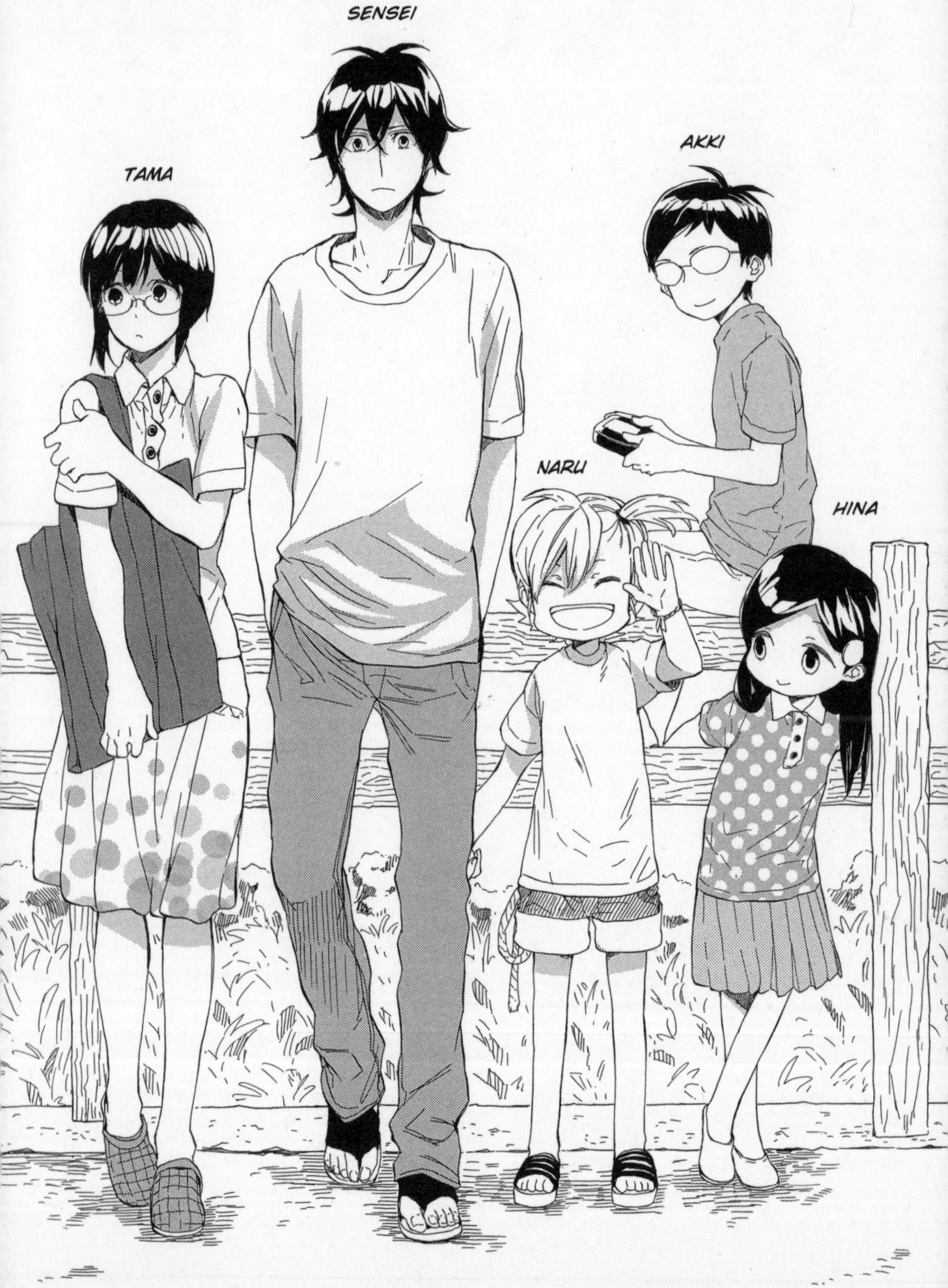
AKKI
HINA
NARU
SENSEI
TAMA

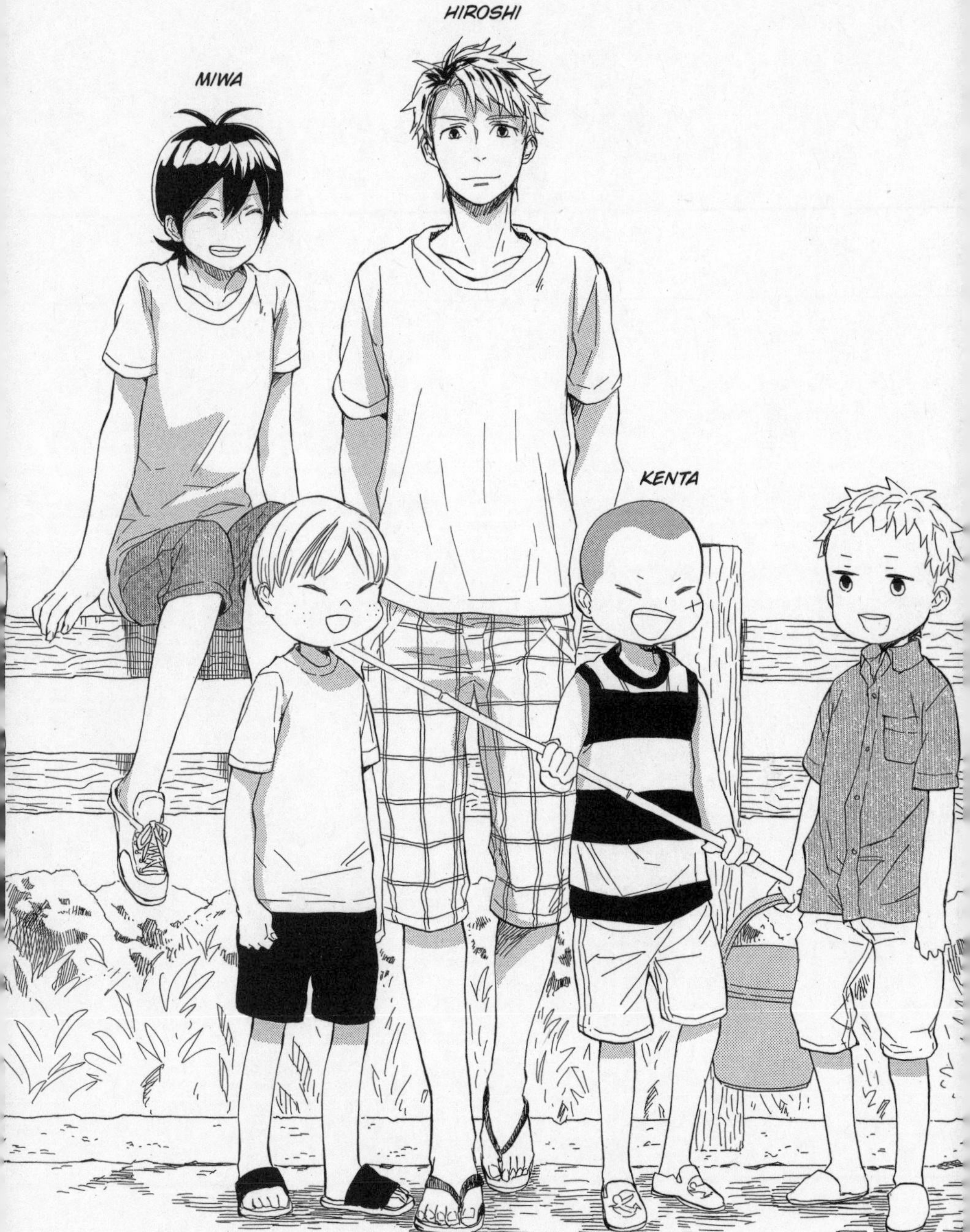
KENTA
HIROSHI
MIWA

Contents

ACT.37
GIPPAKA KAJJA
(Translation: Pretty Hair)

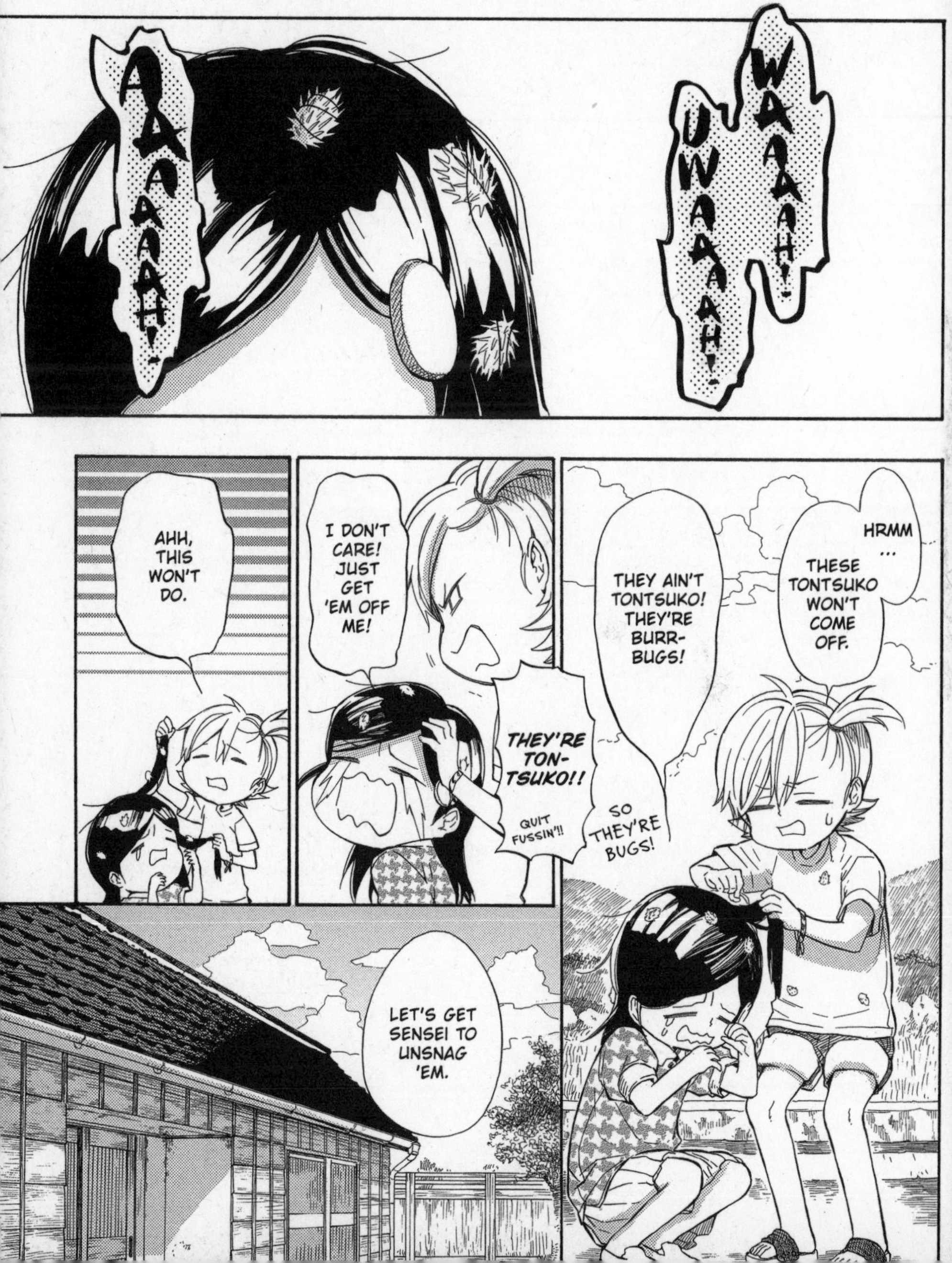
WAAAAH!
UWAAAAH!
AAAAAH!
HRMM... THESE TONTSUKO WON'T COME OFF.
THEY AIN'T TONTSUKO! THEY'RE BURR-BUGS!
THEY'RE TON-TSUKO!!
SO THEY'RE BUGS!
I DON'T CARE! JUST GET 'EM OFF ME!
QUIT FUSSIN'!!
AHH, THIS WON'T DO.
LET'S GET SENSEI TO UNSNAG 'EM.

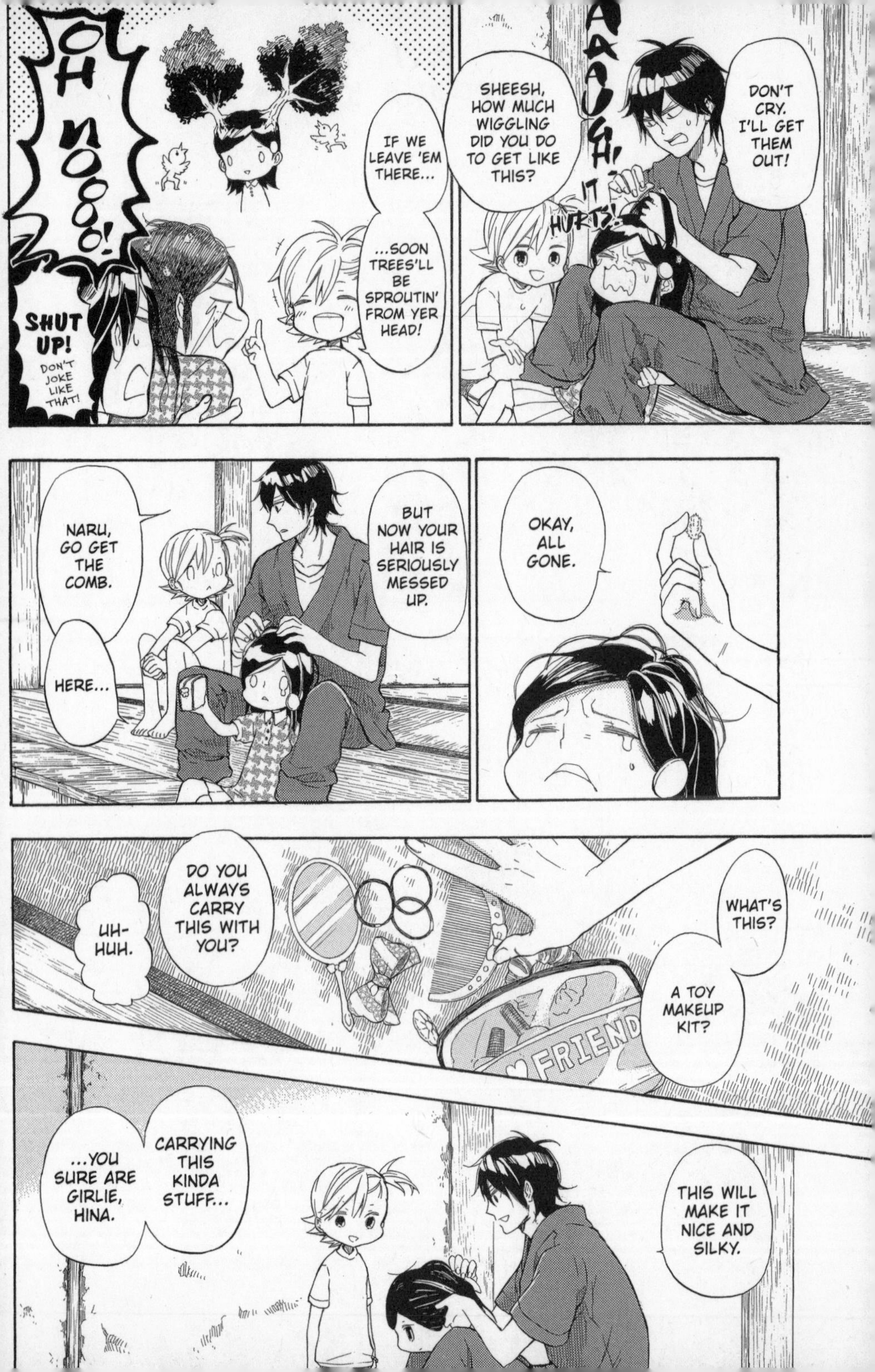

DON'T CRY. I'LL GET THEM OUT!
AAAUGH!
IT HURTS!
SHEESH, HOW MUCH WIGGLING DID YOU DO TO GET LIKE THIS?
IF WE LEAVE 'EM THERE...
...SOON TREES'LL BE SPROUTIN' FROM YER HEAD!
OH NOOOOO!
SHUT UP!
DON'T JOKE LIKE THAT!
OKAY, ALL GONE.
BUT NOW YOUR HAIR IS SERIOUSLY MESSED UP.
NARU, GO GET THE COMB.
HERE...
WHAT'S THIS?
A TOY MAKEUP KIT?
DO YOU ALWAYS CARRY THIS WITH YOU?
UH-HUH.
FRIEND
THIS WILL MAKE IT NICE AND SILKY.
CARRYING THIS KINDA STUFF...
...YOU SURE ARE GIRLIE, HINA.

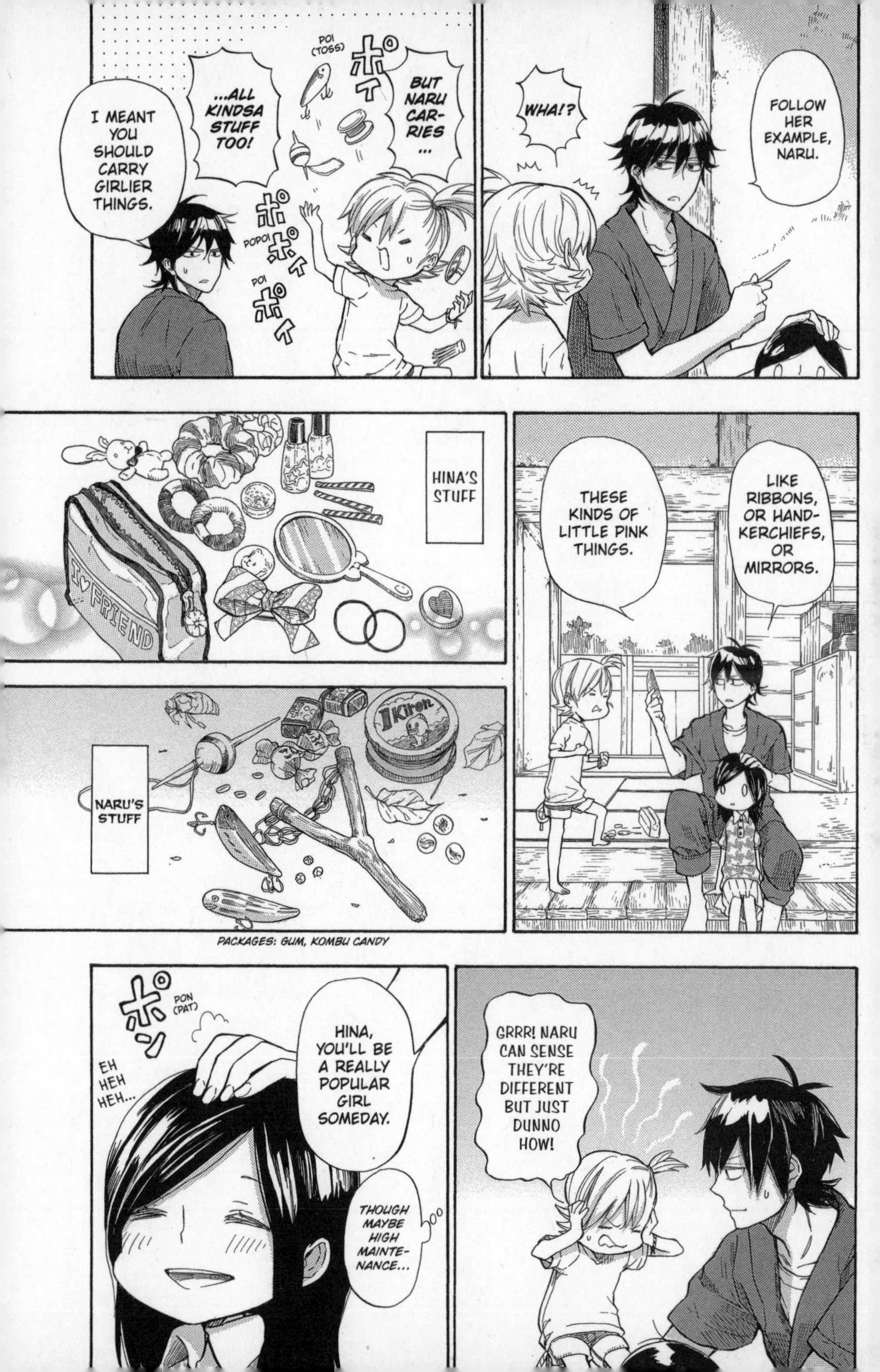
FOLLOW HER EXAMPLE, NARU.
WHA!?
BUT NARU CARRIES...
ポイ
POI (TOSS)
...ALL KINDSA STUFF TOO!
ポポイ
POPOI
ポイ
POI
I MEANT YOU SHOULD CARRY GIRLIER THINGS.
LIKE RIBBONS, OR HANDKERCHIEFS, OR MIRRORS.
THESE KINDS OF LITTLE PINK THINGS.
HINA'S STUFF
I ♥ FRIEND
Kiren
NARU'S STUFF
PACKAGES: GUM, KOMBU CANDY
GRRR! NARU CAN SENSE THEY'RE DIFFERENT BUT JUST DUNNO HOW!
ポン
PON (PAT)
HINA, YOU'LL BE A REALLY POPULAR GIRL SOMEDAY.
EH HEH HEH...
THOUGH MAYBE HIGH MAINTENANCE...

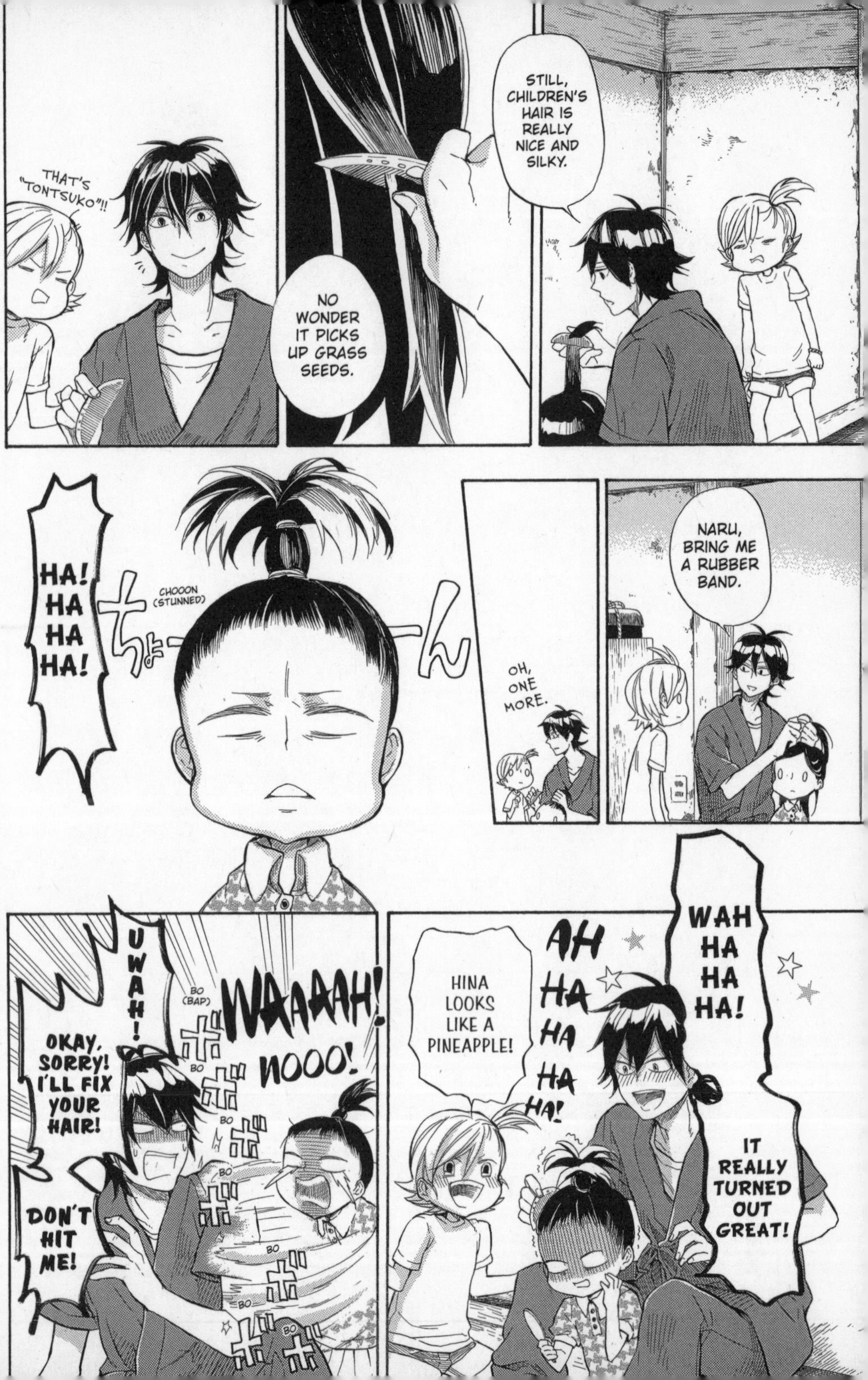
STILL, CHILDREN'S HAIR IS REALLY NICE AND SILKY.
NO WONDER IT PICKS UP GRASS SEEDS.
THAT'S "TONTSUKO"!!
NARU, BRING ME A RUBBER BAND.
OH, ONE MORE.
CHOOON (STUNNED)
ちょーん
HA! HA HA HA!
WAH HA HA HA!
AH HA HA HA HA!
HINA LOOKS LIKE A PINEAPPLE!
IT REALLY TURNED OUT GREAT!
WAAAAH!
NOOO!
UWAH!
BO (BAP)
ボ
OKAY, SORRY! I'LL FIX YOUR HAIR!
DON'T HIT ME!

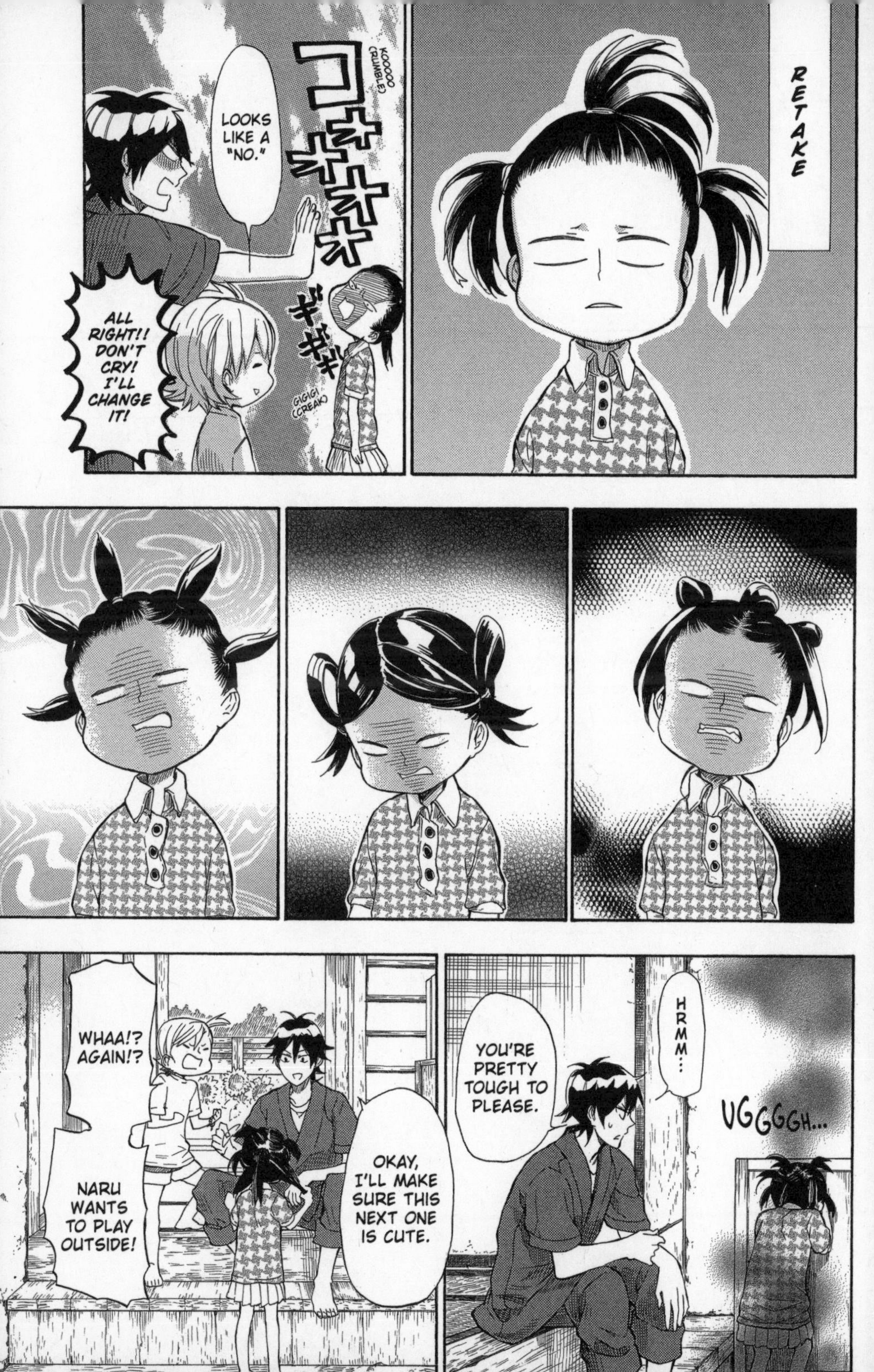
RETAKE
KOOOOO (RUMBLE)
LOOKS LIKE A "NO."
GIGIGI (CREAK)
ALL RIGHT!! DON'T CRY! I'LL CHANGE IT!
HRMM...
YOU'RE PRETTY TOUGH TO PLEASE.
UGGGGH...
OKAY, I'LL MAKE SURE THIS NEXT ONE IS CUTE.
WHAA!? AGAIN!?
NARU WANTS TO PLAY OUTSIDE!

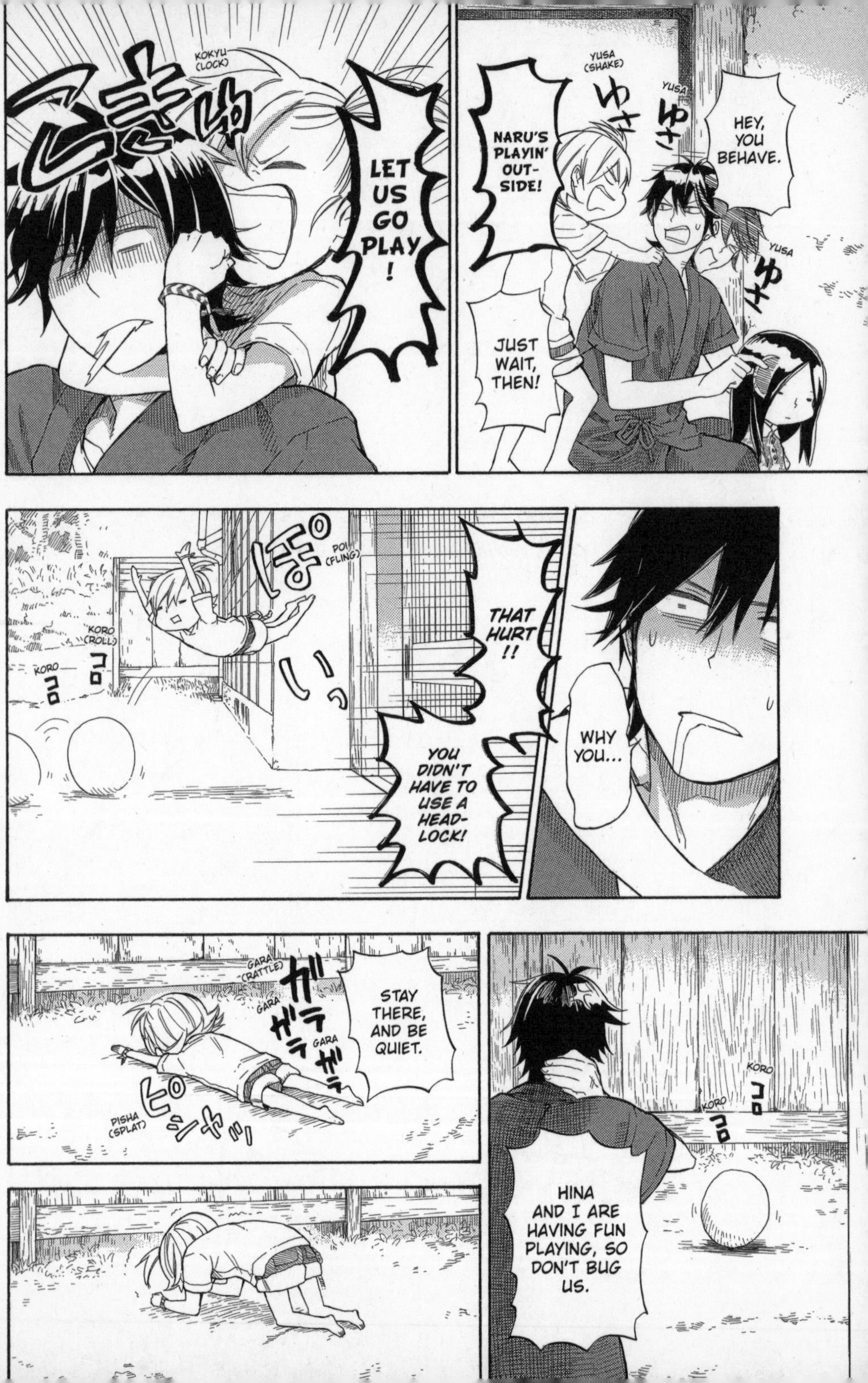
HEY, YOU BEHAVE.
YUSA
ゆさ
YUSA
ゆさ
YUSA (SHAKE)
ゆさ
NARU'S PLAYIN' OUT-SIDE!
JUST WAIT, THEN!
LET US GO PLAY!
KOKYU (LOCK)
こきゅ
WHY YOU...
THAT HURT!!
YOU DIDN'T HAVE TO USE A HEAD-LOCK!
POI (FLING)
ぽい
KORO (ROLL)
コロ
KORO
コロ
KORO
コロ
KORO
コロ
HINA AND I ARE HAVING FUN PLAYING, SO DON'T BUG US.
STAY THERE, AND BE QUIET.
GARA (RATTLE)
ガラ
GARA
ガラ
GARA
ガラ
PISHA (SPLAT)
ぴしゃ

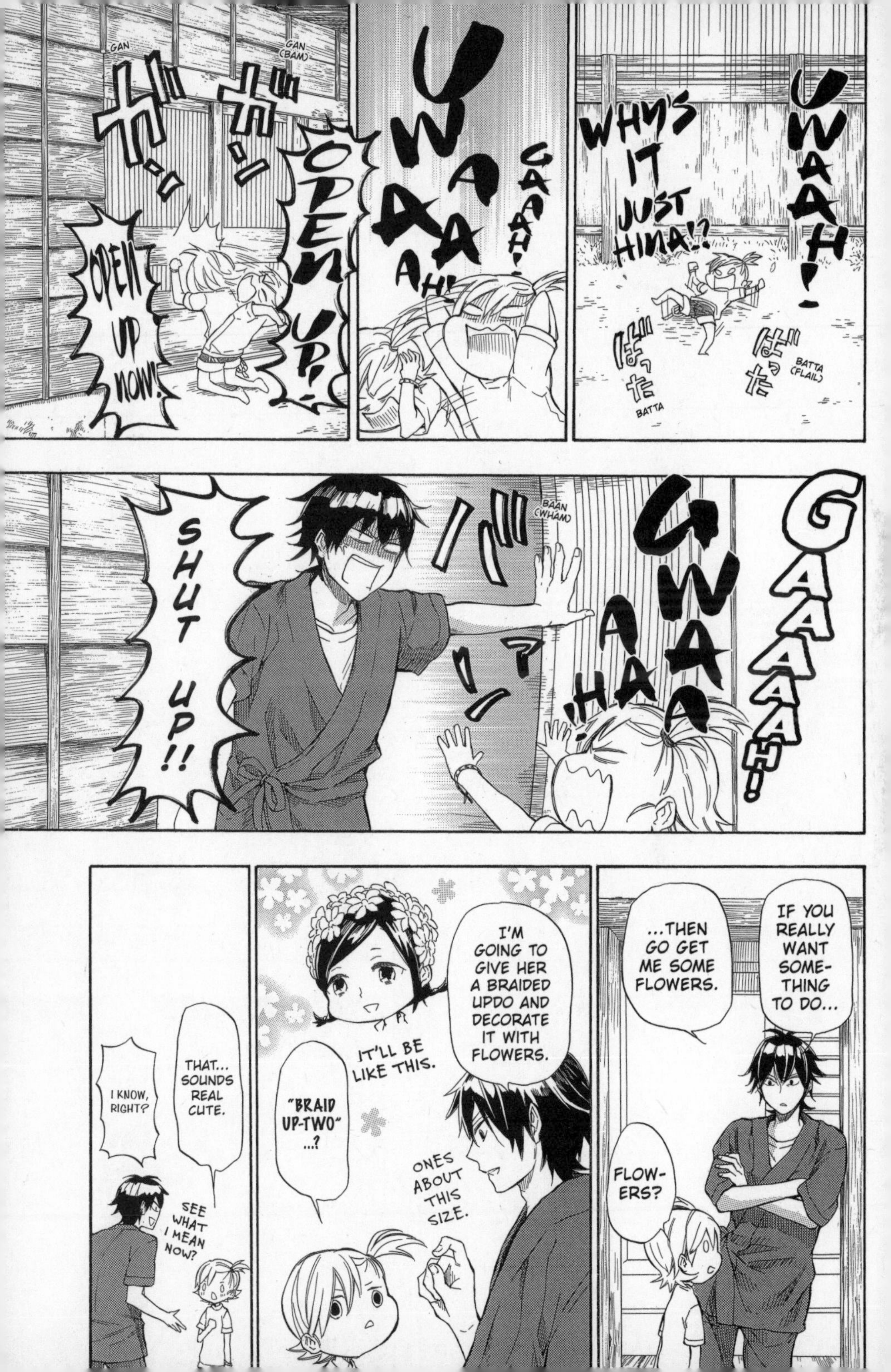
UWAAH!
WHY'S IT JUST HINA!?
BATTA (FLAIL)
BATTA
UWAAAAH!
GAAAH!
OPEN UP!
GAN (BAM)
GAN
OPEN UP NOW!
GAAAAAAH!
UWAAHAHA!
BAAN (WHAM)
SHUT UP!!
IF YOU REALLY WANT SOMETHING TO DO...
...THEN GO GET ME SOME FLOWERS.
FLOWERS?
I'M GOING TO GIVE HER A BRAIDED UPDO AND DECORATE IT WITH FLOWERS.
IT'LL BE LIKE THIS.
ONES ABOUT THIS SIZE.
"BRAID UP-TWO" ...?
THAT... SOUNDS REAL CUTE.
I KNOW, RIGHT?
SEE WHAT I MEAN NOW?

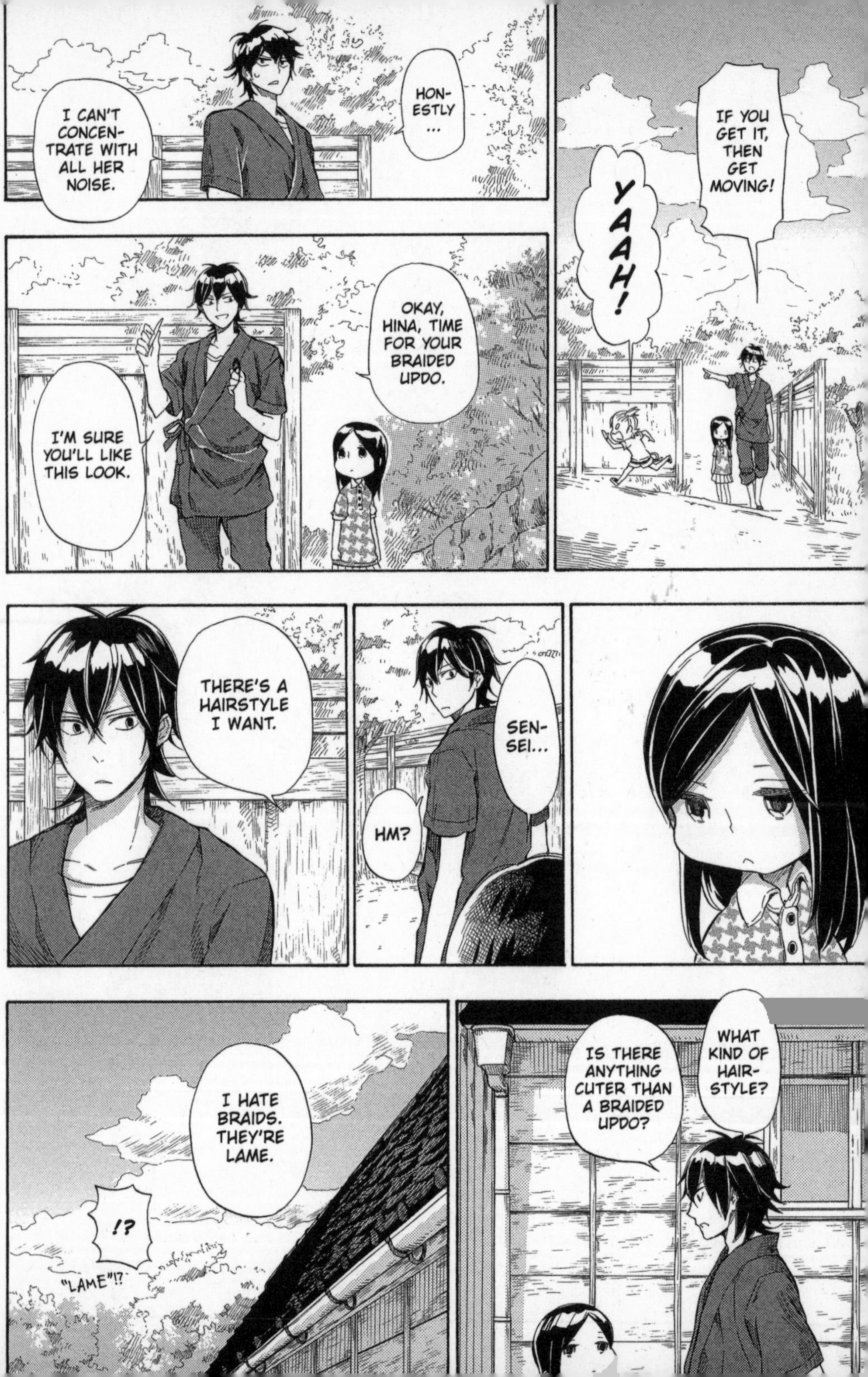
IF YOU GET IT, THEN GET MOVING!
YAAAH!
HON-ESTLY...
I CAN'T CONCEN-TRATE WITH ALL HER NOISE.
OKAY, HINA, TIME FOR YOUR BRAIDED UPDO.
I'M SURE YOU'LL LIKE THIS LOOK.
SEN-SEI...
HM?
THERE'S A HAIRSTYLE I WANT.
WHAT KIND OF HAIR-STYLE?
IS THERE ANYTHING CUTER THAN A BRAIDED UPDO?
I HATE BRAIDS. THEY'RE LAME.
!?
"LAME"!?

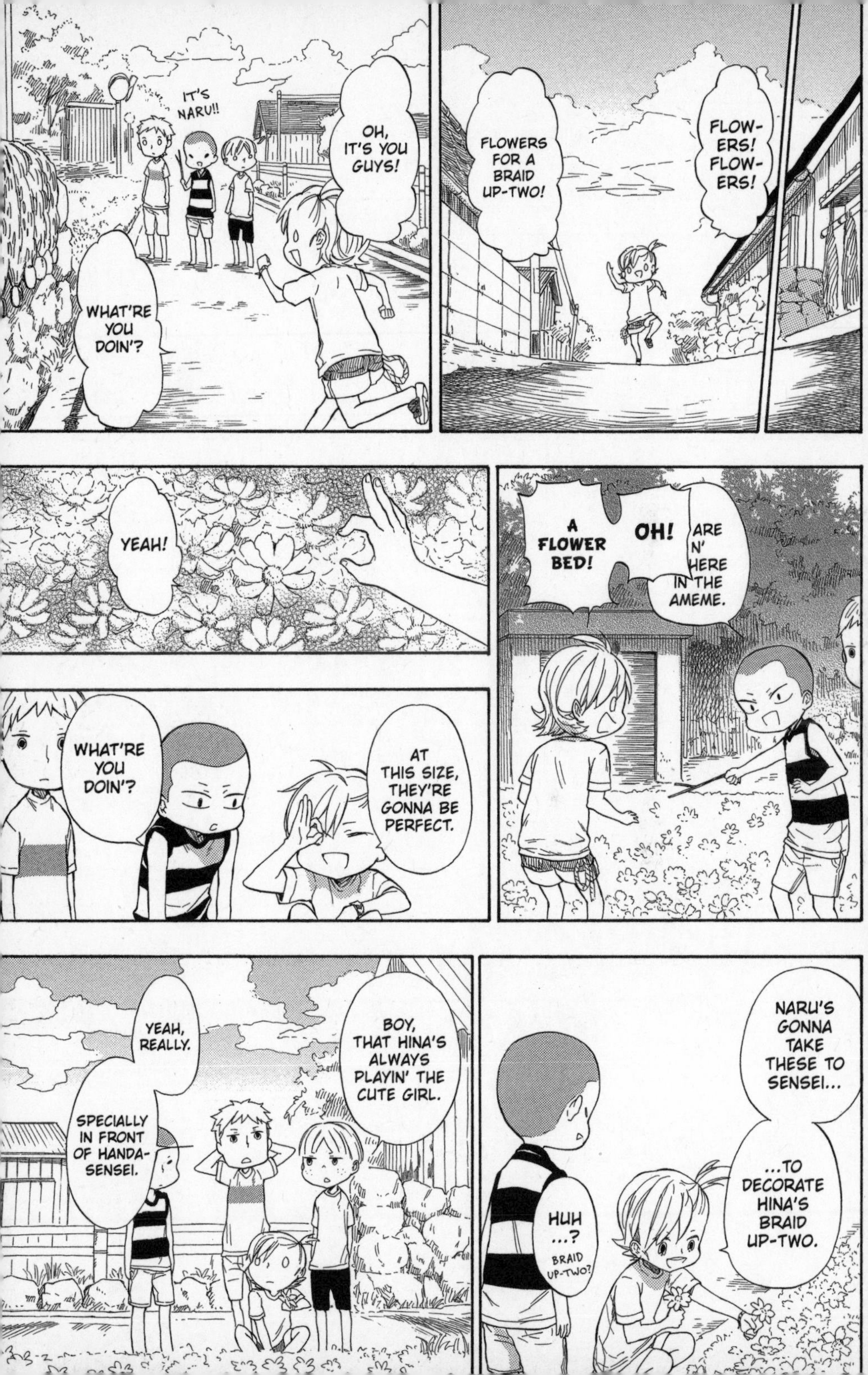
FLOWERS! FLOWERS!
FLOWERS FOR A BRAID UP-TWO!
OH, IT'S YOU GUYS!
IT'S NARU!!
WHAT'RE YOU DOIN'?
ARE N' HERE IN THE AMEME.
OH!
A FLOWER BED!
YEAH!
AT THIS SIZE, THEY'RE GONNA BE PERFECT.
WHAT'RE YOU DOIN'?
NARU'S GONNA TAKE THESE TO SENSEI...
...TO DECORATE HINA'S BRAID UP-TWO.
HUH ...?
BRAID UP-TWO?
BOY, THAT HINA'S ALWAYS PLAYIN' THE CUTE GIRL.
YEAH, REALLY.
SPECIALLY IN FRONT OF HANDA-SENSEI.

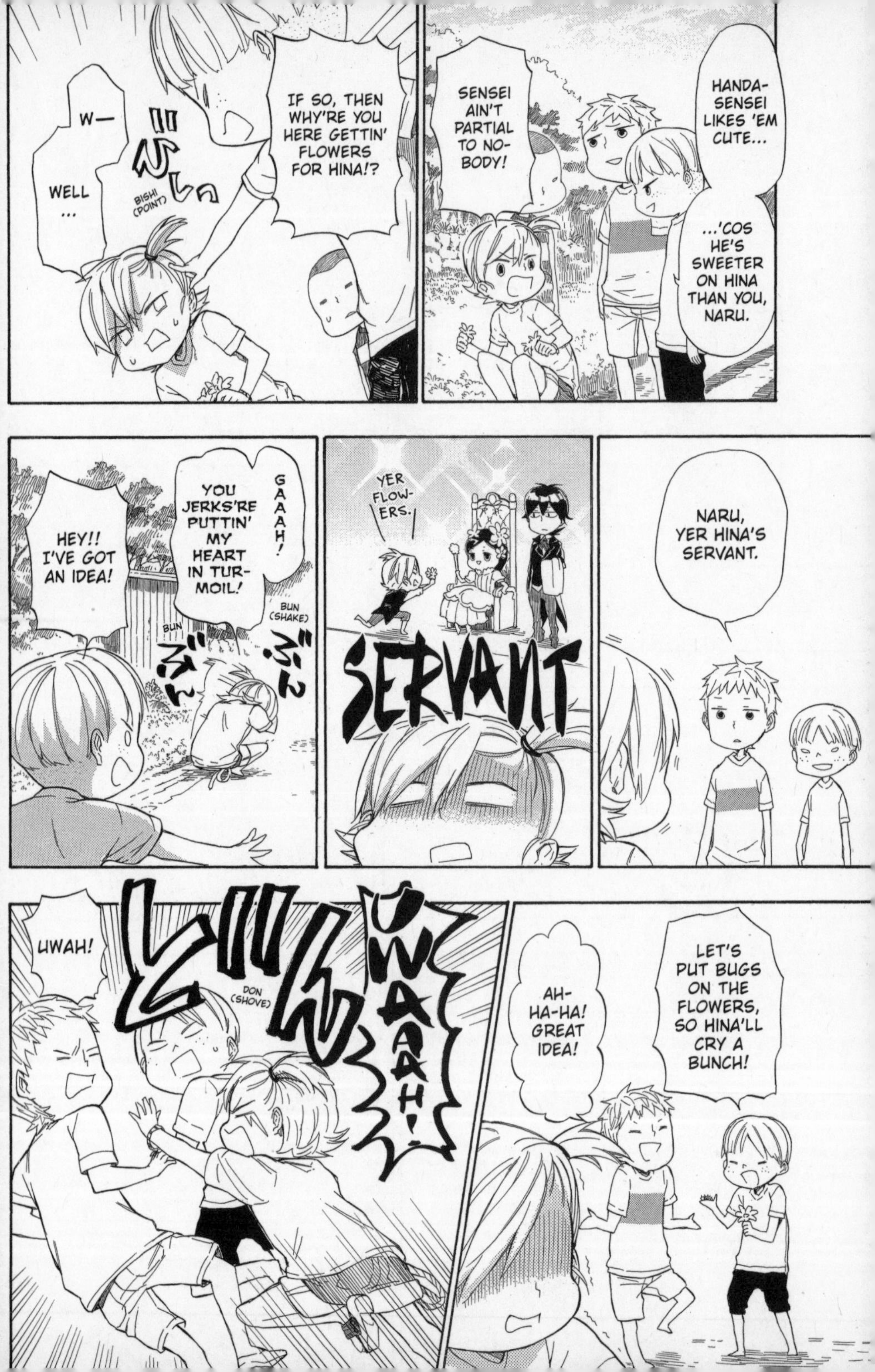
HANDA-SENSEI LIKES 'EM CUTE...
...'COS HE'S SWEETER ON HINA THAN YOU, NARU.
SENSEI AIN'T PARTIAL TO NO-BODY!
IF SO, THEN WHY'RE YOU HERE GETTIN' FLOWERS FOR HINA!?
W— WELL ...
BISHI (POINT)
NARU, YER HINA'S SERVANT.
YER FLOW-ERS.
SERVANT
GAAAAH!
YOU JERKS'RE PUTTIN' MY HEART IN TUR-MOIL!
BUN (SHAKE)
BUN
HEY!! I'VE GOT AN IDEA!
LET'S PUT BUGS ON THE FLOWERS, SO HINA'LL CRY A BUNCH!
AH-HA-HA! GREAT IDEA!
WAAAAH!
DON (SHOVE)
UWAH!

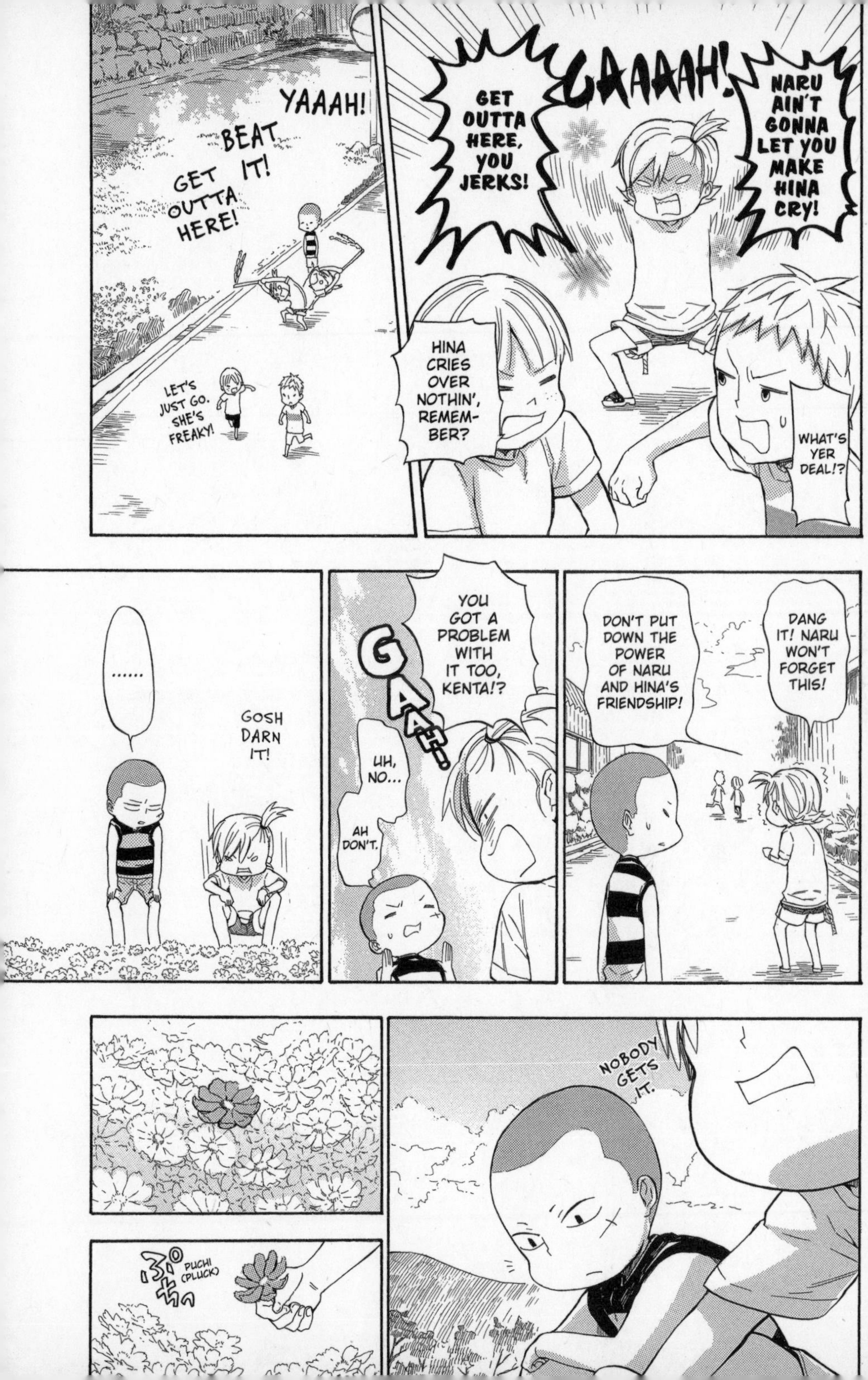
NARU AIN'T GONNA LET YOU MAKE HINA CRY!
GAAAAH!
GET OUTTA HERE, YOU JERKS!
WHAT'S YER DEAL!?
HINA CRIES OVER NOTHIN', REMEMBER?
YAAAH!
BEAT IT!
GET OUTTA HERE!
LET'S JUST GO. SHE'S FREAKY!
DANG IT! NARU WON'T FORGET THIS!
DON'T PUT DOWN THE POWER OF NARU AND HINA'S FRIENDSHIP!
YOU GOT A PROBLEM WITH IT TOO, KENTA!?
GAAAH!
UH, NO...
AH DON'T.
GOSH DARN IT!
......
NOBODY GETS IT.
ぷち PUCHI (PLUCK)

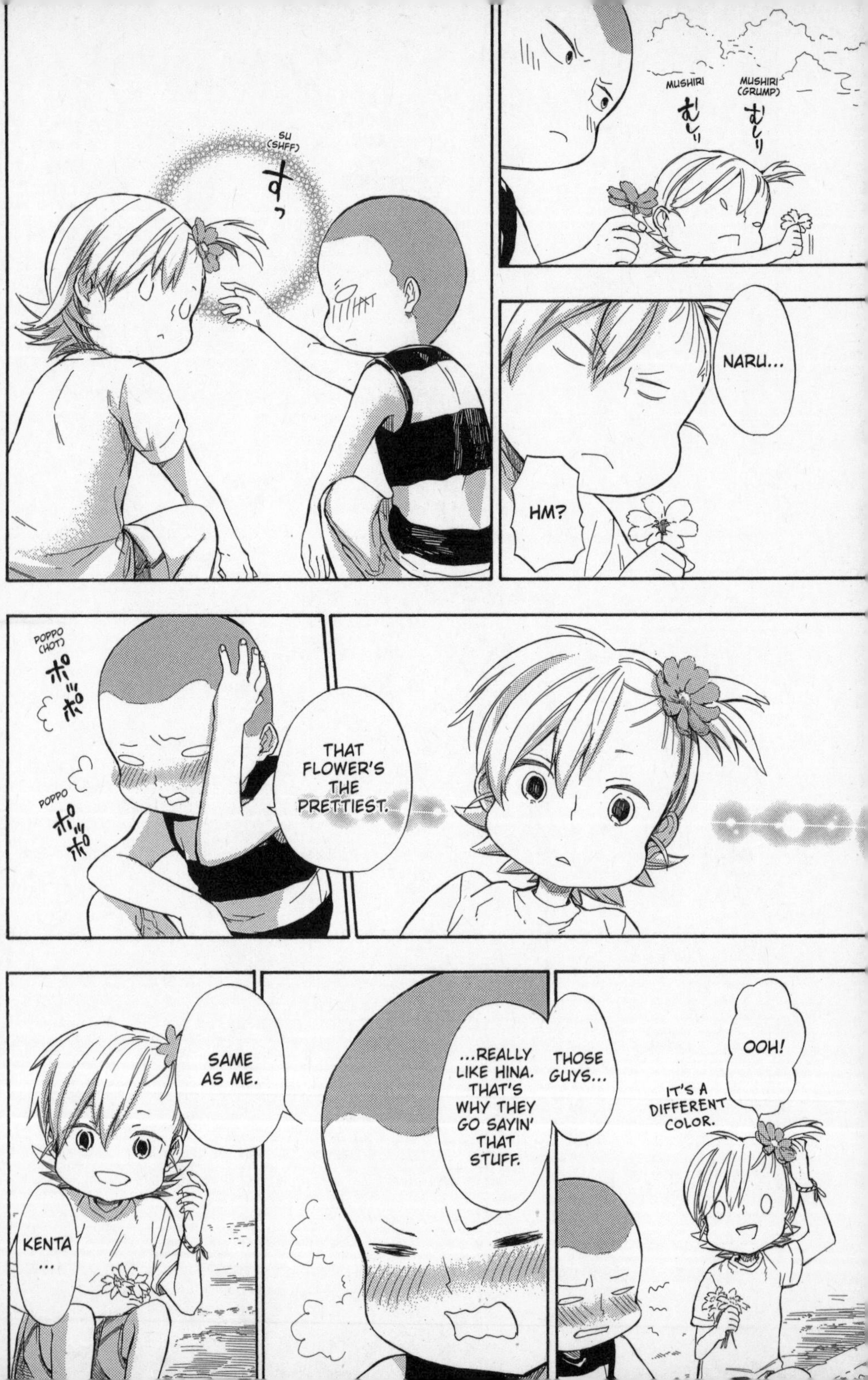
MUSHIRI (GRUMP)
むしり
MUSHIRI
むしり
NARU...
HM?
SU (SHFF)
すっ
THAT FLOWER'S THE PRETTIEST.
POPPO (HOT)
ポッポ
POPPO
ポッポ
OOH!
IT'S A DIFFERENT COLOR.
THOSE GUYS...
...REALLY LIKE HINA. THAT'S WHY THEY GO SAYIN' THAT STUFF.
SAME AS ME.
KENTA ...

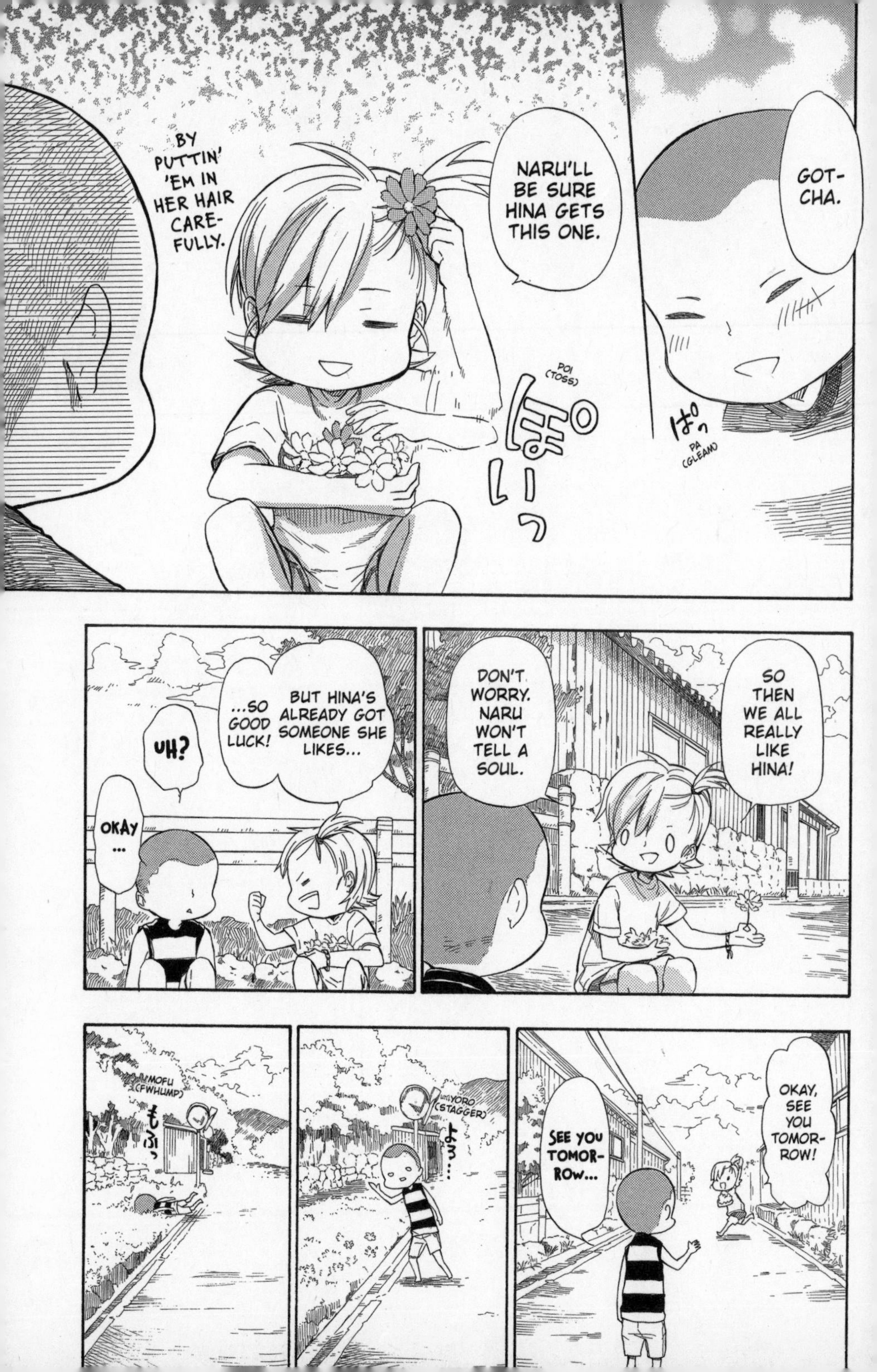
GOT-CHA.
ぱっ
PA (GLEAM)
NARU'LL BE SURE HINA GETS THIS ONE.
ぽいっ
POI (TOSS)
BY PUTTIN' 'EM IN HER HAIR CARE-FULLY.
SO THEN WE ALL REALLY LIKE HINA!
DON'T WORRY. NARU WON'T TELL A SOUL.
BUT HINA'S ALREADY GOT SOMEONE SHE LIKES...
...SO GOOD LUCK!
UH?
OKAY ...
OKAY, SEE YOU TOMOR-ROW!
SEE YOU TOMOR-ROW...
よろ...
YORO (STAGGER)
もふっ
MOFU (FWHUMP)

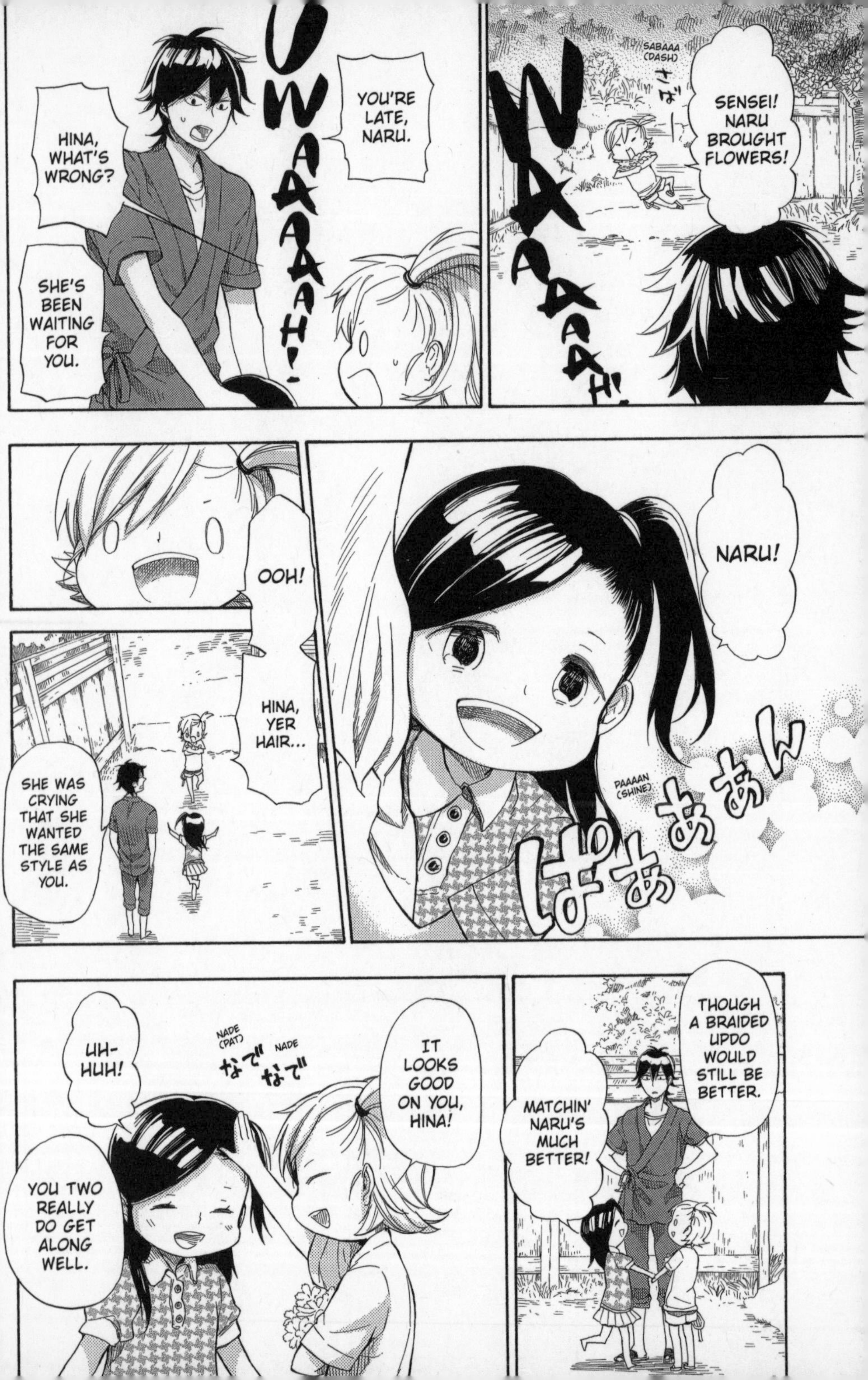
SABAAA (DASH)
さばー
SENSEI! NARU BROUGHT FLOWERS!
WAAAAAH!
UWAAAAAH!
YOU'RE LATE, NARU.
HINA, WHAT'S WRONG?
SHE'S BEEN WAITING FOR YOU.
NARU!
PAAAAN (SHINE)
ぱあああん
OOH!
HINA, YER HAIR...
SHE WAS CRYING THAT SHE WANTED THE SAME STYLE AS YOU.
THOUGH A BRAIDED UPDO WOULD STILL BE BETTER.
MATCHIN' NARU'S MUCH BETTER!
IT LOOKS GOOD ON YOU, HINA!
NADE (PAT)
なで
NADE
なで
UH-HUH!
YOU TWO REALLY DO GET ALONG WELL.

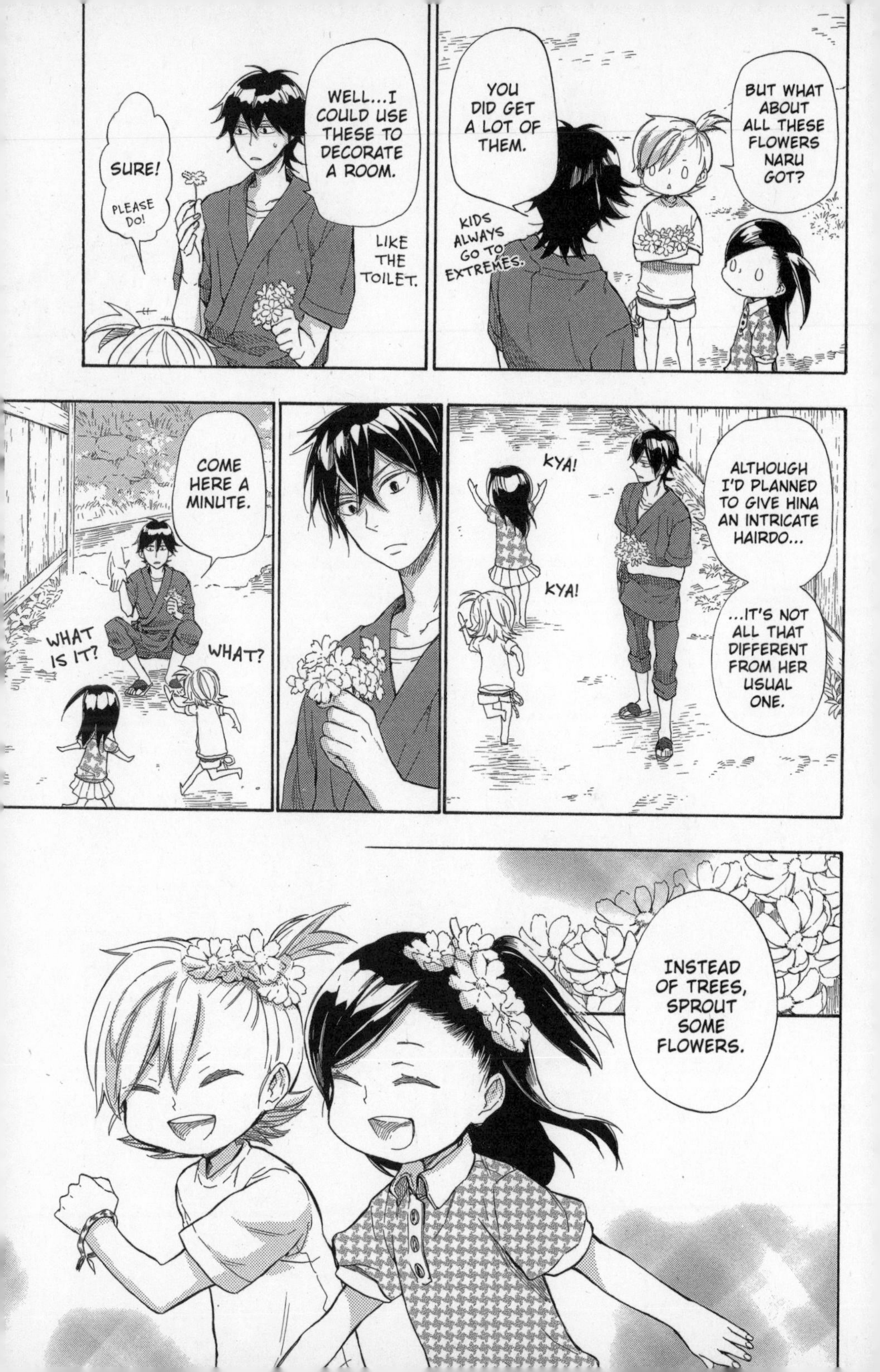
BUT WHAT ABOUT ALL THESE FLOWERS NARU GOT?
YOU DID GET A LOT OF THEM.
KIDS ALWAYS GO TO EXTREMES.
WELL...I COULD USE THESE TO DECORATE A ROOM.
LIKE THE TOILET.
SURE!
PLEASE DO!
ALTHOUGH I'D PLANNED TO GIVE HINA AN INTRICATE HAIRDO...
...IT'S NOT ALL THAT DIFFERENT FROM HER USUAL ONE.
KYA!
KYA!
COME HERE A MINUTE.
WHAT?
WHAT IS IT?
INSTEAD OF TREES, SPROUT SOME FLOWERS.

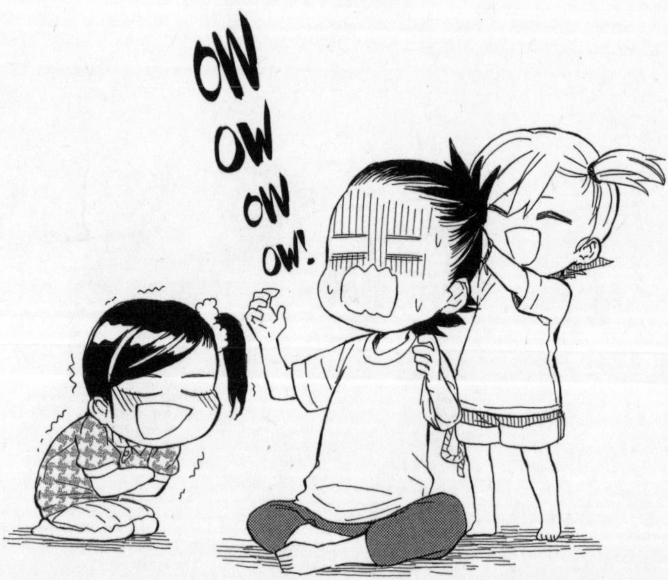
OW
OW
OW
OW!

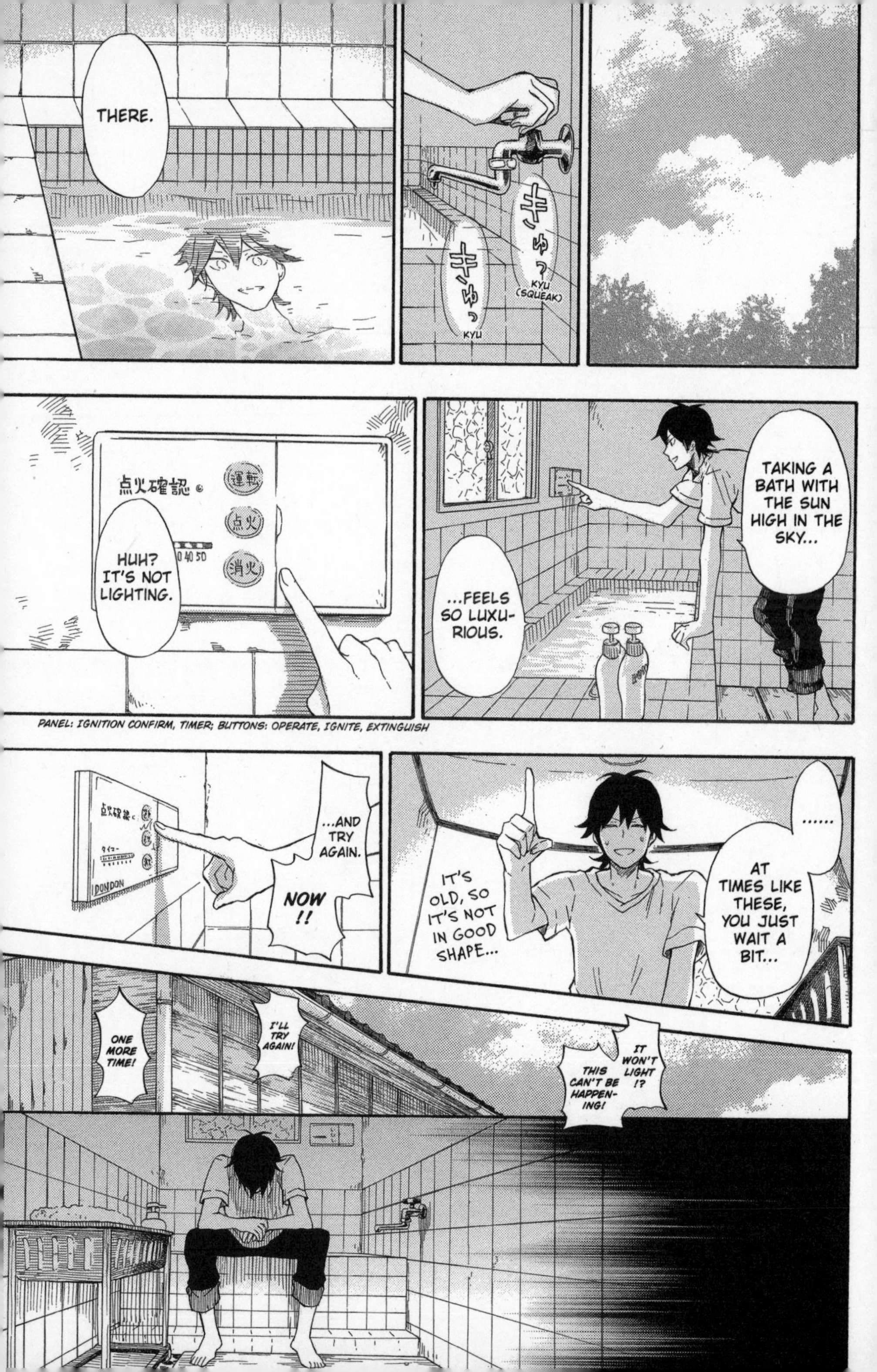
きゅっ
KYU (SQUEAK)
きゅっ
KYU
THERE.
TAKING A BATH WITH THE SUN HIGH IN THE SKY...
...FEELS SO LUXURIOUS.
点火確認
運転
点火
消火
HUH? IT'S NOT LIGHTING.
PANEL: IGNITION CONFIRM, TIMER; BUTTONS: OPERATE, IGNITE, EXTINGUISH
......
AT TIMES LIKE THESE, YOU JUST WAIT A BIT...
IT'S OLD, SO IT'S NOT IN GOOD SHAPE...
...AND TRY AGAIN.
NOW!!
DONDON
IT WON'T LIGHT!?
THIS CAN'T BE HAPPENING!
I'LL TRY AGAIN!
ONE MORE TIME!

ACT.38 BYARA

(Translation: Dry Twigs)

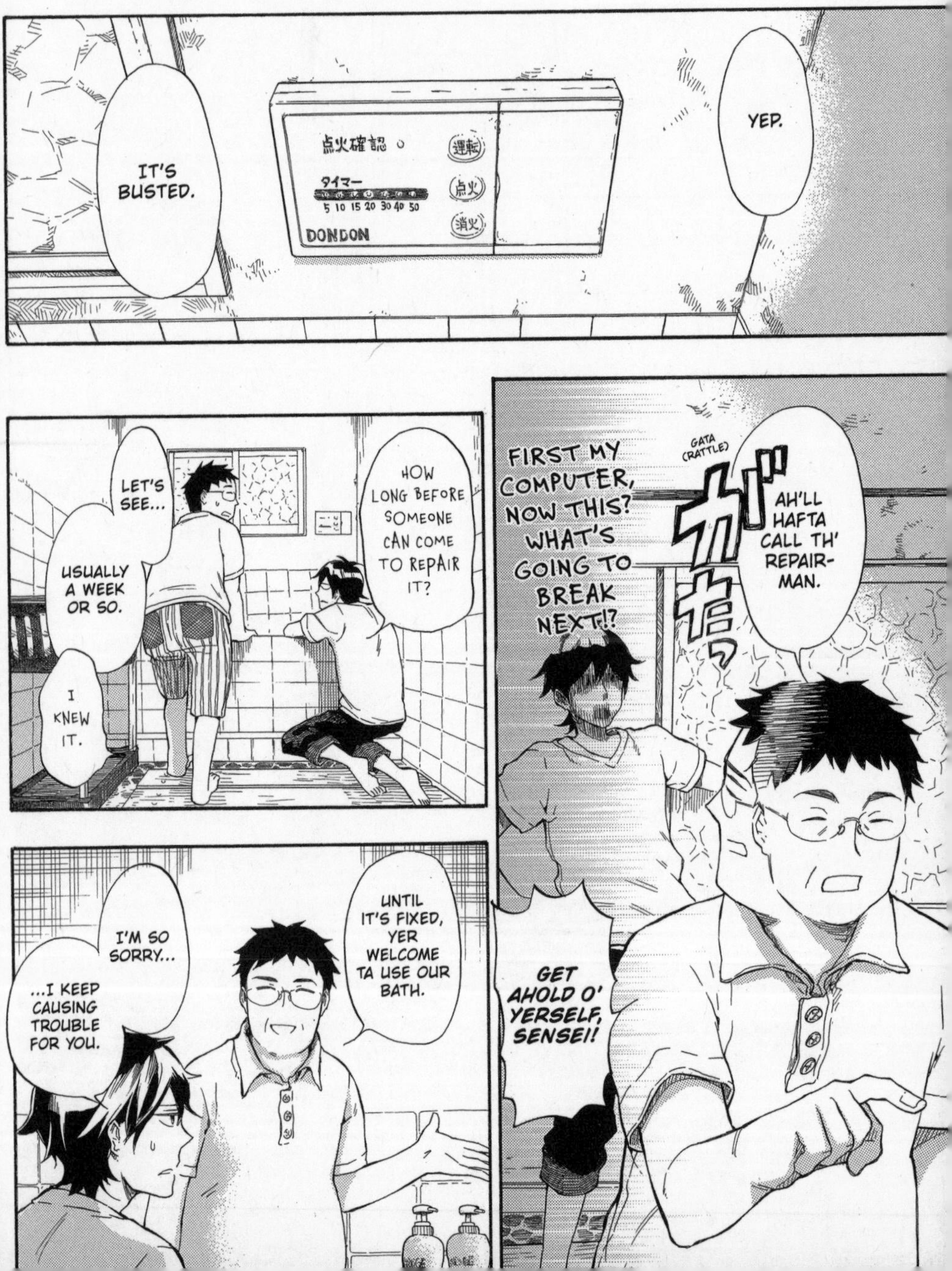
YEP.
点火確認
運転
タイマー
点火
5 10 15 20 30 40 50
消火
DONDON
IT'S BUSTED.
GATA (RATTLE)
AH'LL HAFTA CALL TH' REPAIR-MAN.
FIRST MY COMPUTER, NOW THIS? WHAT'S GOING TO BREAK NEXT!?
GET AHOLD O' YERSELF, SENSEI!
HOW LONG BEFORE SOMEONE CAN COME TO REPAIR IT?
LET'S SEE...
USUALLY A WEEK OR SO.
I KNEW IT.
UNTIL IT'S FIXED, YER WELCOME TA USE OUR BATH.
I'M SO SORRY...
...I KEEP CAUSING TROUBLE FOR YOU.

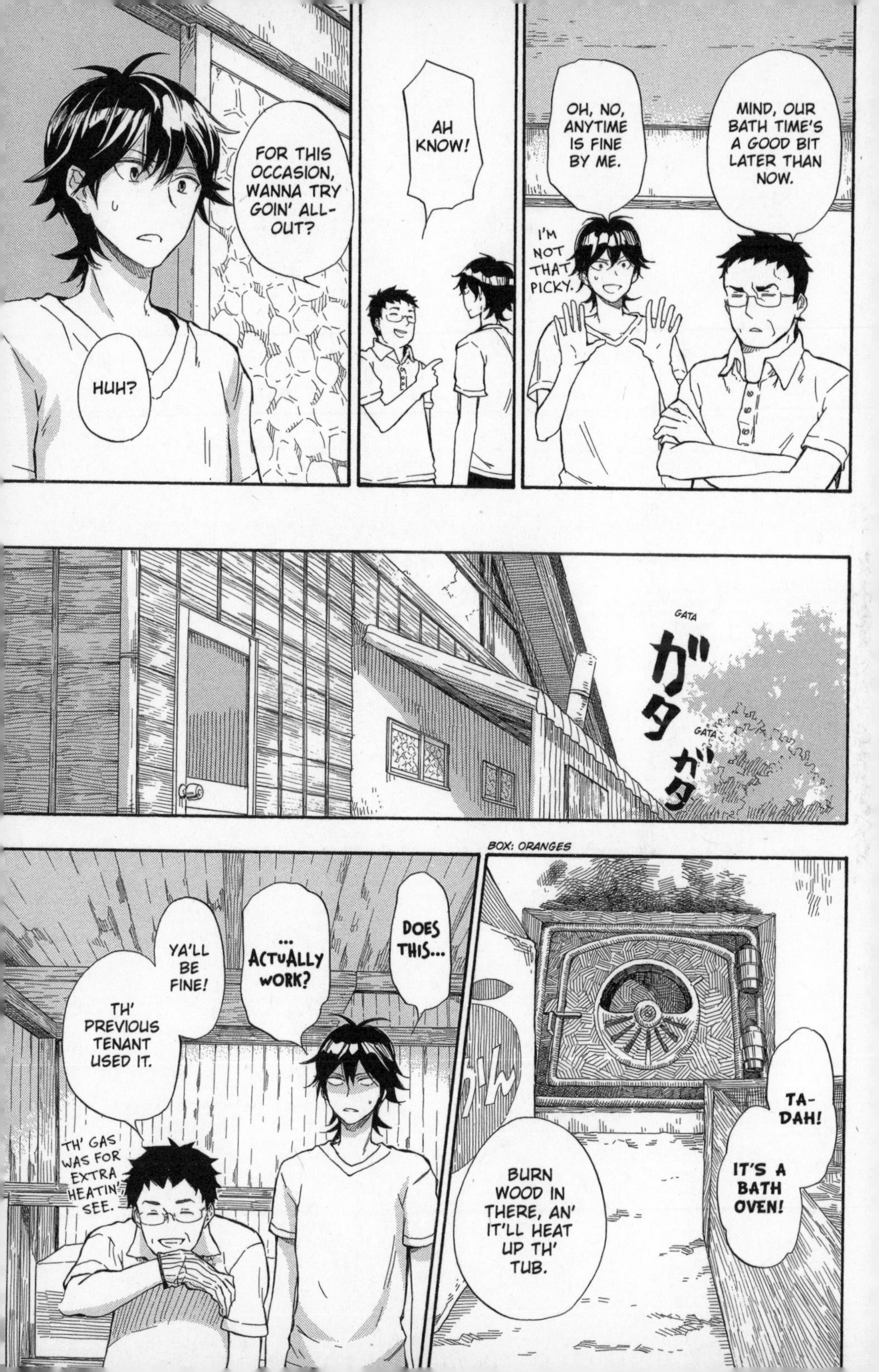
MIND, OUR BATH TIME'S A GOOD BIT LATER THAN NOW.
OH, NO, ANYTIME IS FINE BY ME.
I'M NOT THAT PICKY.
AH KNOW!
FOR THIS OCCASION, WANNA TRY GOIN' ALL-OUT?
HUH?
GATA
ガタ
GATA
ガタ
BOX: ORANGES
TA-DAH!
IT'S A BATH OVEN!
BURN WOOD IN THERE, AN' IT'LL HEAT UP TH' TUB.
DOES THIS...
...ACTUALLY WORK?
YA'LL BE FINE!
TH' PREVIOUS TENANT USED IT.
TH' GAS WAS FOR EXTRA HEATIN', SEE.

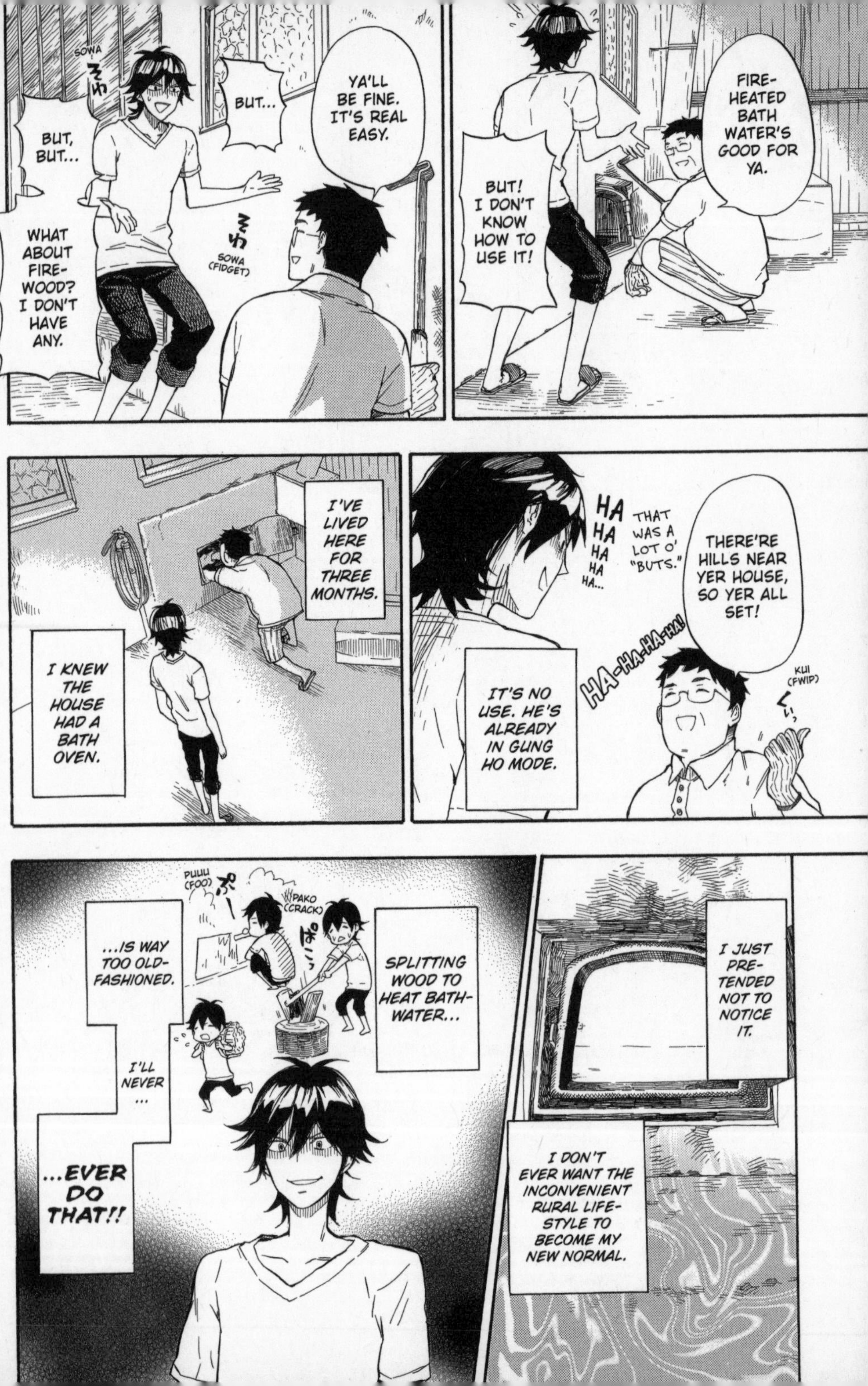
FIRE-HEATED BATH WATER'S GOOD FOR YA.
BUT! I DON'T KNOW HOW TO USE IT!
YA'LL BE FINE. IT'S REAL EASY.
BUT...
SOWA
BUT, BUT...
WHAT ABOUT FIRE-WOOD? I DON'T HAVE ANY.
SOWA (FIDGET)
THERE'RE HILLS NEAR YER HOUSE, SO YER ALL SET!
THAT WAS A LOT O' "BUTS."
HA HA HA HA HA...
HA-HA-HA-HA-HA!
KUI (FWIP)
IT'S NO USE. HE'S ALREADY IN GUNG HO MODE.
I'VE LIVED HERE FOR THREE MONTHS.
I KNEW THE HOUSE HAD A BATH OVEN.
I JUST PRE-TENDED NOT TO NOTICE IT.
I DON'T EVER WANT THE INCONVENIENT RURAL LIFE-STYLE TO BECOME MY NEW NORMAL.
SPLITTING WOOD TO HEAT BATH-WATER...
...IS WAY TOO OLD-FASHIONED.
PAKO (CRACK)
PUUU (FOO)
I'LL NEVER...
...EVER DO THAT!!

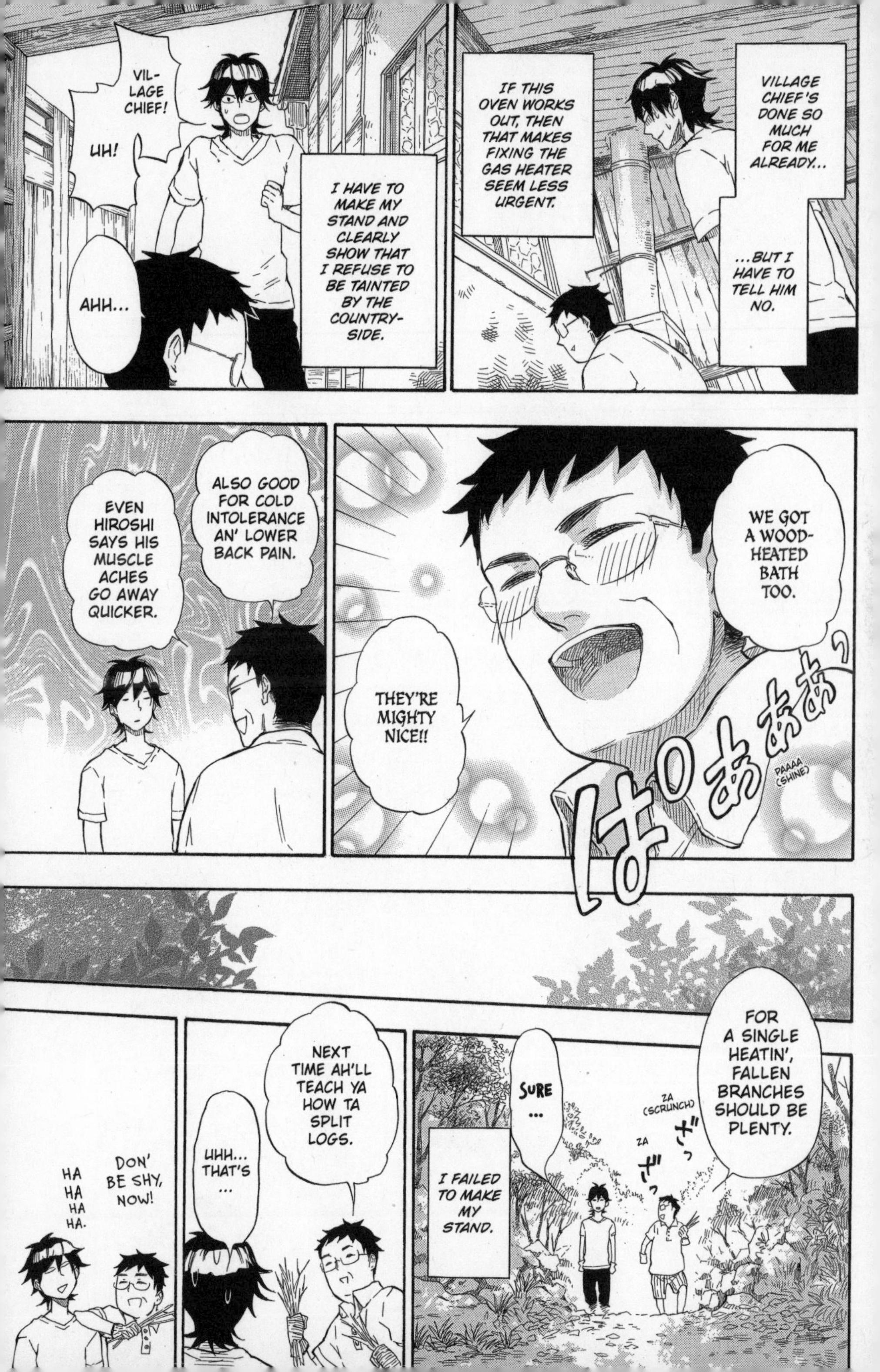
VILLAGE CHIEF'S DONE SO MUCH FOR ME ALREADY...
IF THIS OVEN WORKS OUT, THEN THAT MAKES FIXING THE GAS HEATER SEEM LESS URGENT.
...BUT I HAVE TO TELL HIM NO.
VIL-LAGE CHIEF!
UH!
I HAVE TO MAKE MY STAND AND CLEARLY SHOW THAT I REFUSE TO BE TAINTED BY THE COUNTRY-SIDE.
AHH...
WE GOT A WOOD-HEATED BATH TOO.
THEY'RE MIGHTY NICE!!
ぱあああっ
PAAAA (SHINE)
ALSO GOOD FOR COLD INTOLERANCE AN' LOWER BACK PAIN.
EVEN HIROSHI SAYS HIS MUSCLE ACHES GO AWAY QUICKER.
FOR A SINGLE HEATIN', FALLEN BRANCHES SHOULD BE PLENTY.
ざっ
ZA (SCRUNCH)
ざっ
ZA
SURE ...
I FAILED TO MAKE MY STAND.
NEXT TIME AH'LL TEACH YA HOW TA SPLIT LOGS.
UHH... THAT'S ...
DON' BE SHY, NOW!
HA HA HA HA.

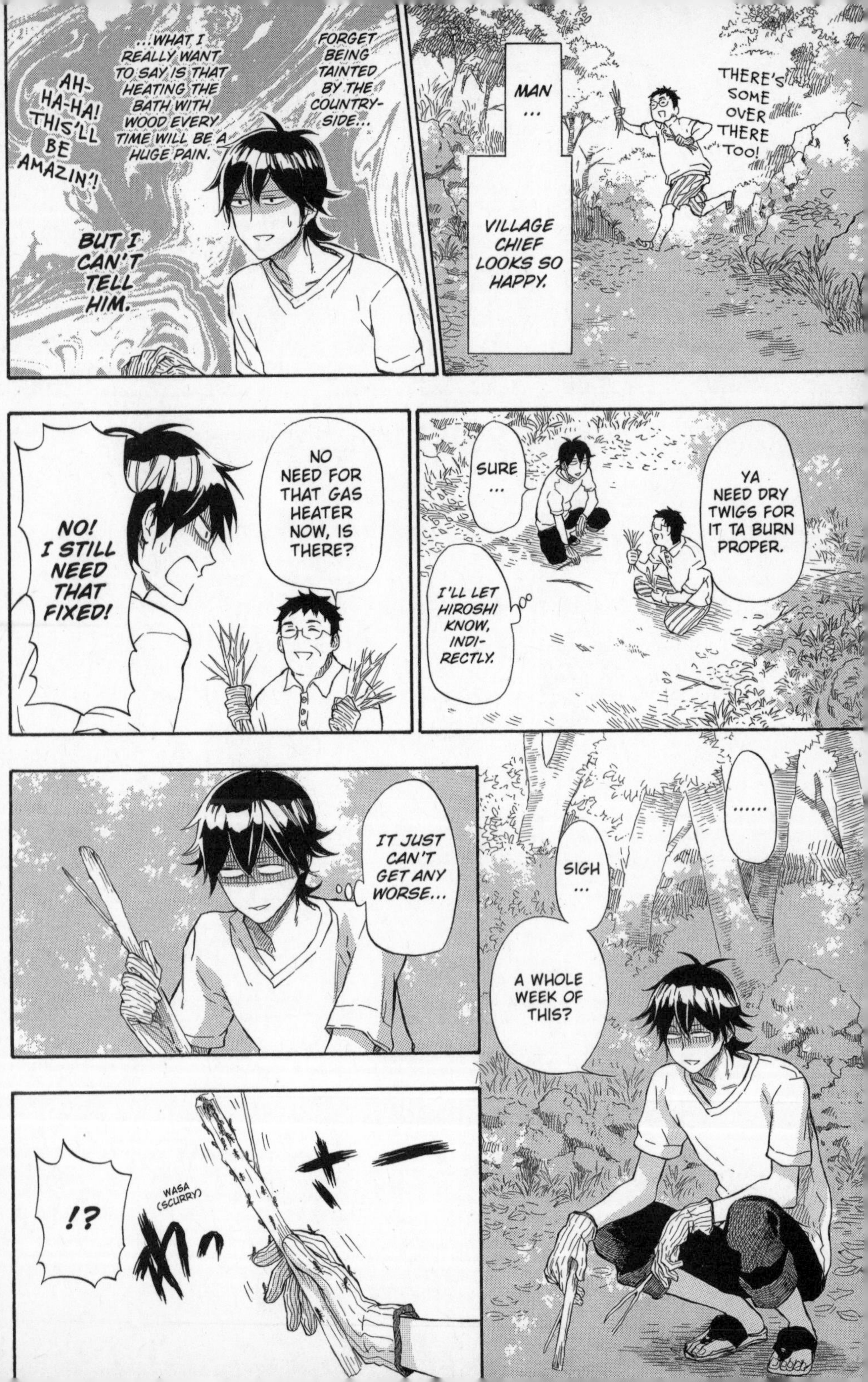
THERE'S SOME OVER THERE TOO!
MAN ...
VILLAGE CHIEF LOOKS SO HAPPY.
FORGET BEING TAINTED BY THE COUNTRY-SIDE...
...WHAT I REALLY WANT TO SAY IS THAT HEATING THE BATH WITH WOOD EVERY TIME WILL BE A HUGE PAIN.
AH-HA-HA! THIS'LL BE AMAZIN'!
BUT I CAN'T TELL HIM.
YA NEED DRY TWIGS FOR IT TA BURN PROPER.
SURE ...
I'LL LET HIROSHI KNOW, INDI-RECTLY.
NO NEED FOR THAT GAS HEATER NOW, IS THERE?
NO! I STILL NEED THAT FIXED!
......
SIGH ...
A WHOLE WEEK OF THIS?
IT JUST CAN'T GET ANY WORSE...
WASA (SCURRY)
!?

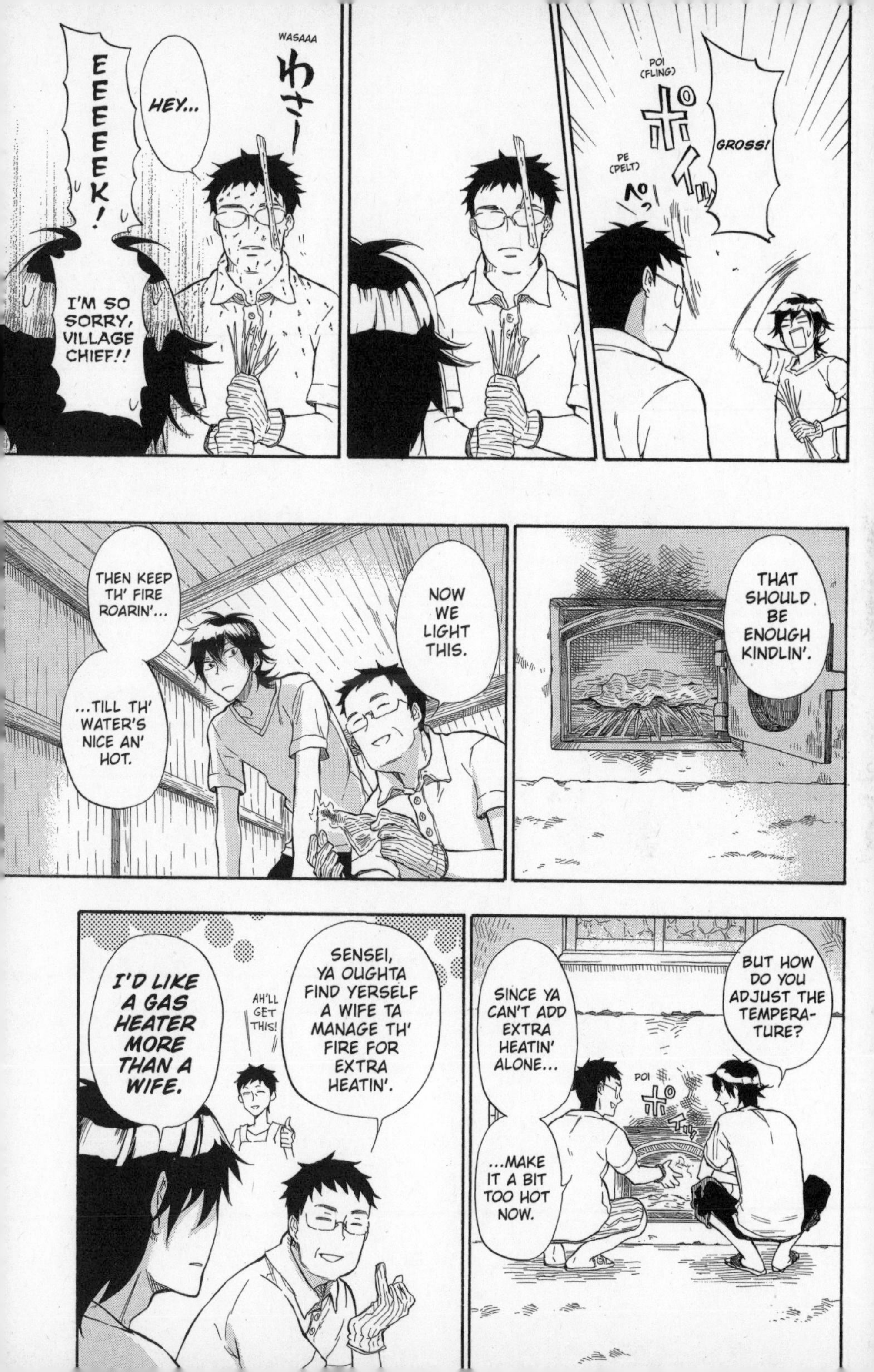
GROSS!
POI (FLING)
ポイッ
PE (PELT)
ぺっ
WASAAA
わさー
HEY...
EEEEEK!
I'M SO SORRY, VILLAGE CHIEF!!
THAT SHOULD BE ENOUGH KINDLIN'.
NOW WE LIGHT THIS.
THEN KEEP TH' FIRE ROARIN'...
...TILL TH' WATER'S NICE AN' HOT.
BUT HOW DO YOU ADJUST THE TEMPERA-TURE?
SINCE YA CAN'T ADD EXTRA HEATIN' ALONE...
POI
ポイッ
...MAKE IT A BIT TOO HOT NOW.
SENSEI, YA OUGHTA FIND YERSELF A WIFE TA MANAGE TH' FIRE FOR EXTRA HEATIN'.
AH'LL GET THIS!
I'D LIKE A GAS HEATER MORE THAN A WIFE.

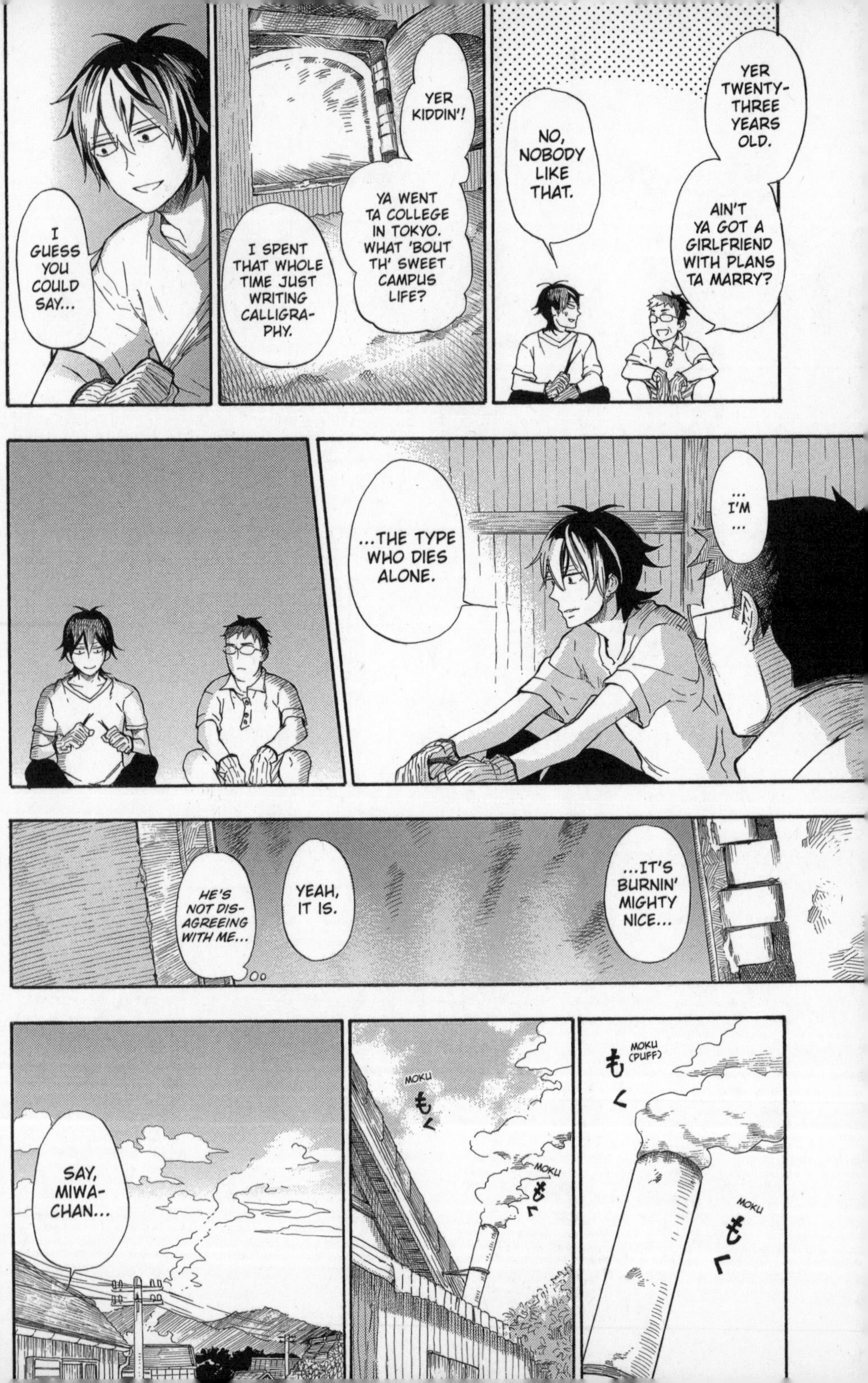
YER TWENTY-THREE YEARS OLD.
AIN'T YA GOT A GIRLFRIEND WITH PLANS TA MARRY?
NO, NOBODY LIKE THAT.
YER KIDDIN'!
YA WENT TA COLLEGE IN TOKYO. WHAT 'BOUT TH' SWEET CAMPUS LIFE?
I SPENT THAT WHOLE TIME JUST WRITING CALLIGRA-PHY.
I GUESS YOU COULD SAY...
... I'M ...
...THE TYPE WHO DIES ALONE.
...IT'S BURNIN' MIGHTY NICE...
YEAH, IT IS.
HE'S NOT DIS-AGREEING WITH ME...
もく
MOKU (PUFF)
もく
MOKU
もく
MOKU
もく
MOKU
SAY, MIWA-CHAN...

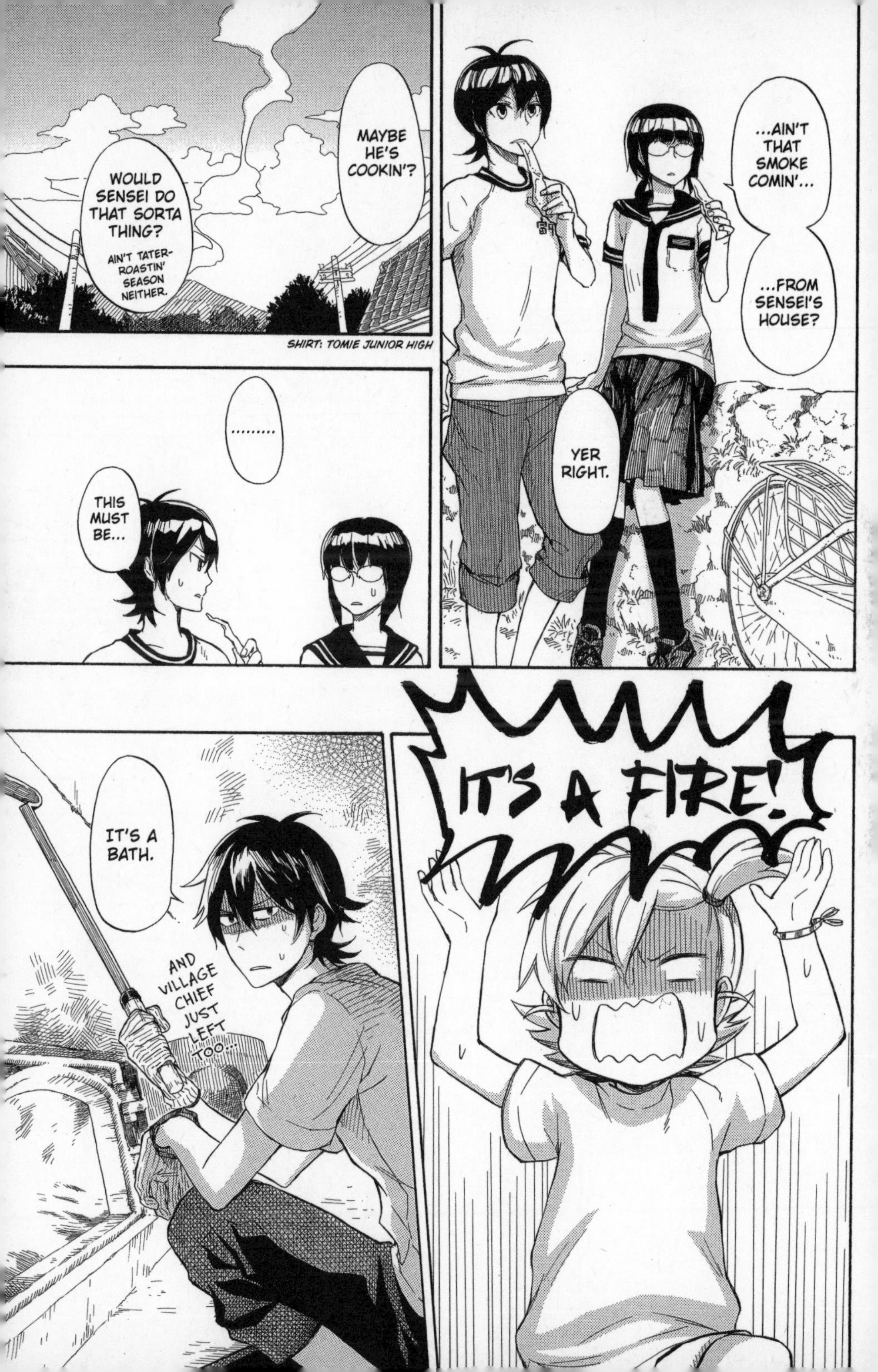

...AIN'T THAT SMOKE COMIN'...
...FROM SENSEI'S HOUSE?
YER RIGHT.
MAYBE HE'S COOKIN'?
WOULD SENSEI DO THAT SORTA THING?
AIN'T TATER-ROASTIN' SEASON NEITHER.
SHIRT: TOMIE JUNIOR HIGH
....
THIS MUST BE...
IT'S A FIRE!
IT'S A BATH.
AND VILLAGE CHIEF JUST LEFT TOO...

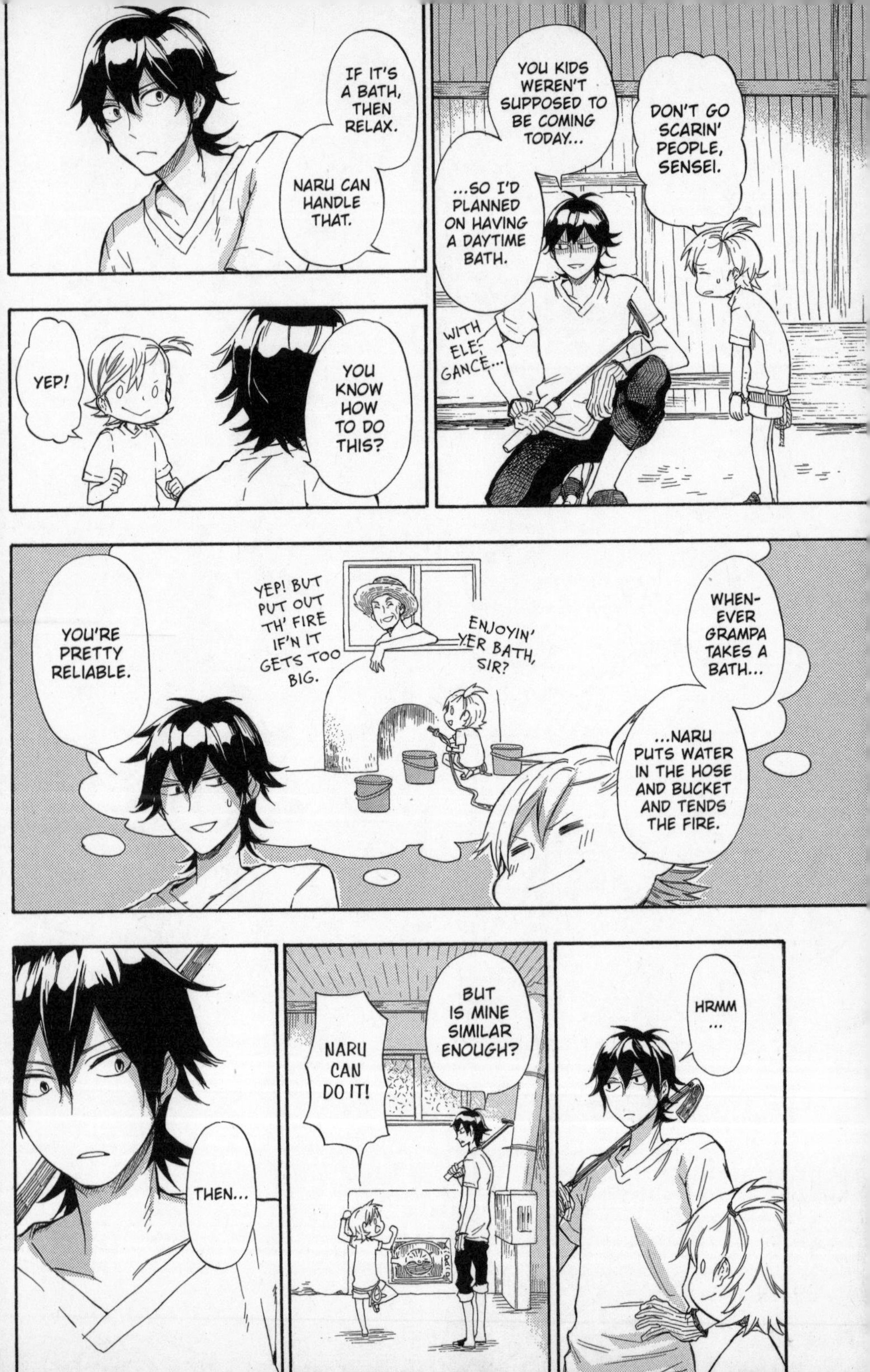
DON'T GO SCARIN' PEOPLE, SENSEI.
YOU KIDS WEREN'T SUPPOSED TO BE COMING TODAY...
...SO I'D PLANNED ON HAVING A DAYTIME BATH.
WITH ELE-GANCE...
IF IT'S A BATH, THEN RELAX.
NARU CAN HANDLE THAT.
YOU KNOW HOW TO DO THIS?
YEP!
WHEN-EVER GRAMPA TAKES A BATH...
...NARU PUTS WATER IN THE HOSE AND BUCKET AND TENDS THE FIRE.
ENJOYIN' YER BATH, SIR?
YEP! BUT PUT OUT TH' FIRE IF'N IT GETS TOO BIG.
YOU'RE PRETTY RELIABLE.
HRMM...
BUT IS MINE SIMILAR ENOUGH?
NARU CAN DO IT!
THEN...

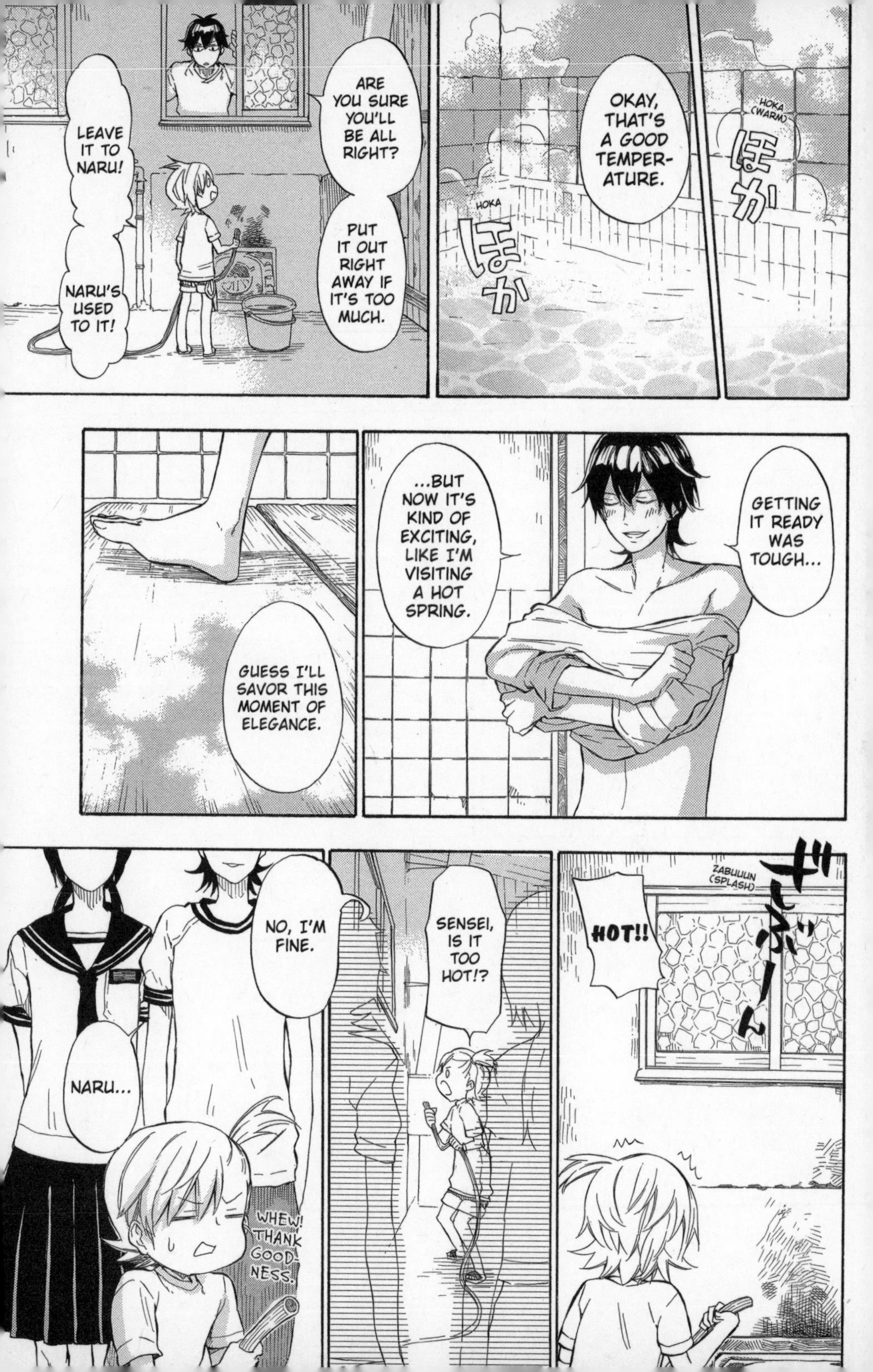

HOKA (WARM)
ほか
OKAY, THAT'S A GOOD TEMPERATURE.
HOKA
ほか
ARE YOU SURE YOU'LL BE ALL RIGHT?
PUT IT OUT RIGHT AWAY IF IT'S TOO MUCH.
LEAVE IT TO NARU!
NARU'S USED TO IT!
GETTING IT READY WAS TOUGH...
...BUT NOW IT'S KIND OF EXCITING, LIKE I'M VISITING A HOT SPRING.
GUESS I'LL SAVOR THIS MOMENT OF ELEGANCE.
ZABUUUN (SPLASH)
ざぶーん
HOT!!
SENSEI, IS IT TOO HOT!?
NO, I'M FINE.
NARU...
WHEW! THANK GOODNESS.

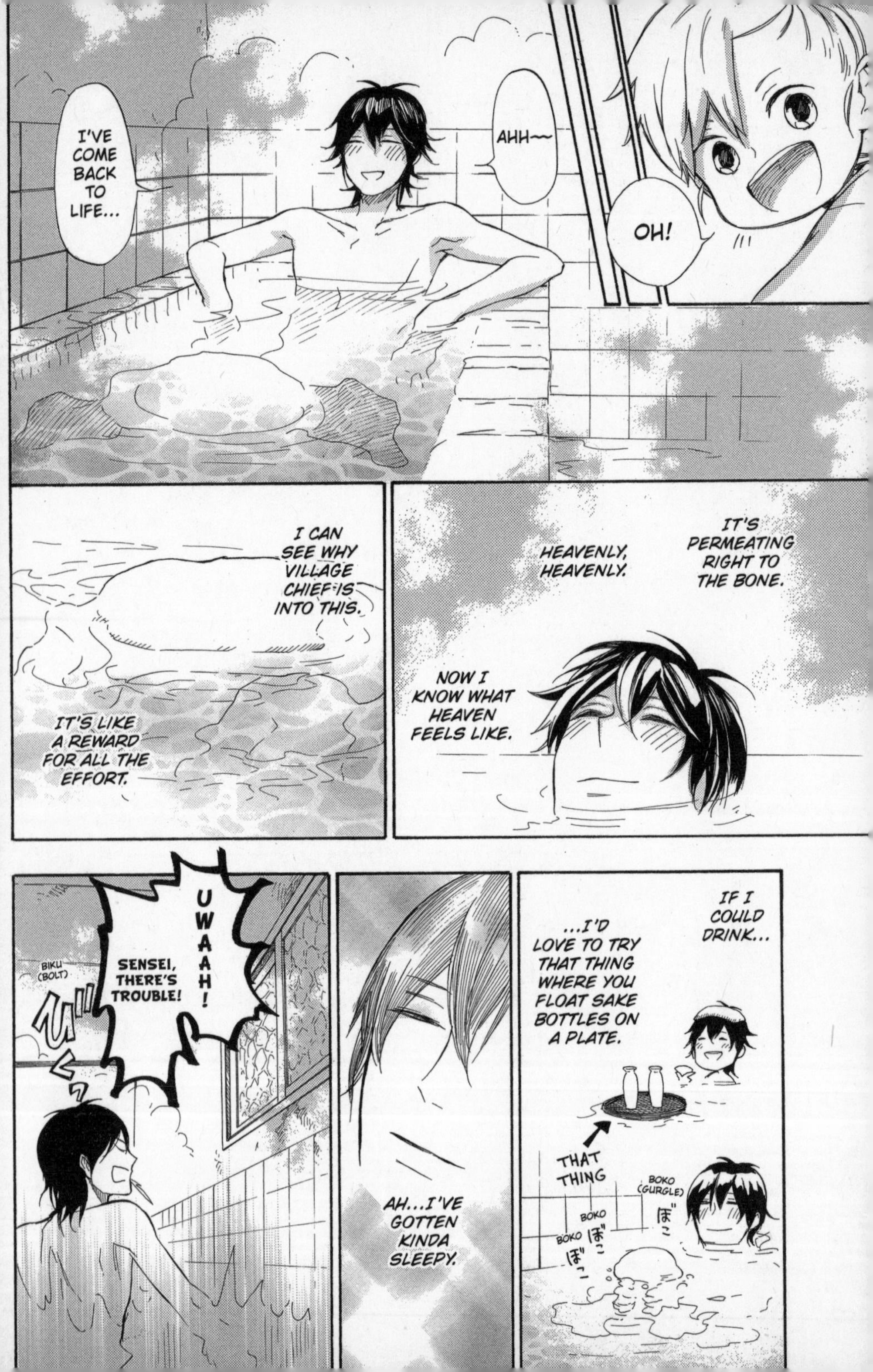

OH!
AHH~~
I'VE COME BACK TO LIFE...
IT'S PERMEATING RIGHT TO THE BONE.
HEAVENLY, HEAVENLY.
NOW I KNOW WHAT HEAVEN FEELS LIKE.
I CAN SEE WHY VILLAGE CHIEF IS INTO THIS.
IT'S LIKE A REWARD FOR ALL THE EFFORT.
IF I COULD DRINK...
...I'D LOVE TO TRY THAT THING WHERE YOU FLOAT SAKE BOTTLES ON A PLATE.
THAT THING
BOKO (GURGLE)
ぼこ
BOKO
ぼこ
BOKO
ぼこ
AH...I'VE GOTTEN KINDA SLEEPY.
UWAAAH!
SENSEI, THERE'S TROUBLE!
BIKU (BOLT)

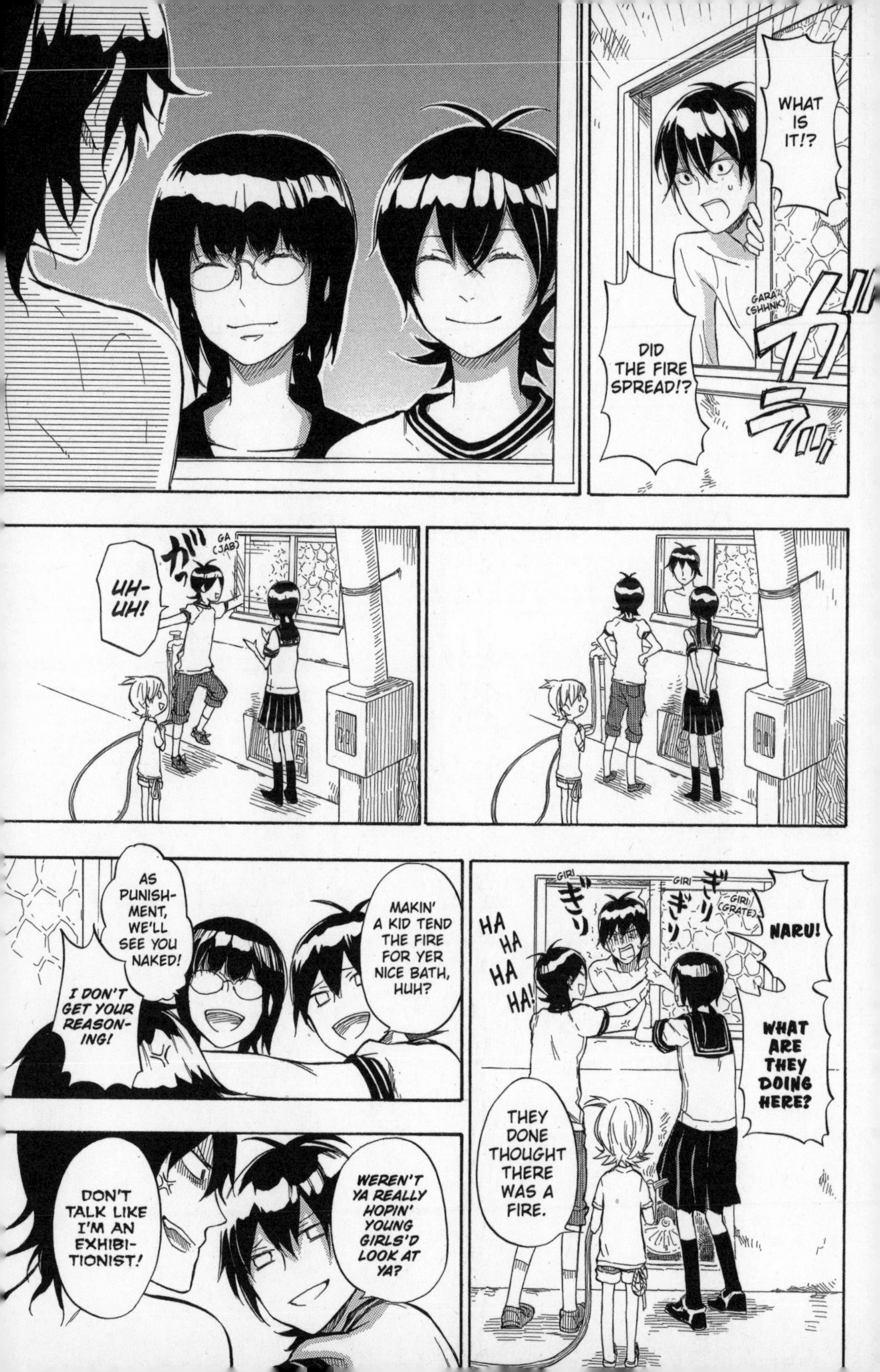
WHAT IS IT!?
ガラッ
GARA (SHHNK)
DID THE FIRE SPREAD!?
がっ
GA (JAB)
UH-UH!
NARU!
ぎり ぎり ぎり
GIRI
GIRI
GIRI (GRATE)
WHAT ARE THEY DOING HERE?
HA HA HA HA!
THEY DONE THOUGHT THERE WAS A FIRE.
MAKIN' A KID TEND THE FIRE FOR YER NICE BATH, HUH?
AS PUNISHMENT, WE'LL SEE YOU NAKED!
I DON'T GET YOUR REASONING!
WEREN'T YA REALLY HOPIN' YOUNG GIRLS'D LOOK AT YA?
DON'T TALK LIKE I'M AN EXHIBITIONIST!

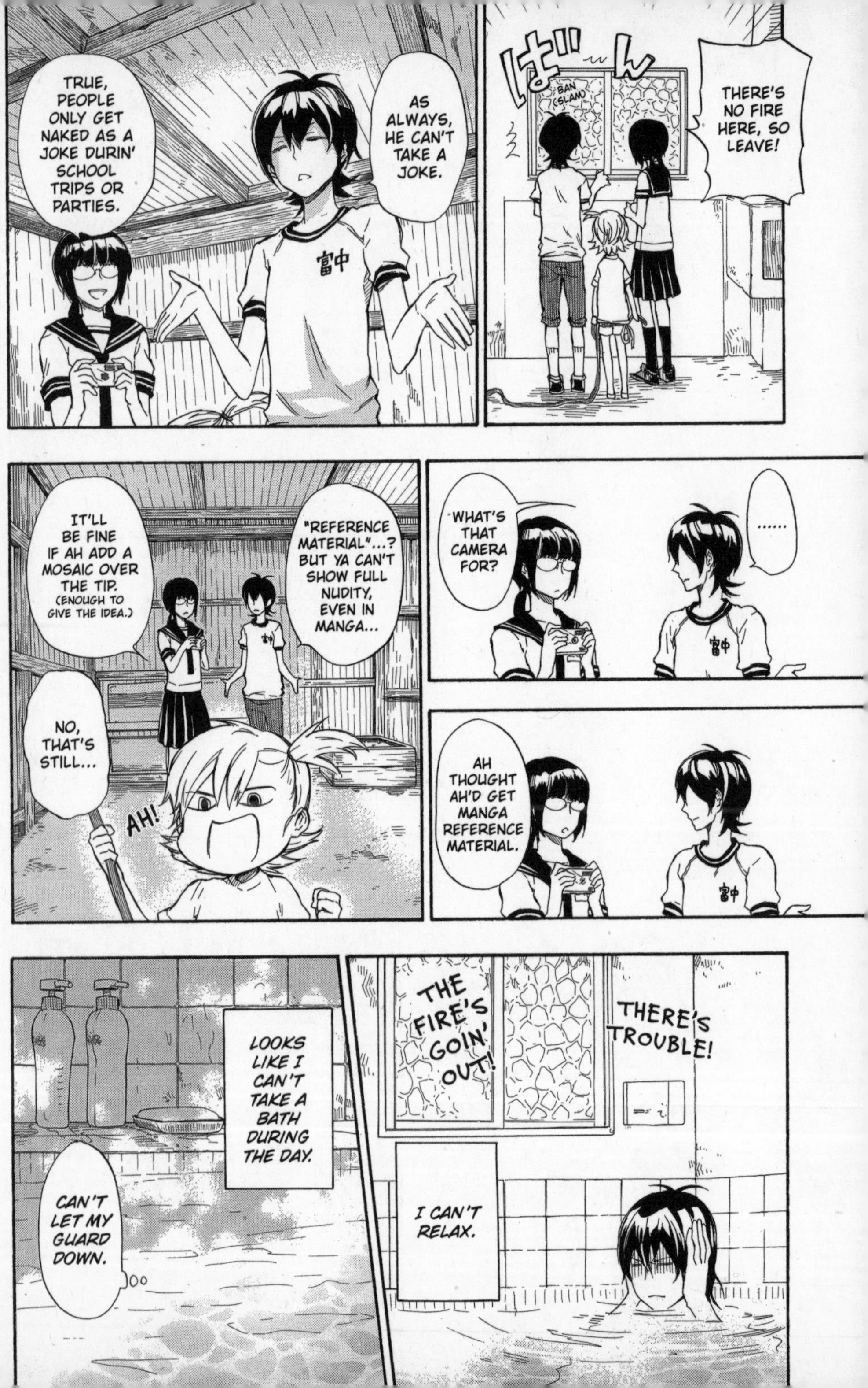

ば〜ん
BAN (SLAM)
THERE'S NO FIRE HERE, SO LEAVE!
AS ALWAYS, HE CAN'T TAKE A JOKE.
TRUE, PEOPLE ONLY GET NAKED AS A JOKE DURIN' SCHOOL TRIPS OR PARTIES.
......
WHAT'S THAT CAMERA FOR?
AH THOUGHT AH'D GET MANGA REFERENCE MATERIAL.
"REFERENCE MATERIAL"...? BUT YA CAN'T SHOW FULL NUDITY, EVEN IN MANGA...
IT'LL BE FINE IF AH ADD A MOSAIC OVER THE TIP. (ENOUGH TO GIVE THE IDEA.)
NO, THAT'S STILL...
AH!
THERE'S TROUBLE!
THE FIRE'S GOIN' OUT!
I CAN'T RELAX.
LOOKS LIKE I CAN'T TAKE A BATH DURING THE DAY.
CAN'T LET MY GUARD DOWN.

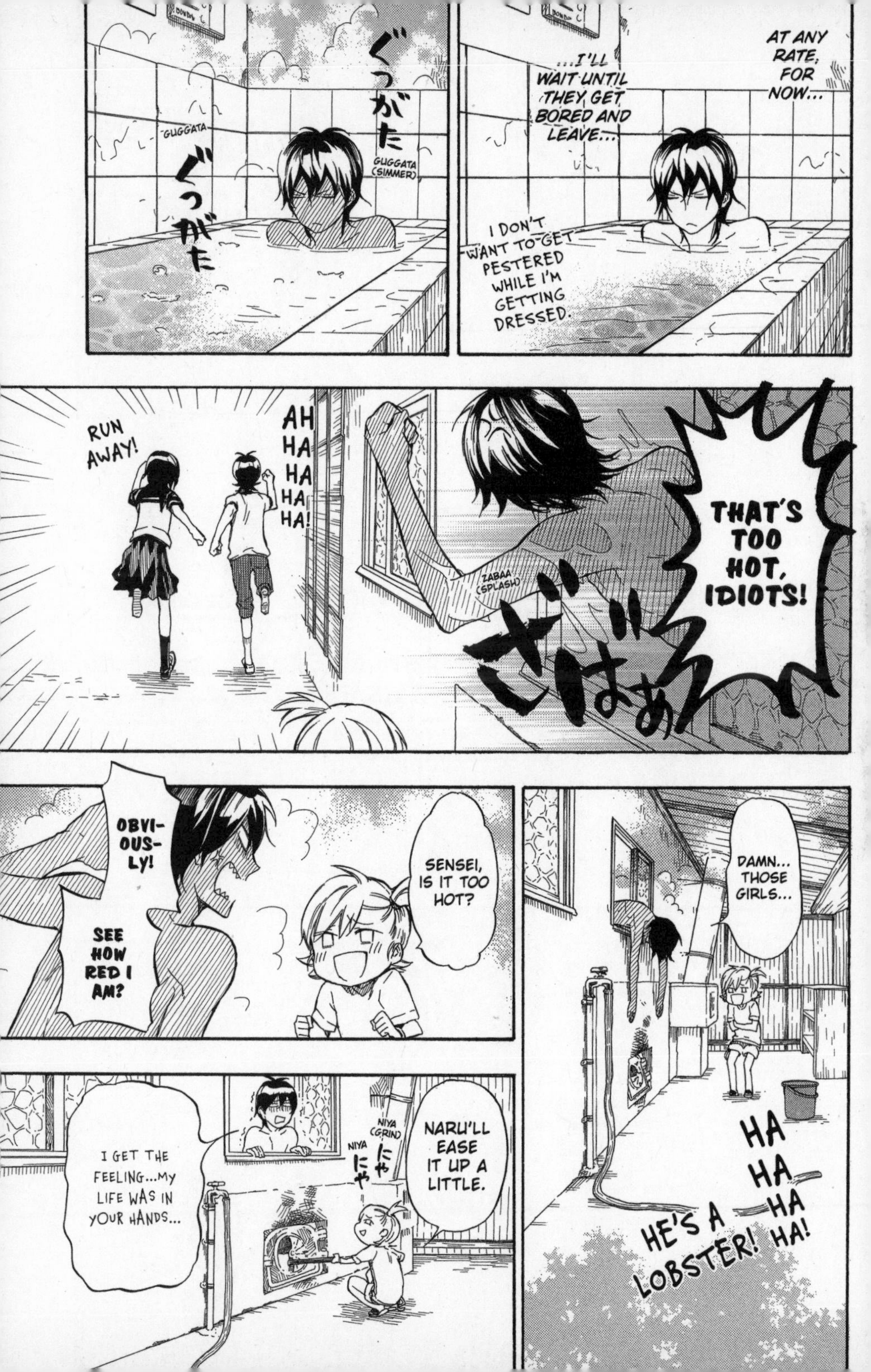
AT ANY RATE, FOR NOW...
...I'LL WAIT UNTIL THEY GET BORED AND LEAVE...
I DON'T WANT TO GET PESTERED WHILE I'M GETTING DRESSED.
ぐっがた
GUGGATA (SIMMER)
ぐっがた
GUGGATA
THAT'S TOO HOT, IDIOTS!
ざばあ
ZABAA (SPLASH)
AH HA HA HA HA!
RUN AWAY!
DAMN... THOSE GIRLS...
HE'S A LOBSTER!
HA HA HA HA!
SENSEI, IS IT TOO HOT?
OBVI-OUS-LY!
SEE HOW RED I AM?
NARU'LL EASE IT UP A LITTLE.
にや
NIYA (GRIN)
にや
NIYA
I GET THE FEELING...MY LIFE WAS IN YOUR HANDS...

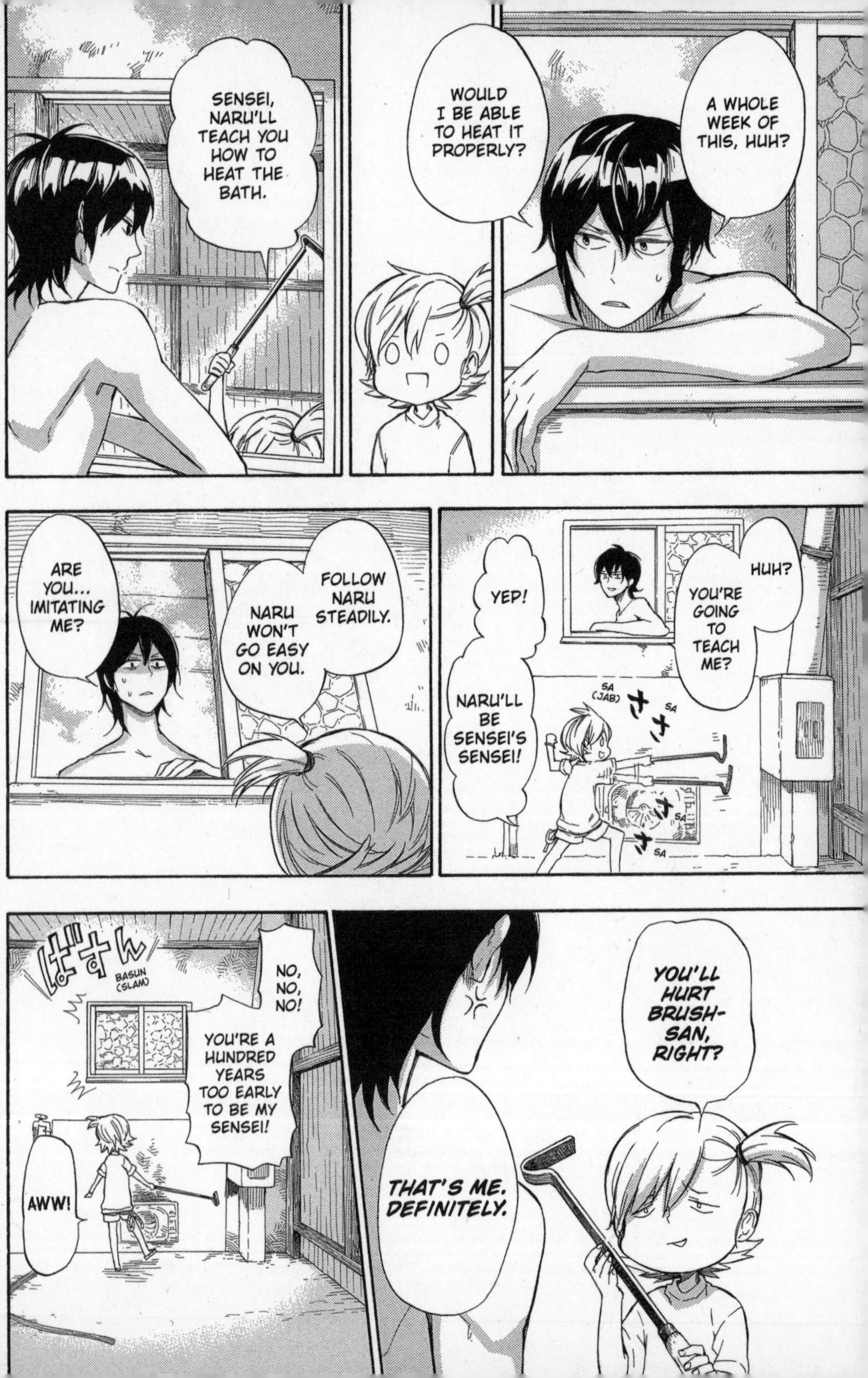
A WHOLE WEEK OF THIS, HUH?
WOULD I BE ABLE TO HEAT IT PROPERLY?
SENSEI, NARU'LL TEACH YOU HOW TO HEAT THE BATH.
HUH? YOU'RE GOING TO TEACH ME?
YEP!
NARU'LL BE SENSEI'S SENSEI!
さ SA (JAB)
さ SA
さ SA
さ SA
FOLLOW NARU STEADILY.
NARU WON'T GO EASY ON YOU.
ARE YOU... IMITATING ME?
YOU'LL HURT BRUSH-SAN, RIGHT?
THAT'S ME. DEFINITELY.
ばすん BASUN (SLAM)
NO, NO, NO!
YOU'RE A HUNDRED YEARS TOO EARLY TO BE MY SENSEI!
AWW!

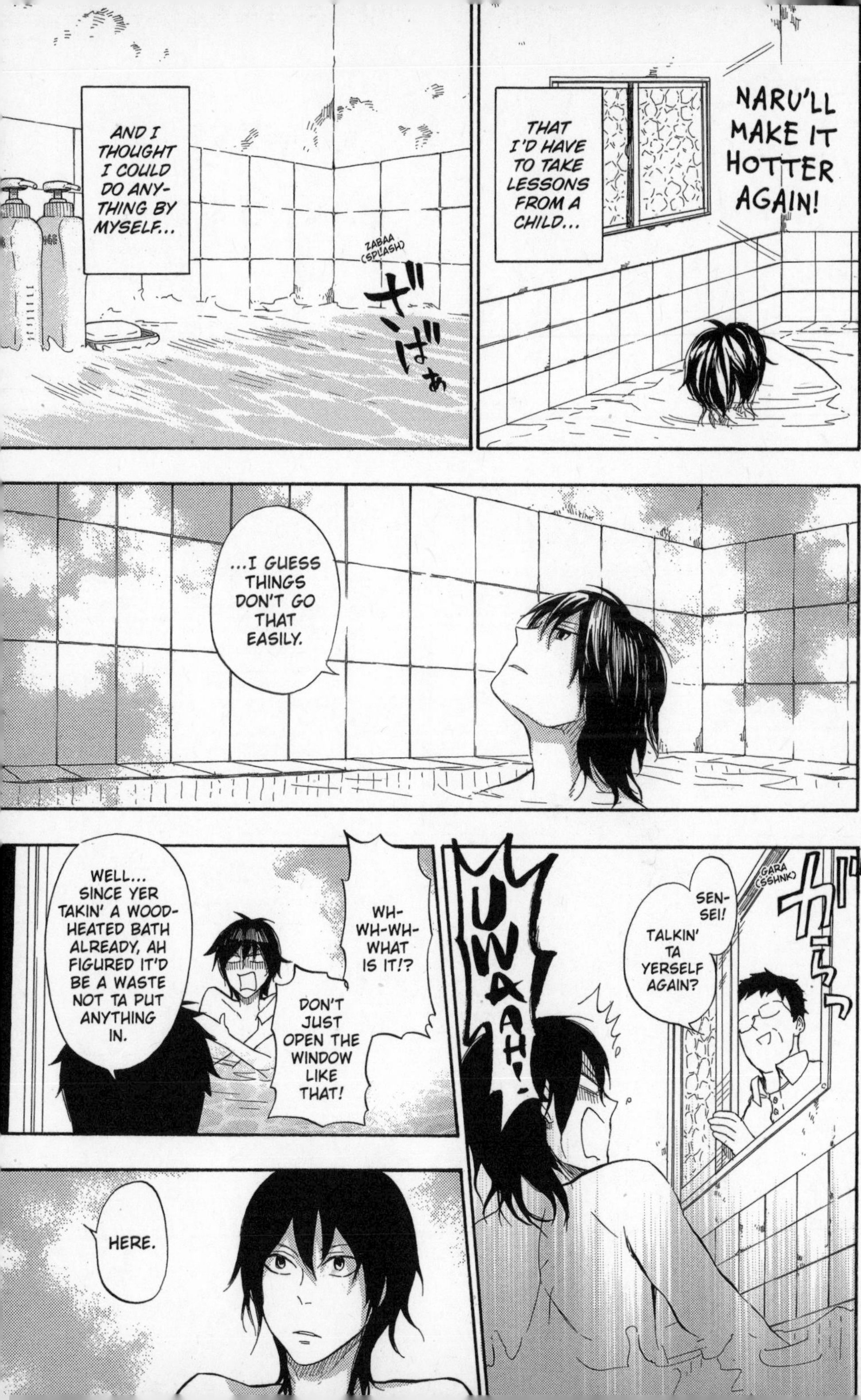
NARU'LL MAKE IT HOTTER AGAIN!
THAT I'D HAVE TO TAKE LESSONS FROM A CHILD...
AND I THOUGHT I COULD DO ANYTHING BY MYSELF...
ZABAA (SPLASH)
ざばぁ
...I GUESS THINGS DON'T GO THAT EASILY.
ガラッ
GARA (SSHNK)
SEN-SEI!
TALKIN' TA YERSELF AGAIN?
UWAAH!!
WH-WH-WH-WHAT IS IT!?
DON'T JUST OPEN THE WINDOW LIKE THAT!
WELL... SINCE YER TAKIN' A WOOD-HEATED BATH ALREADY, AH FIGURED IT'D BE A WASTE NOT TA PUT ANYTHING IN.
HERE.

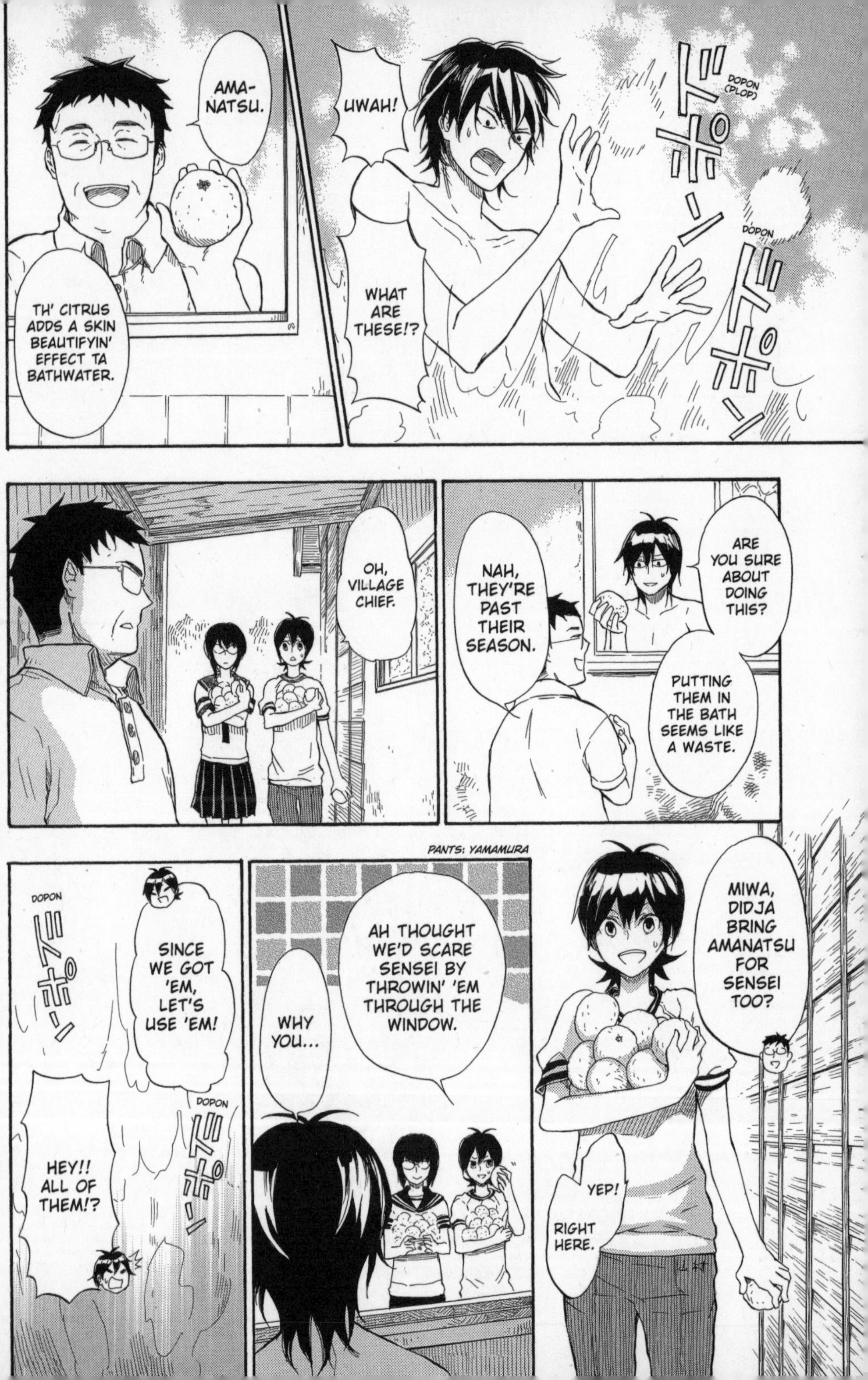
DOPON (PLOP)
UWAH!
WHAT ARE THESE!?
DOPON
AMA-NATSU.
TH' CITRUS ADDS A SKIN BEAUTIFYIN' EFFECT TA BATHWATER.
ARE YOU SURE ABOUT DOING THIS?
PUTTING THEM IN THE BATH SEEMS LIKE A WASTE.
NAH, THEY'RE PAST THEIR SEASON.
OH, VILLAGE CHIEF.
PANTS: YAMAMURA
MIWA, DIDJA BRING AMANATSU FOR SENSEI TOO?
YEP!
RIGHT HERE.
AH THOUGHT WE'D SCARE SENSEI BY THROWIN' 'EM THROUGH THE WINDOW.
WHY YOU...
DOPON
SINCE WE GOT 'EM, LET'S USE 'EM!
DOPON
HEY!! ALL OF THEM!?

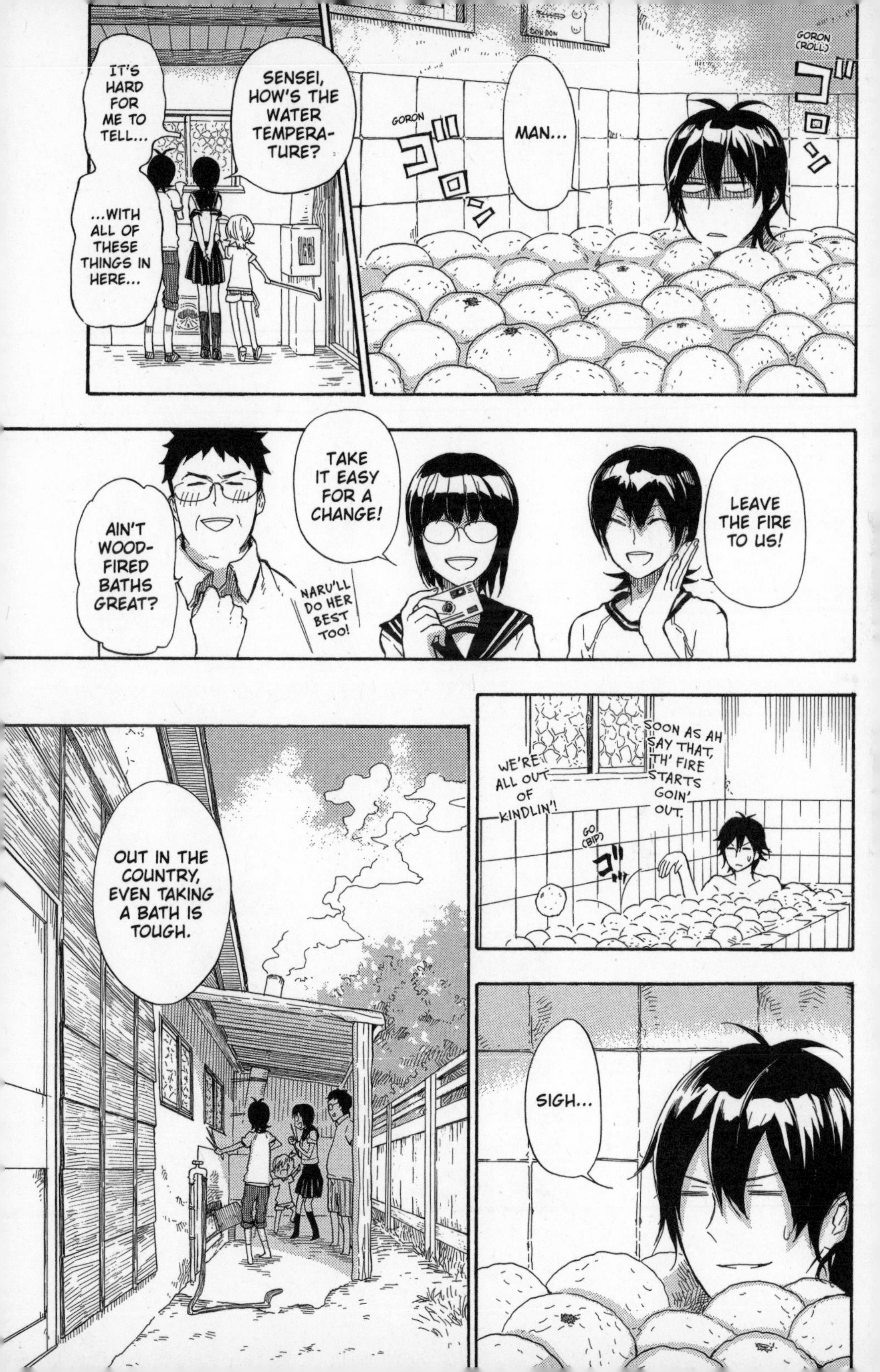
GORON (ROLL)
MAN...
GORON
SENSEI, HOW'S THE WATER TEMPERATURE?
IT'S HARD FOR ME TO TELL...
...WITH ALL OF THESE THINGS IN HERE...
LEAVE THE FIRE TO US!
TAKE IT EASY FOR A CHANGE!
NARU'LL DO HER BEST TOO!
AIN'T WOOD-FIRED BATHS GREAT?
SOON AS AH SAY THAT, TH' FIRE STARTS GOIN' OUT.
WE'RE ALL OUT OF KINDLIN'!
GO (BIP)
SIGH...
OUT IN THE COUNTRY, EVEN TAKING A BATH IS TOUGH.

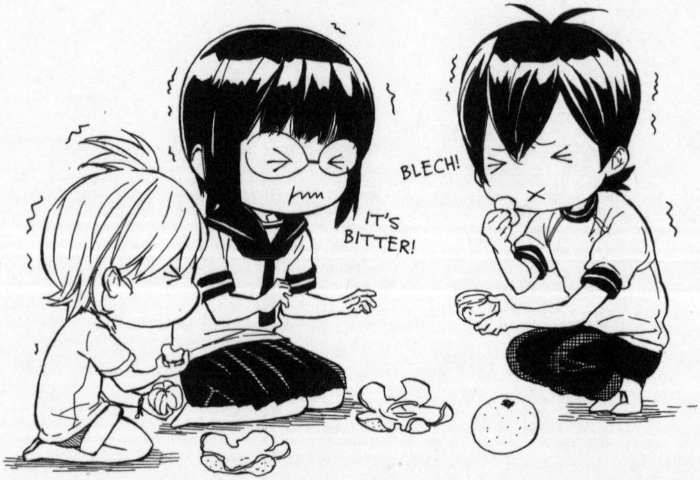
BLECH!
IT'S BITTER!

ACT.39
OKEGA MAKUCCHI SHITA
(Translation: Almost Got Badly Hurt)

PEI
(BIP)

THAT'S HOW MUCH I NEED FOR A BATH.

OKAY.

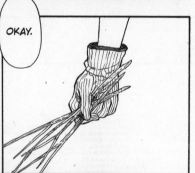

SIGH...

PAN
(CLAP)

PAN

JUST WHAT AM I DOING?

WHILE THE NARUKA DEADLINE'S CLOSING IN...

...I'M OUT GATHERING TWIGS.

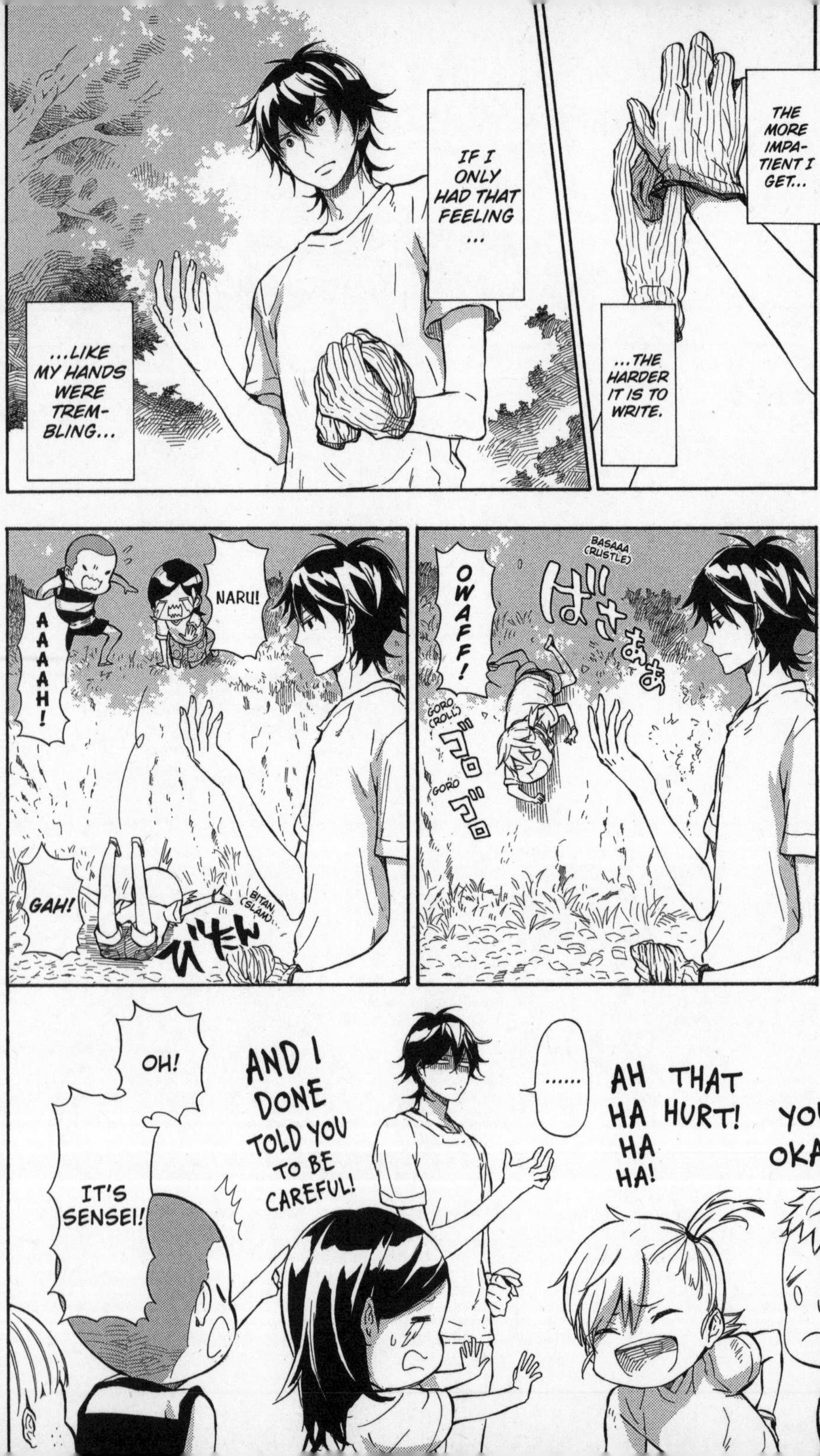
THE MORE IMPATIENT I GET...
...THE HARDER IT IS TO WRITE.
IF I ONLY HAD THAT FEELING...
...LIKE MY HANDS WERE TREMBLING...
BASAAA (RUSTLE)
ばさぁぁ
OWAFF!
GORO (ROLL)
ゴロ
GORO
ゴロ
NARU!
AAAAAH!
GAH!
BITAN (SLAM)
びたん
YOU OKAY?
THAT HURT!
AH HA HA HA!
......
AND I DONE TOLD YOU TO BE CAREFUL!
OH!
IT'S SENSEI!

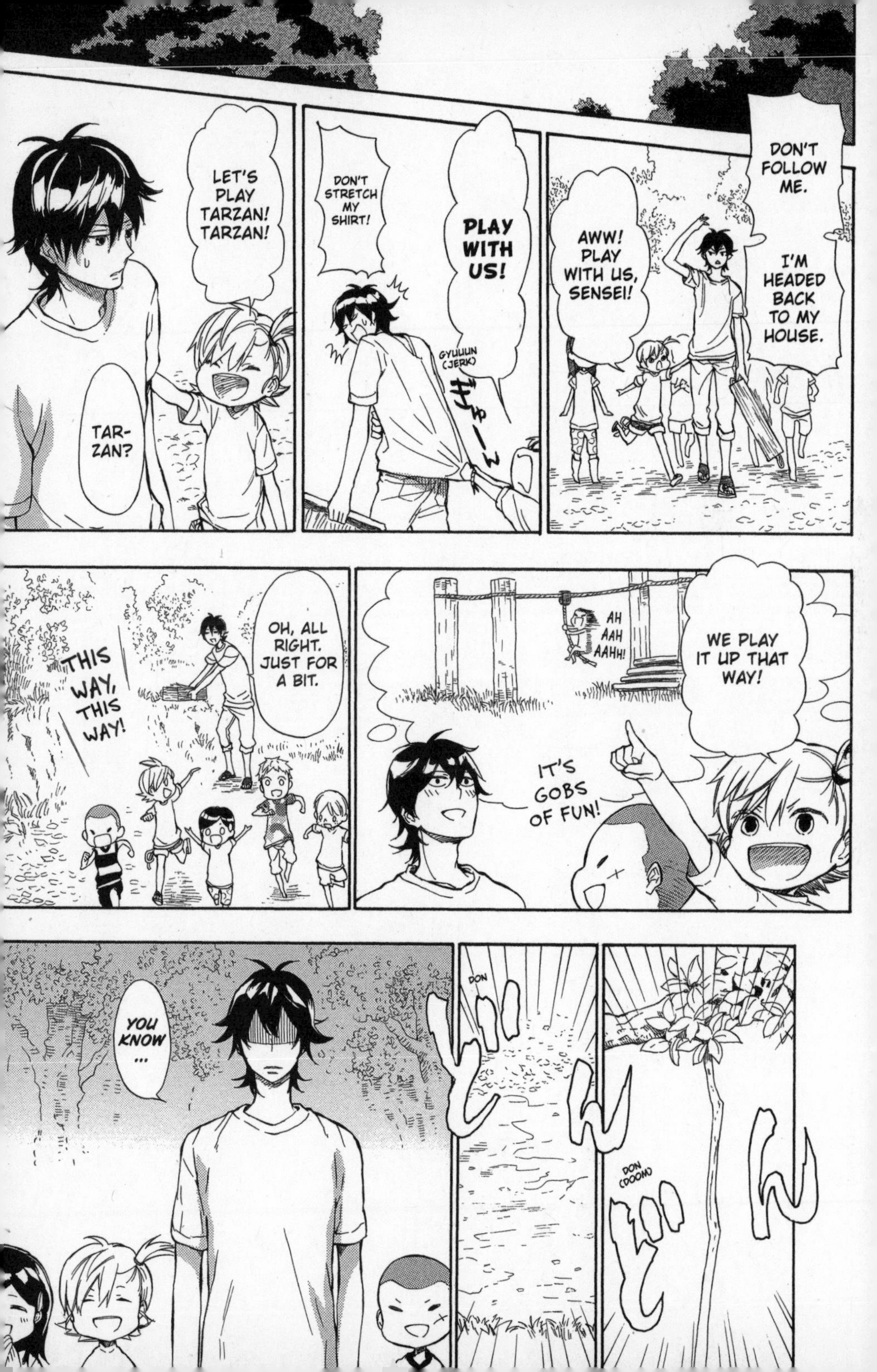
DON'T FOLLOW ME.
I'M HEADED BACK TO MY HOUSE.
AWW! PLAY WITH US, SENSEI!
PLAY WITH US!
DON'T STRETCH MY SHIRT!
GYUUUN (JERK)
ぎゅーん
LET'S PLAY TARZAN! TARZAN!
TAR-ZAN?
AH AAH AAHH!
WE PLAY IT UP THAT WAY!
IT'S GOBS OF FUN!
OH, ALL RIGHT. JUST FOR A BIT.
THIS WAY, THIS WAY!
DON (DOOM)
どん
DON
どん
YOU KNOW ...

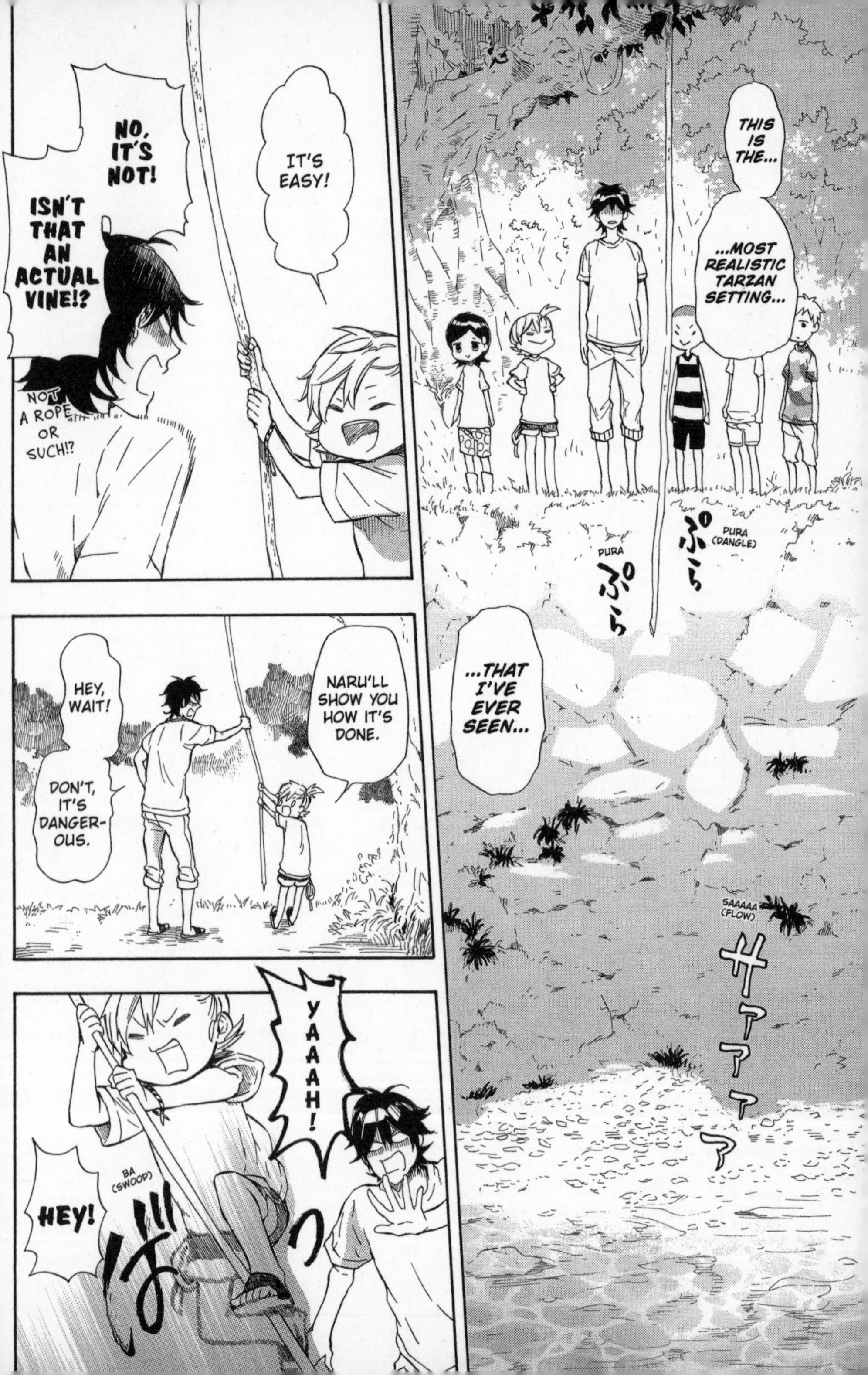
THIS IS THE...
...MOST REALISTIC TARZAN SETTING...
ぷら
PURA (DANGLE)
ぷら
PURA
...THAT I'VE EVER SEEN...
サァァァァ
SAAAAA (FLOW)
IT'S EASY!
NO, IT'S NOT!
ISN'T THAT AN ACTUAL VINE!?
NOT A ROPE OR SUCH!?
NARU'LL SHOW YOU HOW IT'S DONE.
HEY, WAIT!
DON'T, IT'S DANGEROUS.
YAAAH!
ばっ
BA (SWOOP)
HEY!

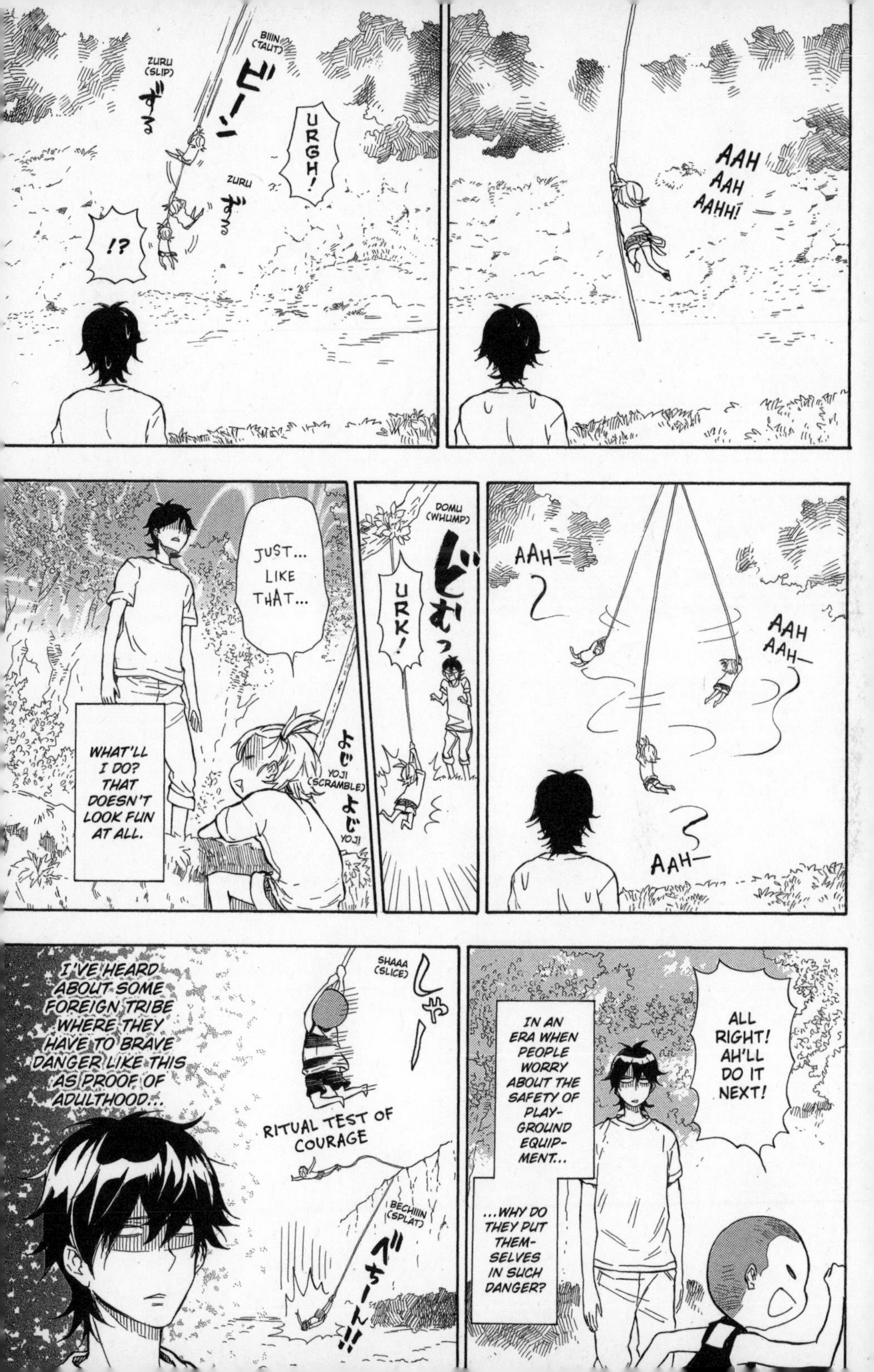
AAH AAH AAHH!
BIIN (TAUT)
ビーン
URGH!
ZURU (SLIP)
ずる
ZURU
ずる
!?
AAH—
AAH AAH—
AAH—
DOMU (WHUMP)
どむっ
URK!
よじ
YOJI (SCRAMBLE)
よじ
YOJI
JUST... LIKE THAT...
WHAT'LL I DO? THAT DOESN'T LOOK FUN AT ALL.
ALL RIGHT! AH'LL DO IT NEXT!
IN AN ERA WHEN PEOPLE WORRY ABOUT THE SAFETY OF PLAY-GROUND EQUIP-MENT...
...WHY DO THEY PUT THEM-SELVES IN SUCH DANGER?
SHAAA (SLICE)
しゃー
I'VE HEARD ABOUT SOME FOREIGN TRIBE WHERE THEY HAVE TO BRAVE DANGER LIKE THIS AS PROOF OF ADULTHOOD...
RITUAL TEST OF COURAGE
BECHIIIN (SPLAT)
べちーん!!

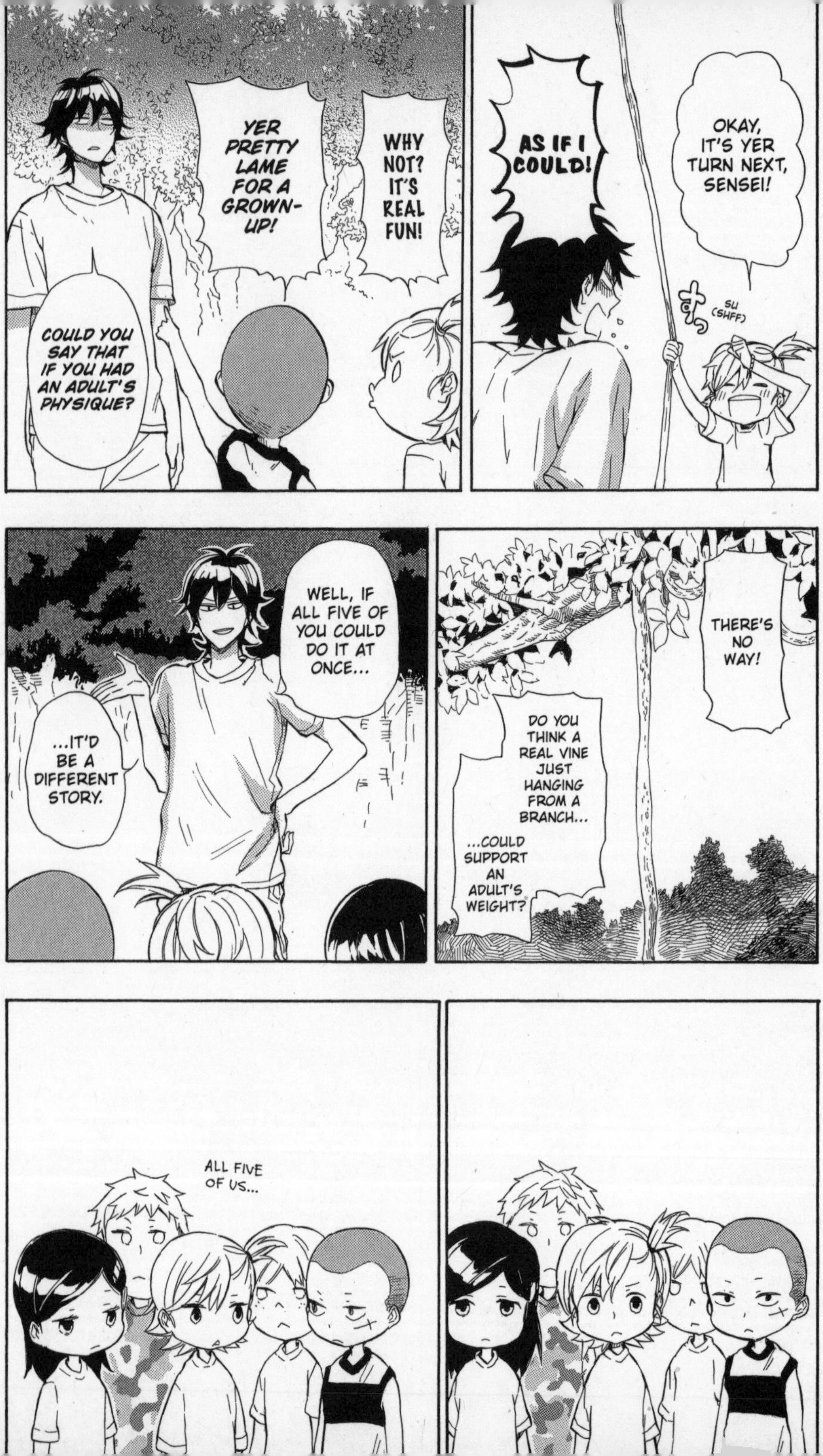
OKAY, IT'S YER TURN NEXT, SENSEI!
すっ
SU (SHFF)
AS IF I COULD!
WHY NOT? IT'S REAL FUN!
YER PRETTY LAME FOR A GROWN-UP!
COULD YOU SAY THAT IF YOU HAD AN ADULT'S PHYSIQUE?
THERE'S NO WAY!
DO YOU THINK A REAL VINE JUST HANGING FROM A BRANCH...
...COULD SUPPORT AN ADULT'S WEIGHT?
WELL, IF ALL FIVE OF YOU COULD DO IT AT ONCE...
...IT'D BE A DIFFERENT STORY.
ALL FIVE OF US...

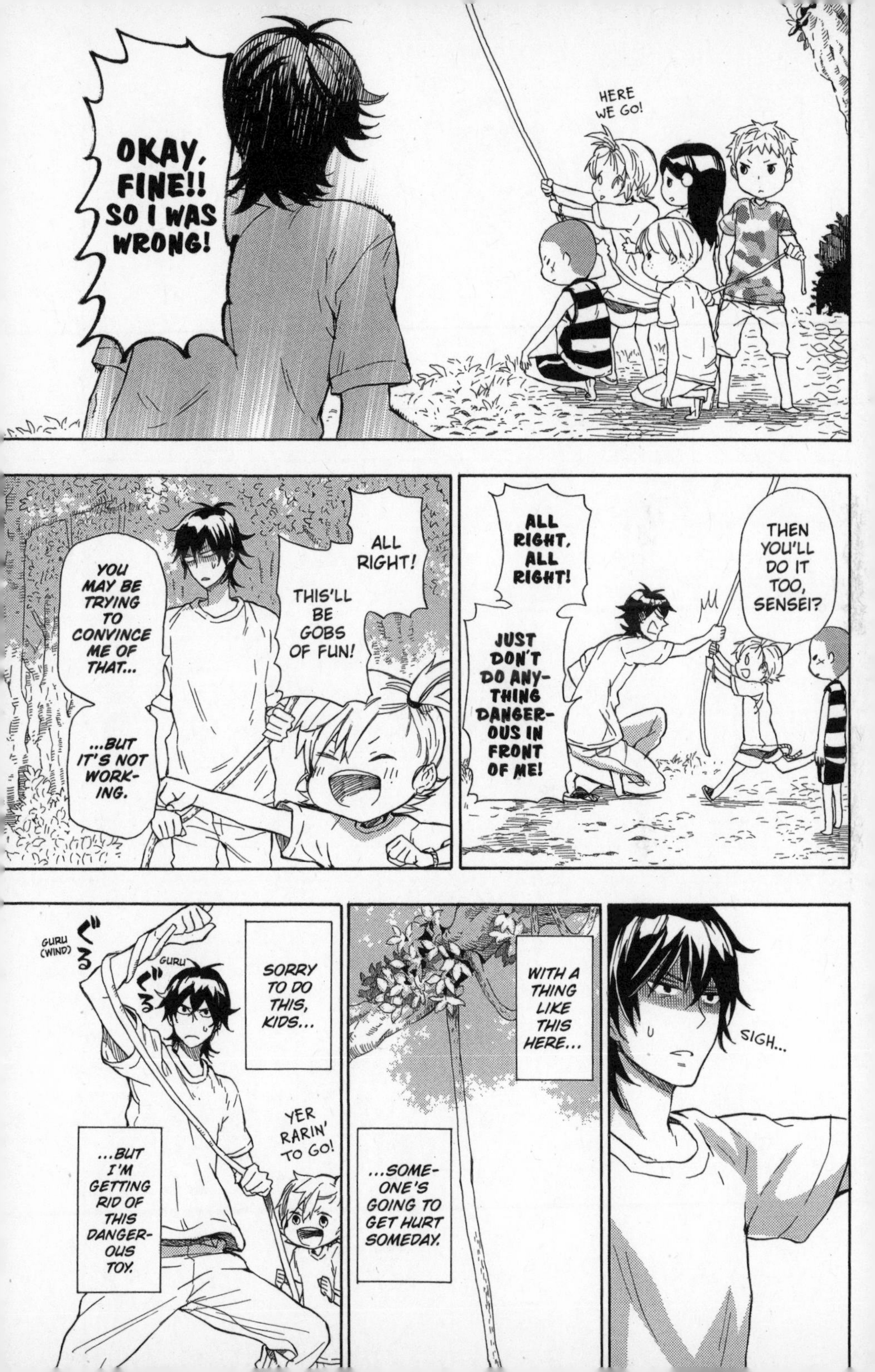
HERE WE GO!
OKAY, FINE!! SO I WAS WRONG!
THEN YOU'LL DO IT TOO, SENSEI?
ALL RIGHT, ALL RIGHT!
JUST DON'T DO ANYTHING DANGEROUS IN FRONT OF ME!
ALL RIGHT!
THIS'LL BE GOBS OF FUN!
YOU MAY BE TRYING TO CONVINCE ME OF THAT...
...BUT IT'S NOT WORKING.
SIGH...
WITH A THING LIKE THIS HERE...
...SOMEONE'S GOING TO GET HURT SOMEDAY.
SORRY TO DO THIS, KIDS...
GURU ぐる
ぐる GURU (WIND)
YER RARIN' TO GO!
...BUT I'M GETTING RID OF THIS DANGEROUS TOY.

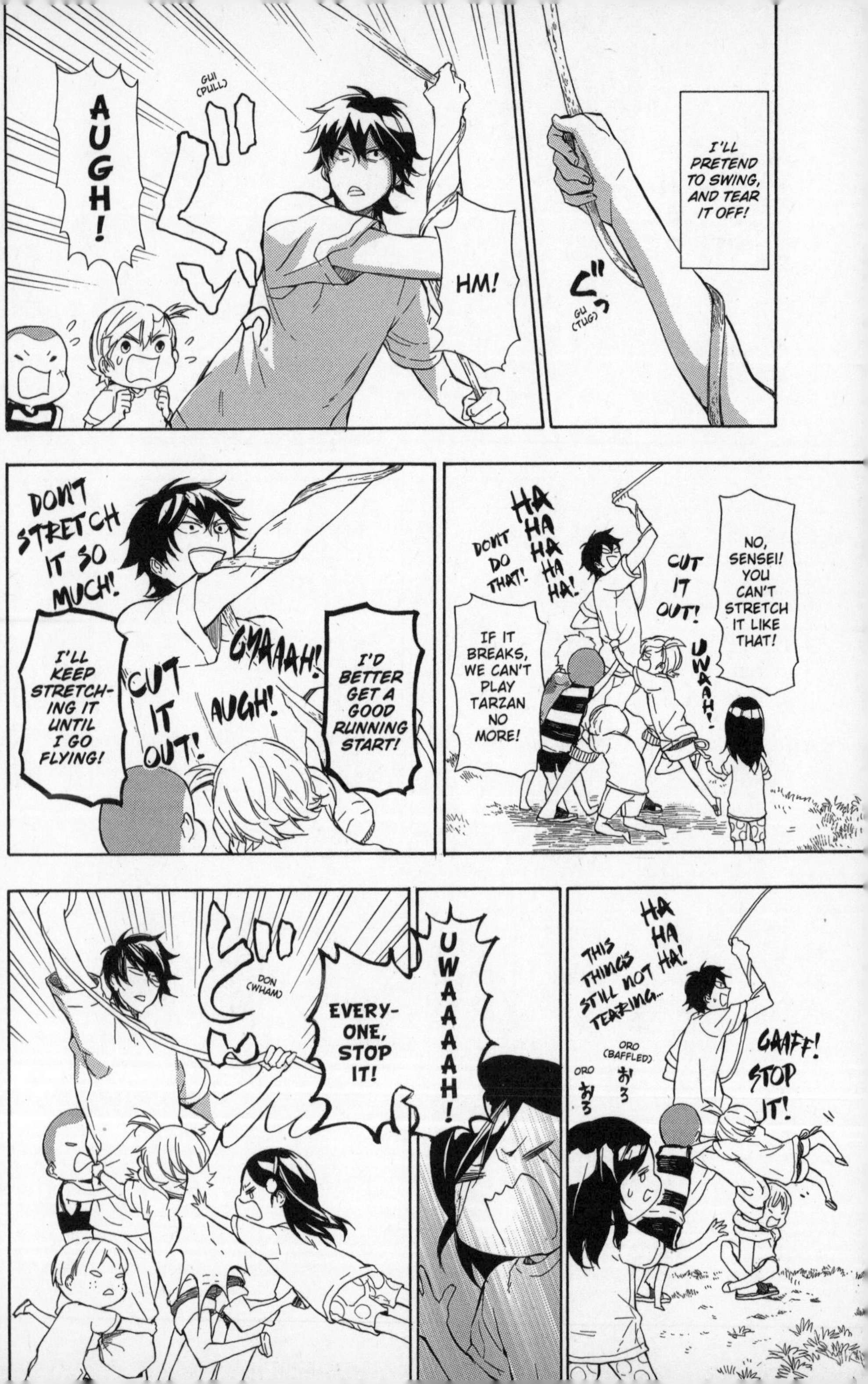
I'LL PRETEND TO SWING, AND TEAR IT OFF!
GU (TUG)
HM!
GUI (PULL)
AUGH!
NO, SENSEI! YOU CAN'T STRETCH IT LIKE THAT!
CUT IT OUT!
UWAAAH!
HA HA HA HA HA!
DON'T DO THAT!
IF IT BREAKS, WE CAN'T PLAY TARZAN NO MORE!
I'D BETTER GET A GOOD RUNNING START!
GYAAAAH!
DON'T STRETCH IT SO MUCH!
AUGH!
CUT IT OUT!
I'LL KEEP STRETCHING IT UNTIL I GO FLYING!
HA HA HA!
THIS THING'S STILL NOT TEARING...
GAAFF! STOP IT!
ORO (BAFFLED)
ORO
UWAAAAAH!
EVERY-ONE, STOP IT!
DON (WHAM)

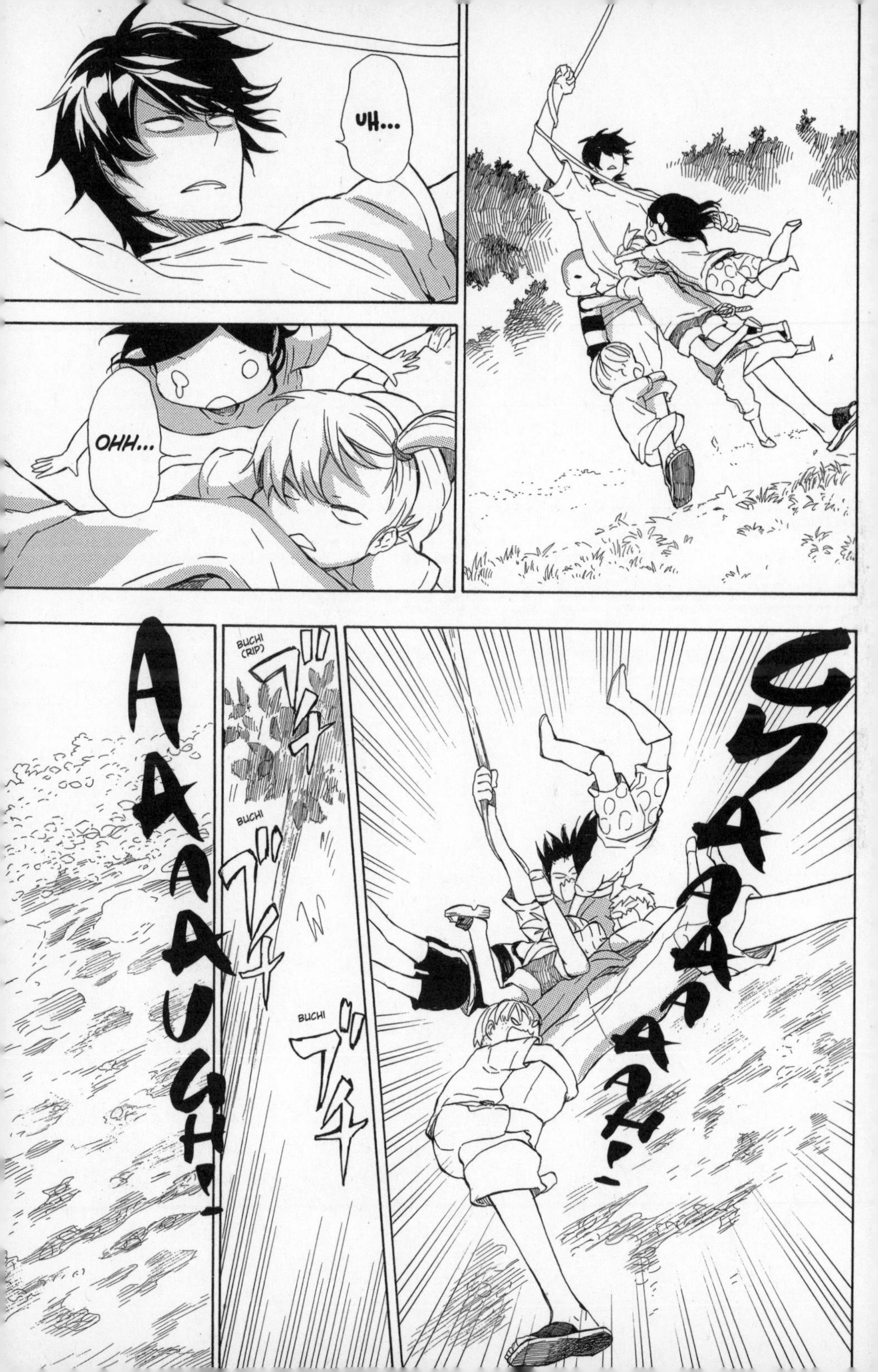
UH...
OHH...
GYAAAAAH!
BUCHI (RIP)
ブチ
BUCHI
ブチ
BUCHI
ブチ
AAAAUGH!

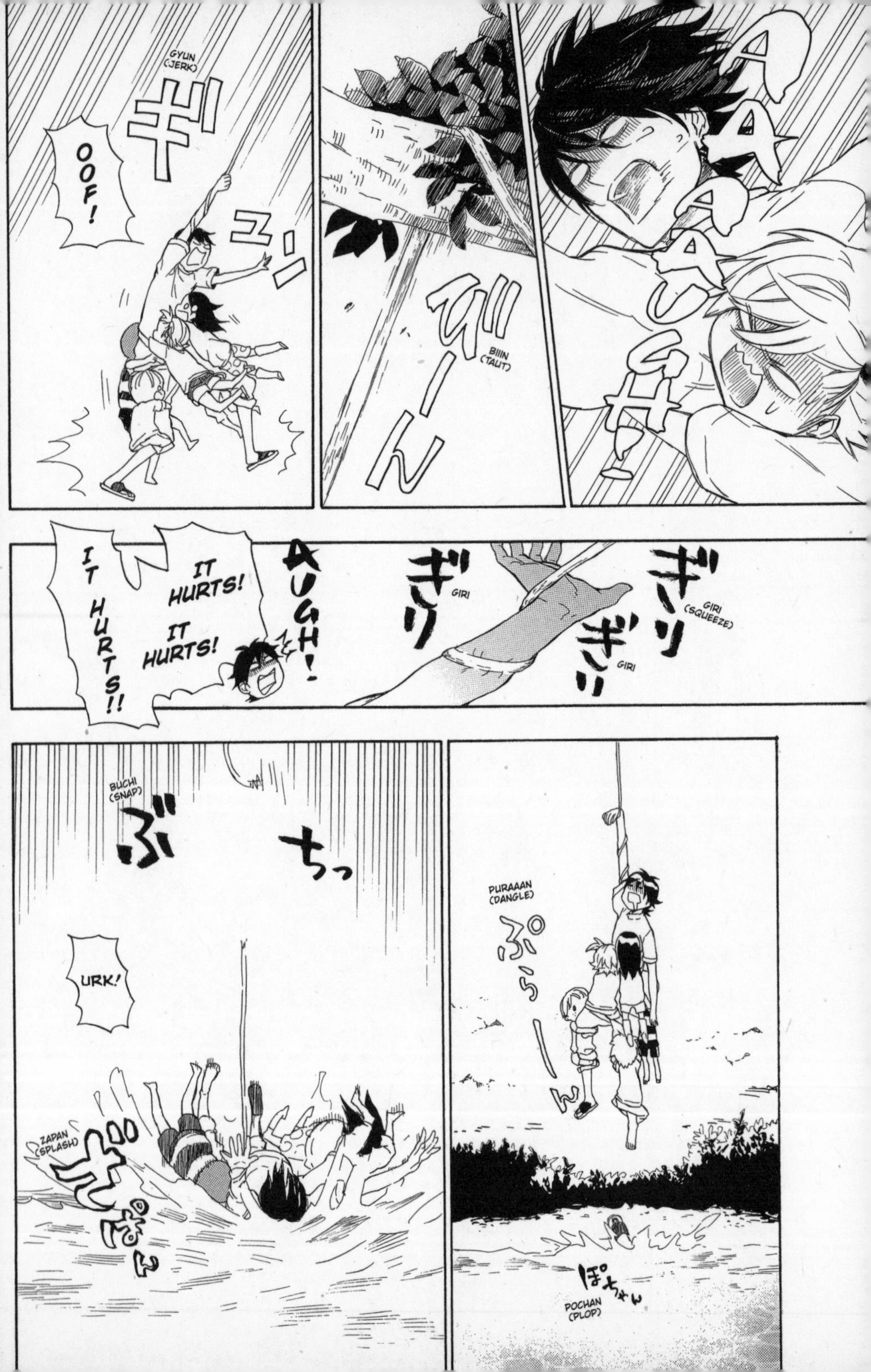
AAAA
ぴーん
BIIN (TAUT)
GYUN (JERK)
ギュン
OOF!
ギリ
GIRI (SQUEEZE)
ぎり
GIRI
ぎり
GIRI
AUGH!
IT HURTS! IT HURTS!
IT HURTS!!
PURAAAN (DANGLE)
ぷらーん
ぽちゃん
POCHAN (PLOP)
BUCHI (SNAP)
ぶちっ
URK!
ZAPAN (SPLASH)

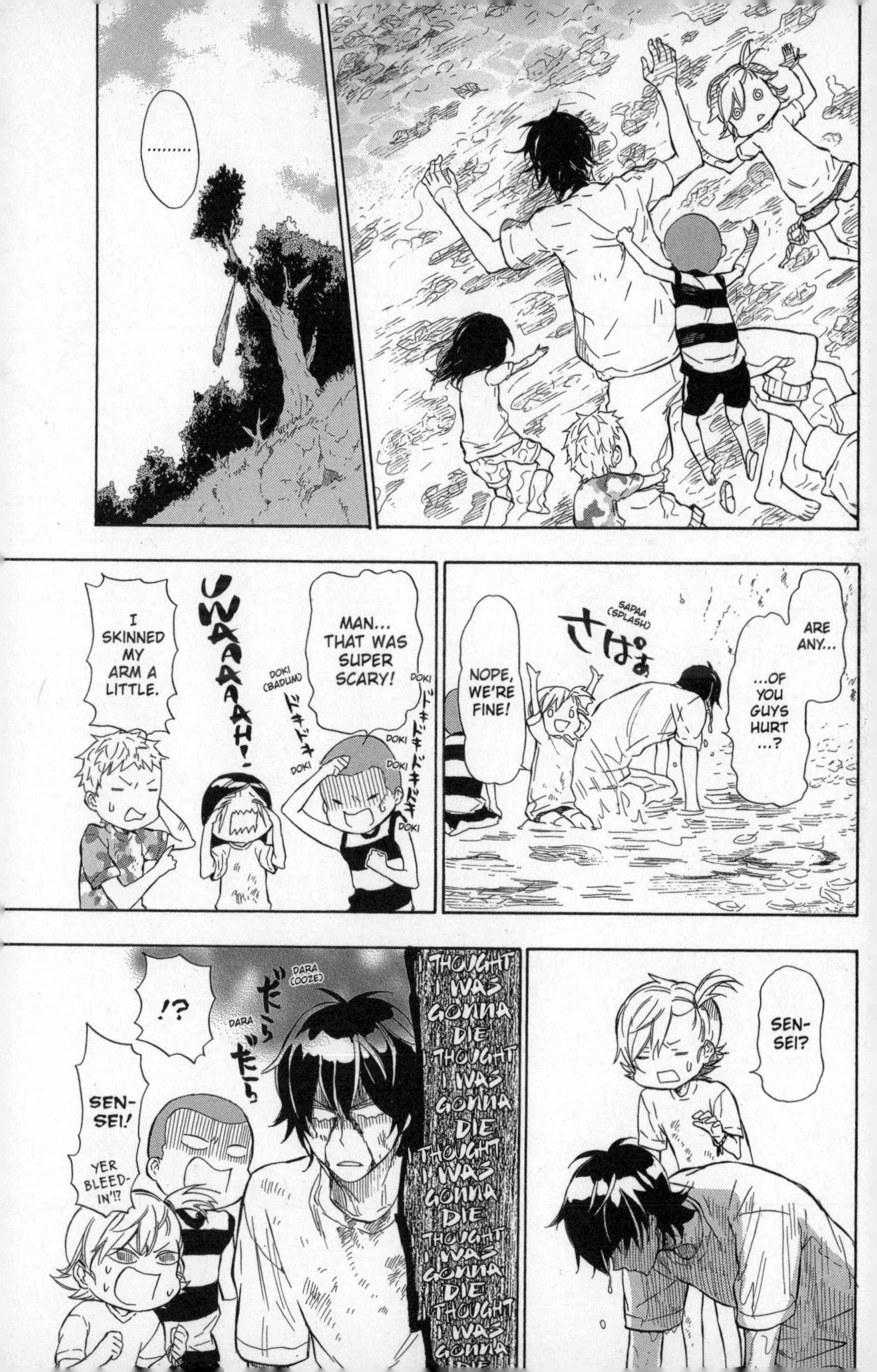

....
ARE ANY... ...OF YOU GUYS HURT ...?
SAPAA (SPLASH)
さぱぁ
NOPE, WE'RE FINE!
MAN... THAT WAS SUPER SCARY!
DOKI (BADUM) DOKI DOKI DOKI DOKI
ドキドキ ドキドキドキドキ
WAAAAAH!
I SKINNED MY ARM A LITTLE.
SEN-SEI?
THOUGHT I WAS GONNA DIE THOUGHT I WAS GONNA DIE THOUGHT I WAS GONNA DIE THOUGHT I WAS GONNA DIE THOUGHT I WAS GONNA
DARA (OOZE) DARA
だらだら
!?
SEN-SEI!
YER BLEED-IN'!?

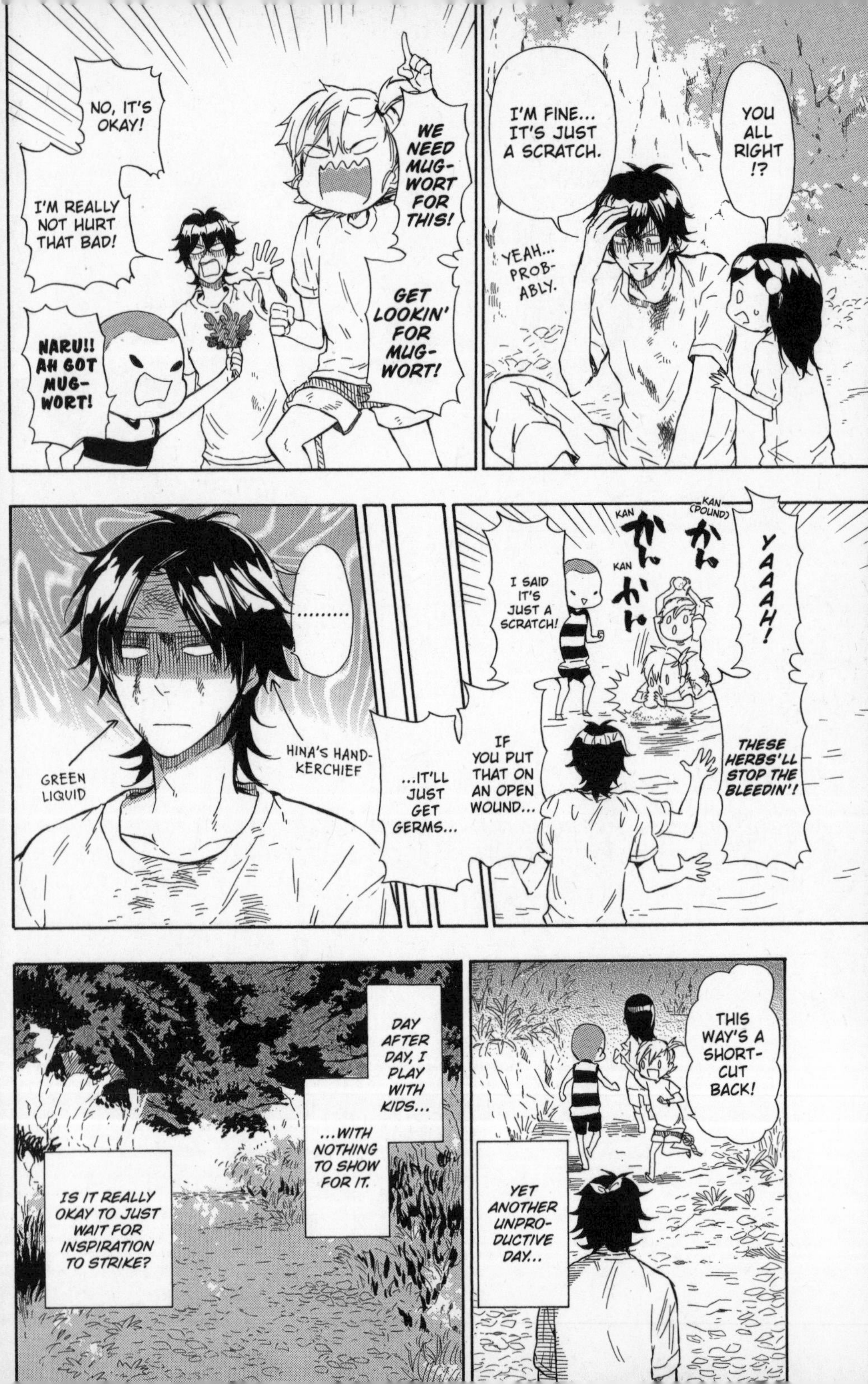
YOU ALL RIGHT!?
I'M FINE... IT'S JUST A SCRATCH.
YEAH... PROBABLY.
WE NEED MUG-WORT FOR THIS!
NO, IT'S OKAY!
GET LOOKIN' FOR MUG-WORT!
I'M REALLY NOT HURT THAT BAD!
NARU!! AH GOT MUG-WORT!
YAAAH!
KAN (POUND)
かん
KAN
KAN
かんかん
I SAID IT'S JUST A SCRATCH!
THESE HERBS'LL STOP THE BLEEDIN'!
IF YOU PUT THAT ON AN OPEN WOUND...
...IT'LL JUST GET GERMS...
....
HINA'S HAND-KERCHIEF
GREEN LIQUID
THIS WAY'S A SHORT-CUT BACK!
YET ANOTHER UNPRO-DUCTIVE DAY...
DAY AFTER DAY, I PLAY WITH KIDS...
...WITH NOTHING TO SHOW FOR IT.
IS IT REALLY OKAY TO JUST WAIT FOR INSPIRATION TO STRIKE?

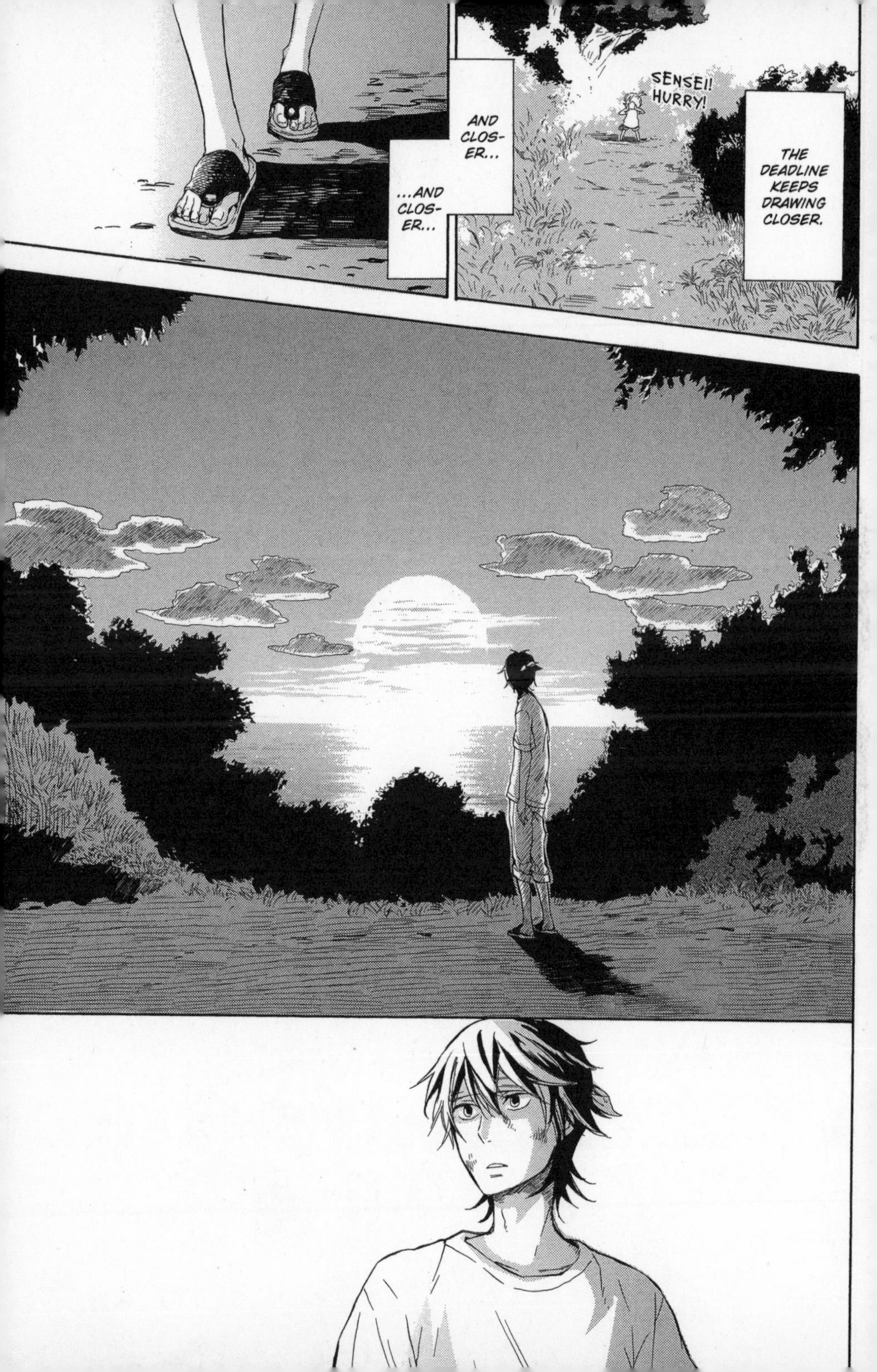
THE DEADLINE KEEPS DRAWING CLOSER.
SENSEI! HURRY!
AND CLOSER...
...AND CLOSER...

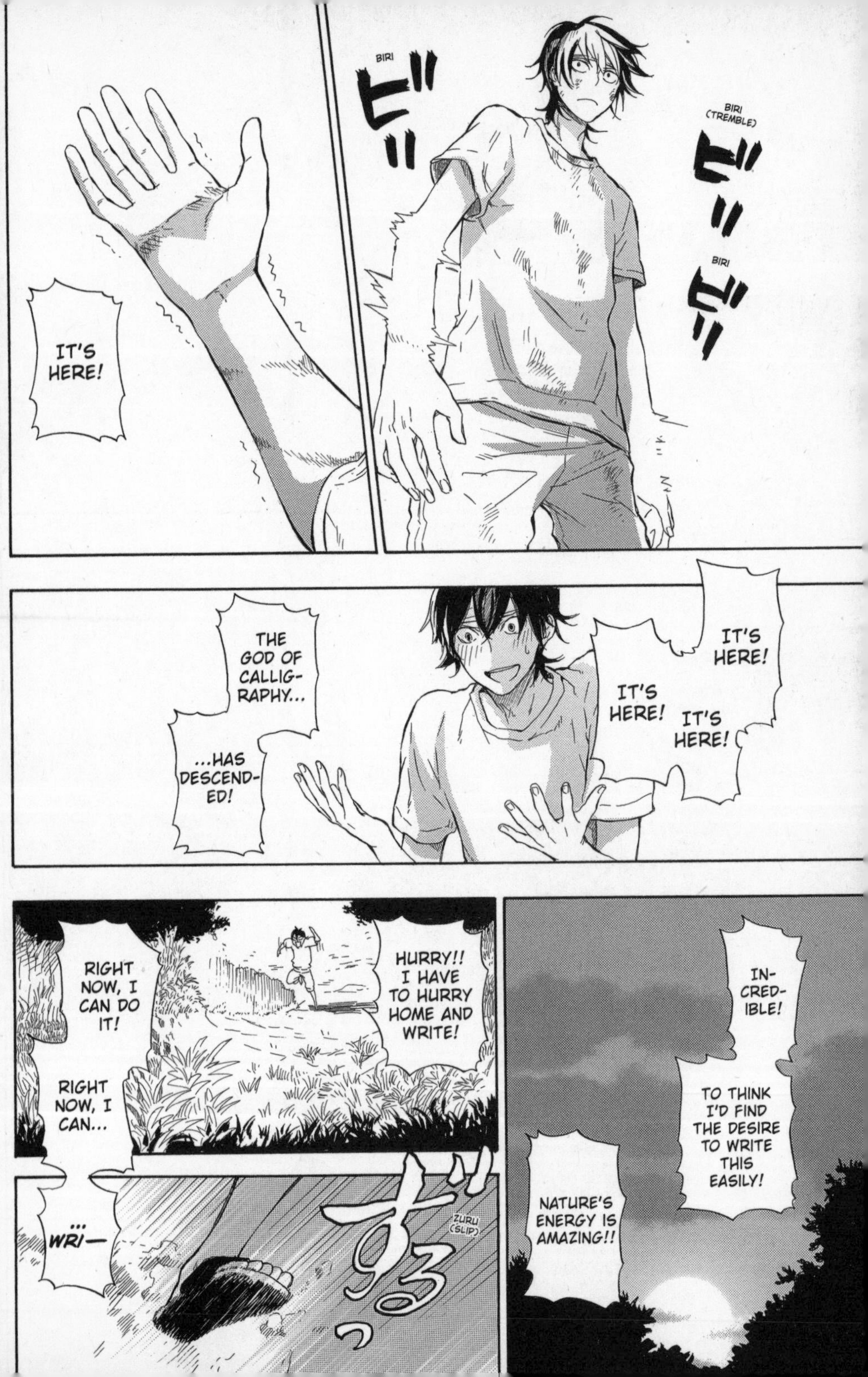

BIRI
ビッ
BIRI (TREMBLE)
ビッ
BIRI
ビリ
IT'S HERE!
IT'S HERE!
IT'S HERE!
IT'S HERE!
THE GOD OF CALLIG-RAPHY...
...HAS DESCEND-ED!
IN-CRED-IBLE!
TO THINK I'D FIND THE DESIRE TO WRITE THIS EASILY!
NATURE'S ENERGY IS AMAZING!!
HURRY!! I HAVE TO HURRY HOME AND WRITE!
RIGHT NOW, I CAN DO IT!
RIGHT NOW, I CAN...
ZURU (SLIP)
ずるっ
... WRI—

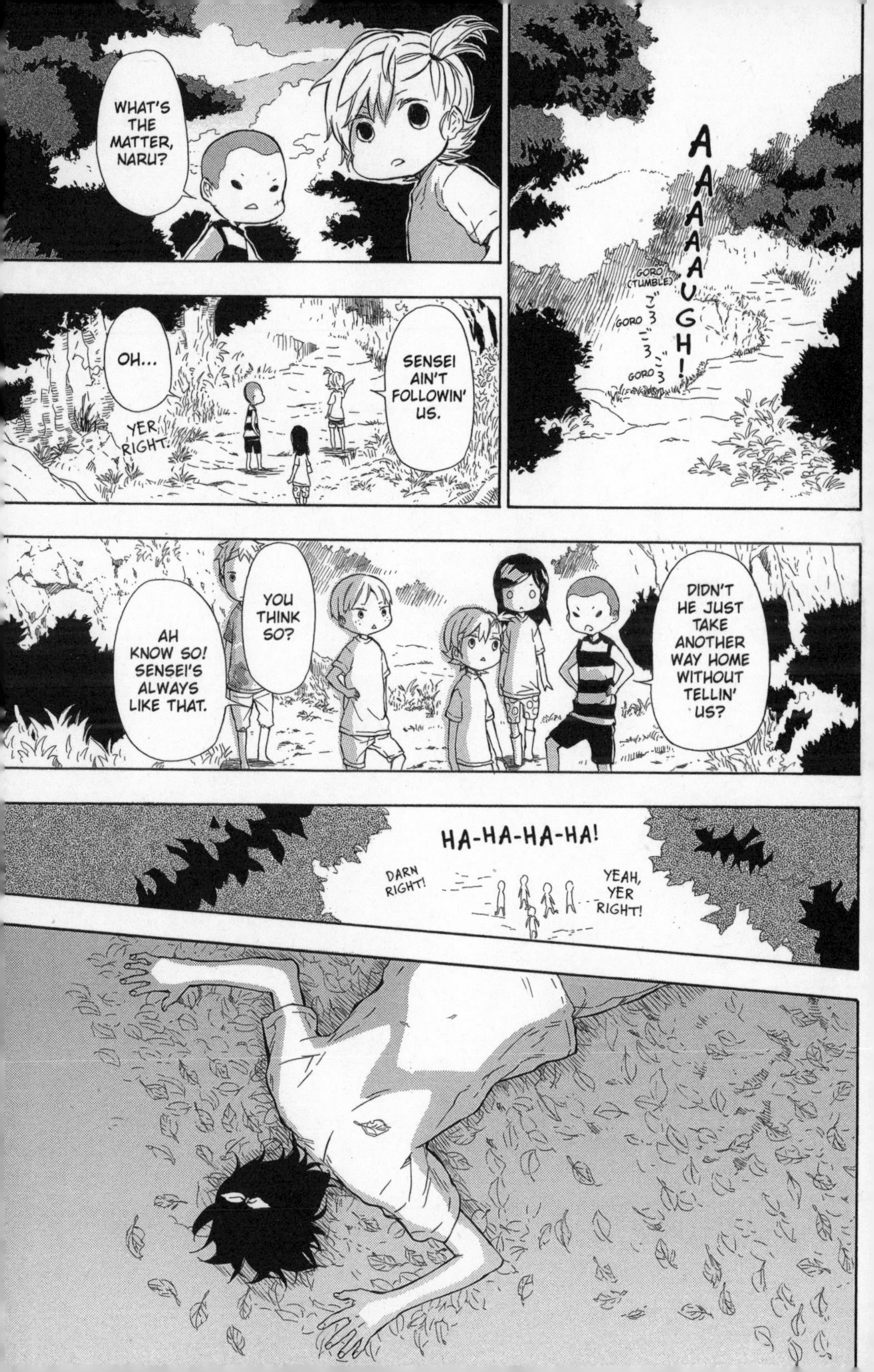
AAAAAUGH!
GORO (TUMBLE)
GORO
GORO
WHAT'S THE MATTER, NARU?
SENSEI AIN'T FOLLOWIN' US.
OH...
YER RIGHT.
DIDN'T HE JUST TAKE ANOTHER WAY HOME WITHOUT TELLIN' US?
YOU THINK SO?
AH KNOW SO! SENSEI'S ALWAYS LIKE THAT.
HA-HA-HA-HA!
YEAH, YER RIGHT!
DARN RIGHT!

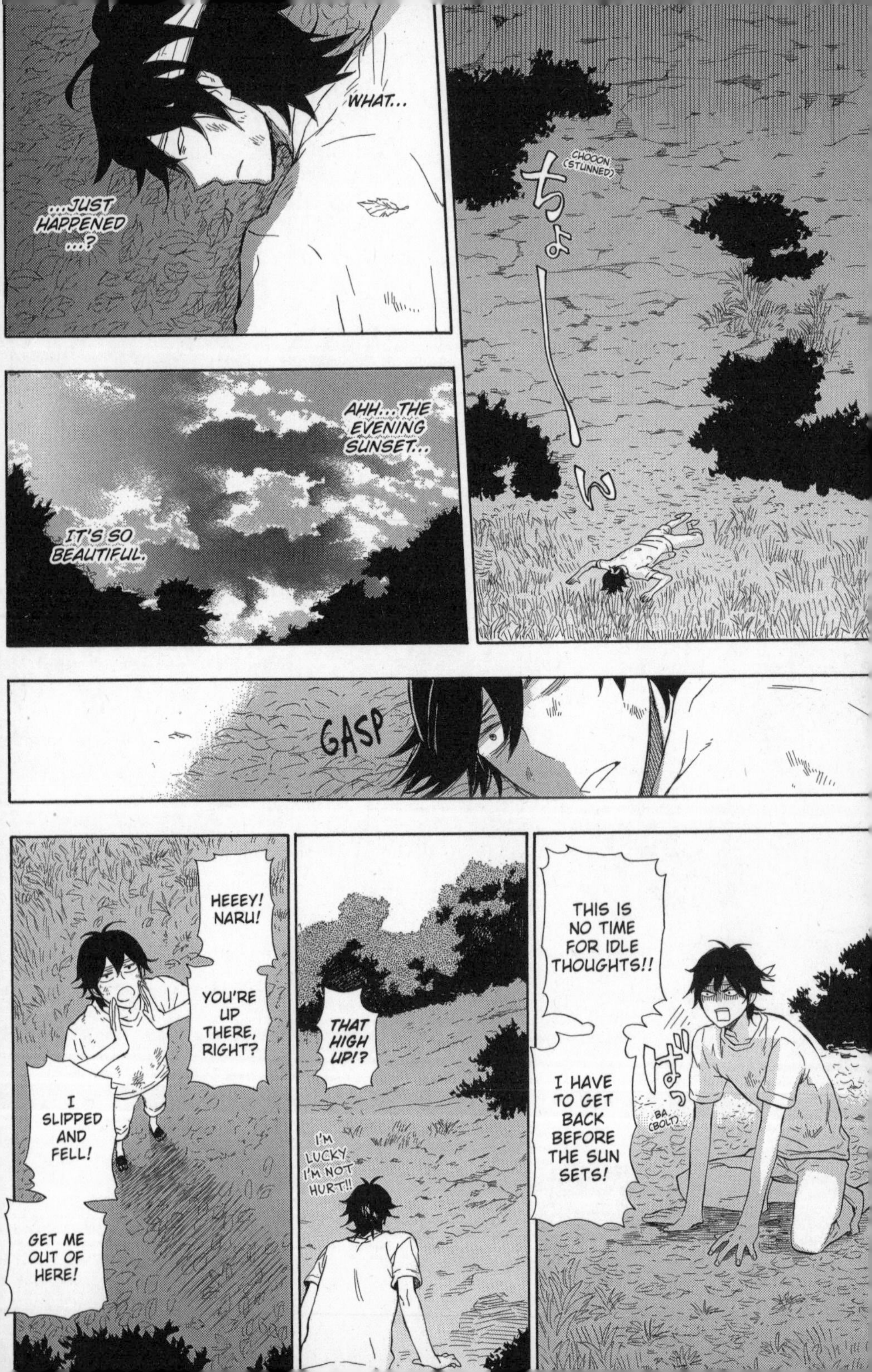
CHOOON (STUNNED)
ちょーーん
WHAT...
...JUST HAPPENED ...?
AHH...THE EVENING SUNSET...
IT'S SO BEAUTIFUL.
GASP
THIS IS NO TIME FOR IDLE THOUGHTS!!
ばっ
BA (BOLT)
I HAVE TO GET BACK BEFORE THE SUN SETS!
THAT HIGH UP!?
I'M LUCKY I'M NOT HURT!!
HEEEY! NARU!
YOU'RE UP THERE, RIGHT?
I SLIPPED AND FELL!
GET ME OUT OF HERE!

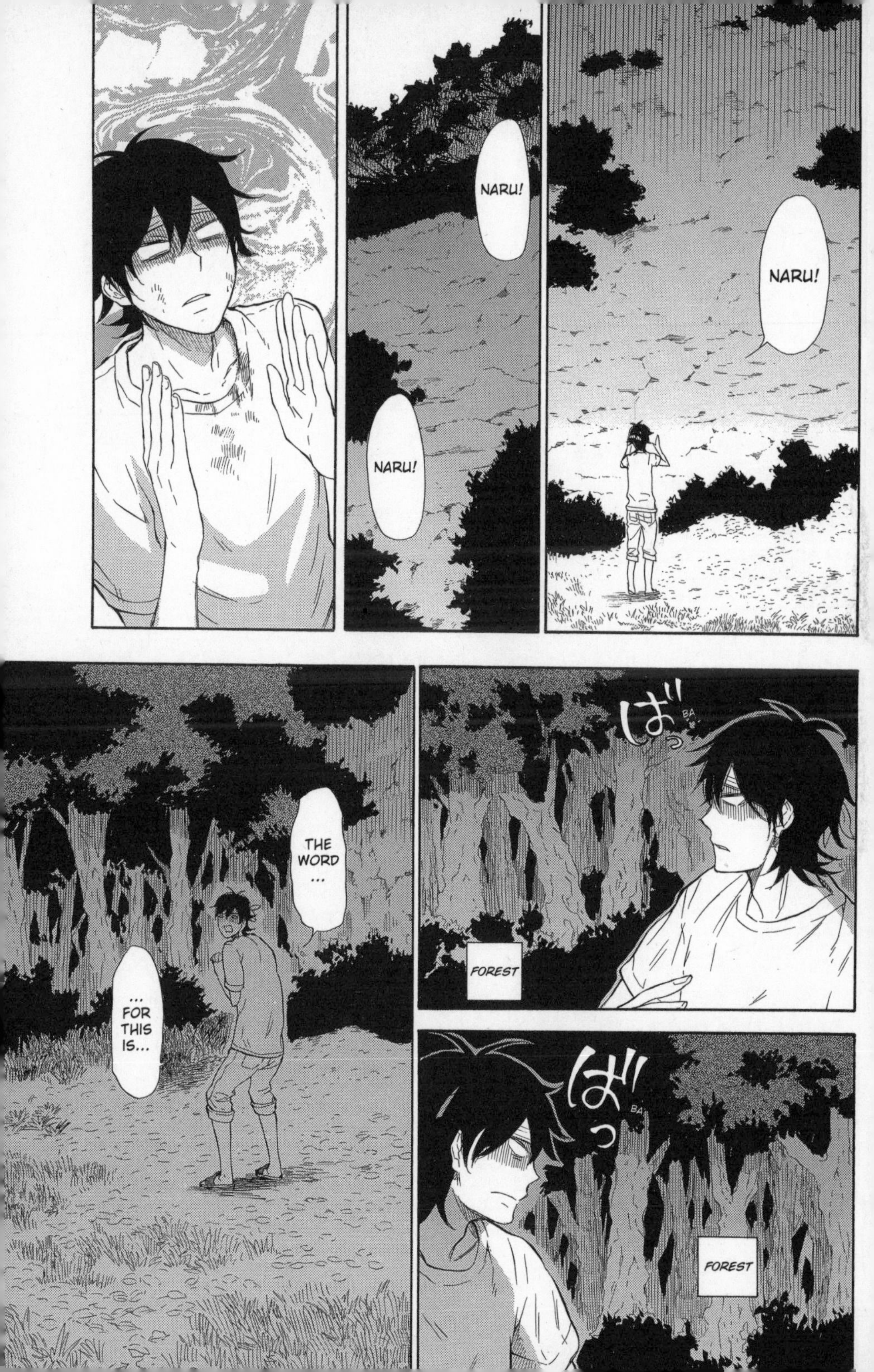
NARU!
NARU!
NARU!
ばっ
BA
FOREST
ばっ
BA
FOREST
THE WORD ...
... FOR THIS IS...

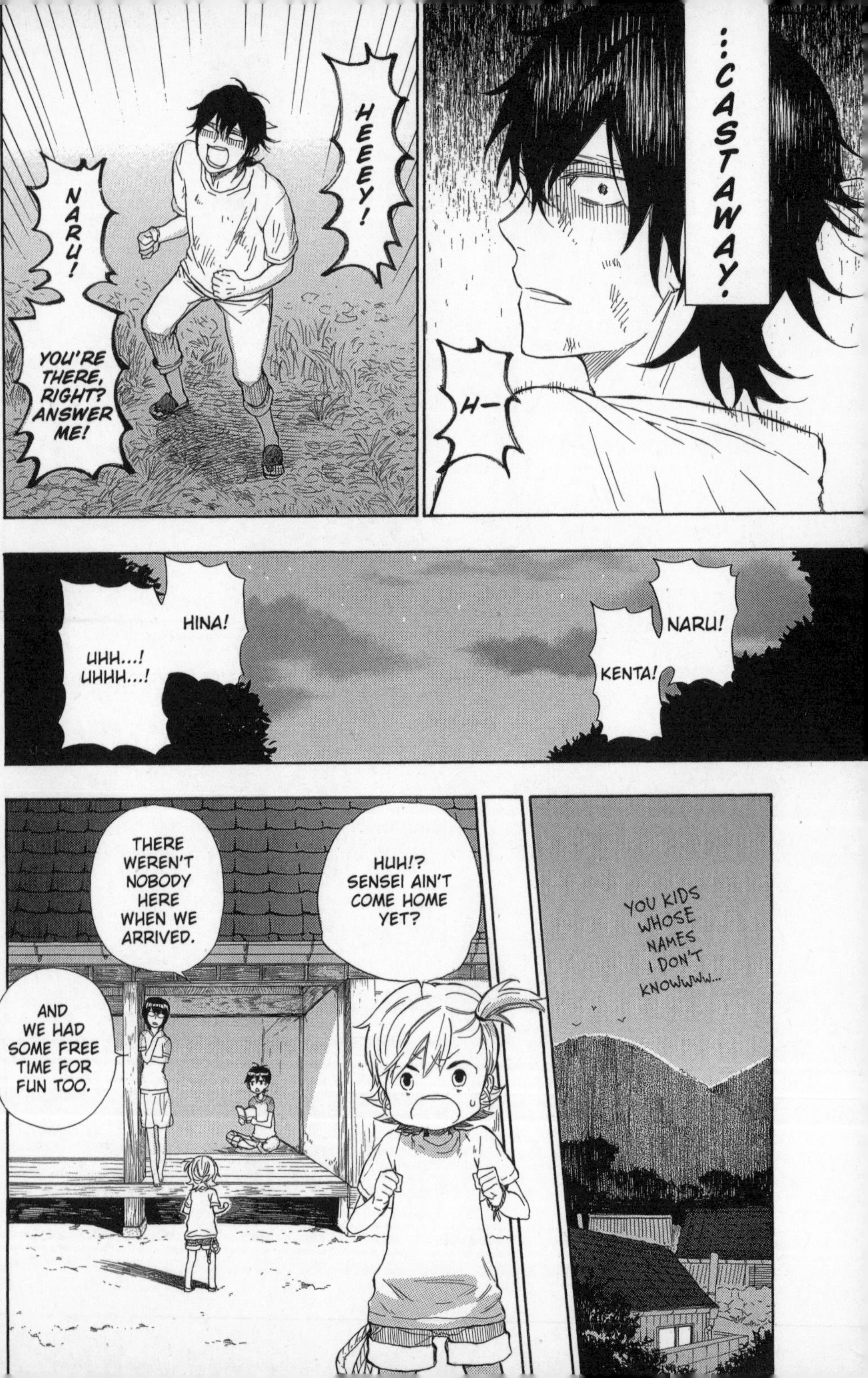
...CASTAWAY.
H—
HEEEEY!
NARU!
YOU'RE THERE, RIGHT? ANSWER ME!
NARU!
KENTA!
HINA!
UHH...! UHHH...!
YOU KIDS WHOSE NAMES I DON'T KNOWWWW...
HUH!? SENSEI AIN'T COME HOME YET?
THERE WEREN'T NOBODY HERE WHEN WE ARRIVED.
AND WE HAD SOME FREE TIME FOR FUN TOO.

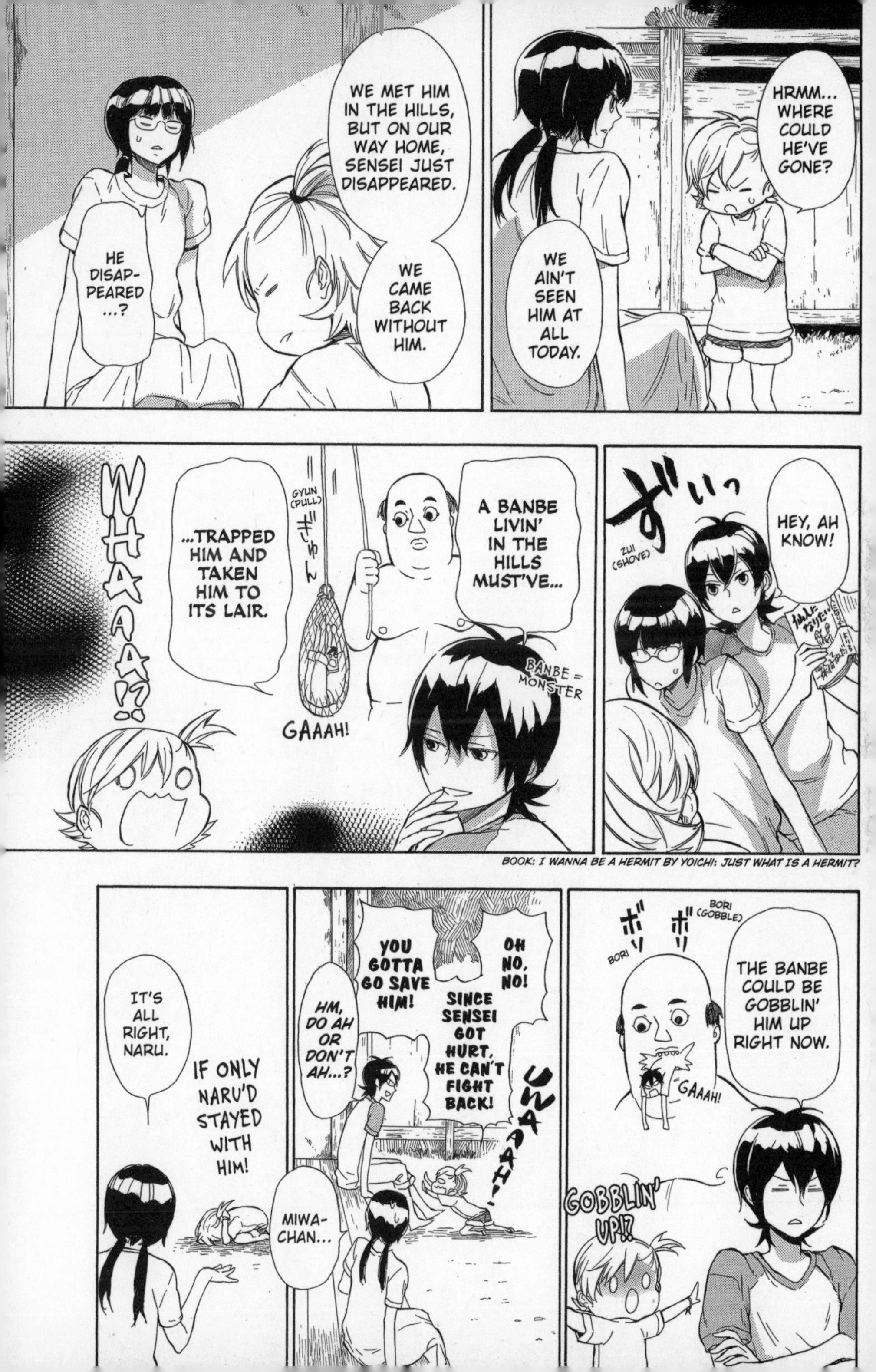
HRMM... WHERE COULD HE'VE GONE?
WE AIN'T SEEN HIM AT ALL TODAY.
WE MET HIM IN THE HILLS, BUT ON OUR WAY HOME, SENSEI JUST DISAPPEARED.
WE CAME BACK WITHOUT HIM.
HE DISAP-PEARED ...?
ZUI (SHOVE)
HEY, AH KNOW!
A BANBE LIVIN' IN THE HILLS MUST'VE...
BANBE = MONSTER
GYUN (PULL)
...TRAPPED HIM AND TAKEN HIM TO ITS LAIR.
GAAAH!
WHAAAA!?
BOOK: I WANNA BE A HERMIT BY YOICHI: JUST WHAT IS A HERMIT?
BORI (GOBBLE)
BORI
THE BANBE COULD BE GOBBLIN' HIM UP RIGHT NOW.
GAAAH!
GOBBLIN' UP!?
OH NO, NO!
SINCE SENSEI GOT HURT, HE CAN'T FIGHT BACK!
YOU GOTTA GO SAVE HIM!
HM, DO AH OR DON'T AH...?
UWAAAAH!
MIWA-CHAN...
IT'S ALL RIGHT, NARU.
IF ONLY NARU'D STAYED WITH HIM!

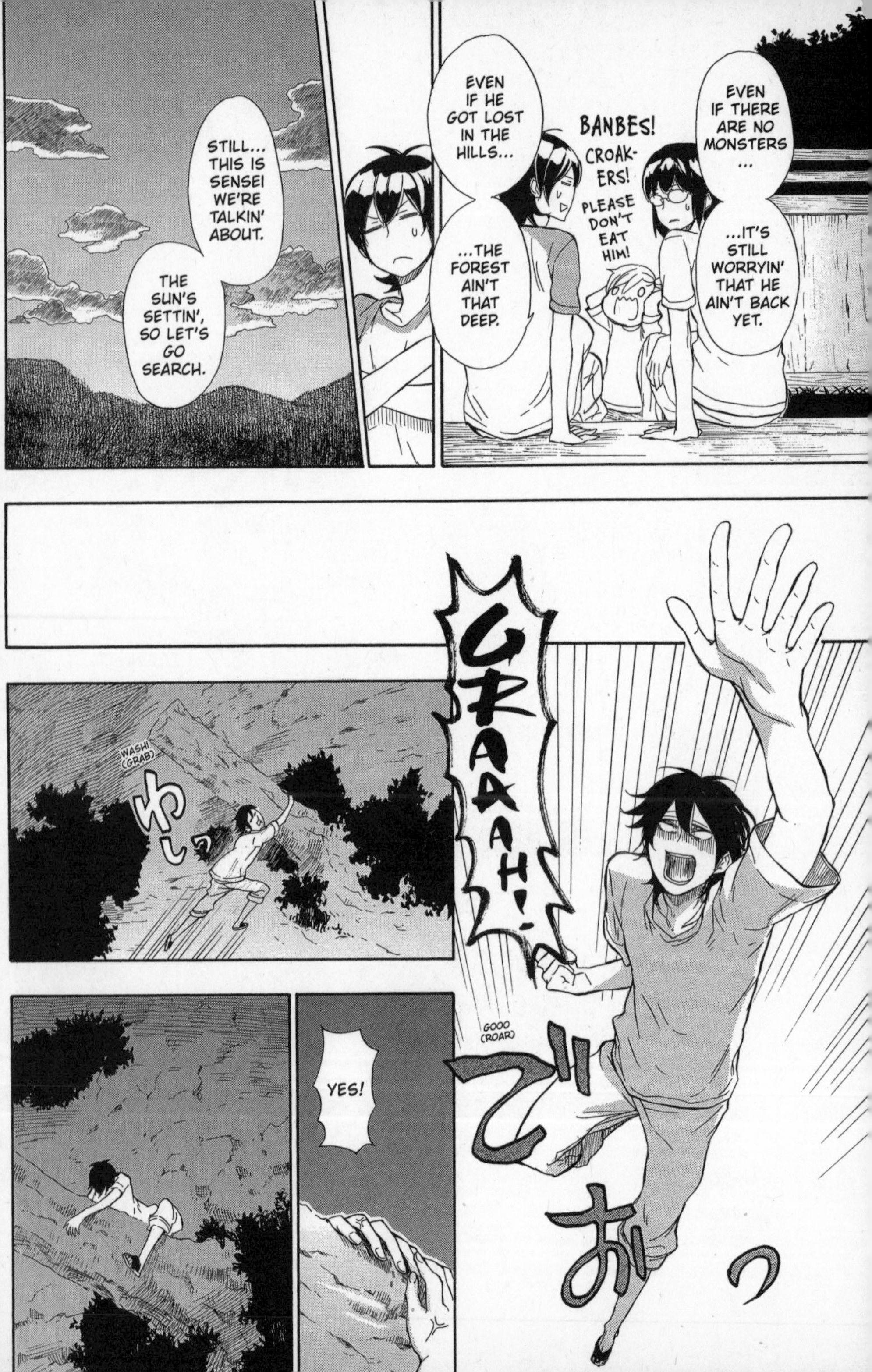
EVEN IF THERE ARE NO MONSTERS...
...IT'S STILL WORRYIN' THAT HE AIN'T BACK YET.
BANBES!
CROAK-ERS!
PLEASE DON'T EAT HIM!
EVEN IF HE GOT LOST IN THE HILLS...
...THE FOREST AIN'T THAT DEEP.
STILL... THIS IS SENSEI WE'RE TALKIN' ABOUT.
THE SUN'S SETTIN', SO LET'S GO SEARCH.
GRAAAAH!
GOOO (ROAR)
ごおっ
WASHI (GRAB)
わしっ
YES!

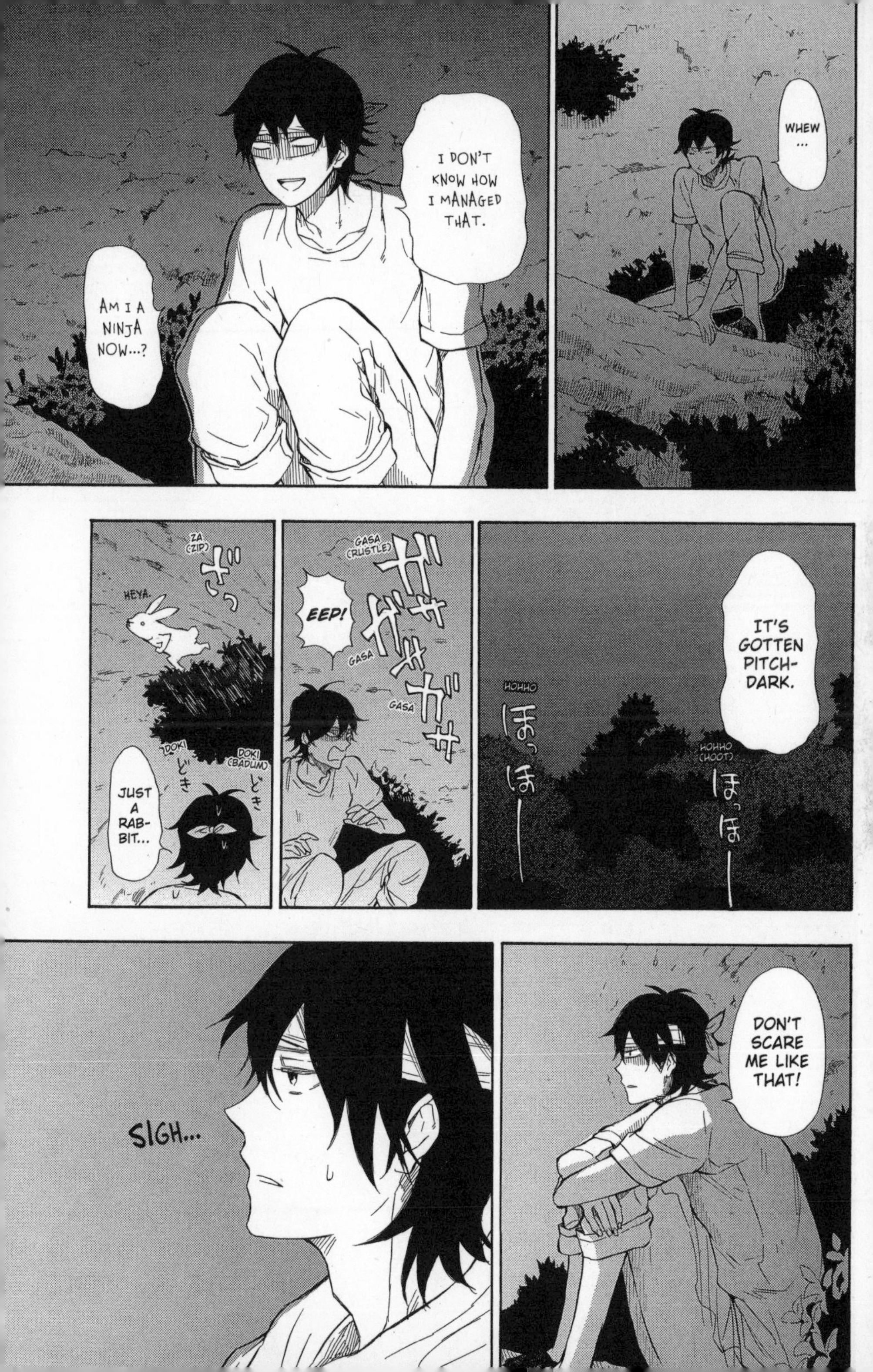
WHEW...
I DON'T KNOW HOW I MANAGED THAT.
AM I A NINJA NOW...?
IT'S GOTTEN PITCH-DARK.
HOHHO (HOOT)
ほっほー
HOHHO
ほっほー
GASA (RUSTLE)
ガサガサガサ
EEP!
GASA
GASA
ZA (ZIP)
ざっ
HEYA.
DOKI (BADUM)
どき
DOKI
どき
JUST A RAB-BIT...
DON'T SCARE ME LIKE THAT!
SIGH...

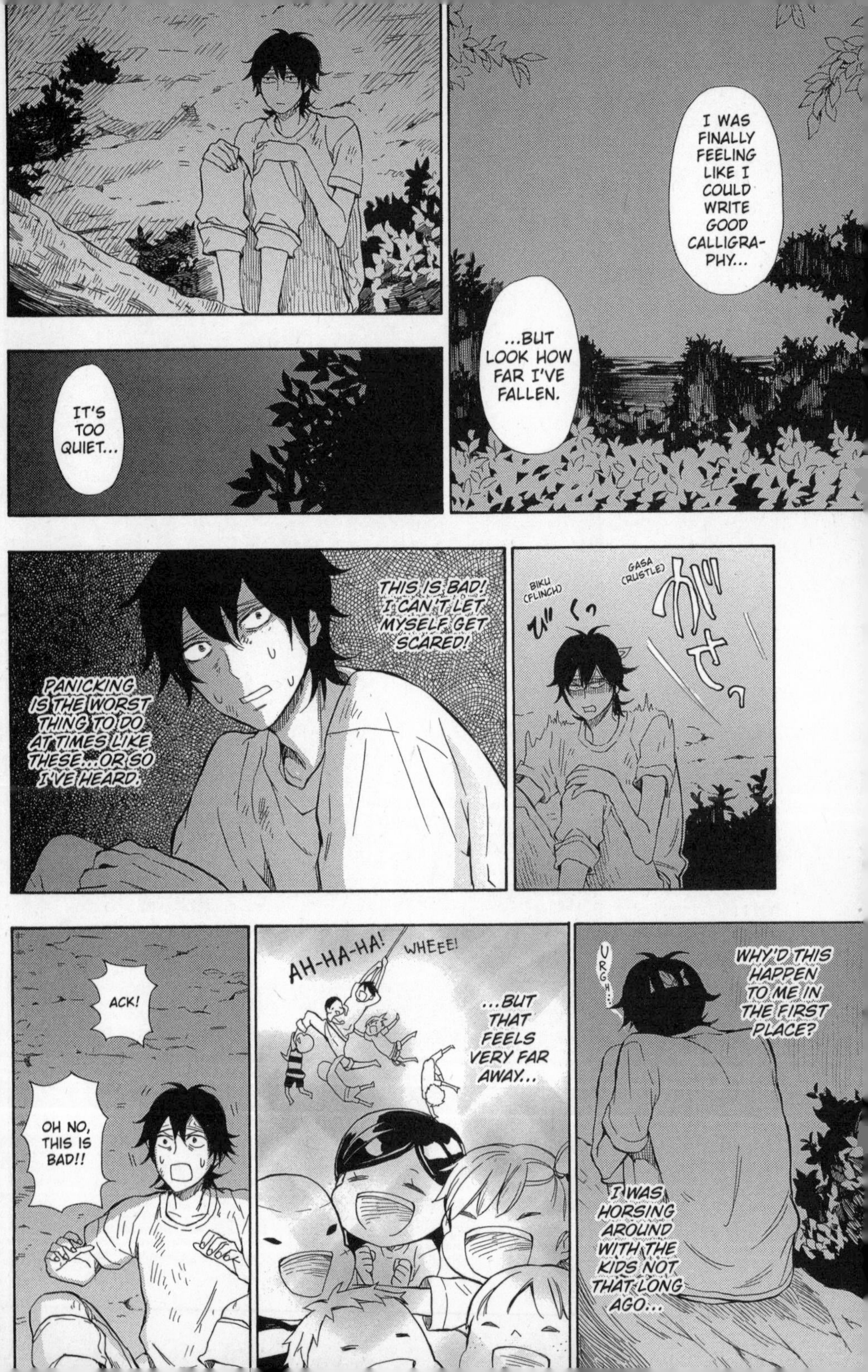

I WAS FINALLY FEELING LIKE I COULD WRITE GOOD CALLIGRA-PHY...
...BUT LOOK HOW FAR I'VE FALLEN.
IT'S TOO QUIET...
GASA (RUSTLE)
がさっ
BIKU (FLINCH)
びくっ
THIS IS BAD! I CAN'T LET MYSELF GET SCARED!
PANICKING IS THE WORST THING TO DO AT TIMES LIKE THESE...OR SO I'VE HEARD.
WHY'D THIS HAPPEN TO ME IN THE FIRST PLACE?
URGH...
I WAS HORSING AROUND WITH THE KIDS NOT THAT LONG AGO...
WHEEE!
AH-HA-HA!
...BUT THAT FEELS VERY FAR AWAY...
ACK!
OH NO, THIS IS BAD!!

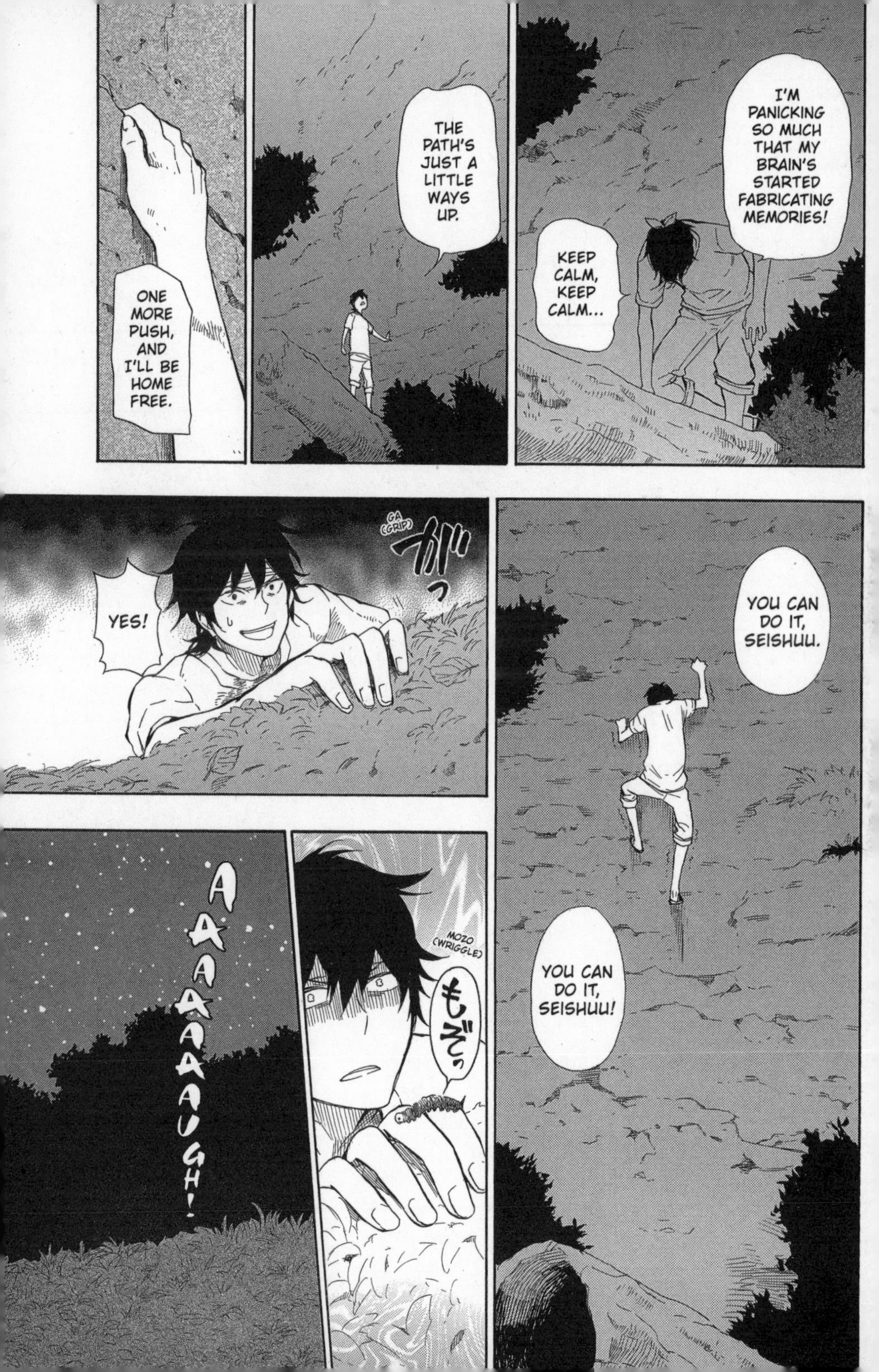
I'M PANICKING SO MUCH THAT MY BRAIN'S STARTED FABRICATING MEMORIES!
KEEP CALM, KEEP CALM...
THE PATH'S JUST A LITTLE WAYS UP.
ONE MORE PUSH, AND I'LL BE HOME FREE.
YOU CAN DO IT, SEISHUU.
YOU CAN DO IT, SEISHUU!
GA (GRIP)
がっ
YES!
MOZO (WRIGGLE)
もぞっ
AAAAAAAUGH!

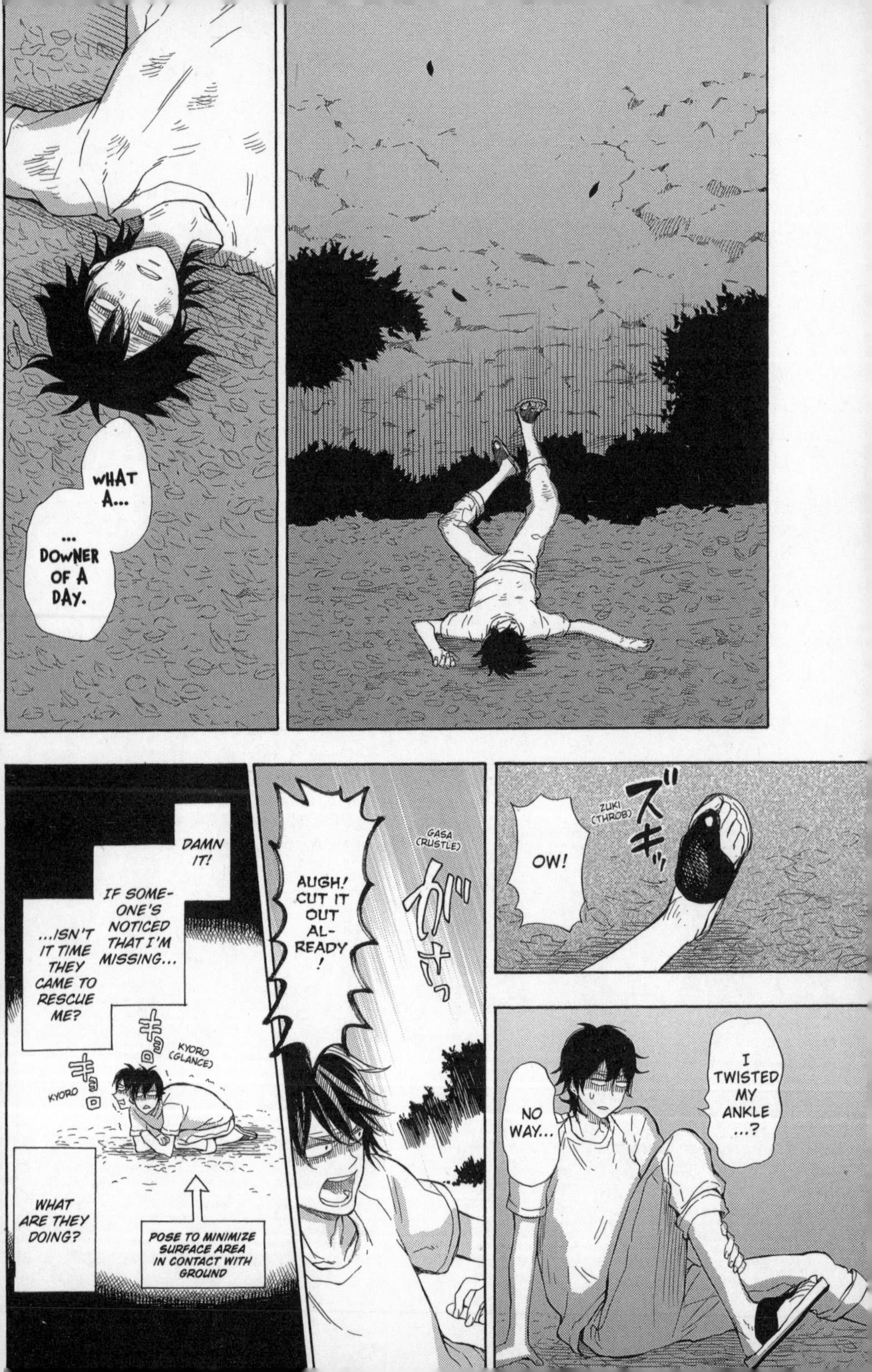
WHAT A...
... DOWNER OF A DAY.
ZUKI (THROB)
ズキッ
OW!
I TWISTED MY ANKLE ...?
NO WAY...
GASA (RUSTLE)
がさっ
AUGH! CUT IT OUT AL-READY!
DAMN IT!
IF SOME-ONE'S NOTICED THAT I'M MISSING...
...ISN'T IT TIME THEY CAME TO RESCUE ME?
キョロ
KYORO (GLANCE)
キョロ
KYORO
WHAT ARE THEY DOING?
POSE TO MINIMIZE SURFACE AREA IN CONTACT WITH GROUND

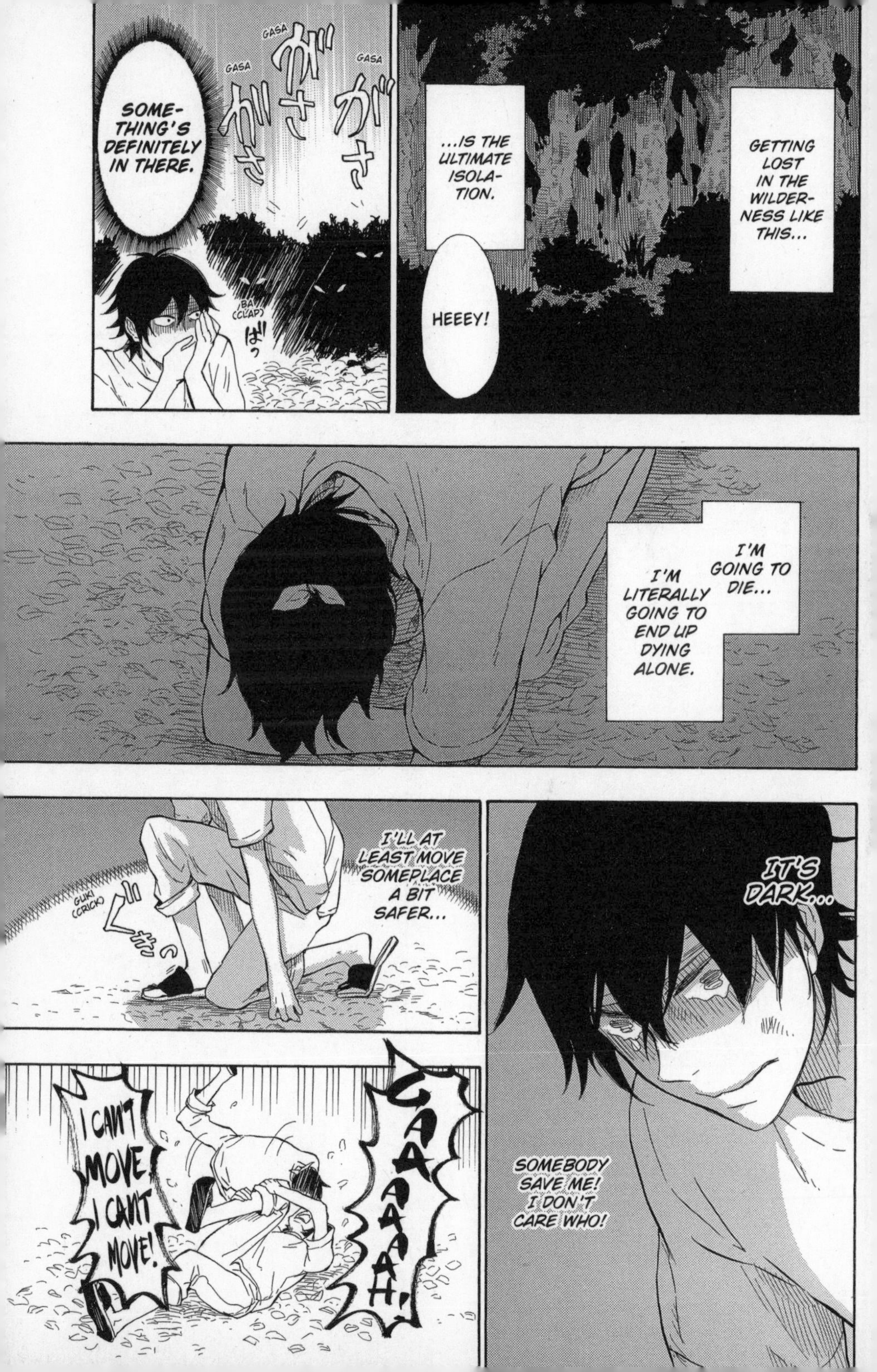
GETTING LOST IN THE WILDERNESS LIKE THIS...
...IS THE ULTIMATE ISOLATION.
HEEEY!
GASA
GASA
GASA
SOMETHING'S DEFINITELY IN THERE.
BA (CLAP)
I'M GOING TO DIE...
I'M LITERALLY GOING TO END UP DYING ALONE.
IT'S DARK...
SOMEBODY SAVE ME! I DON'T CARE WHO!
I'LL AT LEAST MOVE SOMEPLACE A BIT SAFER...
GUKI (CRICK)
GAAAAAAH!
I CAN'T MOVE! I CAN'T MOVE!

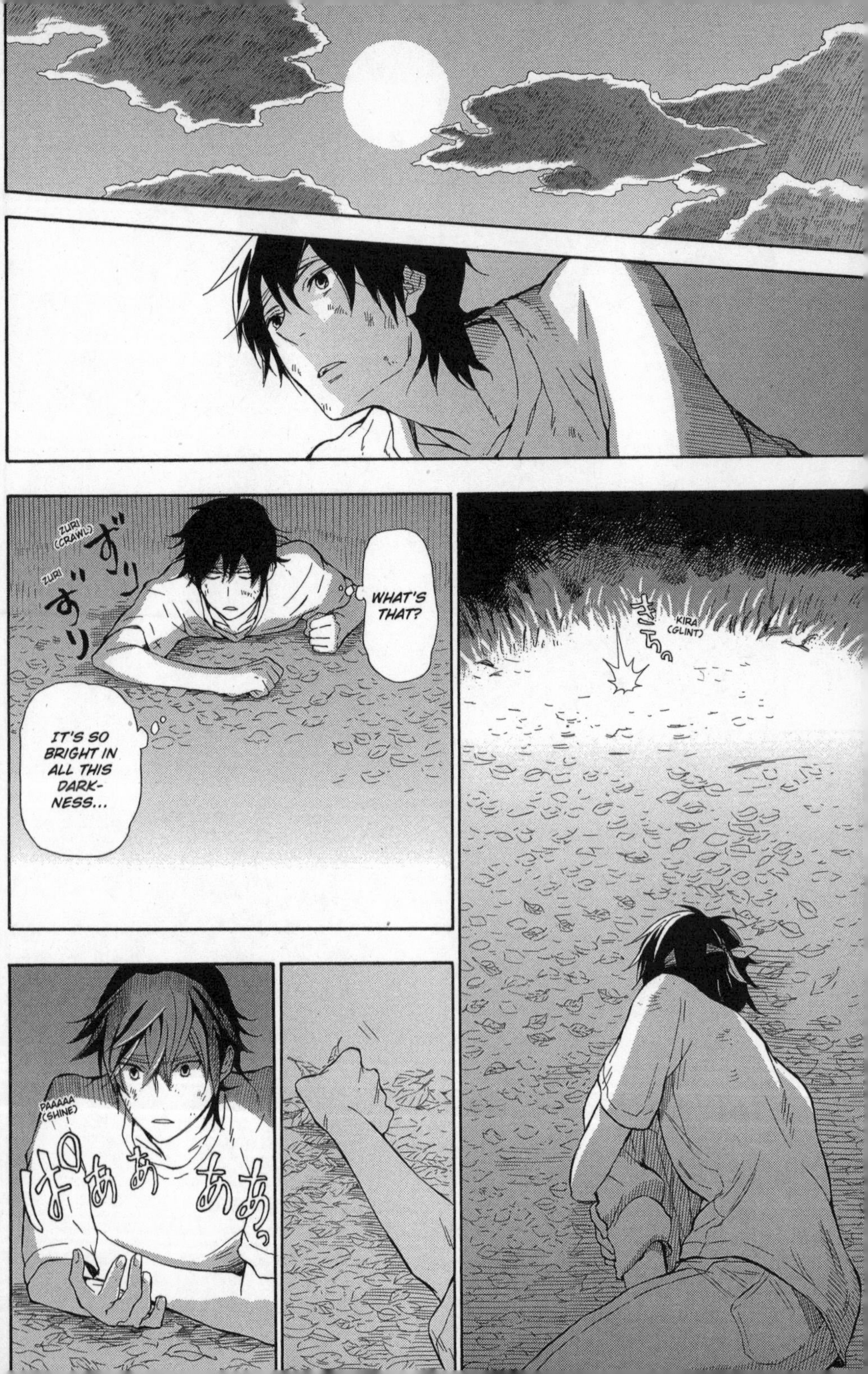

KIRA (GLINT)
ZURI (CRAWL)
ずり
ZURI
ずり
WHAT'S THAT?
IT'S SO BRIGHT IN ALL THIS DARK-NESS...
PAAAAA (SHINE)

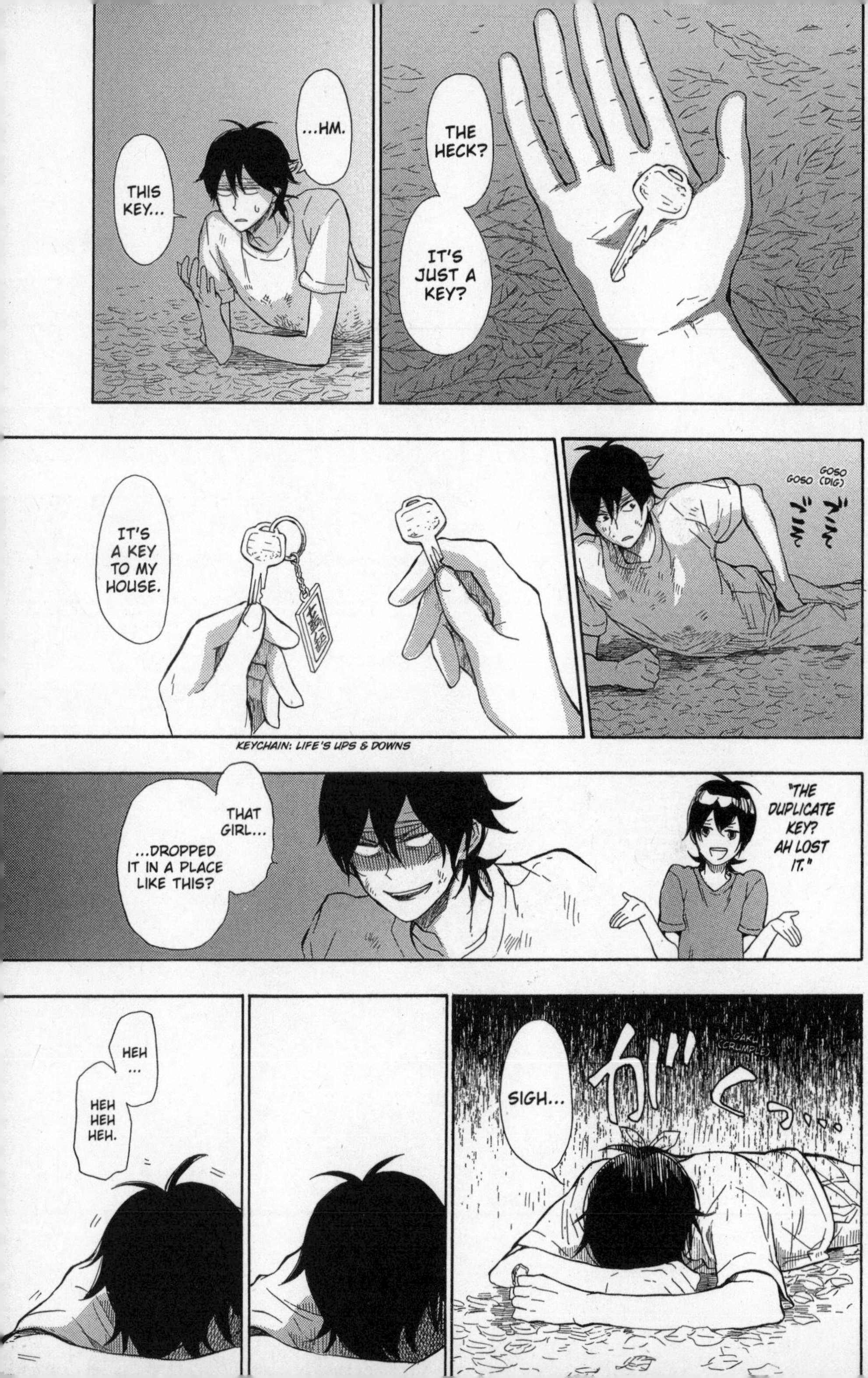
THE HECK?
IT'S JUST A KEY?
...HM.
THIS KEY...
GOSO GOSO (DIG)
IT'S A KEY TO MY HOUSE.
KEYCHAIN: LIFE'S UPS & DOWNS
"THE DUPLICATE KEY? AH LOST IT."
THAT GIRL...
...DROPPED IT IN A PLACE LIKE THIS?
GAKU (CRUMPLE)
SIGH...
HEH ...
HEH HEH HEH.

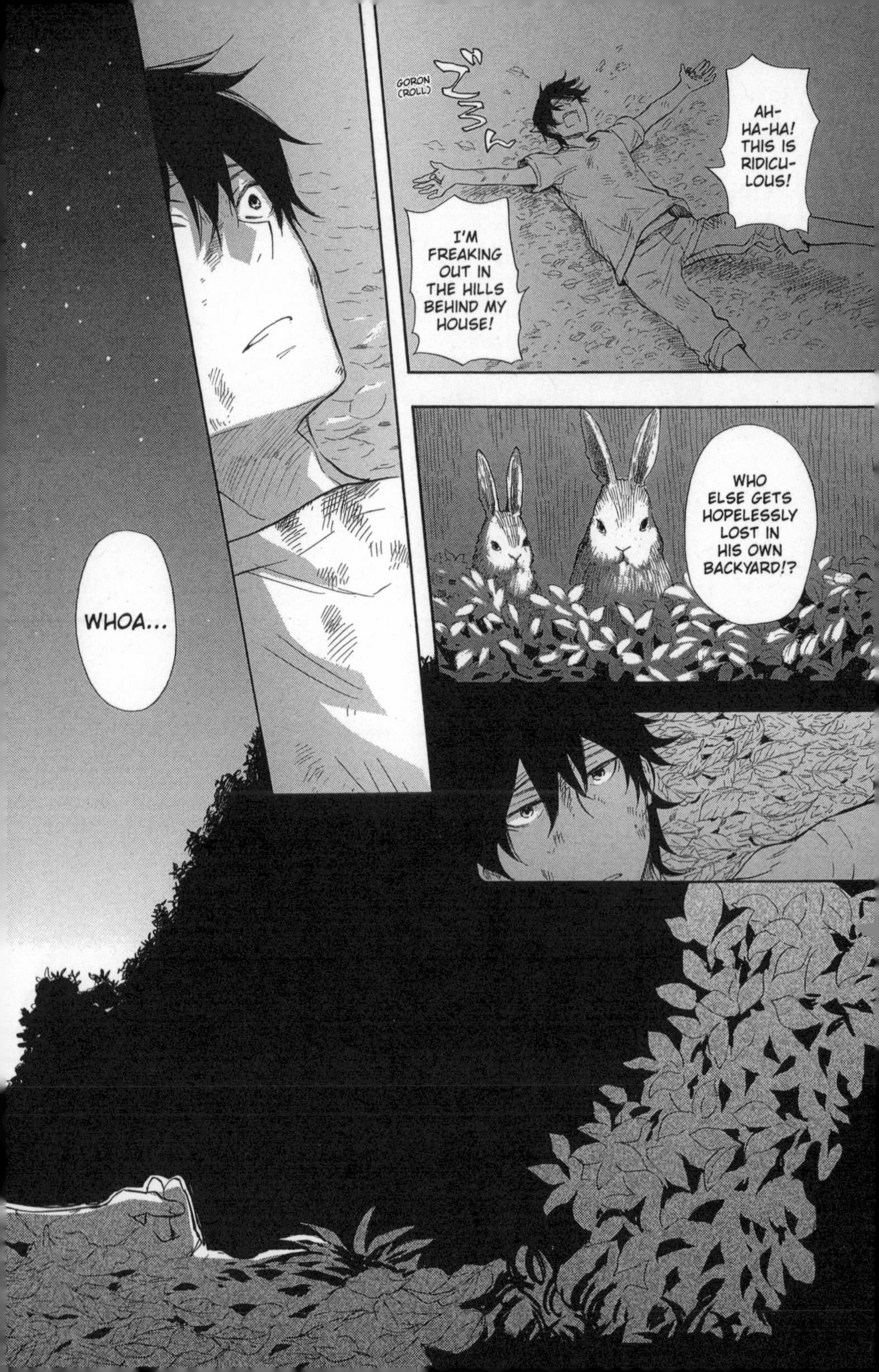
AH-HA-HA! THIS IS RIDICULOUS!
GORON (ROLL)
I'M FREAKING OUT IN THE HILLS BEHIND MY HOUSE!
WHO ELSE GETS HOPELESSLY LOST IN HIS OWN BACKYARD!?
WHOA...

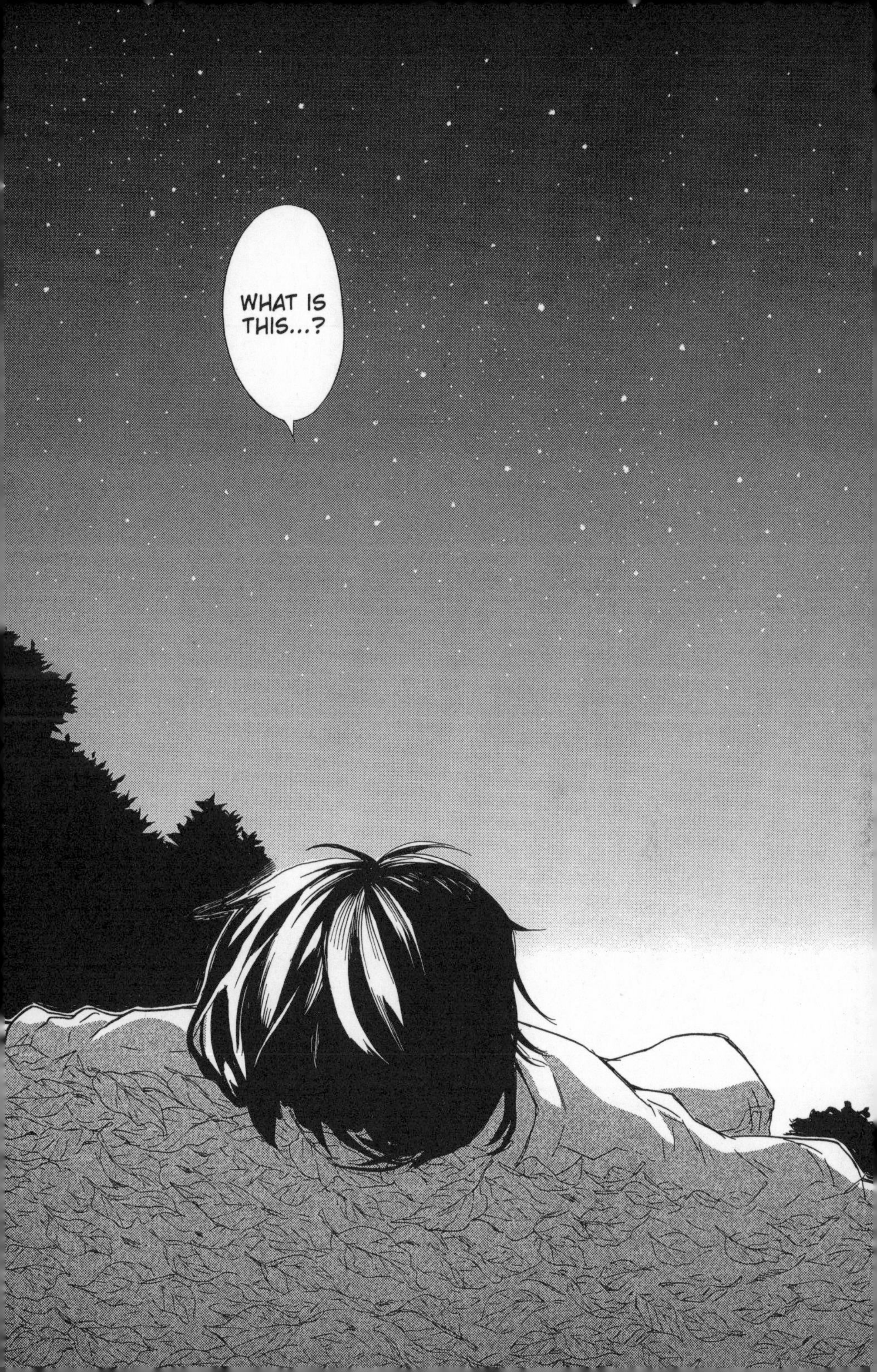
WHAT IS THIS...?

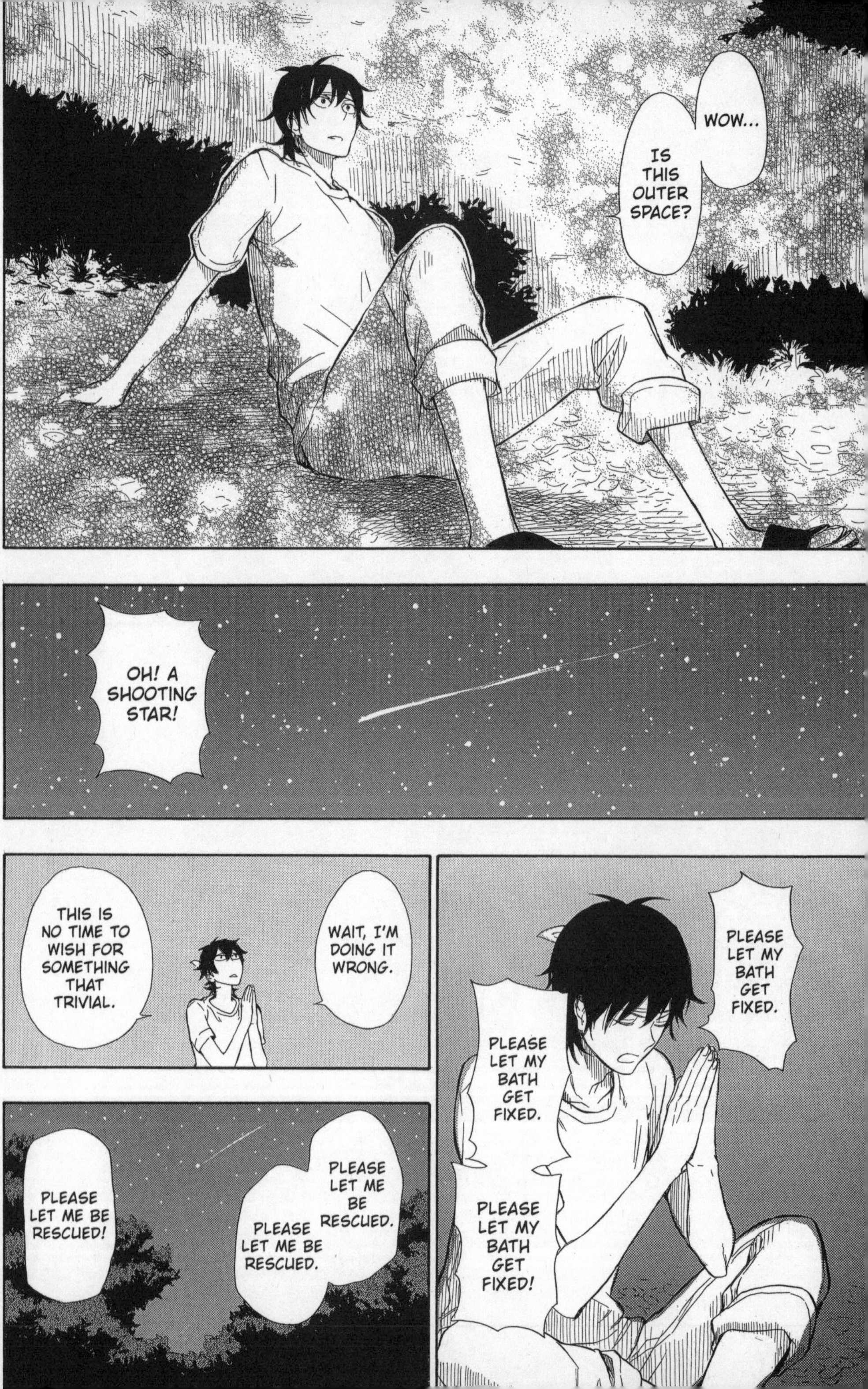
WOW...
IS THIS OUTER SPACE?
OH! A SHOOTING STAR!
PLEASE LET MY BATH GET FIXED.
PLEASE LET MY BATH GET FIXED.
PLEASE LET MY BATH GET FIXED!
WAIT, I'M DOING IT WRONG.
THIS IS NO TIME TO WISH FOR SOMETHING THAT TRIVIAL.
PLEASE LET ME BE RESCUED.
PLEASE LET ME BE RESCUED.
PLEASE LET ME BE RESCUED!

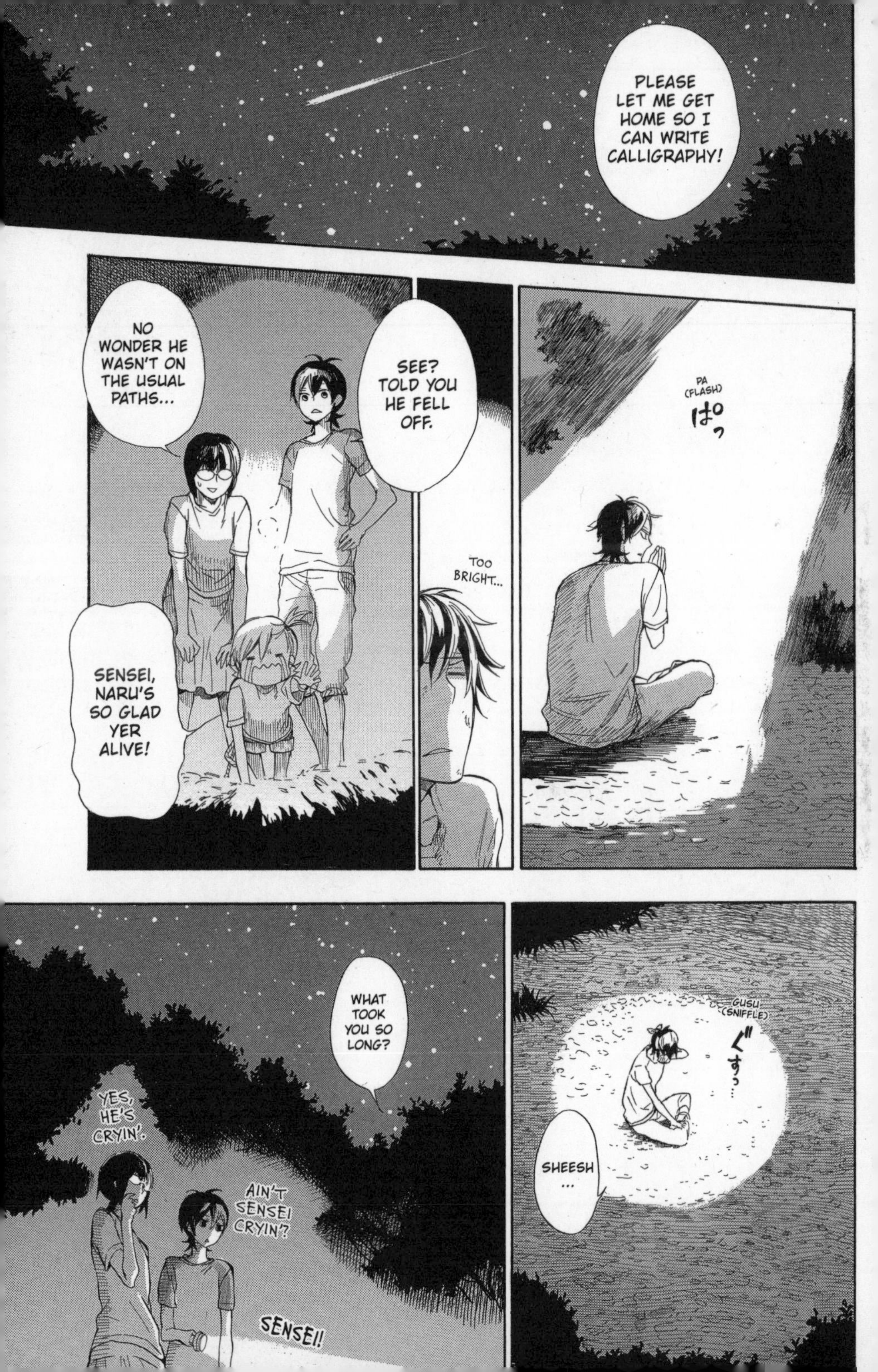
PLEASE LET ME GET HOME SO I CAN WRITE CALLIGRAPHY!
PA (FLASH)
ぱっ
TOO BRIGHT...
SEE? TOLD YOU HE FELL OFF.
NO WONDER HE WASN'T ON THE USUAL PATHS...
SENSEI, NARU'S SO GLAD YER ALIVE!
GUSU (SNIFFLE)
ぐすっ...
SHEESH ...
WHAT TOOK YOU SO LONG?
AIN'T SENSEI CRYIN'?
YES, HE'S CRYIN'.
SENSEI!

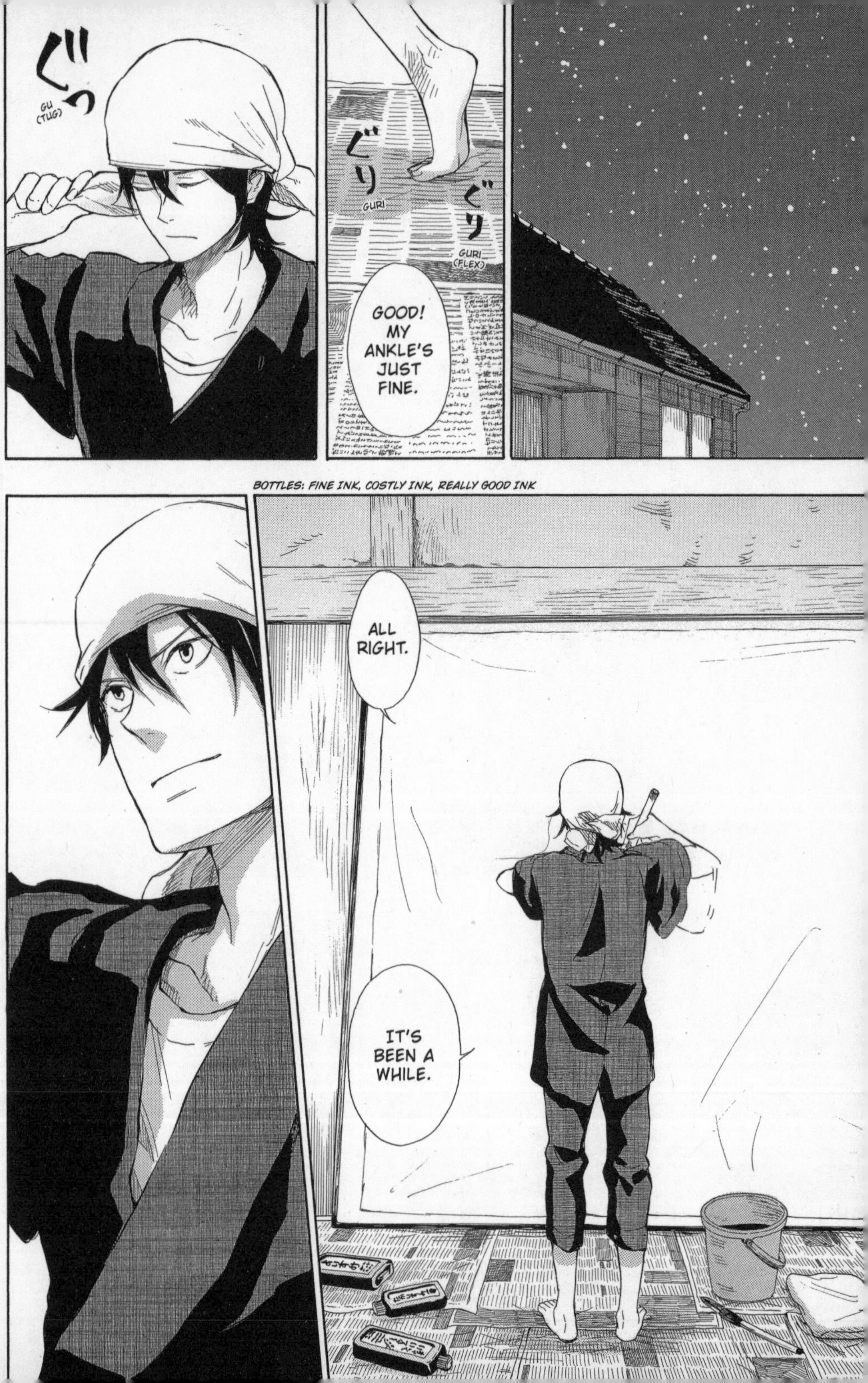
ぐり
GURI
ぐり
GURI (FLEX)
GOOD! MY ANKLE'S JUST FINE.
ぐっ
GU (TUG)
BOTTLES: FINE INK, COSTLY INK, REALLY GOOD INK
ALL RIGHT.
IT'S BEEN A WHILE.

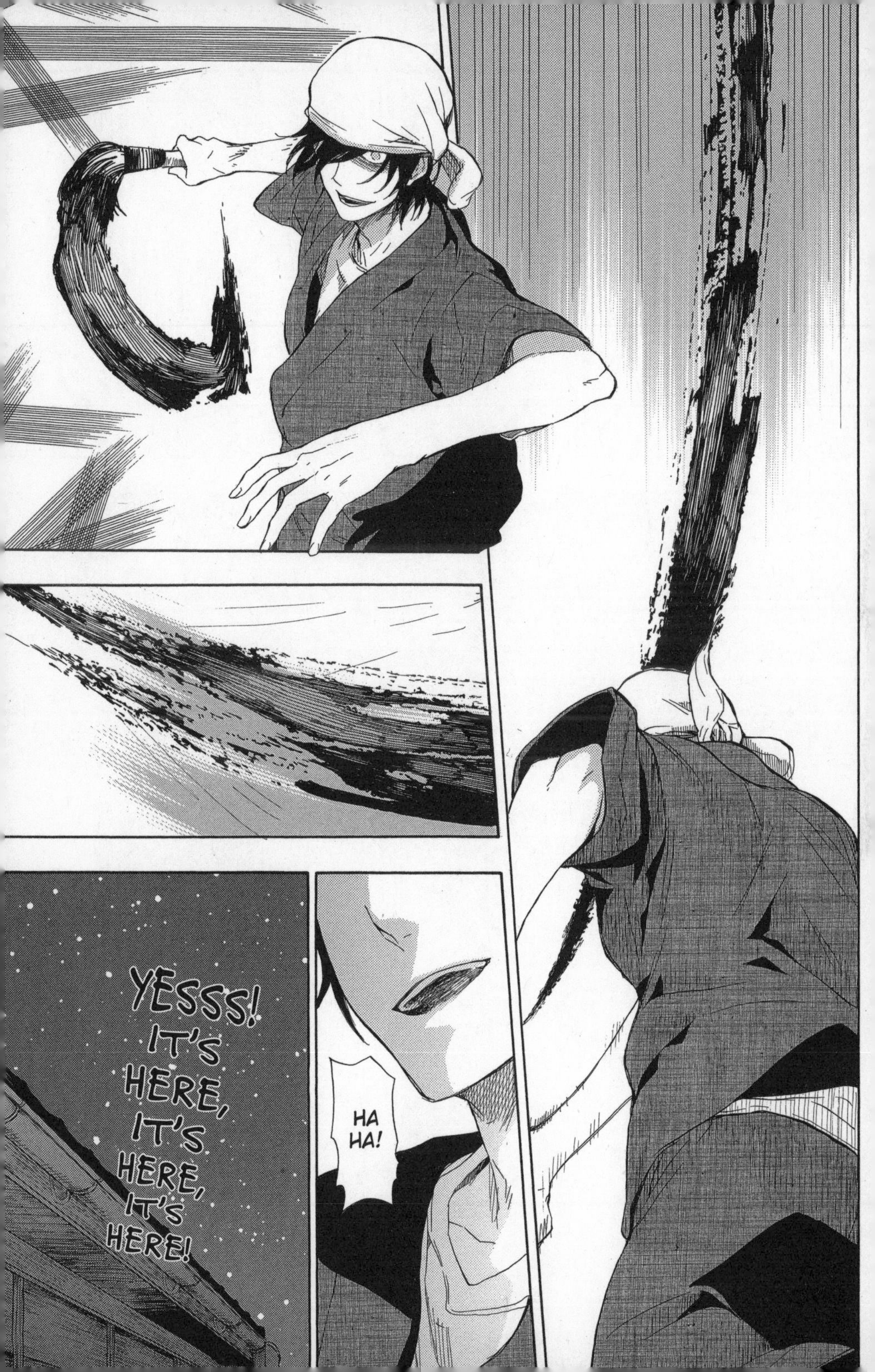
HA HA!
YESSS! IT'S HERE, IT'S HERE, IT'S HERE!

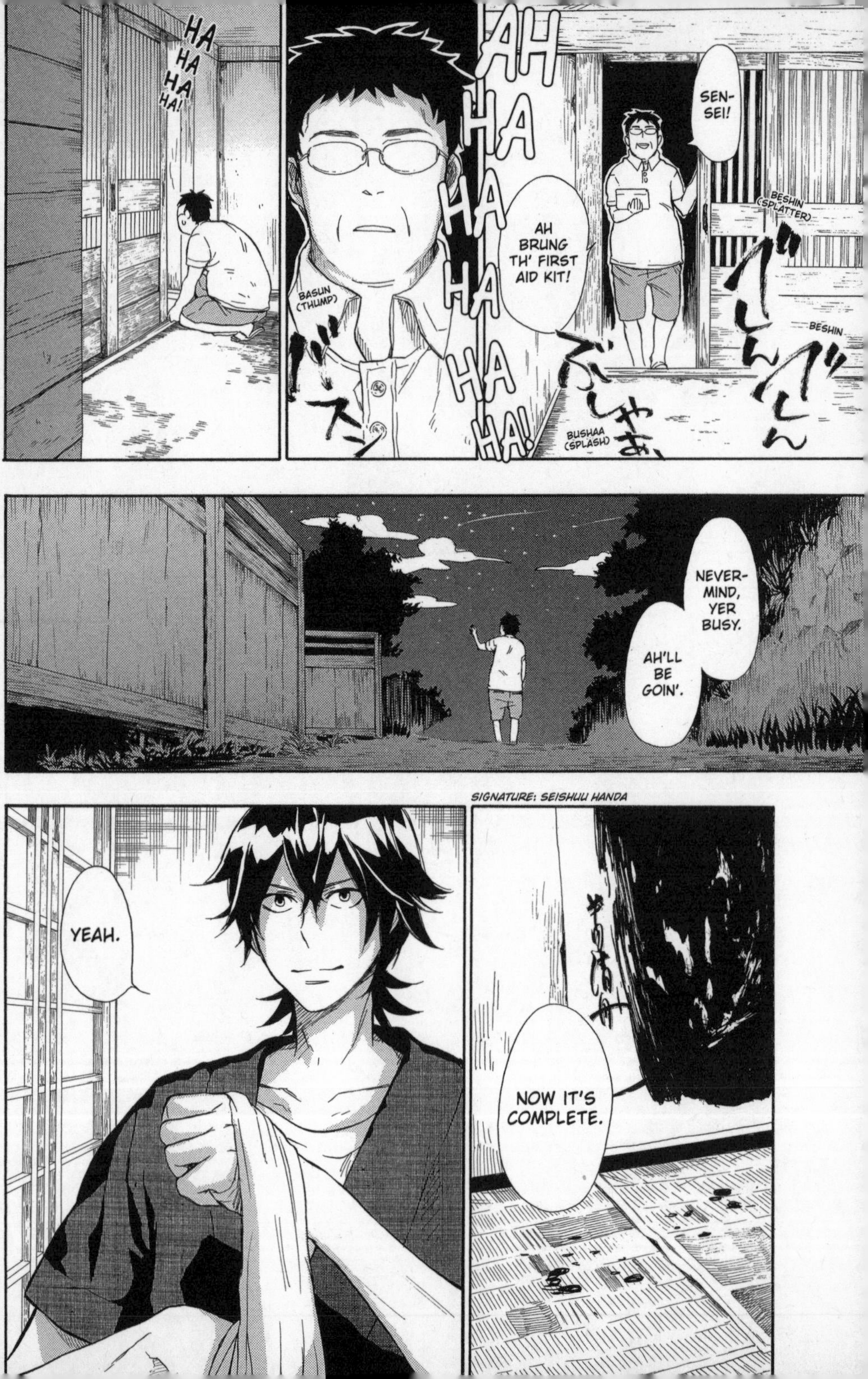
SEN-SEI!
BESHIN (SPLATTER)
BESHIN
BUSHAA (SPLASH)
AH HA HA HA HA HA HA!
AH BRUNG TH' FIRST AID KIT!
BASUN (THUMP)
HA HA HA HA!
NEVER-MIND, YER BUSY.
AH'LL BE GOIN'.
SIGNATURE: SEISHUU HANDA
NOW IT'S COMPLETE.
YEAH.

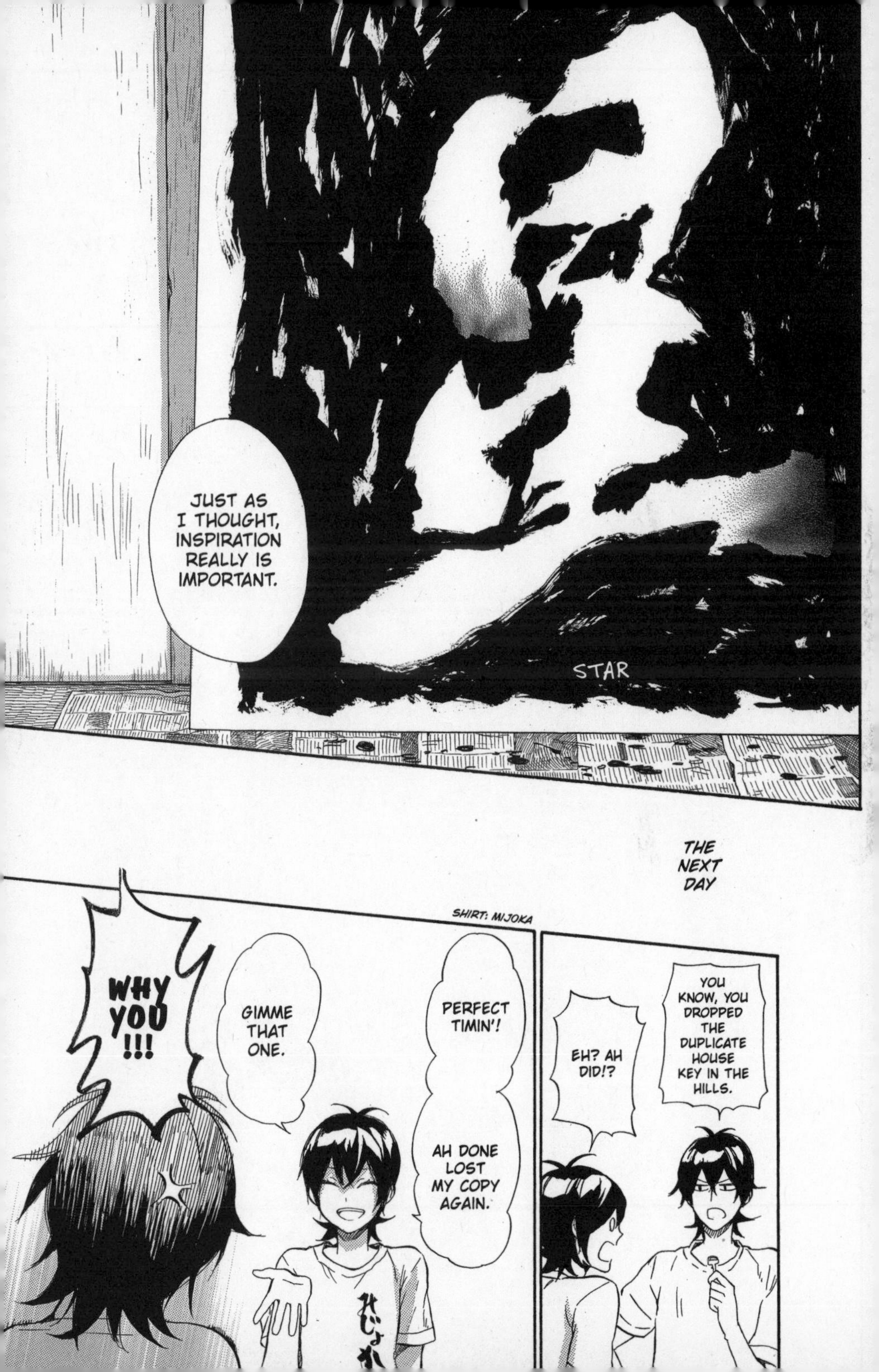
JUST AS I THOUGHT, INSPIRATION REALLY IS IMPORTANT.
STAR
THE NEXT DAY
YOU KNOW, YOU DROPPED THE DUPLICATE HOUSE KEY IN THE HILLS.
EH? AH DID!?
SHIRT: MIJOKA
PERFECT TIMIN'!
AH DONE LOST MY COPY AGAIN.
GIMME THAT ONE.
WHY YOU!!!

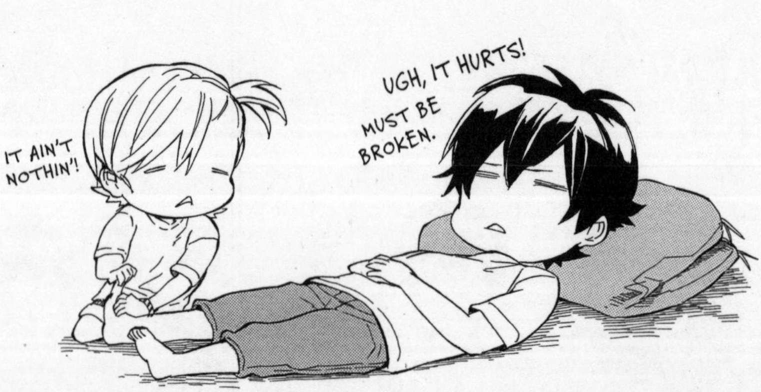
UGH, IT HURTS!
MUST BE BROKEN.
IT AIN'T NOTHIN'!

ACT.40
DOROTAPPE NACCHOTTE

(Translation: Becoming a Morass of Mud)

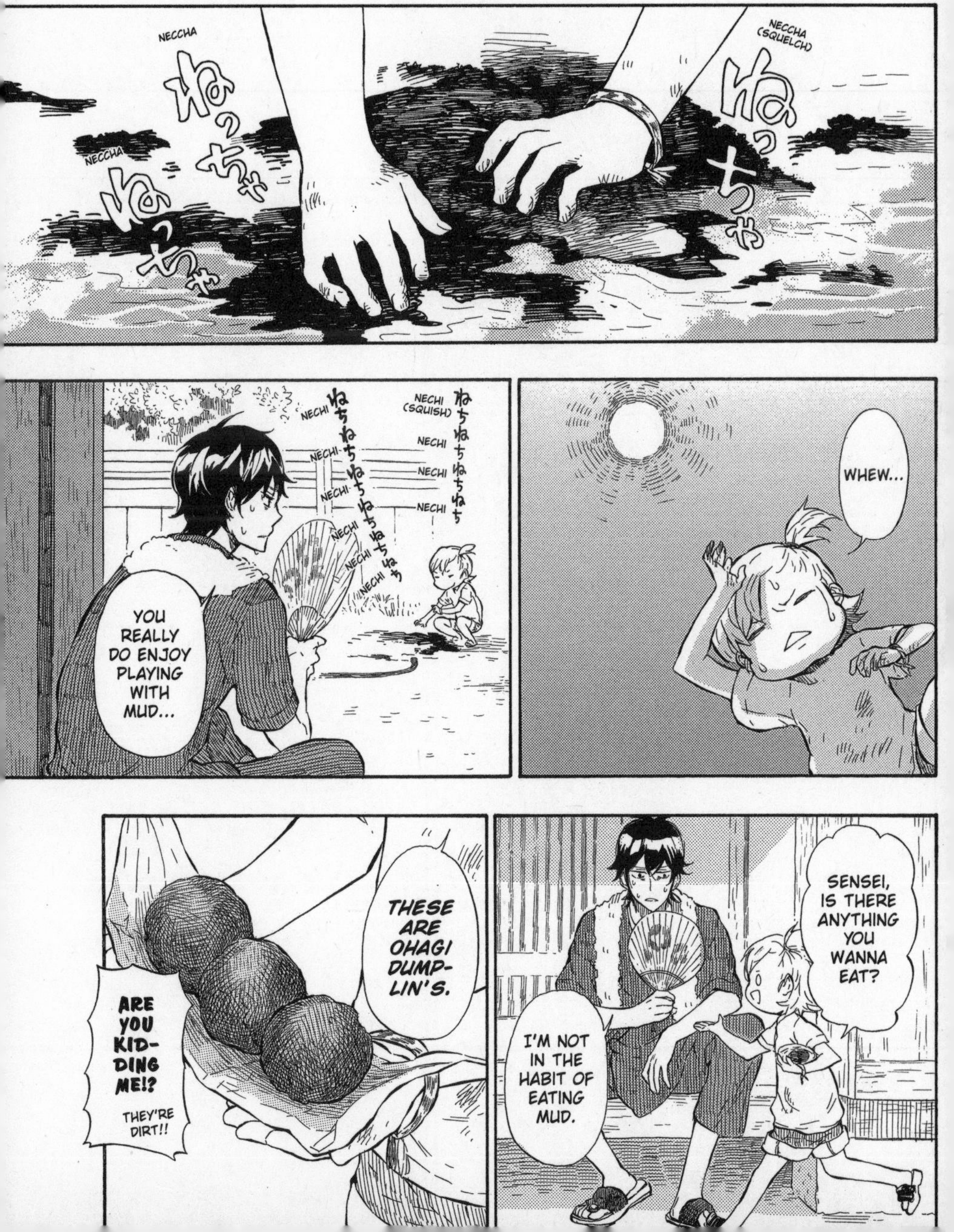
NECCHA (SQUELCH)
ねっちゃ
NECCHA
ねっちゃ
NECCHA
ねっちゃ
WHEW...
NECHI (SQUISH)
ねちねちねちねち
NECHI
NECHI
NECHI
ねちねちねちねちねち
NECHI
NECHI
NECHI
NECHI
YOU REALLY DO ENJOY PLAYING WITH MUD...
SENSEI, IS THERE ANYTHING YOU WANNA EAT?
I'M NOT IN THE HABIT OF EATING MUD.
THESE ARE OHAGI DUMPLIN'S.
ARE YOU KIDDING ME!?
THEY'RE DIRT!!

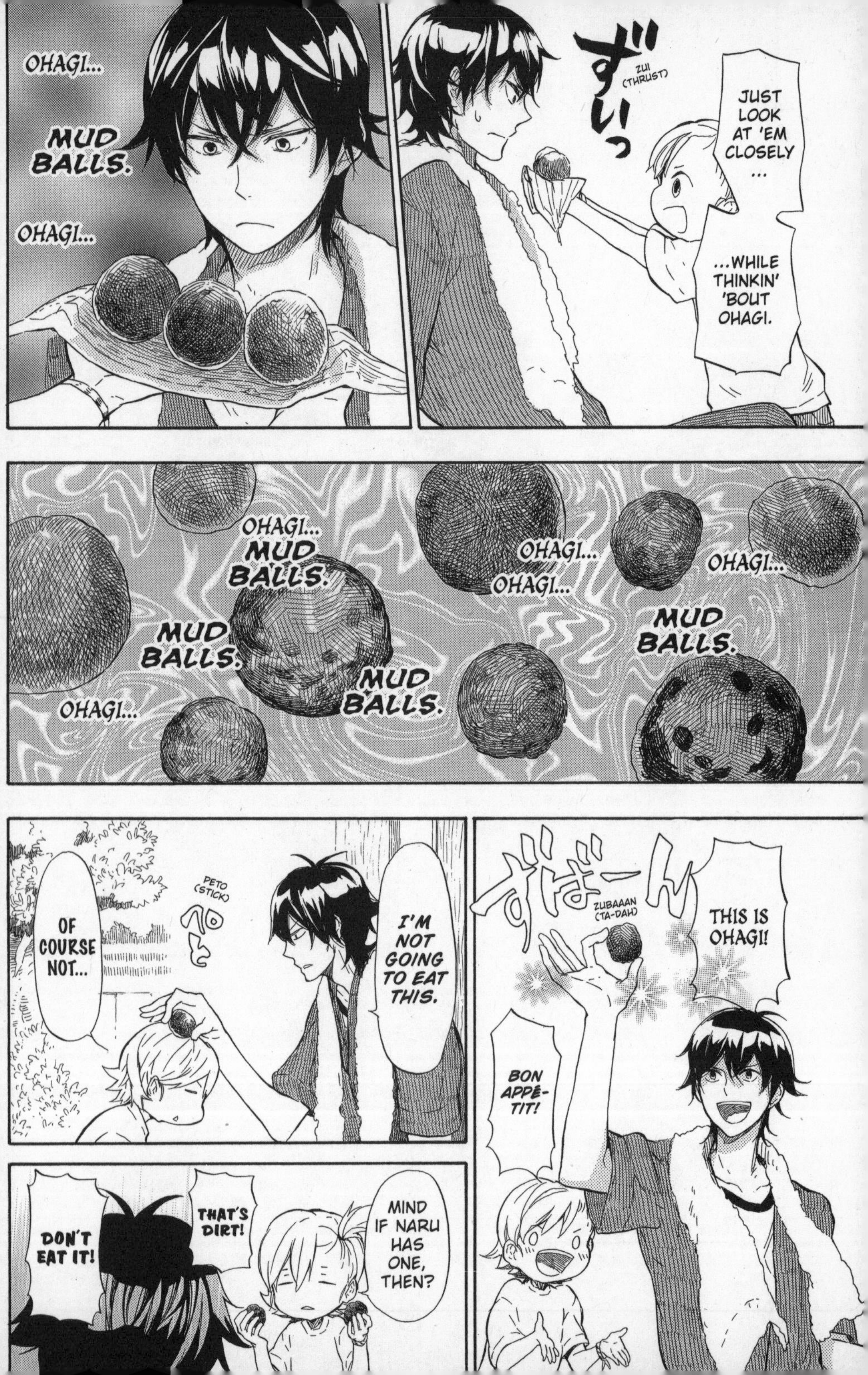ずいっ
ZUI (THRUST)
JUST LOOK AT 'EM CLOSELY ...
...WHILE THINKIN' 'BOUT OHAGI.
OHAGI...
MUD BALLS.
OHAGI...
OHAGI...
OHAGI...
OHAGI...
MUD BALLS.
OHAGI...
MUD BALLS.
MUD BALLS.
MUD BALLS.
OHAGI...
ずばーん
ZUBAAAN (TA-DAH)
THIS IS OHAGI!
BON APPÉTIT!
I'M NOT GOING TO EAT THIS.
ぺと
PETO (STICK)
OF COURSE NOT...
MIND IF NARU HAS ONE, THEN?
THAT'S DIRT!
DON'T EAT IT!

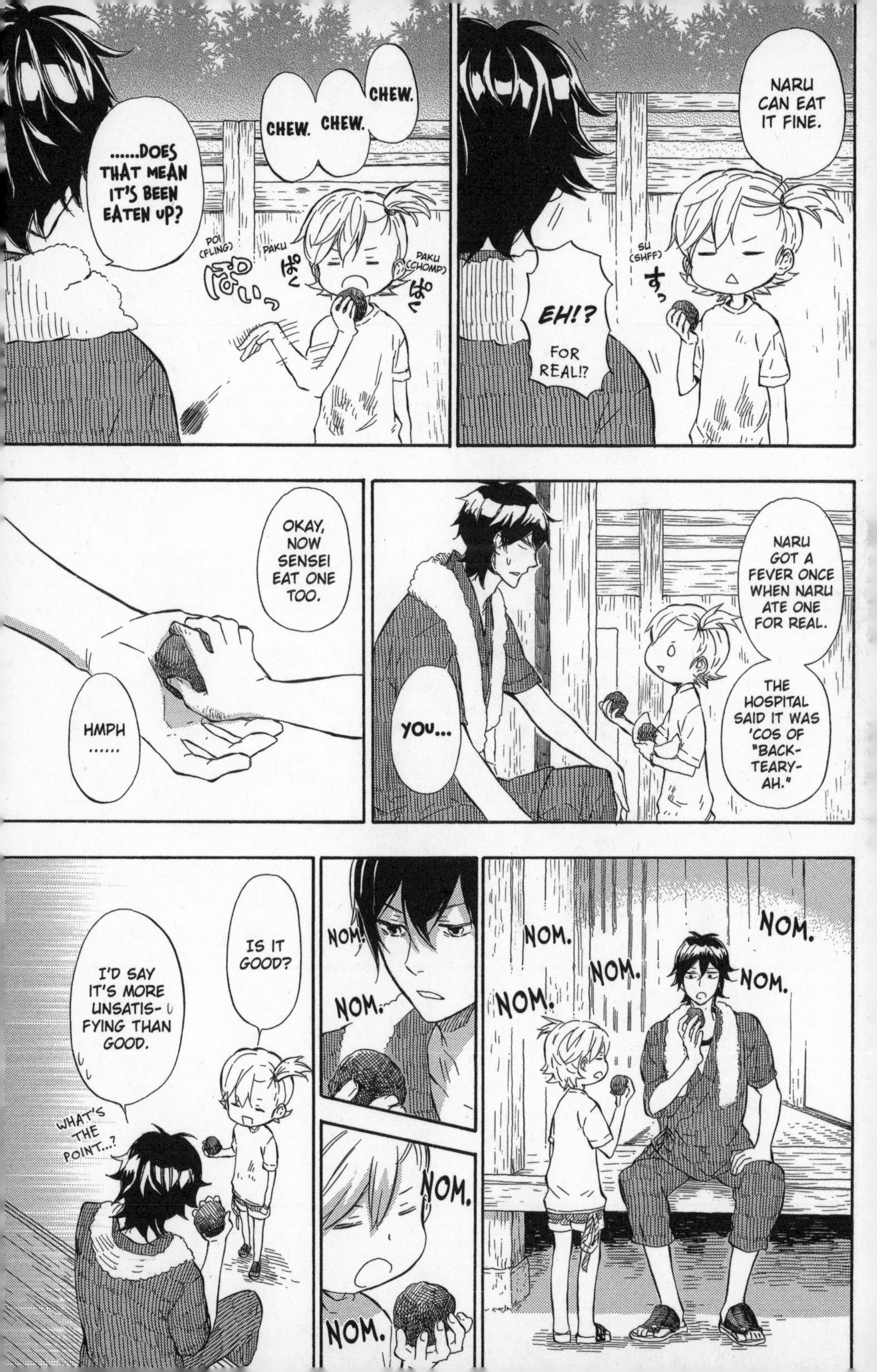
NARU CAN EAT IT FINE.
SU (SHFF)
すっ
EH!?
FOR REAL!?
CHEW.
CHEW.
CHEW.
......DOES THAT MEAN IT'S BEEN EATEN UP?
PAKU (CHOMP)
ぱく
PAKU
ぱく
POI (FLING)
ぽいっ
NARU GOT A FEVER ONCE WHEN NARU ATE ONE FOR REAL.
THE HOSPITAL SAID IT WAS 'COS OF "BACK-TEARY-AH."
YOU...
OKAY, NOW SENSEI EAT ONE TOO.
HMPH ......
NOM.
NOM.
NOM.
NOM.
NOM.
NOM.
NOM.
NOM.
NOM.
IS IT GOOD?
I'D SAY IT'S MORE UNSATIS-FYING THAN GOOD.
WHAT'S THE POINT...?

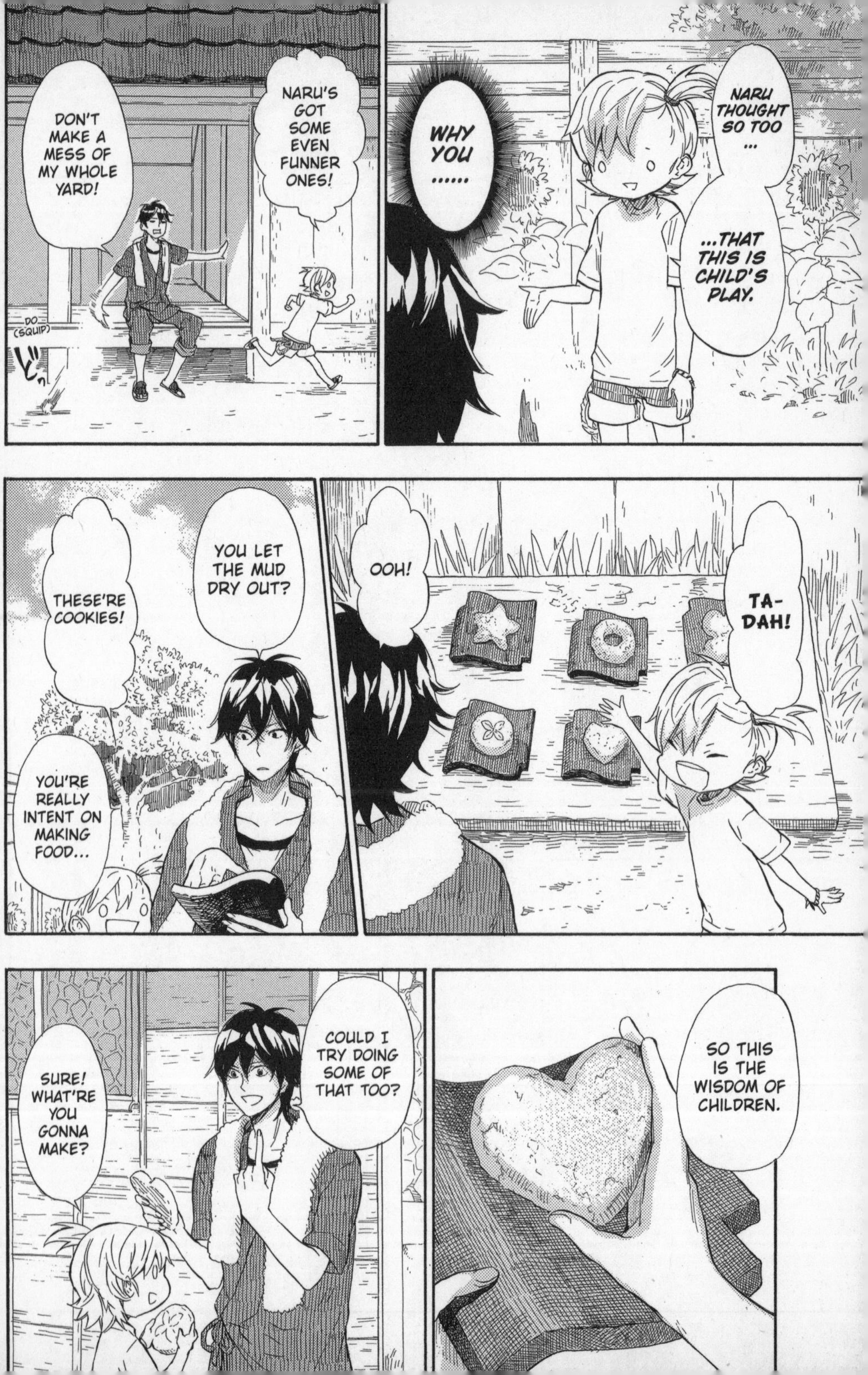
NARU THOUGHT SO TOO ...
...THAT THIS IS CHILD'S PLAY.
WHY YOU ......
NARU'S GOT SOME EVEN FUNNER ONES!
DON'T MAKE A MESS OF MY WHOLE YARD!
DO (SQUIP)
どん
TA-DAH!
OOH!
YOU LET THE MUD DRY OUT?
THESE'RE COOKIES!
YOU'RE REALLY INTENT ON MAKING FOOD...
SO THIS IS THE WISDOM OF CHILDREN.
COULD I TRY DOING SOME OF THAT TOO?
SURE! WHAT'RE YOU GONNA MAKE?

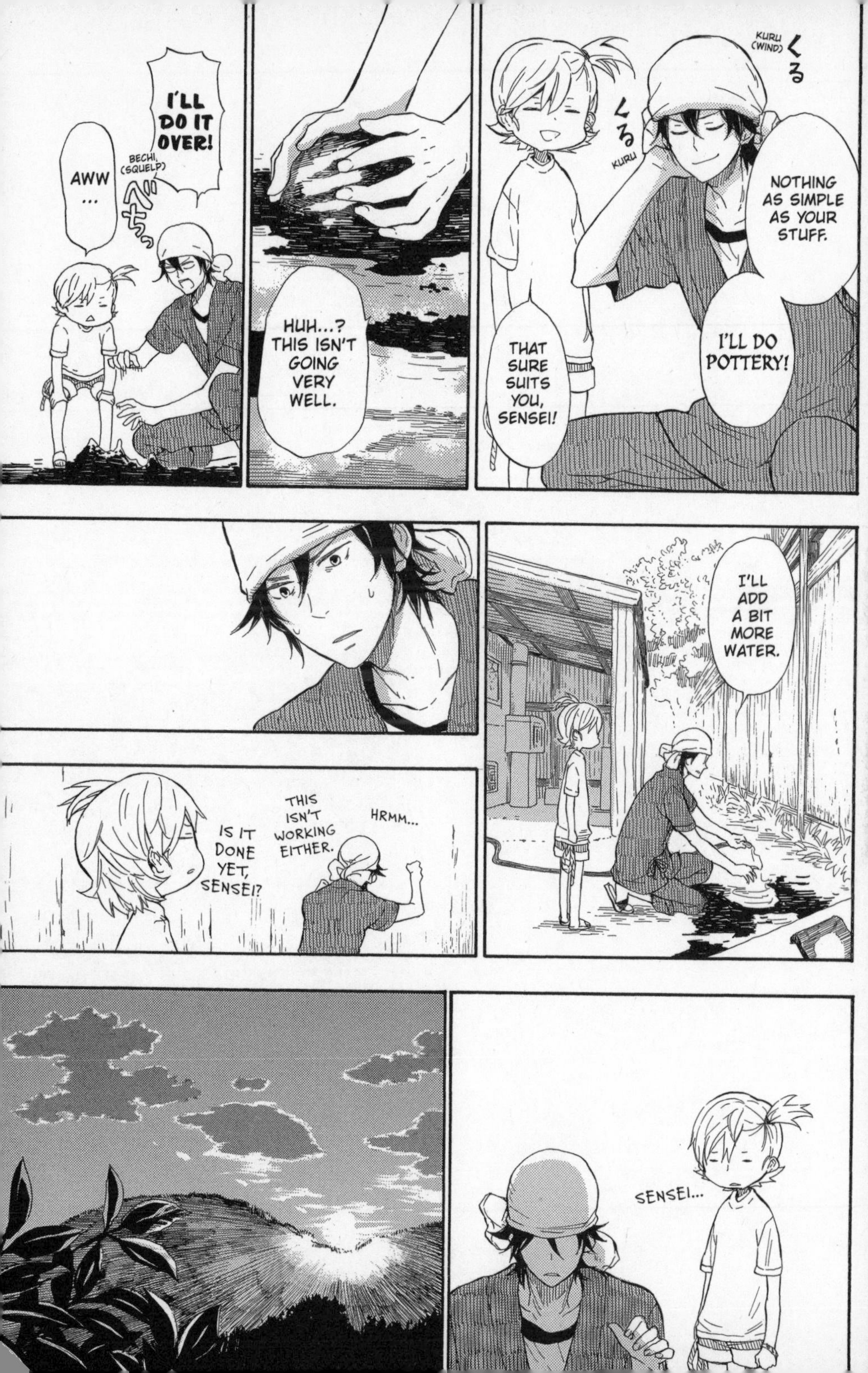
KURU (WIND) くる
NOTHING AS SIMPLE AS YOUR STUFF.
くる KURU
I'LL DO POTTERY!
THAT SURE SUITS YOU, SENSEI!
HUH...? THIS ISN'T GOING VERY WELL.
I'LL DO IT OVER!
BECHI (SQUELP) べちっ
AWW ...
I'LL ADD A BIT MORE WATER.
HRMM...
THIS ISN'T WORKING EITHER.
IS IT DONE YET, SENSEI?
SENSEI...

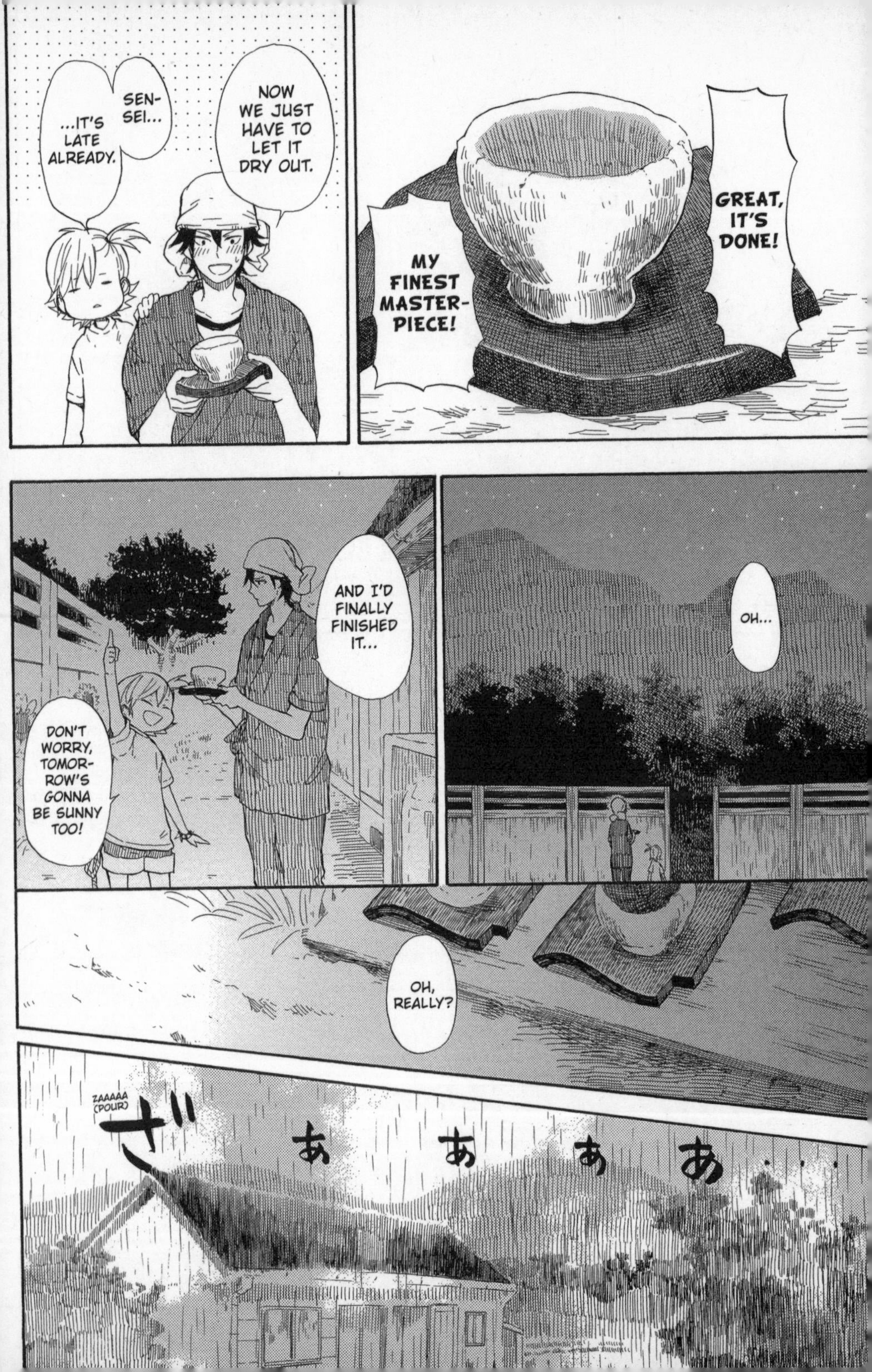
GREAT, IT'S DONE!
MY FINEST MASTER-PIECE!
NOW WE JUST HAVE TO LET IT DRY OUT.
SEN-SEI...
...IT'S LATE ALREADY.
OH...
AND I'D FINALLY FINISHED IT...
DON'T WORRY, TOMOR-ROW'S GONNA BE SUNNY TOO!
OH, REALLY?
ZAAAAA (POUR)
ざあああああ...

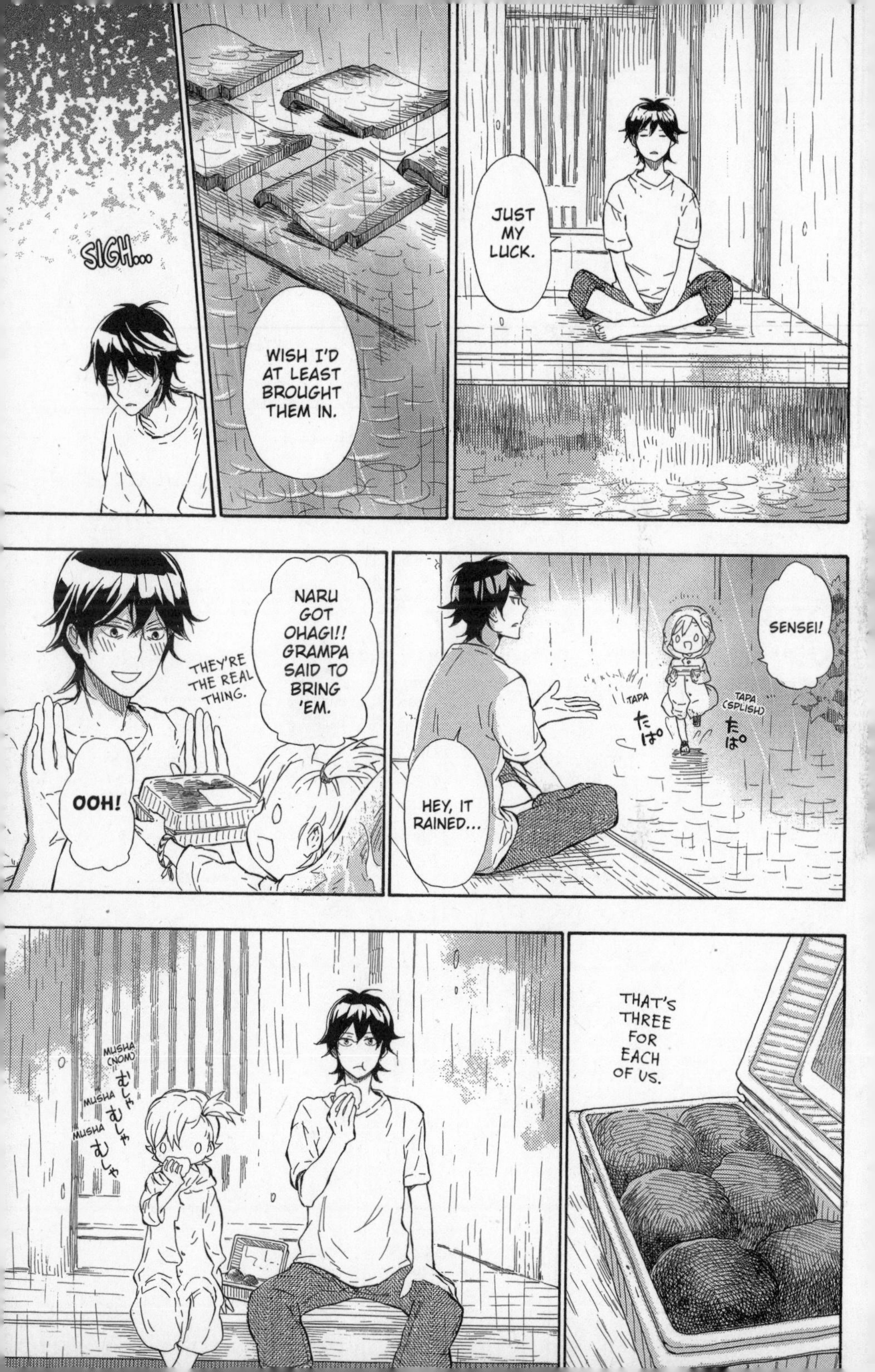
JUST MY LUCK.
WISH I'D AT LEAST BROUGHT THEM IN.
SIGH...
SENSEI!
TAPA (SPLISH) たぱ
TAPA たぱ
HEY, IT RAINED...
NARU GOT OHAGI!! GRAMPA SAID TO BRING 'EM.
THEY'RE THE REAL THING.
OOH!
THAT'S THREE FOR EACH OF US.
MUSHA (NOM) むしゃ
MUSHA むしゃ
MUSHA むしゃ

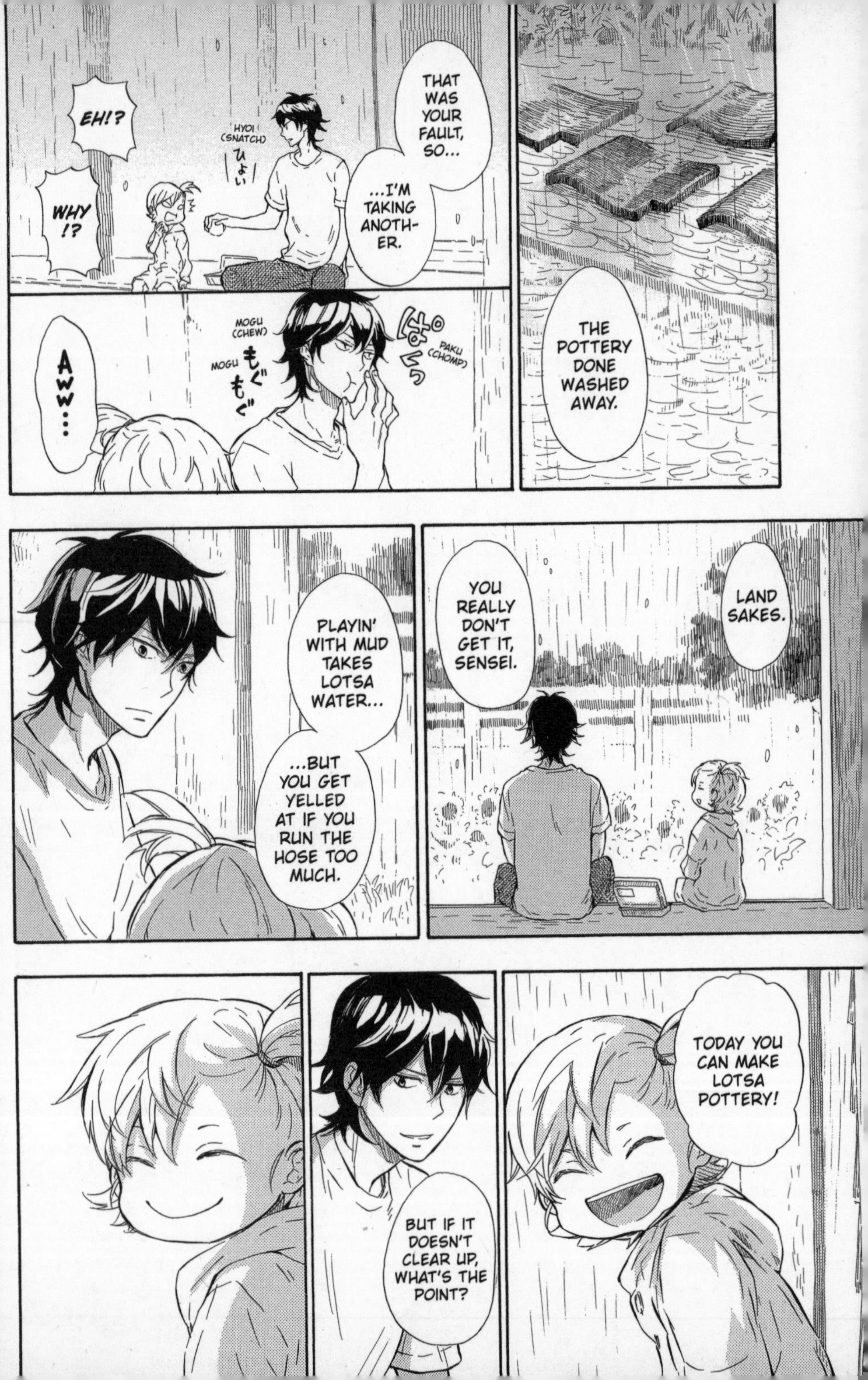
THE POTTERY DONE WASHED AWAY.
THAT WAS YOUR FAULT, SO...
...I'M TAKING ANOTH-ER.
HYOI (SNATCH) ひょい
EH!?
WHY !?
PAKU (CHOMP) ぱく
MOGU (CHEW) もぐ
MOGU もぐ
AWW...
LAND SAKES.
YOU REALLY DON'T GET IT, SENSEI.
PLAYIN' WITH MUD TAKES LOTSA WATER...
...BUT YOU GET YELLED AT IF YOU RUN THE HOSE TOO MUCH.
TODAY YOU CAN MAKE LOTSA POTTERY!
BUT IF IT DOESN'T CLEAR UP, WHAT'S THE POINT?

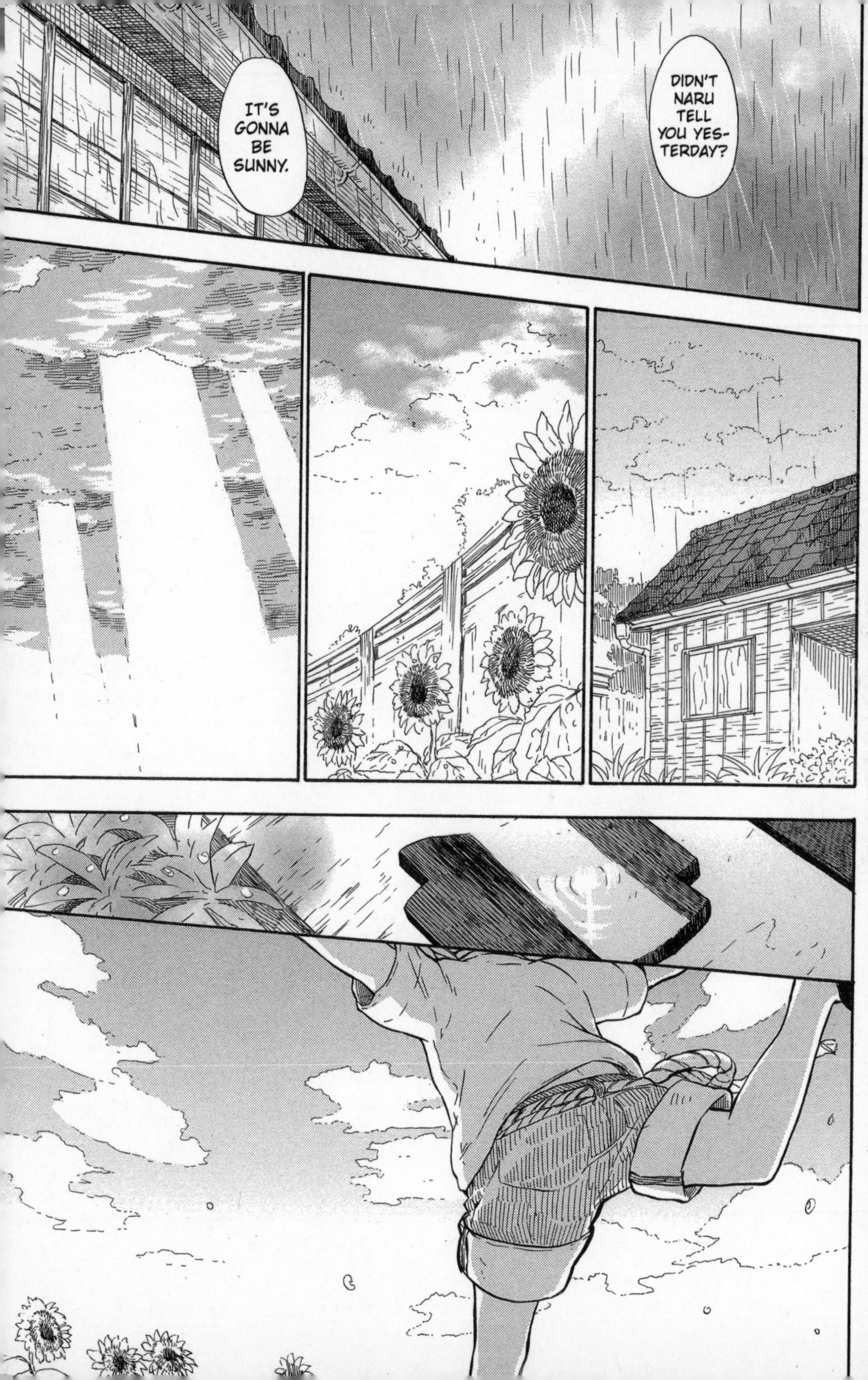
DIDN'T NARU TELL YOU YES-TERDAY?
IT'S GONNA BE SUNNY.

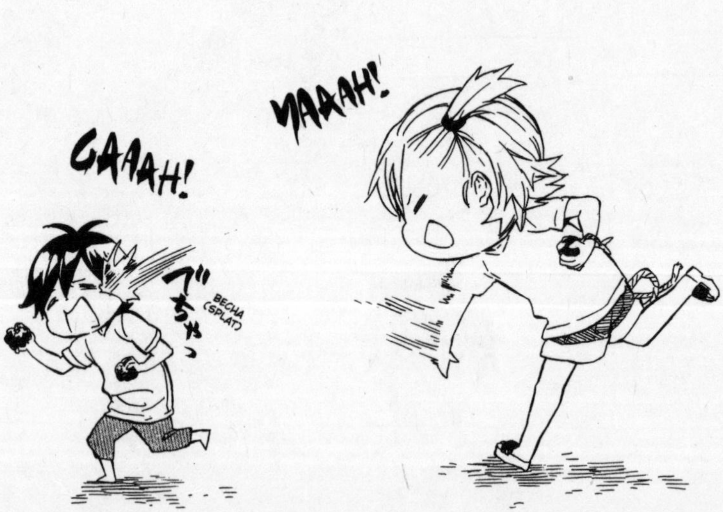
WAAAH!
GAAAH!
べちゃっ
BECHA (SPLAT)

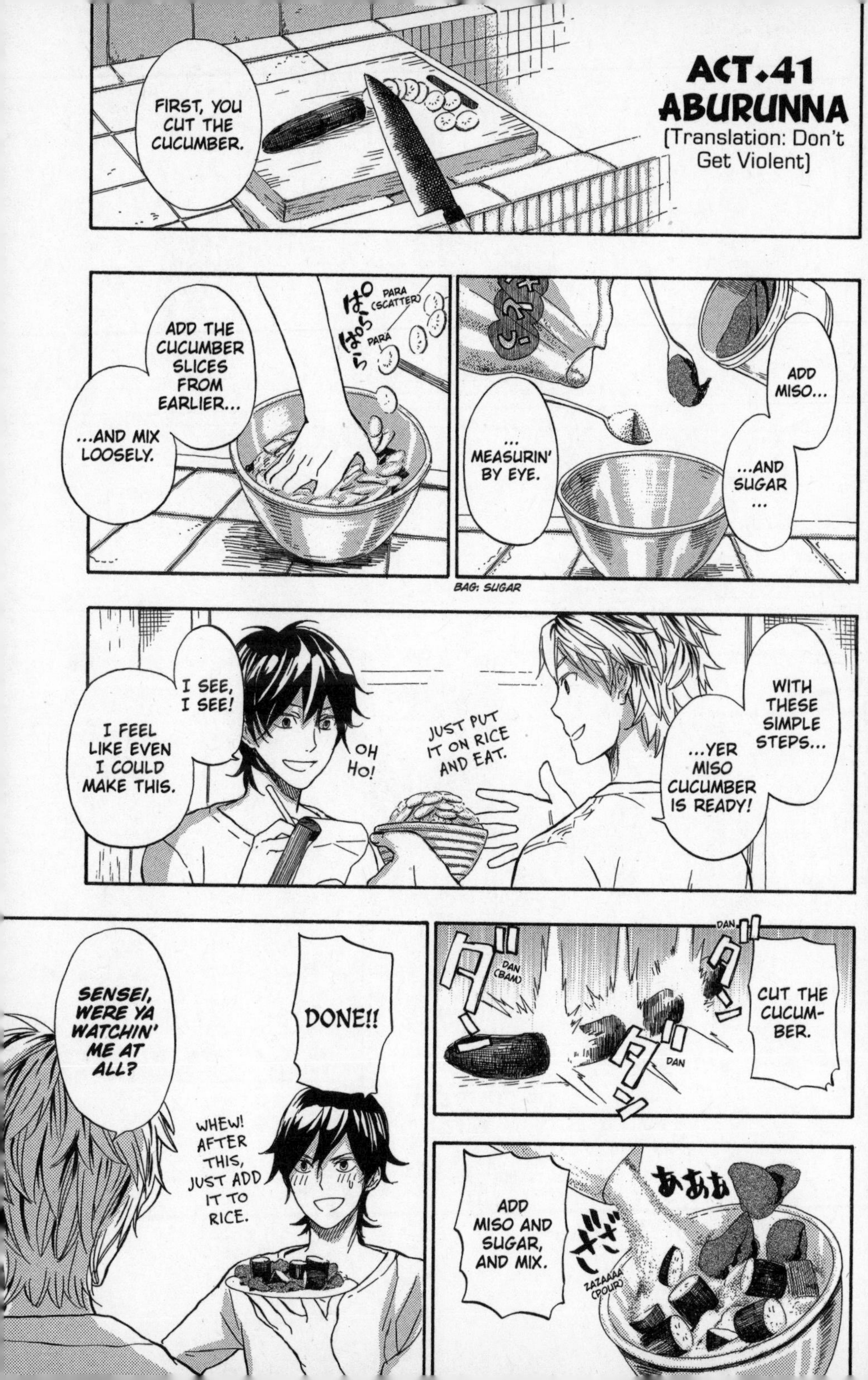
ACT.41
ABURUNNA
(Translation: Don't Get Violent)
FIRST, YOU CUT THE CUCUMBER.
ADD MISO...
...AND SUGAR...
...MEASURIN' BY EYE.
BAG: SUGAR
PARA (SCATTER)
PARA
ADD THE CUCUMBER SLICES FROM EARLIER...
...AND MIX LOOSELY.
WITH THESE SIMPLE STEPS...
...YER MISO CUCUMBER IS READY!
JUST PUT IT ON RICE AND EAT.
OH HO!
I SEE, I SEE!
I FEEL LIKE EVEN I COULD MAKE THIS.
CUT THE CUCUMBER.
DAN
DAN (BAM)
DAN
ADD MISO AND SUGAR, AND MIX.
ZAZAAAA (POUR)
DONE!!
WHEW! AFTER THIS, JUST ADD IT TO RICE.
SENSEI, WERE YA WATCHIN' ME AT ALL?

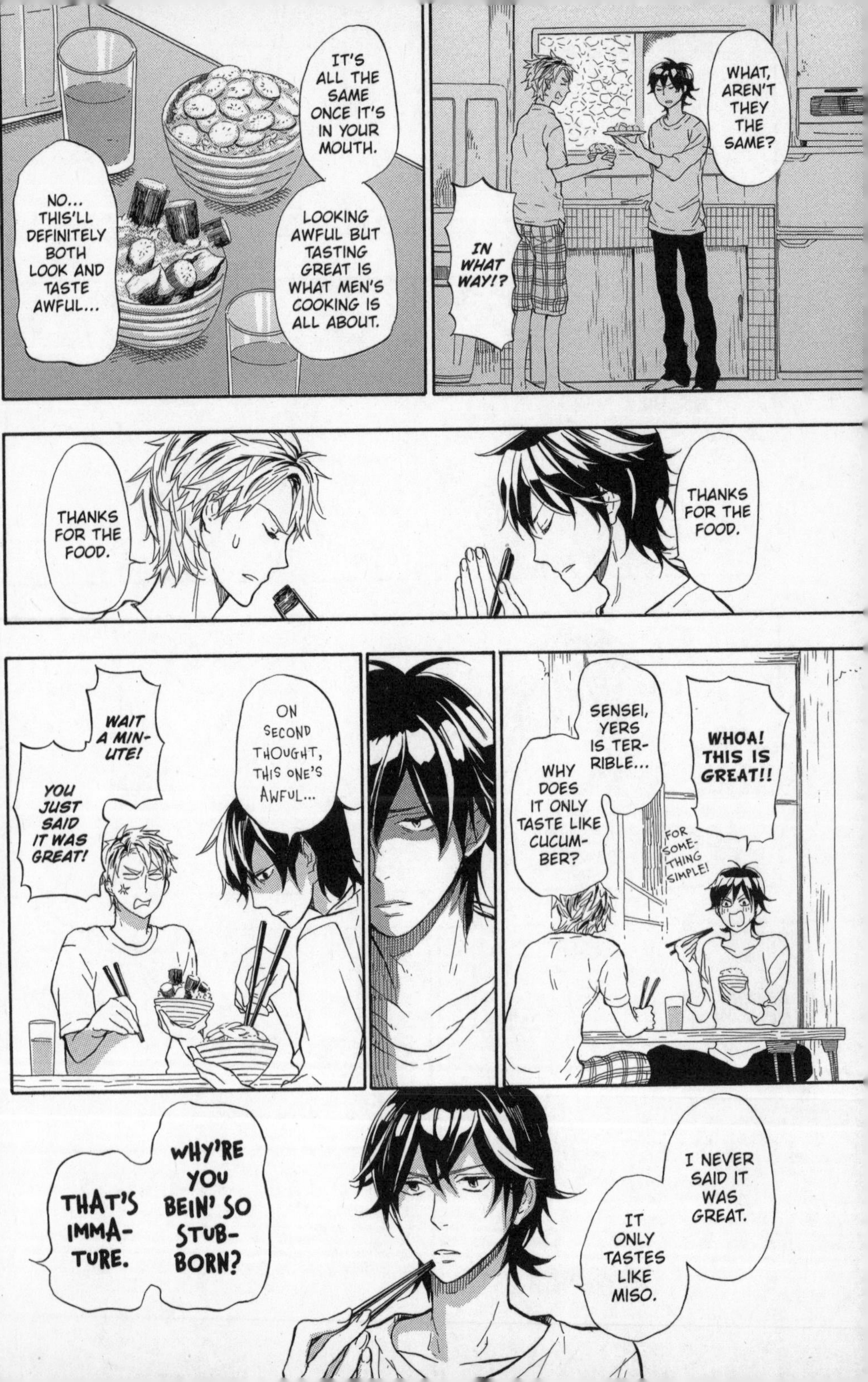
WHAT, AREN'T THEY THE SAME?
IN WHAT WAY!?
IT'S ALL THE SAME ONCE IT'S IN YOUR MOUTH.
LOOKING AWFUL BUT TASTING GREAT IS WHAT MEN'S COOKING IS ALL ABOUT.
NO... THIS'LL DEFINITELY BOTH LOOK AND TASTE AWFUL...
THANKS FOR THE FOOD.
THANKS FOR THE FOOD.
WHOA! THIS IS GREAT!!
FOR SOMETHING SIMPLE!
SENSEI, YERS IS TERRIBLE...
WHY DOES IT ONLY TASTE LIKE CUCUMBER?
ON SECOND THOUGHT, THIS ONE'S AWFUL...
WAIT A MINUTE!
YOU JUST SAID IT WAS GREAT!
I NEVER SAID IT WAS GREAT.
IT ONLY TASTES LIKE MISO.
WHY'RE YOU BEIN' SO STUBBORN?
THAT'S IMMATURE.

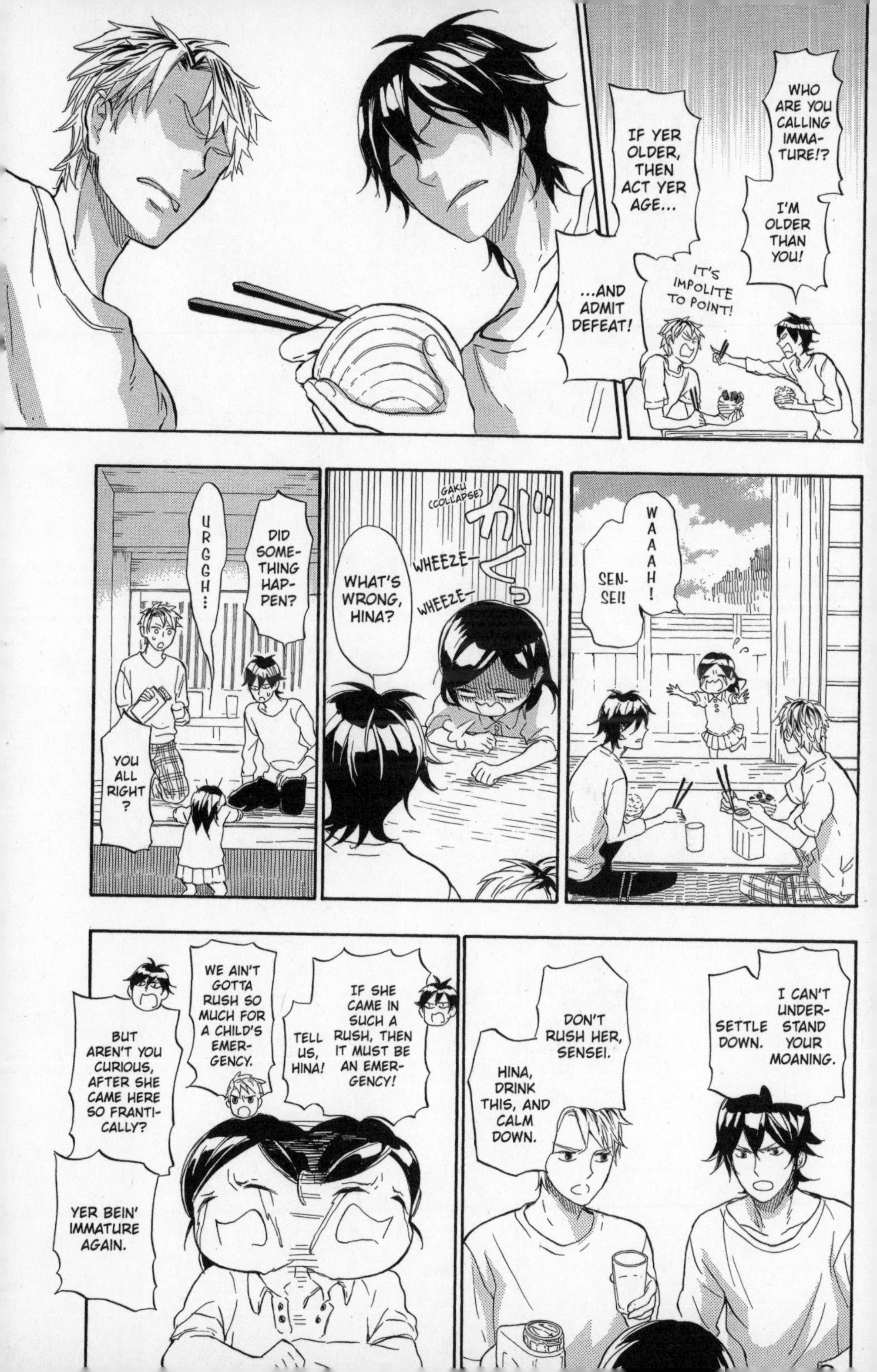
WHO ARE YOU CALLING IMMATURE!?
I'M OLDER THAN YOU!
IF YER OLDER, THEN ACT YER AGE...
IT'S IMPOLITE TO POINT!
...AND ADMIT DEFEAT!
WAAAAH!
SEN-SEI!
GAKU (COLLAPSE)
がくっ
WHEEZE—
WHEEZE—
WHAT'S WRONG, HINA?
DID SOME-THING HAP-PEN?
URGGH...
YOU ALL RIGHT?
I CAN'T UNDER-STAND YOUR MOANING.
SETTLE DOWN.
DON'T RUSH HER, SENSEI.
HINA, DRINK THIS, AND CALM DOWN.
IF SHE CAME IN SUCH A RUSH, THEN IT MUST BE AN EMER-GENCY!
TELL US, HINA!
WE AIN'T GOTTA RUSH SO MUCH FOR A CHILD'S EMER-GENCY.
BUT AREN'T YOU CURIOUS, AFTER SHE CAME HERE SO FRANTI-CALLY?
YER BEIN' IMMATURE AGAIN.

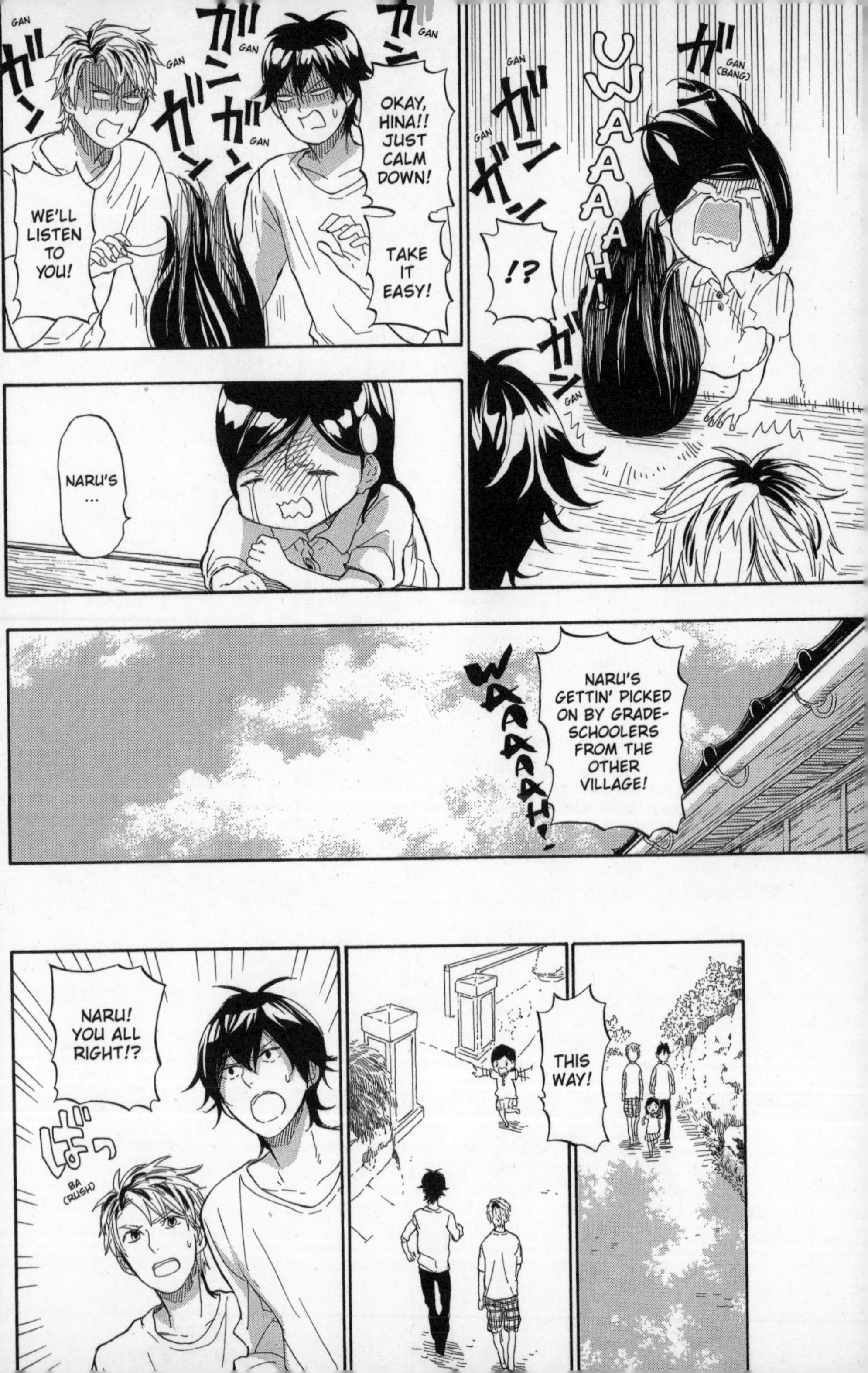
GAN (BANG)
UWAAAAAH!
GAN
GAN
!?
GAN
GAN
OKAY, HINA!! JUST CALM DOWN!
TAKE IT EASY!
GAN
GAN
GAN
WE'LL LISTEN TO YOU!
NARU'S ...
NARU'S GETTIN' PICKED ON BY GRADE-SCHOOLERS FROM THE OTHER VILLAGE!
WAAAAAH!
THIS WAY!
NARU! YOU ALL RIGHT!?
BA (RUSH)

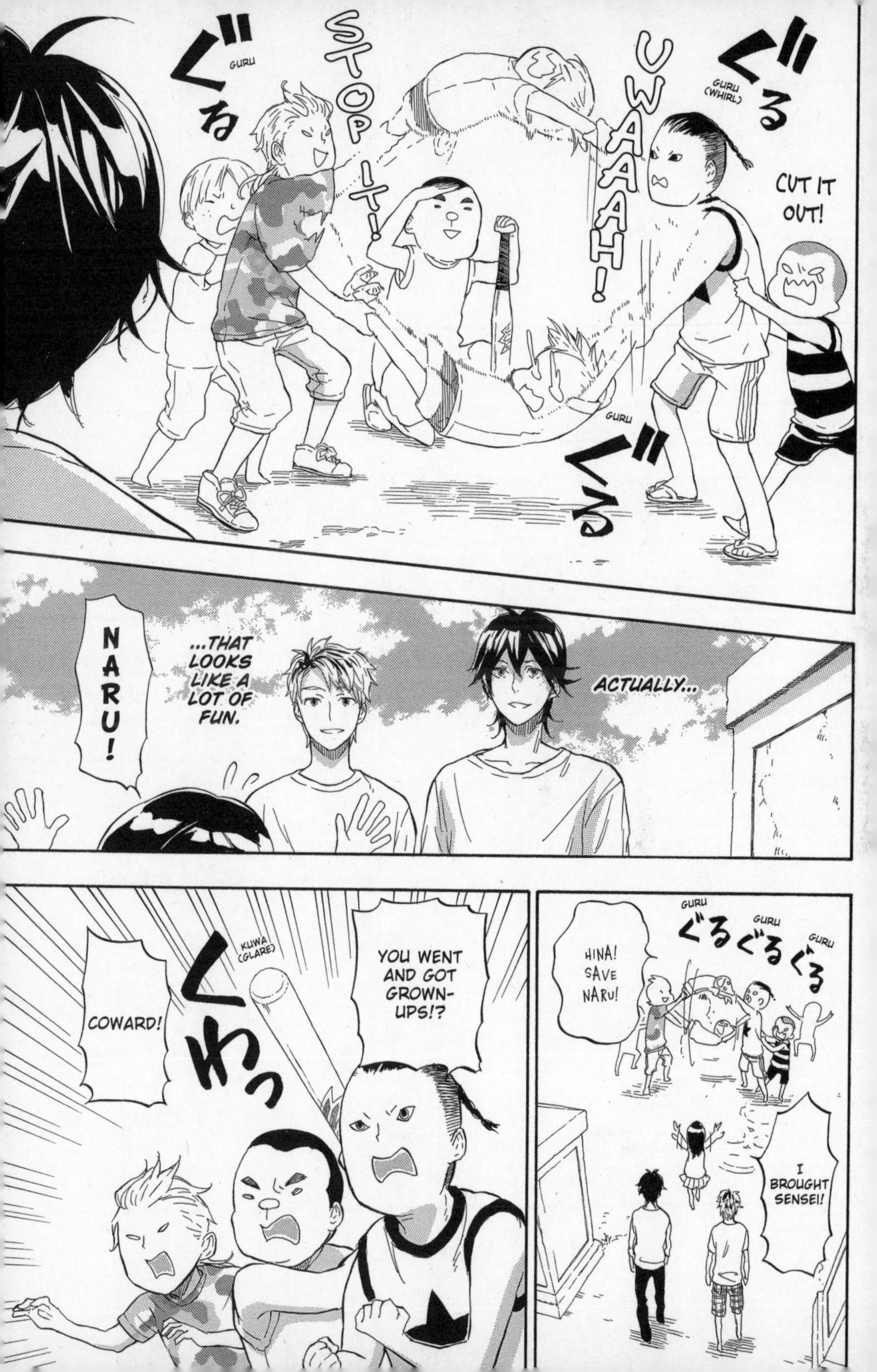
ぐる
GURU (WHIRL)
CUT IT OUT!
UWAAAAH!
STOP IT!
ぐる
GURU
ぐる
GURU
ACTUALLY...
...THAT LOOKS LIKE A LOT OF FUN.
NARU!
ぐるぐるぐる
GURU GURU GURU
HINA! SAVE NARU!
I BROUGHT SENSEI!
YOU WENT AND GOT GROWN-UPS!?
くわっ
KUWA (GLARE)
COWARD!

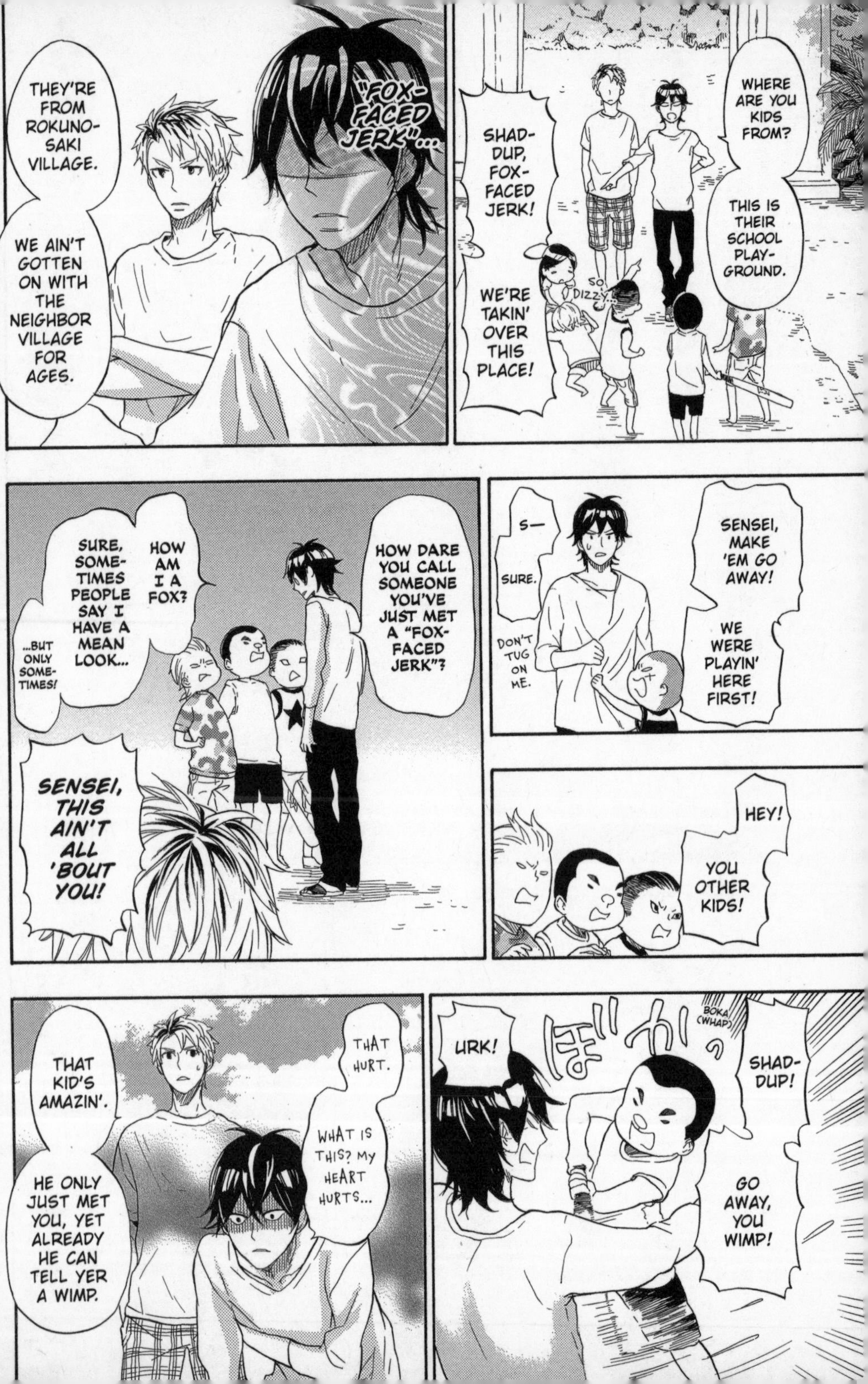
WHERE ARE YOU KIDS FROM?
THIS IS THEIR SCHOOL PLAYGROUND.
SHADDUP, FOX-FACED JERK!
SO DIZZY...
WE'RE TAKIN' OVER THIS PLACE!
"FOX-FACED JERK"...
THEY'RE FROM ROKUNOSAKI VILLAGE.
WE AIN'T GOTTEN ON WITH THE NEIGHBOR VILLAGE FOR AGES.
SENSEI, MAKE 'EM GO AWAY!
WE WERE PLAYIN' HERE FIRST!
S—
SURE.
DON'T TUG ON ME.
HEY!
YOU OTHER KIDS!
HOW DARE YOU CALL SOMEONE YOU'VE JUST MET A "FOX-FACED JERK"?
HOW AM I A FOX?
SURE, SOMETIMES PEOPLE SAY I HAVE A MEAN LOOK...
...BUT ONLY SOMETIMES!
SENSEI, THIS AIN'T ALL 'BOUT YOU!
BOKA (WHAP)
ぼかっ
SHADDUP!
GO AWAY, YOU WIMP!
URK!
THAT HURT.
WHAT IS THIS? MY HEART HURTS...
THAT KID'S AMAZIN'.
HE ONLY JUST MET YOU, YET ALREADY HE CAN TELL YER A WIMP.

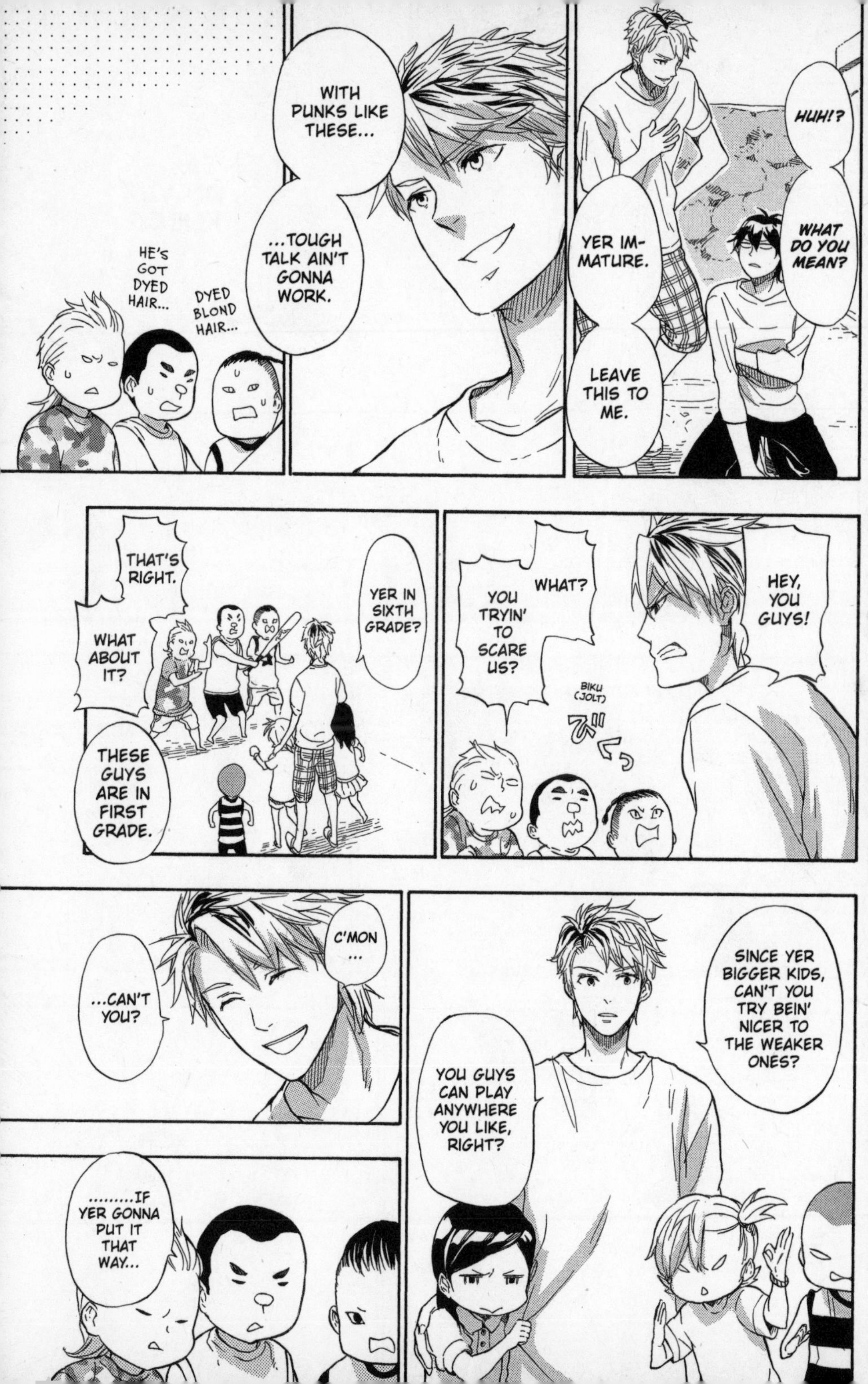
HUH!?
WHAT DO YOU MEAN?
YER IM-MATURE.
LEAVE THIS TO ME.
WITH PUNKS LIKE THESE...
...TOUGH TALK AIN'T GONNA WORK.
HE'S GOT DYED HAIR...
DYED BLOND HAIR...
HEY, YOU GUYS!
WHAT?
YOU TRYIN' TO SCARE US?
BIKU (JOLT)
びくっ
YER IN SIXTH GRADE?
THAT'S RIGHT.
WHAT ABOUT IT?
THESE GUYS ARE IN FIRST GRADE.
SINCE YER BIGGER KIDS, CAN'T YOU TRY BEIN' NICER TO THE WEAKER ONES?
YOU GUYS CAN PLAY ANYWHERE YOU LIKE, RIGHT?
C'MON...
...CAN'T YOU?
.........IF YER GONNA PUT IT THAT WAY...

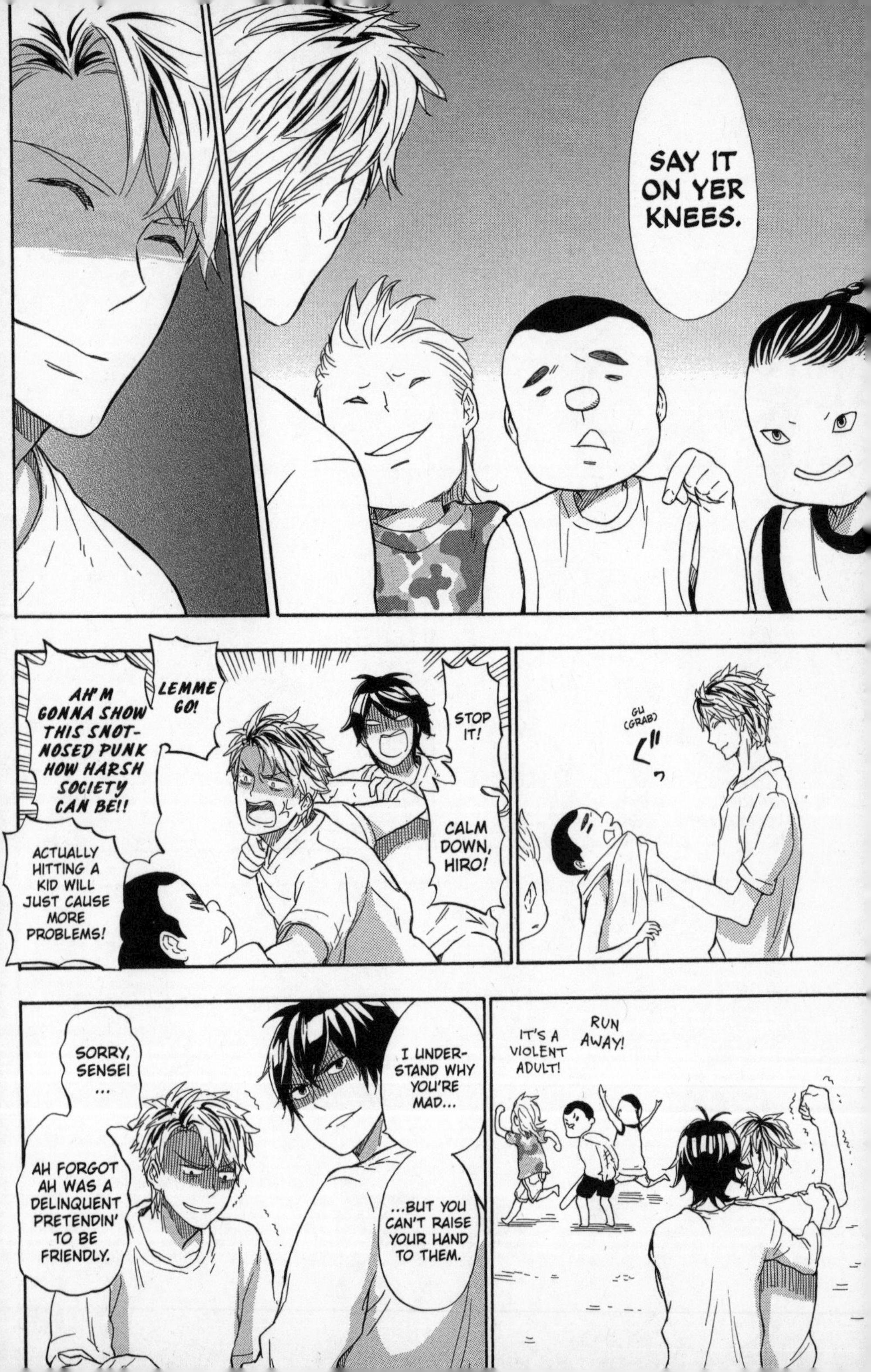
SAY IT ON YER KNEES.
GU (GRAB)
ぐっ
STOP IT!
CALM DOWN, HIRO!
LEMME GO!
AH'M GONNA SHOW THIS SNOT-NOSED PUNK HOW HARSH SOCIETY CAN BE!!
ACTUALLY HITTING A KID WILL JUST CAUSE MORE PROBLEMS!
RUN AWAY!
IT'S A VIOLENT ADULT!
I UNDERSTAND WHY YOU'RE MAD...
...BUT YOU CAN'T RAISE YOUR HAND TO THEM.
SORRY, SENSEI ...
AH FORGOT AH WAS A DELINQUENT PRETENDIN' TO BE FRIENDLY.

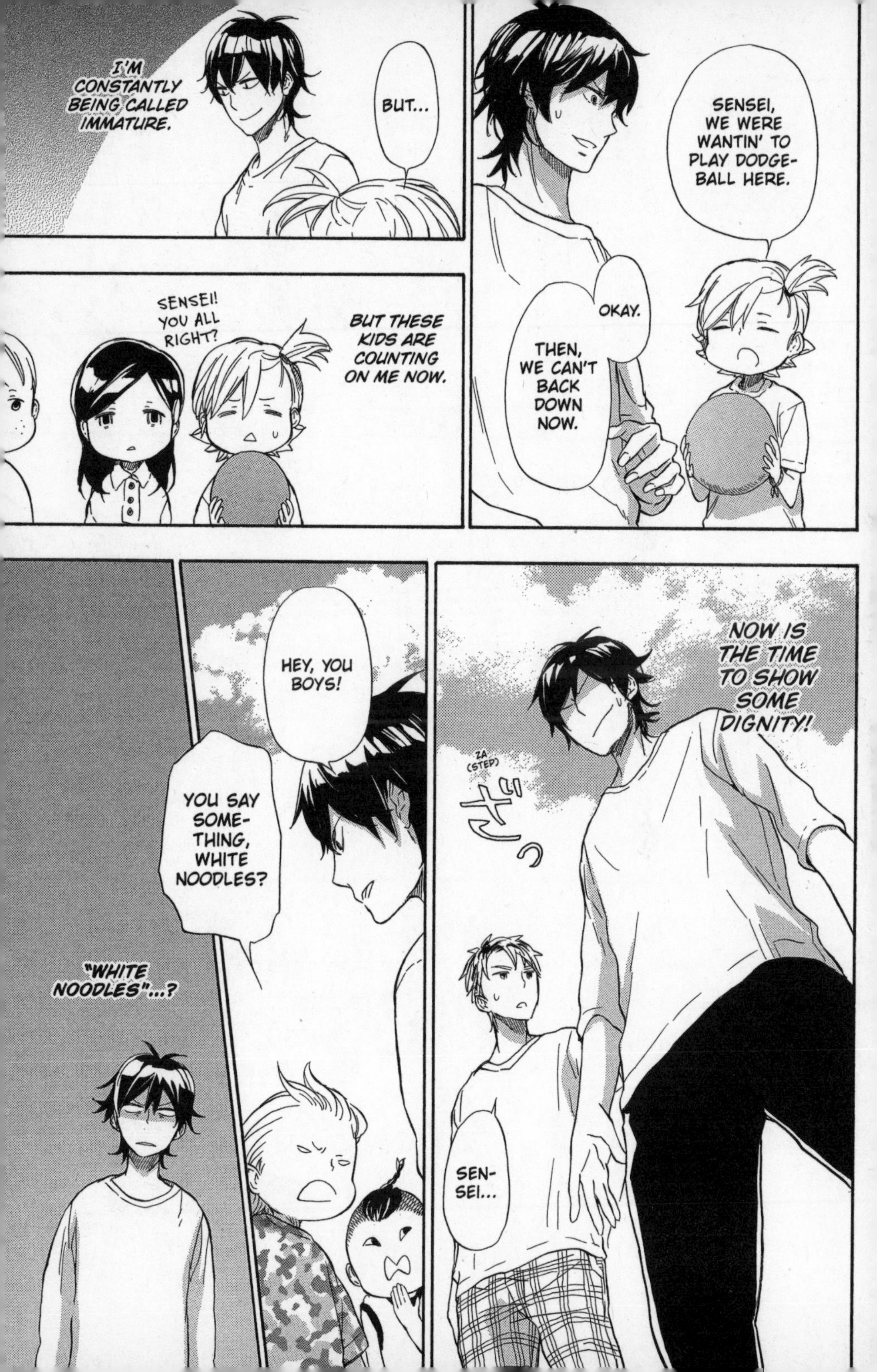
SENSEI, WE WERE WANTIN' TO PLAY DODGE-BALL HERE.
OKAY.
THEN, WE CAN'T BACK DOWN NOW.
BUT...
I'M CONSTANTLY BEING CALLED IMMATURE.
BUT THESE KIDS ARE COUNTING ON ME NOW.
SENSEI! YOU ALL RIGHT?
NOW IS THE TIME TO SHOW SOME DIGNITY!
ZA (STEP)
ざっ
SEN-SEI...
HEY, YOU BOYS!
YOU SAY SOME-THING, WHITE NOODLES?
"WHITE NOODLES"...?

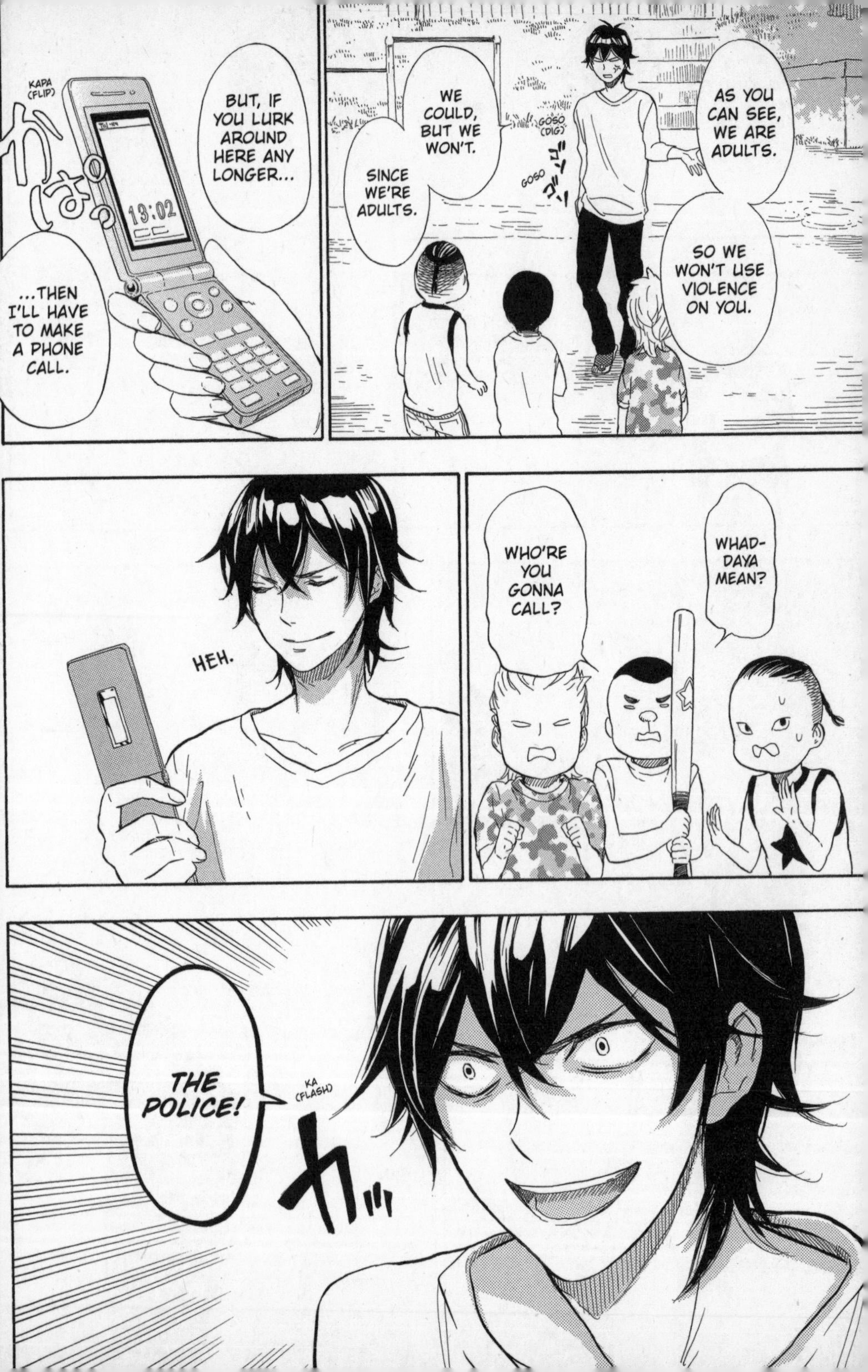
AS YOU CAN SEE, WE ARE ADULTS.
SO WE WON'T USE VIOLENCE ON YOU.
GOSO (DIG)
ゴソゴソ
GOSO
WE COULD, BUT WE WON'T.
SINCE WE'RE ADULTS.
BUT, IF YOU LURK AROUND HERE ANY LONGER...
KAPA (FLIP)
かぱっ
13:02
...THEN I'LL HAVE TO MAKE A PHONE CALL.
WHAD-DAYA MEAN?
WHO'RE YOU GONNA CALL?
HEH.
THE POLICE!
KA (FLASH)
カッ

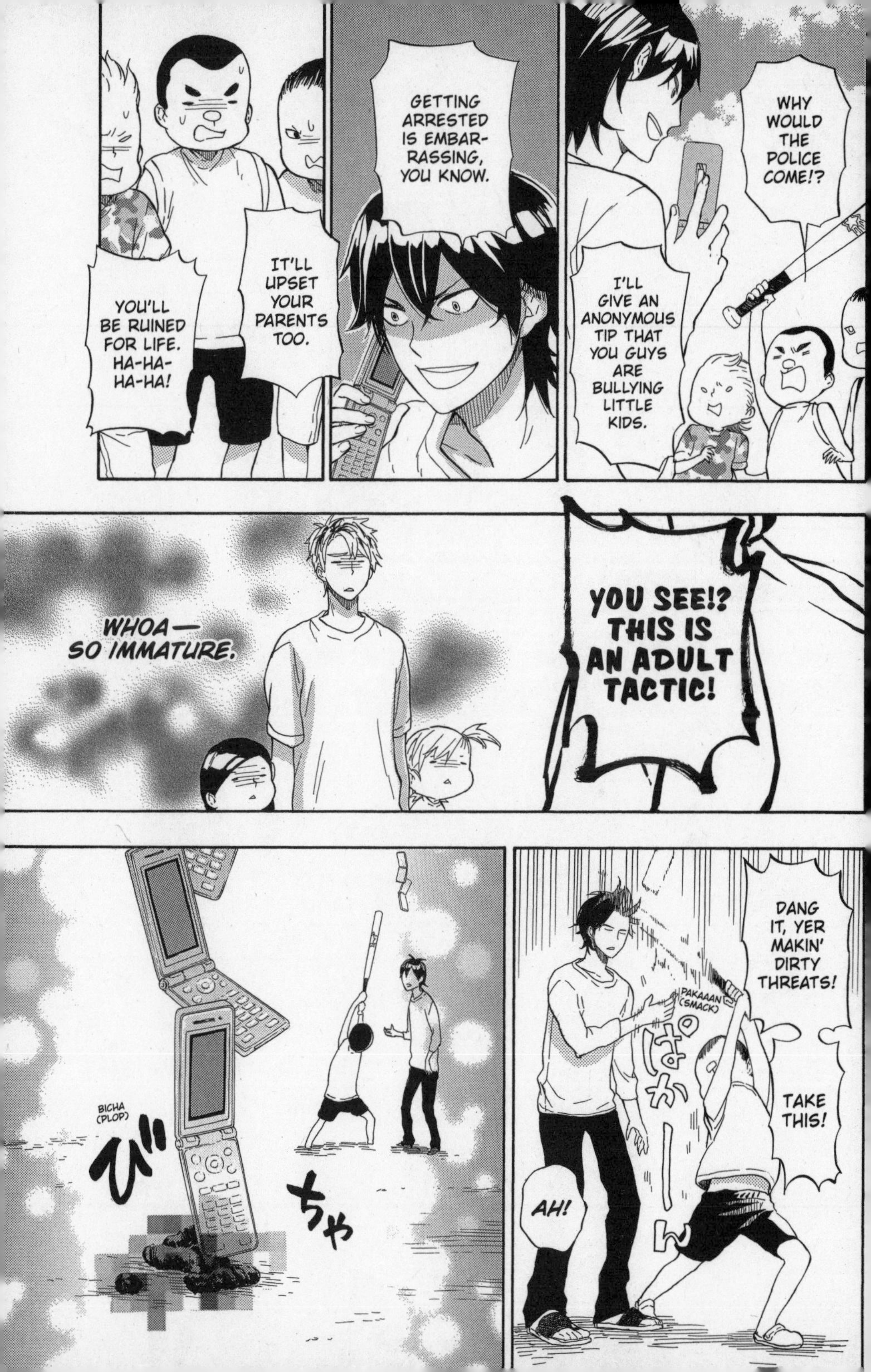
WHY WOULD THE POLICE COME!?
I'LL GIVE AN ANONYMOUS TIP THAT YOU GUYS ARE BULLYING LITTLE KIDS.
GETTING ARRESTED IS EMBARRASSING, YOU KNOW.
IT'LL UPSET YOUR PARENTS TOO.
YOU'LL BE RUINED FOR LIFE. HA-HA-HA-HA!
YOU SEE!? THIS IS AN ADULT TACTIC!
WHOA— SO IMMATURE.
DANG IT, YER MAKIN' DIRTY THREATS!
TAKE THIS!
PAKAAAN (SMACK)
ぱかーん
AH!
BICHA (PLOP)
びちゃ

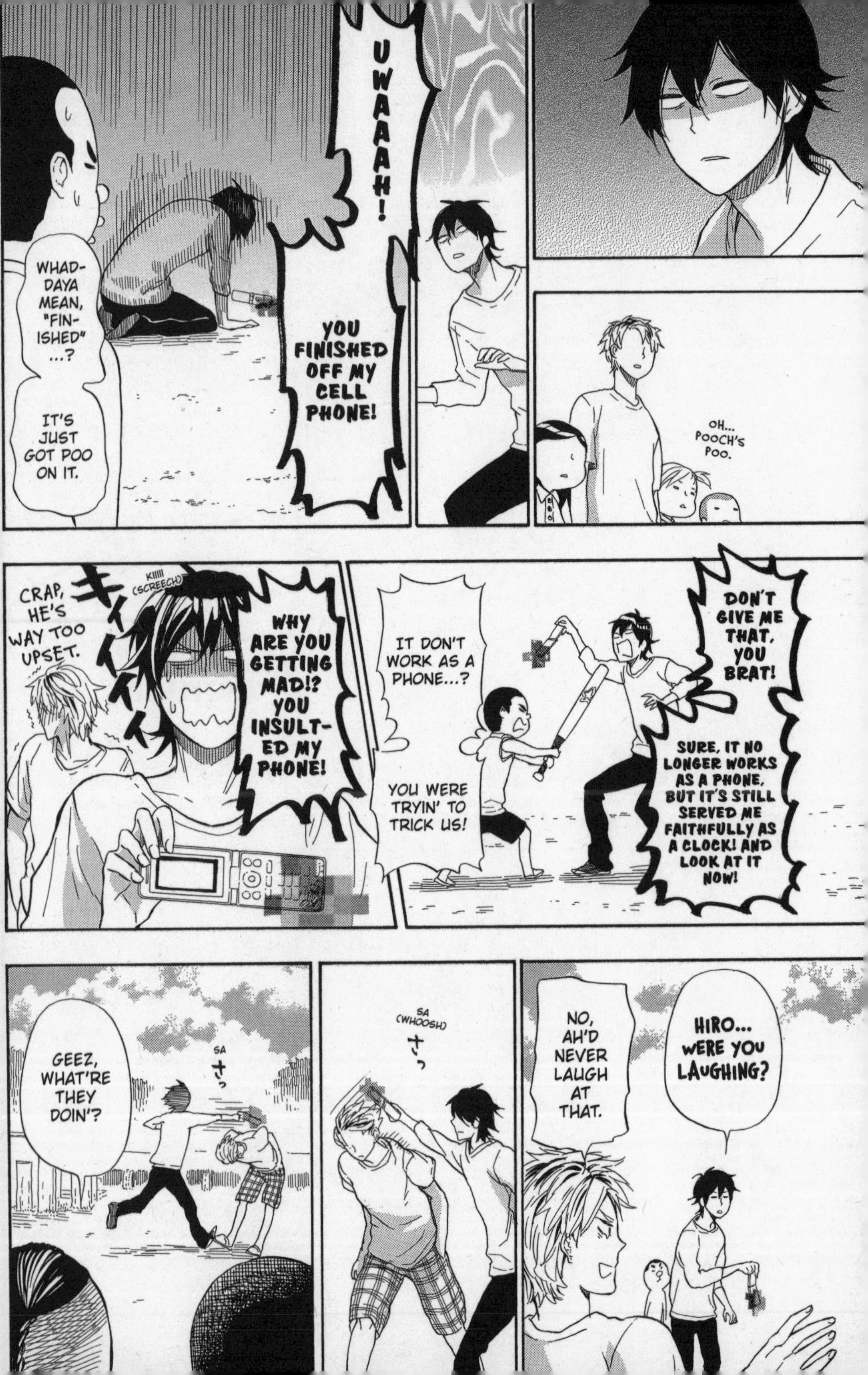
OH... POOCH'S POO.
UWAAAH!
YOU FINISHED OFF MY CELL PHONE!
WHADDAYA MEAN, "FINISHED"...?
IT'S JUST GOT POO ON IT.
DON'T GIVE ME THAT, YOU BRAT!
IT DON'T WORK AS A PHONE...?
SURE, IT NO LONGER WORKS AS A PHONE, BUT IT'S STILL SERVED ME FAITHFULLY AS A CLOCK! AND LOOK AT IT NOW!
YOU WERE TRYIN' TO TRICK US!
KIIII (SCREECH)
キィィィ
WHY ARE YOU GETTING MAD!? YOU INSULTED MY PHONE!
CRAP, HE'S WAY TOO UPSET.
HIRO... WERE YOU LAUGHING?
NO, AH'D NEVER LAUGH AT THAT.
SA (WHOOSH)
さっ
SA
さっ
GEEZ, WHAT'RE THEY DOIN'?

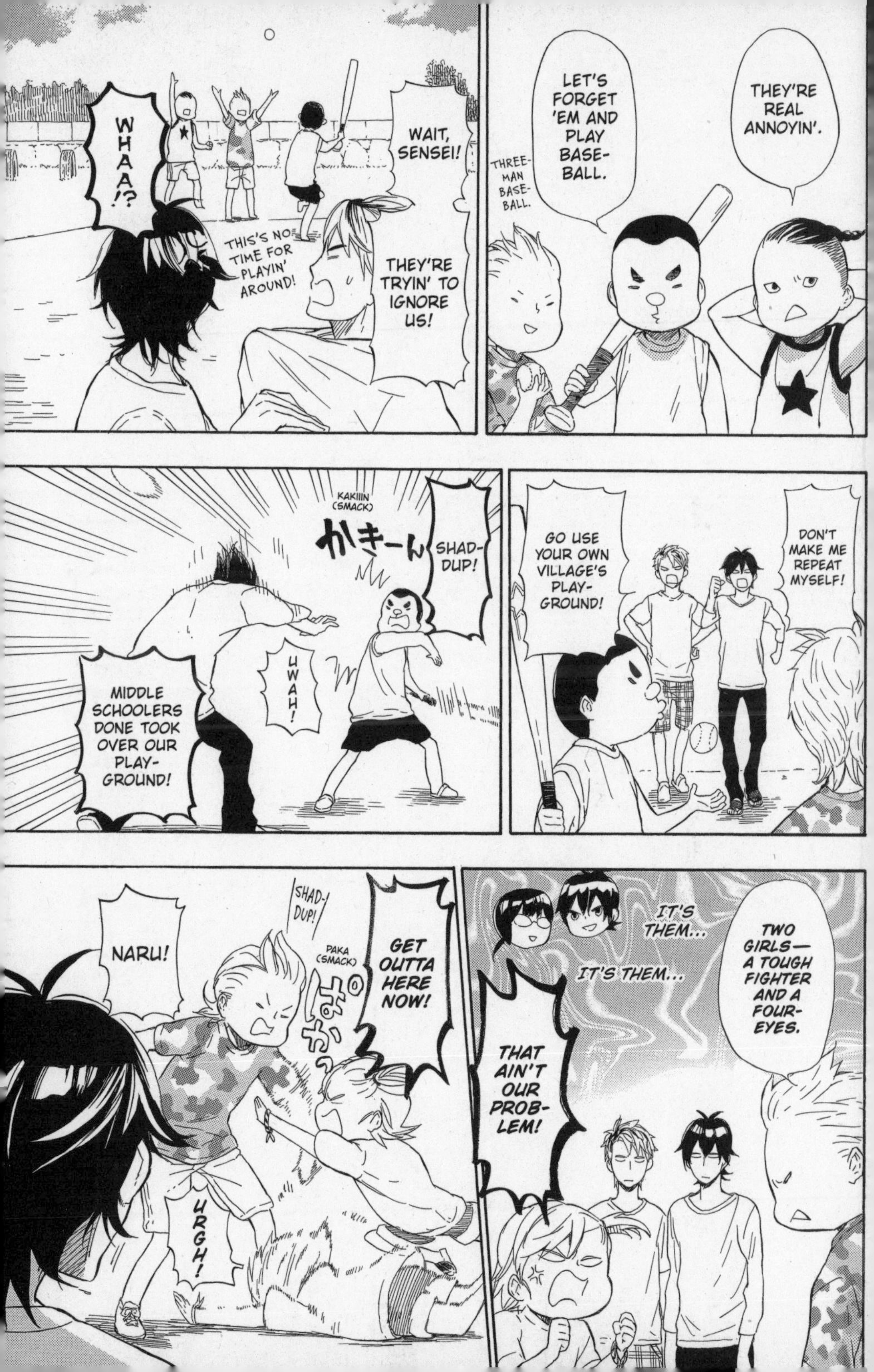
THEY'RE REAL ANNOYIN'.
LET'S FORGET 'EM AND PLAY BASEBALL.
THREE-MAN BASEBALL.
WAIT, SENSEI!
THEY'RE TRYIN' TO IGNORE US!
THIS'S NO TIME FOR PLAYIN' AROUND!
WHAA!?
DON'T MAKE ME REPEAT MYSELF!
GO USE YOUR OWN VILLAGE'S PLAYGROUND!
SHAD-DUP!
KAKIIIN (SMACK)
かきーん
UWAH!
MIDDLE SCHOOLERS DONE TOOK OVER OUR PLAYGROUND!
TWO GIRLS— A TOUGH FIGHTER AND A FOUR-EYES.
IT'S THEM...
IT'S THEM...
THAT AIN'T OUR PROBLEM!
GET OUTTA HERE NOW!
SHAD-DUP!
PAKA (SMACK)
ぱかっ
NARU!
URGH!

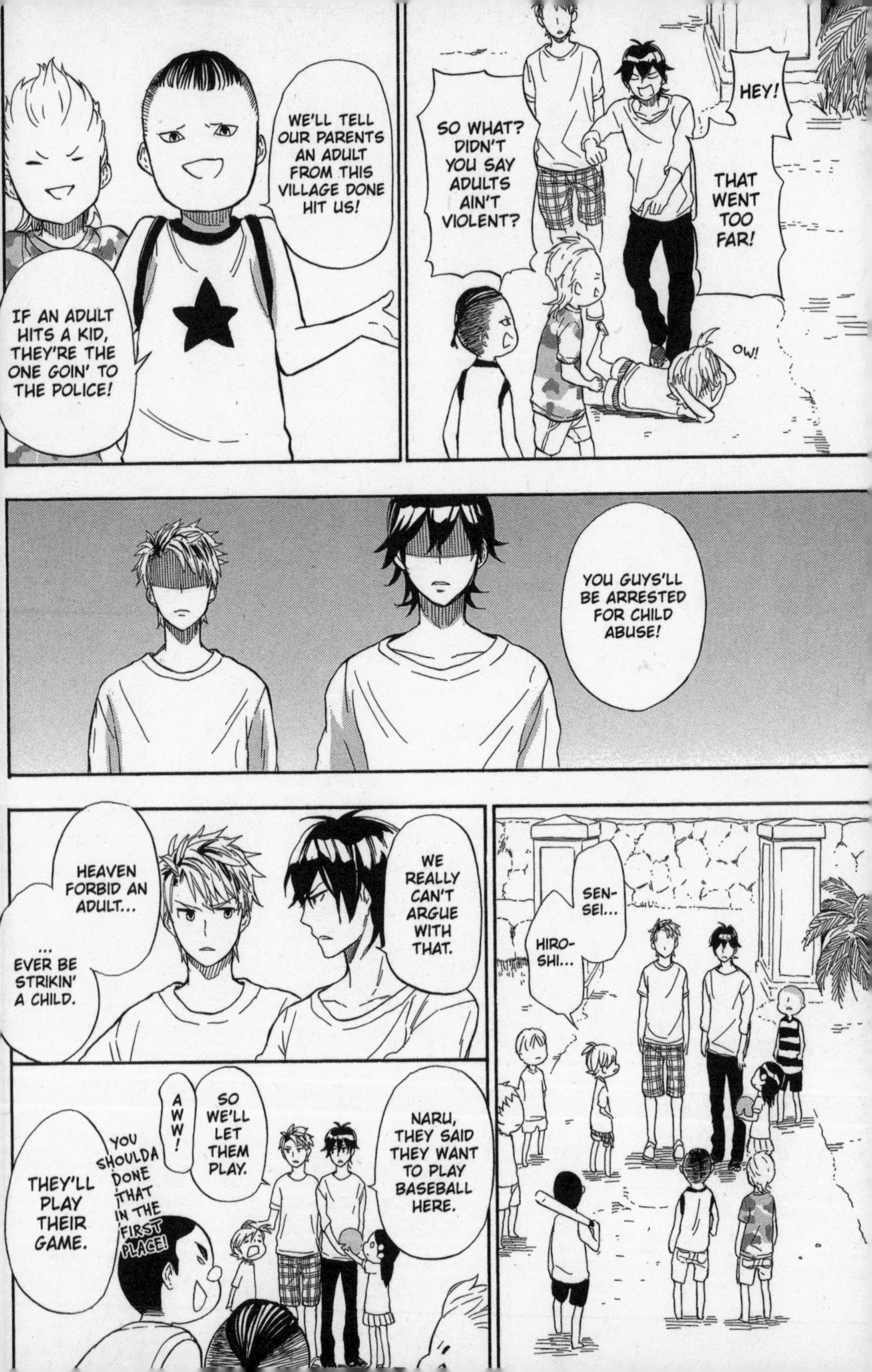
HEY!
THAT WENT TOO FAR!
OW!
SO WHAT? DIDN'T YOU SAY ADULTS AIN'T VIOLENT?
WE'LL TELL OUR PARENTS AN ADULT FROM THIS VILLAGE DONE HIT US!
IF AN ADULT HITS A KID, THEY'RE THE ONE GOIN' TO THE POLICE!
YOU GUYS'LL BE ARRESTED FOR CHILD ABUSE!
SEN-SEI...
HIRO-SHI...
WE REALLY CAN'T ARGUE WITH THAT.
HEAVEN FORBID AN ADULT...
... EVER BE STRIKIN' A CHILD.
NARU, THEY SAID THEY WANT TO PLAY BASEBALL HERE.
SO WE'LL LET THEM PLAY.
AWW!
YOU SHOULDA DONE THAT IN THE FIRST PLACE!
THEY'LL PLAY THEIR GAME.

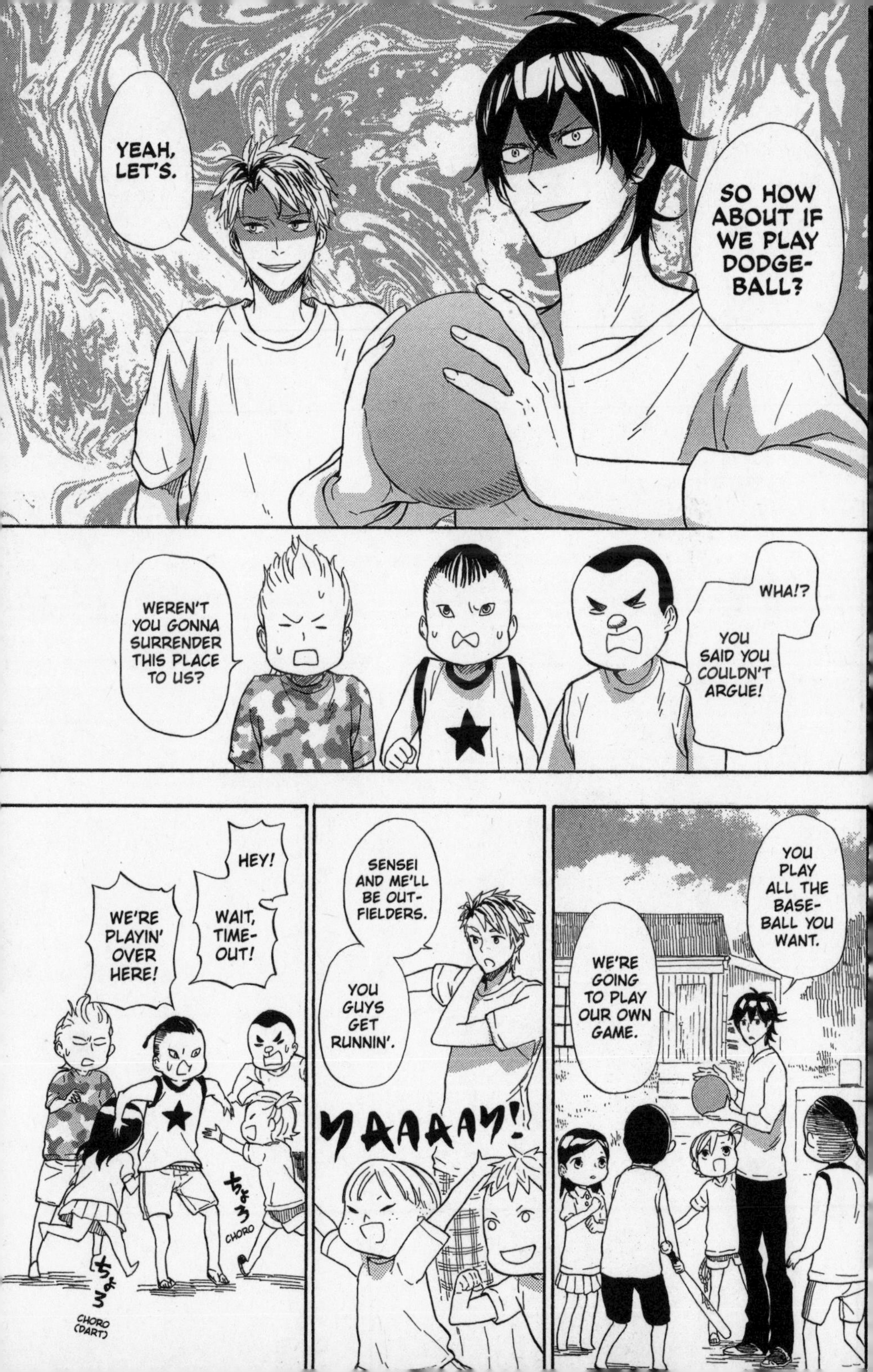
SO HOW ABOUT IF WE PLAY DODGE-BALL?
YEAH, LET'S.
WHA!?
YOU SAID YOU COULDN'T ARGUE!
WEREN'T YOU GONNA SURRENDER THIS PLACE TO US?
YOU PLAY ALL THE BASE-BALL YOU WANT.
WE'RE GOING TO PLAY OUR OWN GAME.
SENSEI AND ME'LL BE OUT-FIELDERS.
YOU GUYS GET RUNNIN'.
YAAAAY!
HEY!
WAIT, TIME-OUT!
WE'RE PLAYIN' OVER HERE!
ちょろ
CHORO
ちょろ
CHORO (DART)

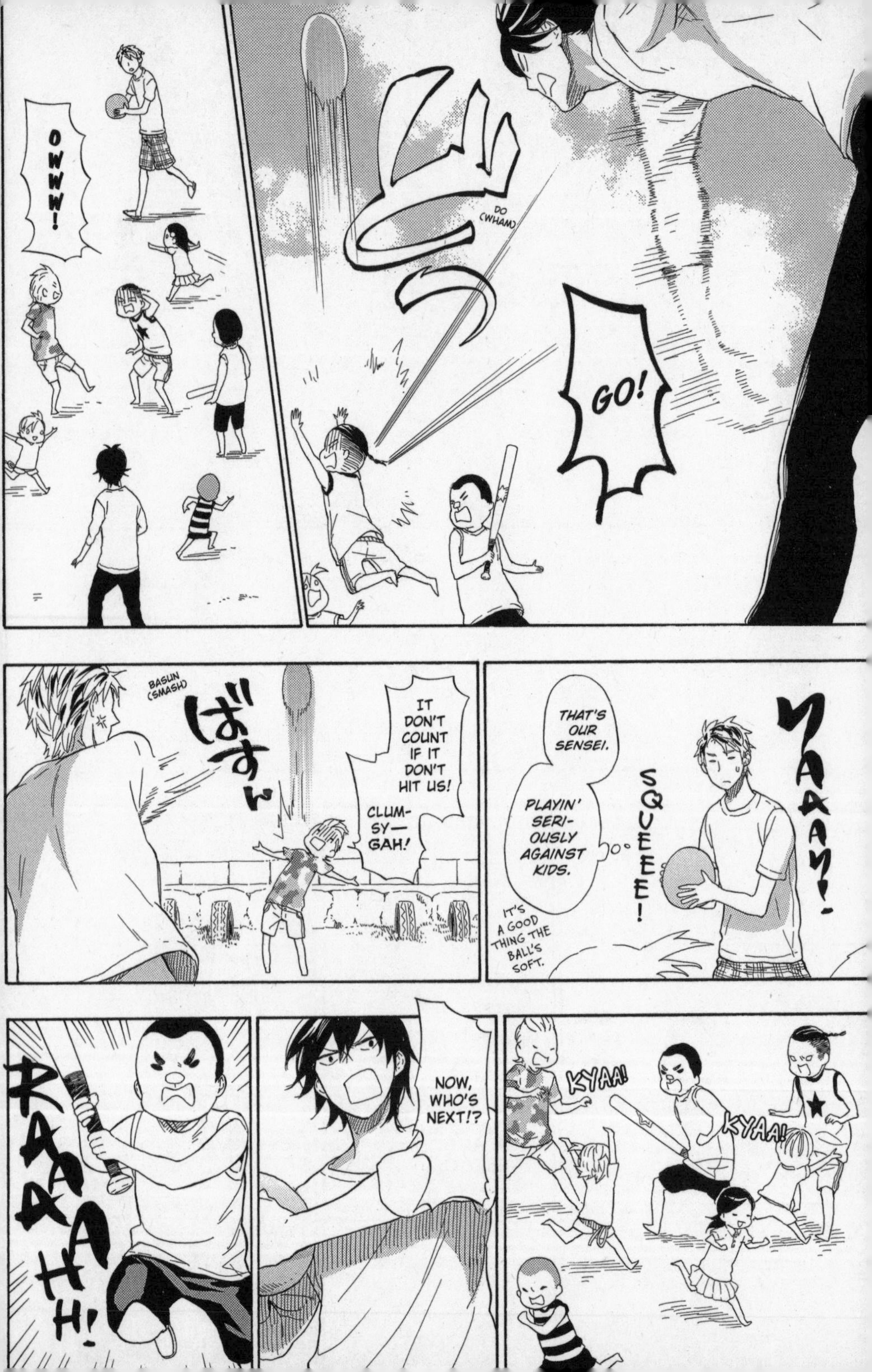
GO!
DO (WHAM)
OWWW!
MAAAN!
SQUEEE!
THAT'S OUR SENSEI.
PLAYIN' SERIOUSLY AGAINST KIDS.
IT'S A GOOD THING THE BALL'S SOFT.
IT DON'T COUNT IF IT DON'T HIT US!
CLUMSY—GAH!
ばすん
BASUN (SMASH)
KYAA!
KYAA!
NOW, WHO'S NEXT!?
RAAAAAHH!

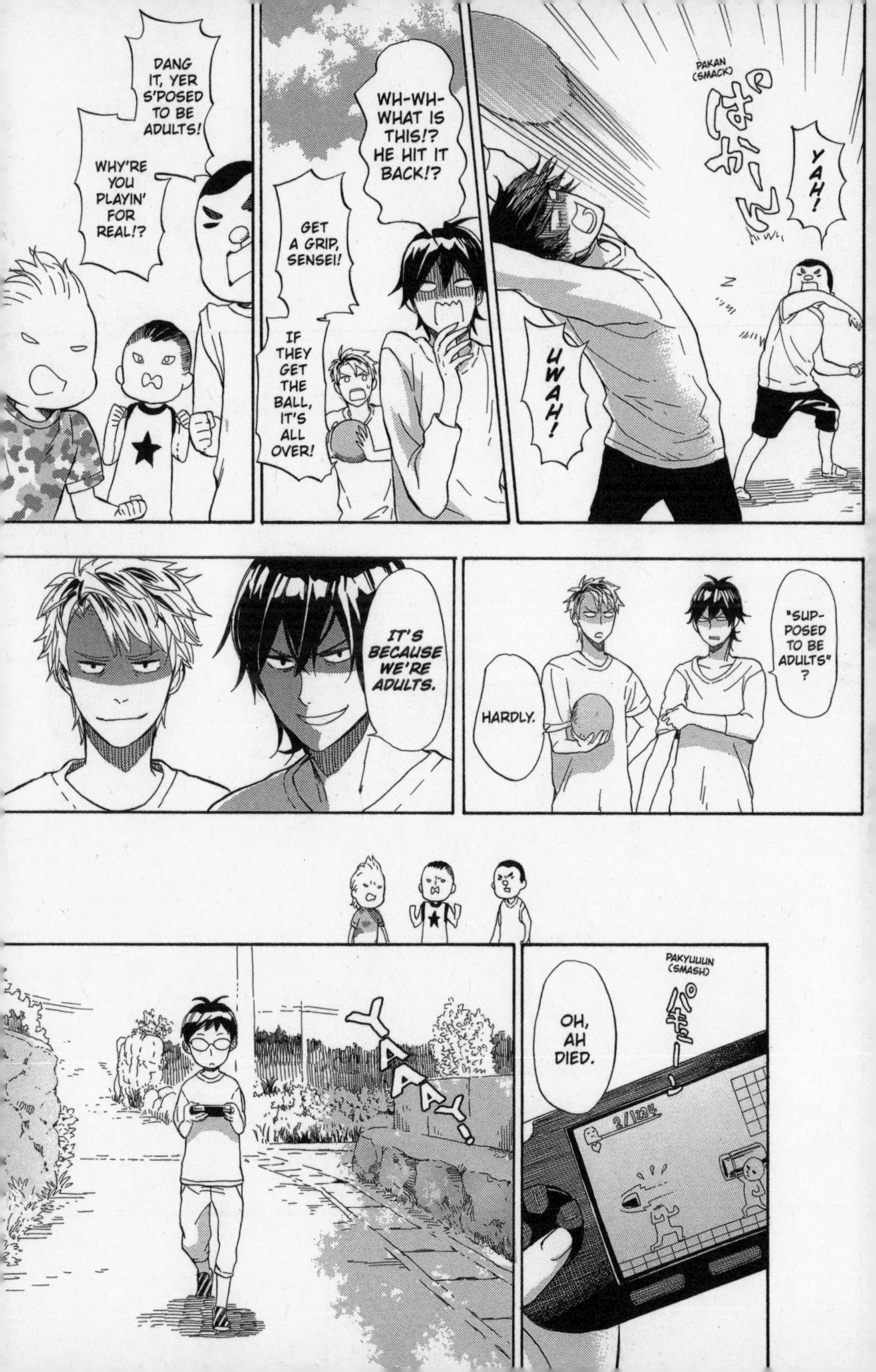
PAKAN (SMACK)
YAH!
UWAH!
WH-WH-WHAT IS THIS!? HE HIT IT BACK!?
GET A GRIP, SENSEI!
IF THEY GET THE BALL, IT'S ALL OVER!
DANG IT, YER S'POSED TO BE ADULTS!
WHY'RE YOU PLAYIN' FOR REAL!?
"SUP-POSED TO BE ADULTS"?
HARDLY.
IT'S BECAUSE WE'RE ADULTS.
PAKYUUUN (SMASH)
OH, AH DIED.
YAAAY!

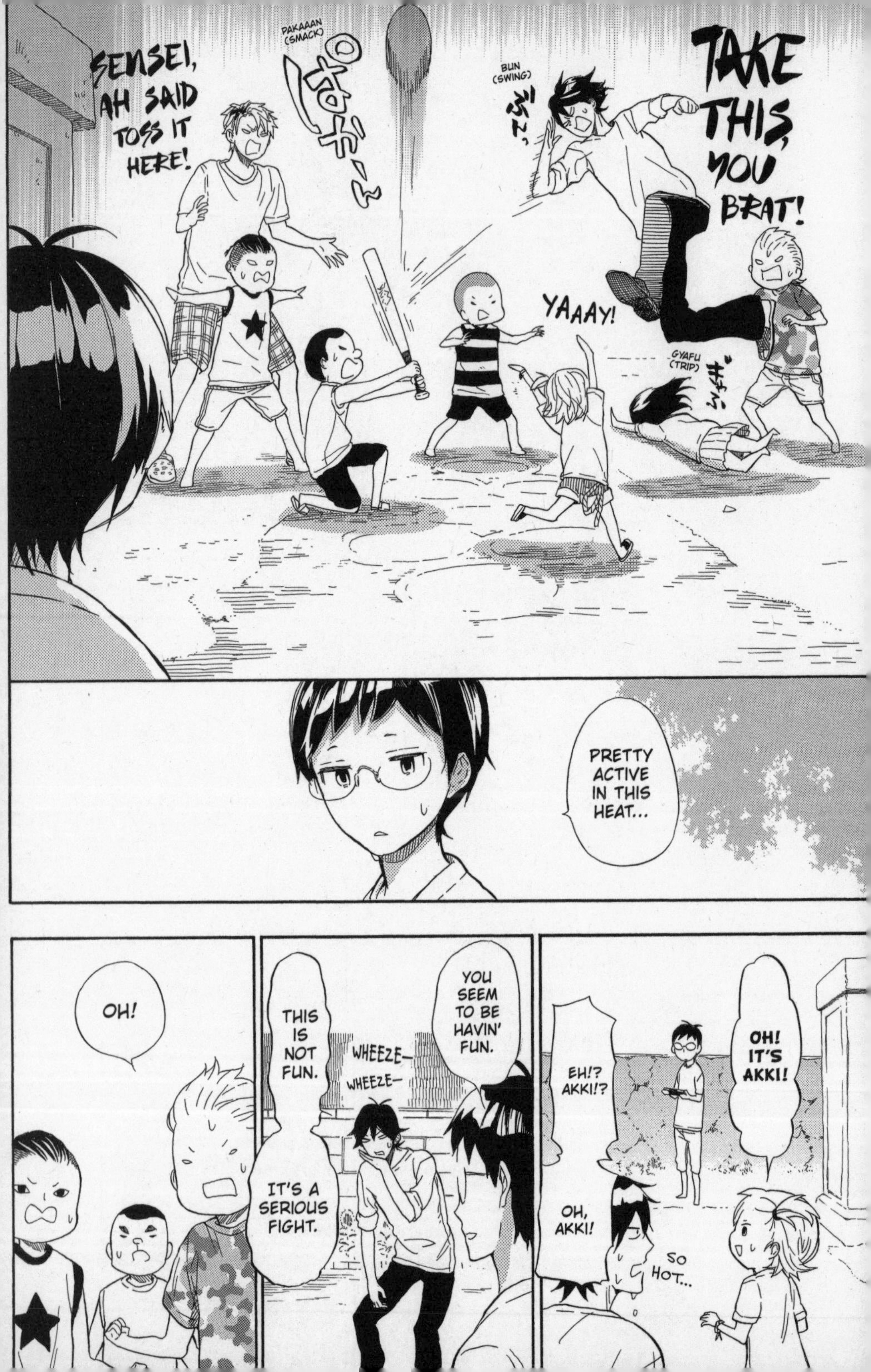
TAKE THIS, YOU BRAT!
BUN (SWING)
ぶん
PAKAAAN (SMACK)
ぱかーん
SENSEI, AH SAID TOSS IT HERE!
YAAAY!
GYAFU (TRIP)
ぎゃふ
PRETTY ACTIVE IN THIS HEAT...
OH! IT'S AKKI!
EH!? AKKI!?
OH, AKKI!
SO HOT...
YOU SEEM TO BE HAVIN' FUN.
WHEEZE—
WHEEZE—
THIS IS NOT FUN.
IT'S A SERIOUS FIGHT.
OH!

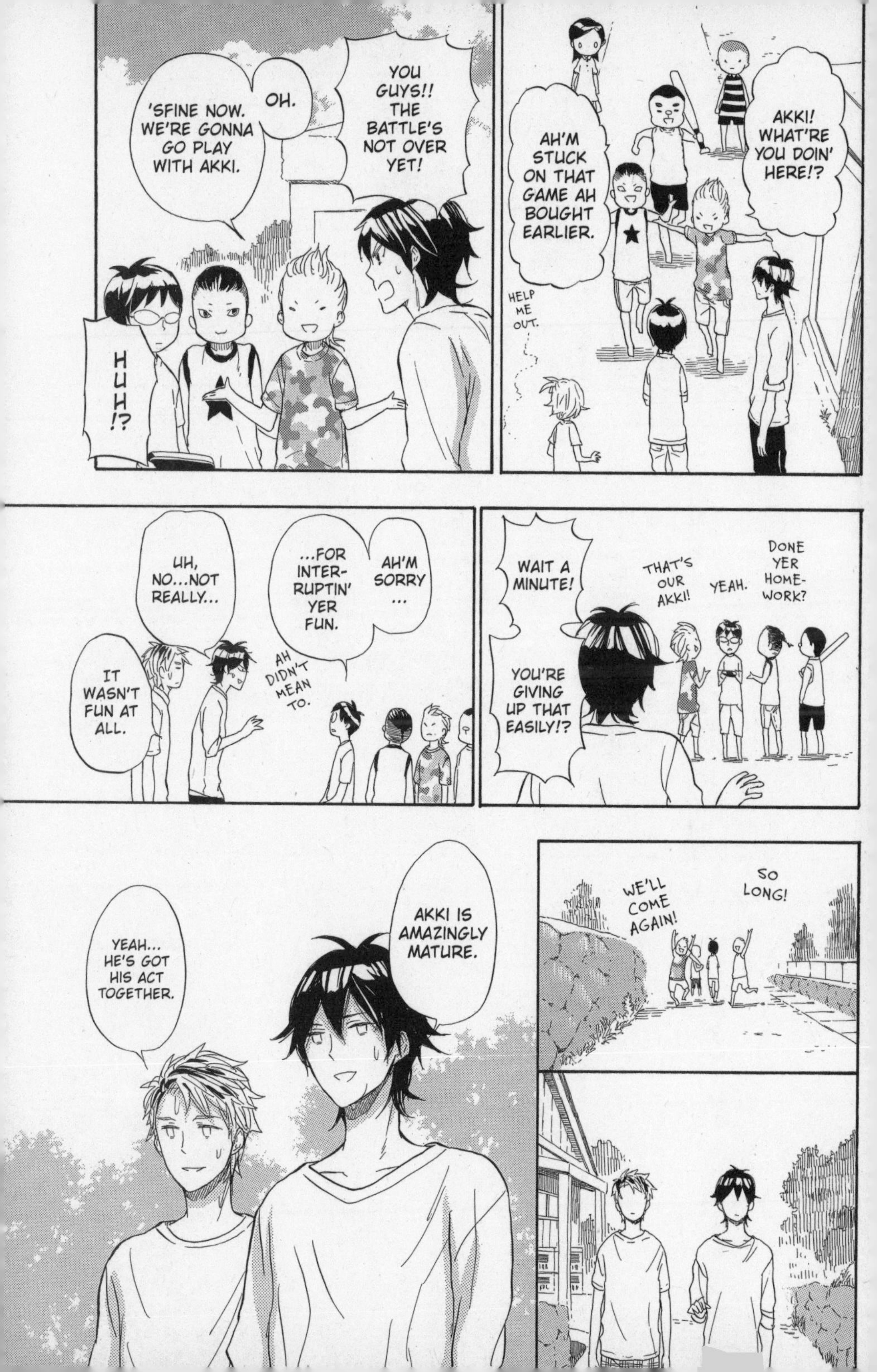
AKKI! WHAT'RE YOU DOIN' HERE!?
AH'M STUCK ON THAT GAME AH BOUGHT EARLIER.
HELP ME OUT.
YOU GUYS!! THE BATTLE'S NOT OVER YET!
OH.
'SFINE NOW. WE'RE GONNA GO PLAY WITH AKKI.
HUH!?
WAIT A MINUTE!
YOU'RE GIVING UP THAT EASILY!?
DONE YER HOMEWORK?
YEAH.
THAT'S OUR AKKI!
AH'M SORRY...
...FOR INTERRUPTIN' YER FUN.
AH DIDN'T MEAN TO.
UH, NO...NOT REALLY...
IT WASN'T FUN AT ALL.
SO LONG!
WE'LL COME AGAIN!
AKKI IS AMAZINGLY MATURE.
YEAH... HE'S GOT HIS ACT TOGETHER.

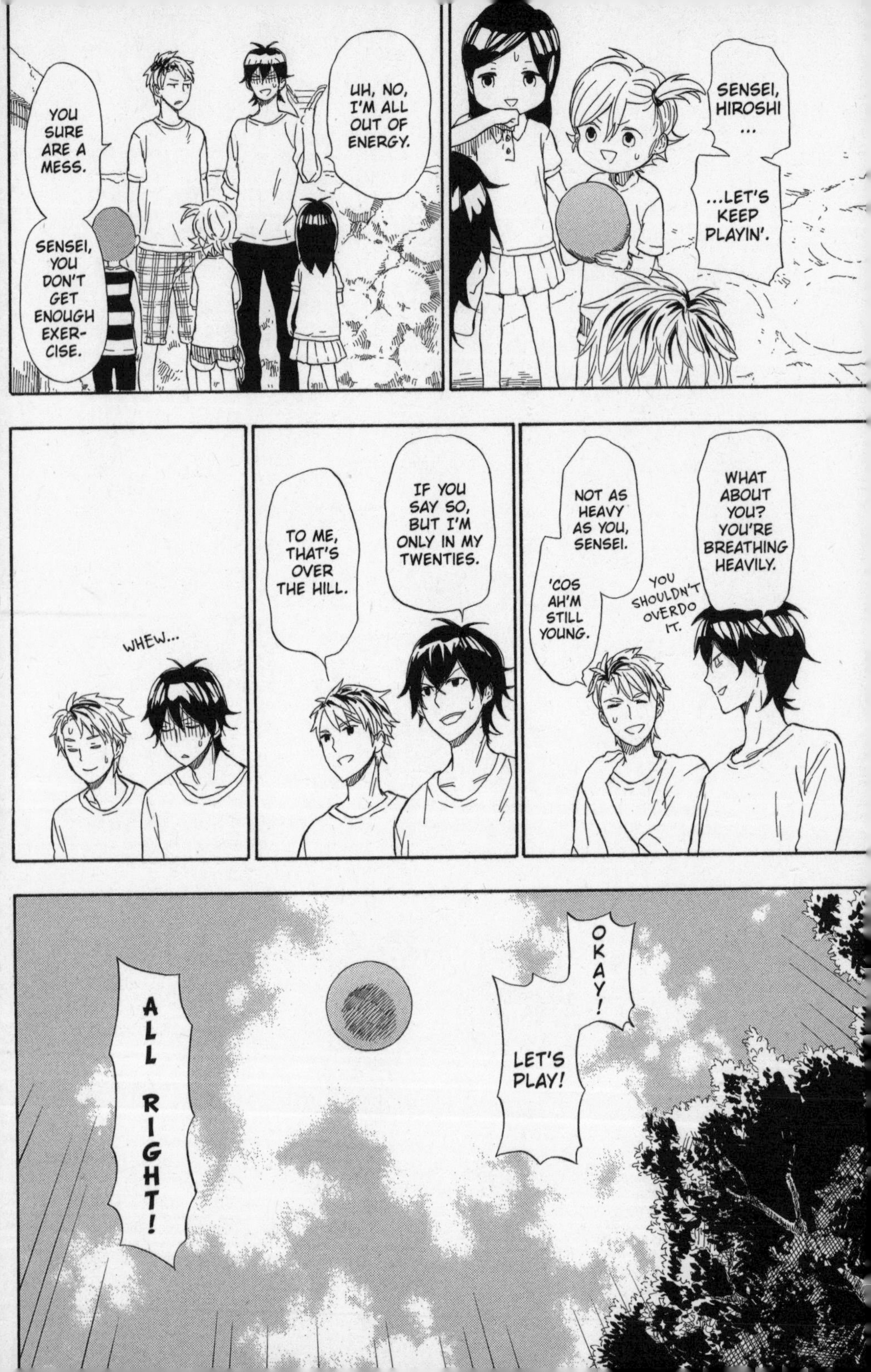
SENSEI, HIROSHI ...
...LET'S KEEP PLAYIN'.
UH, NO, I'M ALL OUT OF ENERGY.
YOU SURE ARE A MESS.
SENSEI, YOU DON'T GET ENOUGH EXER-CISE.
WHAT ABOUT YOU? YOU'RE BREATHING HEAVILY.
YOU SHOULDN'T OVERDO IT.
NOT AS HEAVY AS YOU, SENSEI.
'COS AH'M STILL YOUNG.
IF YOU SAY SO, BUT I'M ONLY IN MY TWENTIES.
TO ME, THAT'S OVER THE HILL.
WHEW...
OKAY!
LET'S PLAY!
ALL RIGHT!

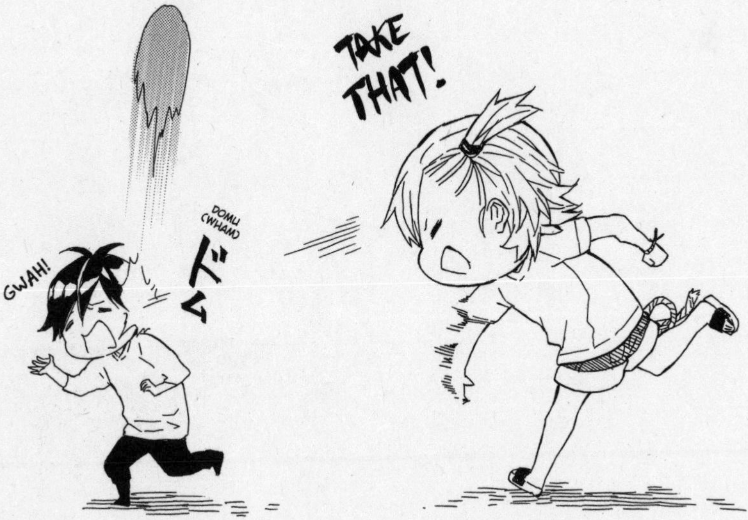
TAKE THAT!
DOMU (WHAM)
GWAH!

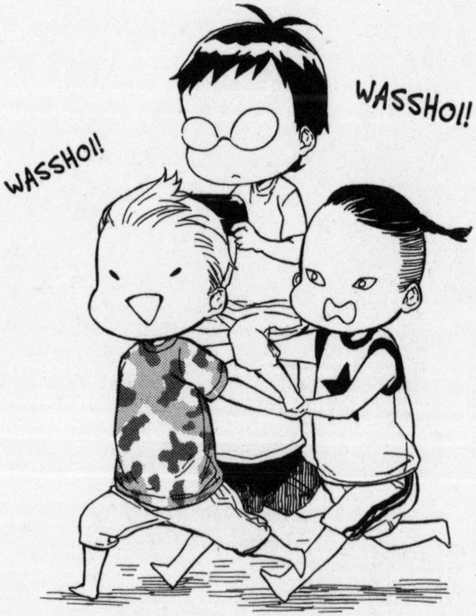
WASSHOI!
WASSHOI!

BONUS KAUKA
(Translation: Mosquito)

PUUUN (WNNNN)
ぷーん
PUUUU
ぷ
PUN
ぷんっ
GOT YOU!
BAAN (WHACK)
ばあん
DOBA (TOPPLE)
どばっ
FUKI (WIPE)
ふき
FUKI
ふき

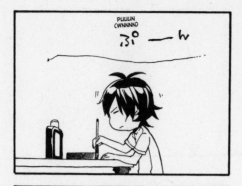

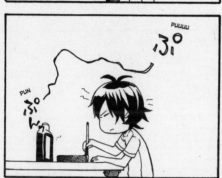

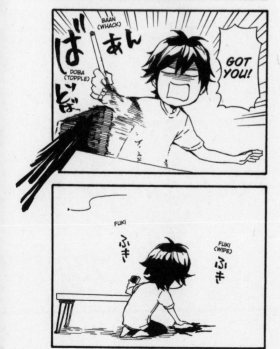

PUUUN (WNNNNN)
IRA (IRK)
イラ
IRA
イラ
BACHIN (CRACKLE)
GASHAN (CRASH)
PUUUN
GRRR!
DIE!
SENSEI! NARU CAME TO PLAY!
I'LL KILL YOU!
!?

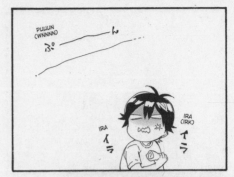

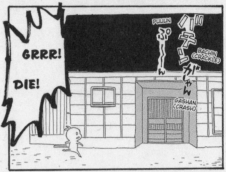

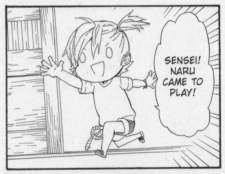

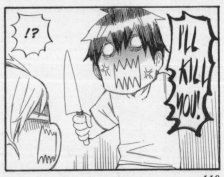

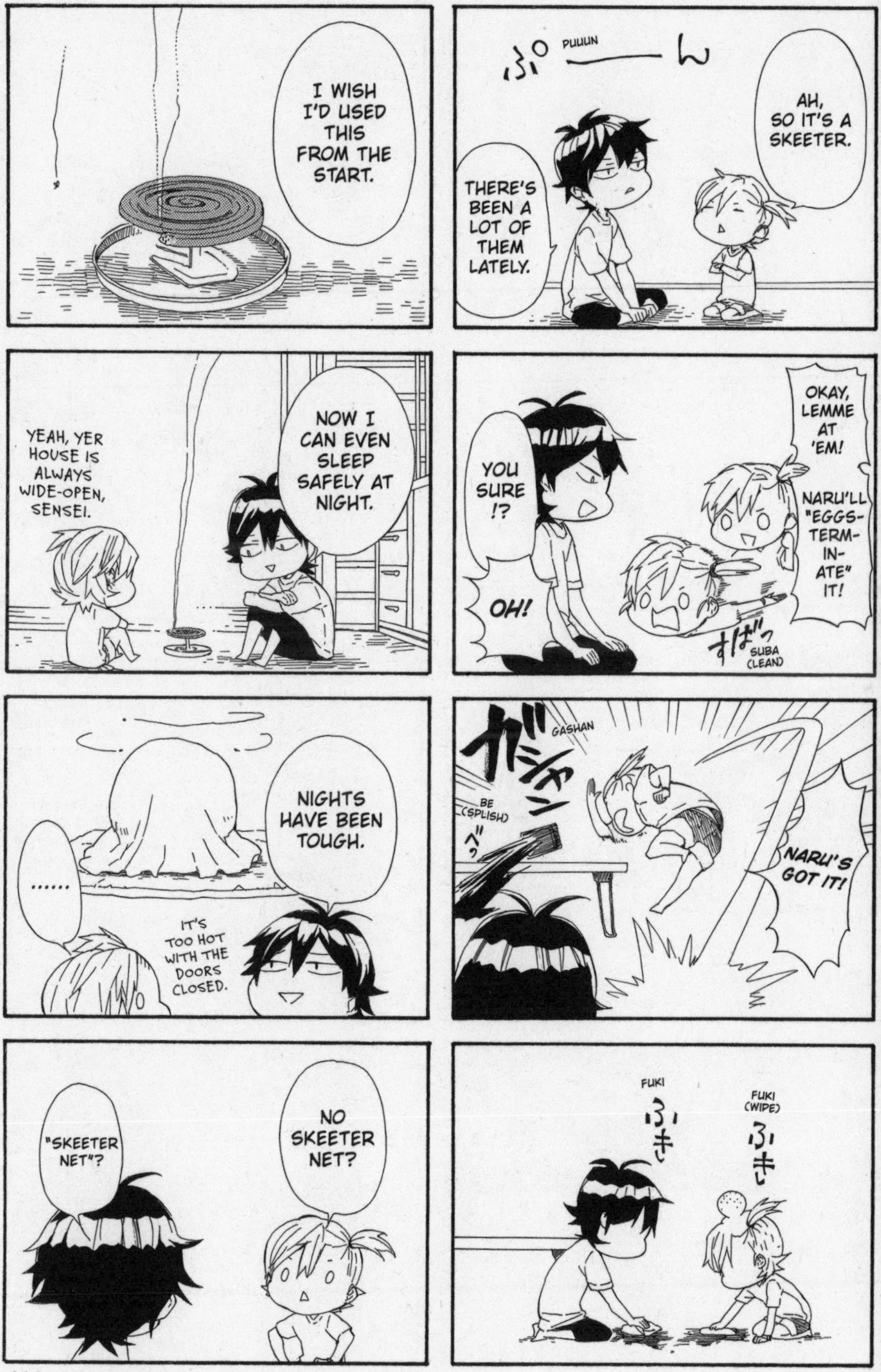
ぷ——ん
PUUUN
AH, SO IT'S A SKEETER.
THERE'S BEEN A LOT OF THEM LATELY.
I WISH I'D USED THIS FROM THE START.
OKAY, LEMME AT 'EM!
NARU'LL "EGGS-TERM-INATE" IT!
YOU SURE !?
OH!
すばっ
SUBA (LEAN)
NOW I CAN EVEN SLEEP SAFELY AT NIGHT.
YEAH, YER HOUSE IS ALWAYS WIDE-OPEN, SENSEI.
ガシャン
GASHAN
NARU'S GOT IT!
べっ
BE (SPLISH)
NIGHTS HAVE BEEN TOUGH.
IT'S TOO HOT WITH THE DOORS CLOSED.
......
ふき
FUKI
ふき
FUKI (WIPE)
NO SKEETER NET?
"SKEETER NET"?

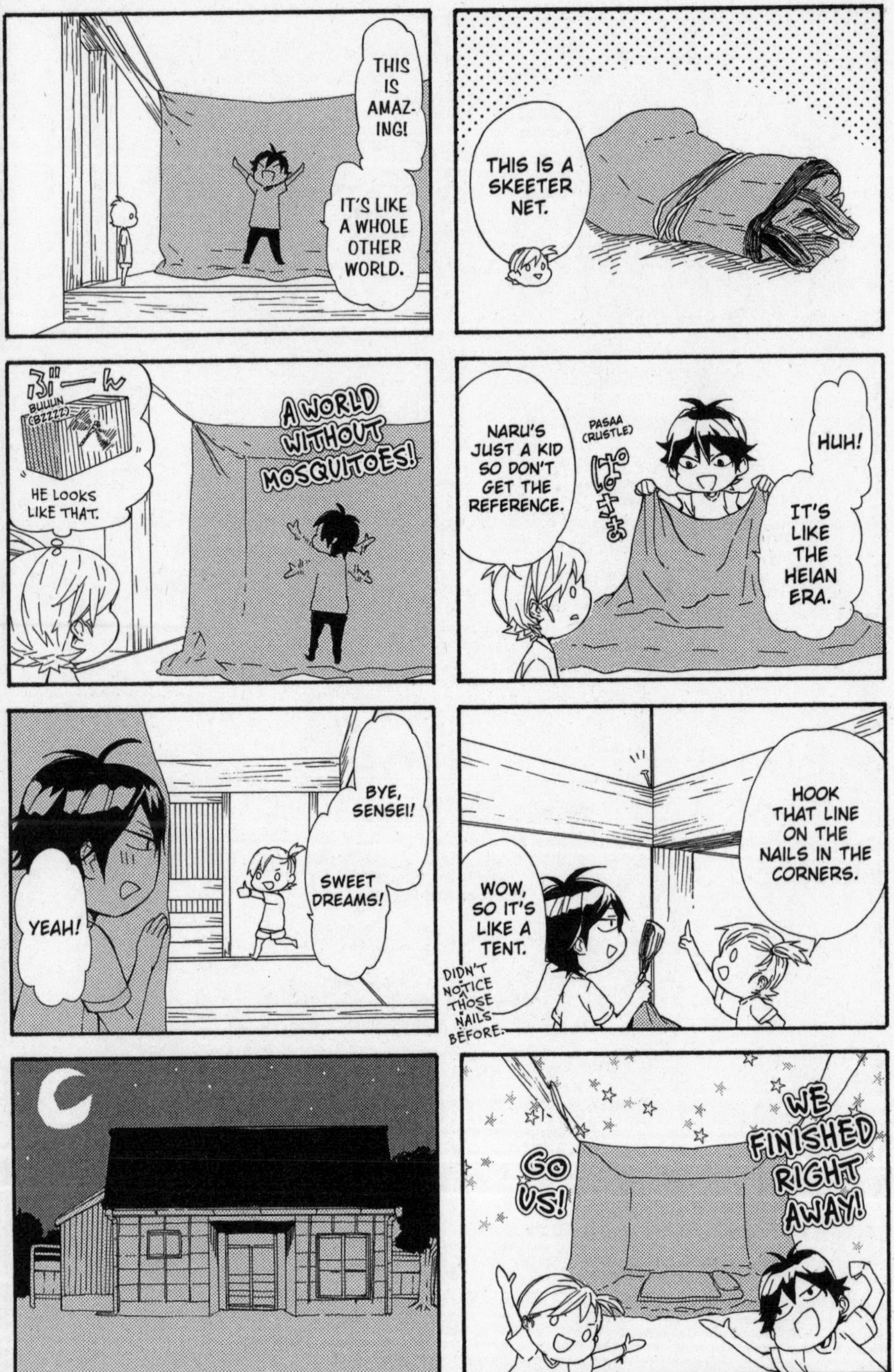
THIS IS A SKEETER NET.
HUH!
IT'S LIKE THE HEIAN ERA.
PASAA (RUSTLE)
ぱさぁ
NARU'S JUST A KID SO DON'T GET THE REFERENCE.
HOOK THAT LINE ON THE NAILS IN THE CORNERS.
WOW, SO IT'S LIKE A TENT.
DIDN'T NOTICE THOSE NAILS BEFORE.
WE FINISHED RIGHT AWAY!
GO US!
THIS IS AMAZING!
IT'S LIKE A WHOLE OTHER WORLD.
A WORLD WITHOUT MOSQUITOES!
ぶーん
BUUUN (BZZZZ)
HE LOOKS LIKE THAT.
BYE, SENSEI!
SWEET DREAMS!
YEAH!

THE NEXT DAY

BORI (WELT) ぼり

BORI ぼり

BORI ぼり

KOKURI (NOD) こくり...

SENSEI... FELL ASLEEP WITH THE SKEETER STILL INSIDE.

PUUUN (WNNNN)

GASHAN (CRASH)

YAAAH!

BE (SPLISH)

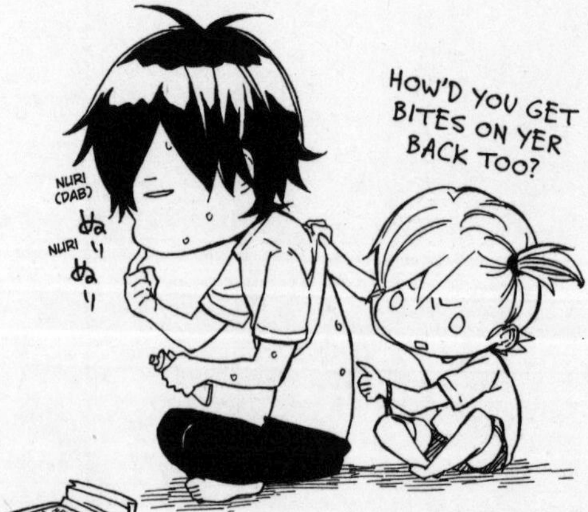
HOW'D YOU GET BITES ON YER BACK TOO?
NURI (DAB)
ぬり
NURI
ぬり

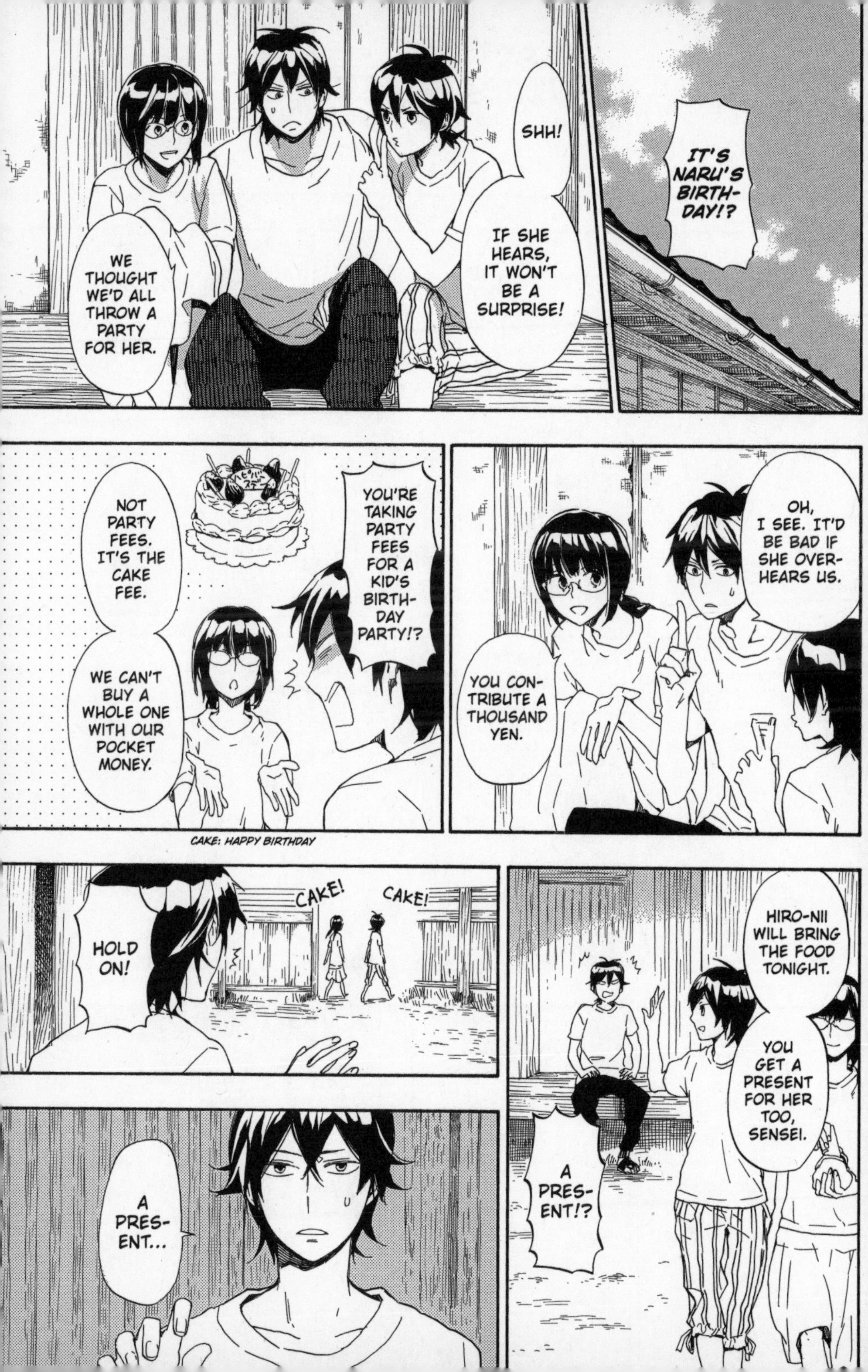
IT'S NARU'S BIRTHDAY!?
SHH!
IF SHE HEARS, IT WON'T BE A SURPRISE!
WE THOUGHT WE'D ALL THROW A PARTY FOR HER.
OH, I SEE. IT'D BE BAD IF SHE OVERHEARS US.
YOU CONTRIBUTE A THOUSAND YEN.
YOU'RE TAKING PARTY FEES FOR A KID'S BIRTHDAY PARTY!?
NOT PARTY FEES. IT'S THE CAKE FEE.
WE CAN'T BUY A WHOLE ONE WITH OUR POCKET MONEY.
HIRO-NII WILL BRING THE FOOD TONIGHT.
YOU GET A PRESENT FOR HER TOO, SENSEI.
A PRESENT!?
CAKE!
CAKE!
HOLD ON!
A PRESENT...
CAKE: HAPPY BIRTHDAY

ACT.42
YOROKOBASUDENO
(Translation: Let's Make Her Happy)

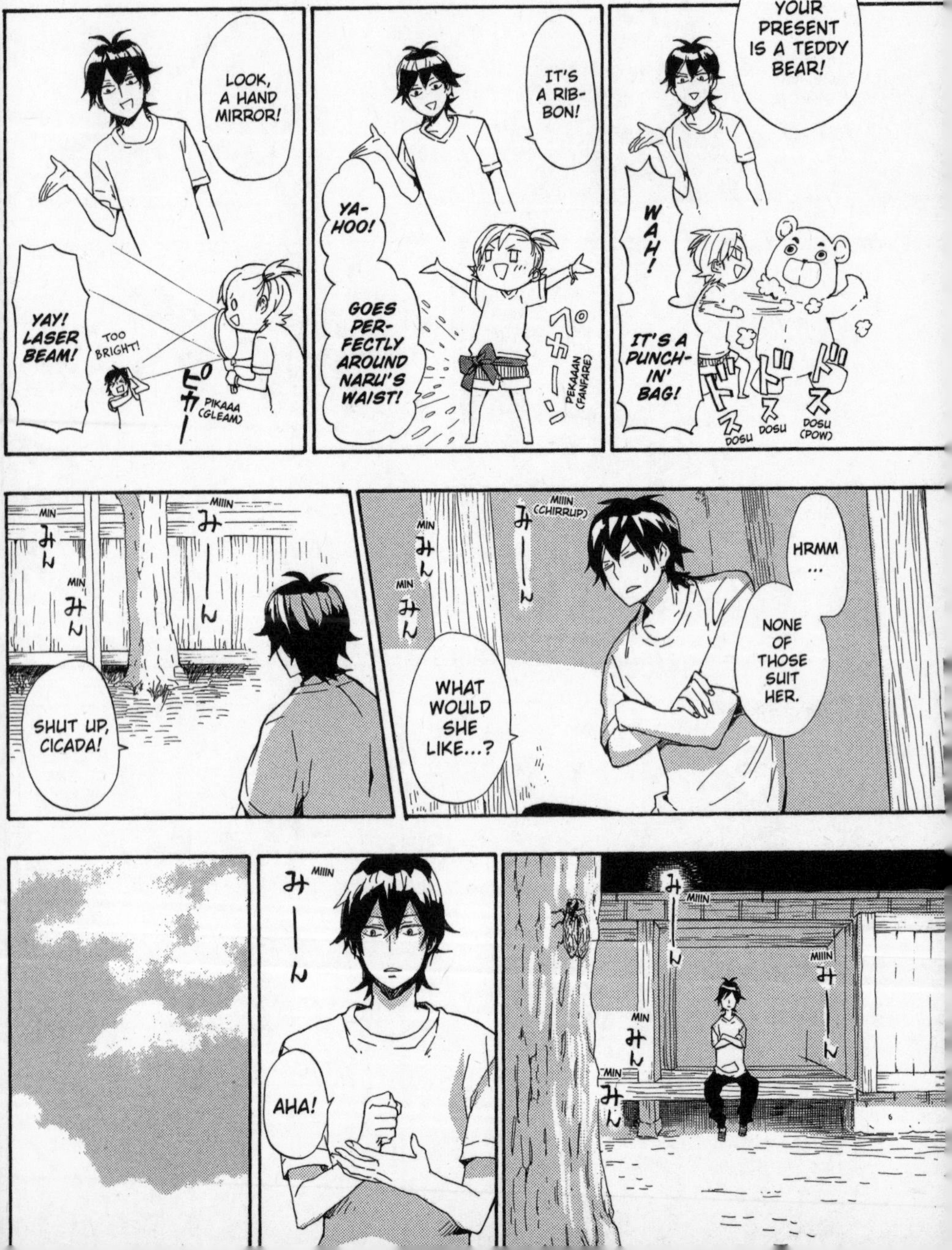
YOUR PRESENT IS A TEDDY BEAR!
WAH!
IT'S A PUNCH-IN' BAG!
DOSU
DOSU
DOSU (POW)
IT'S A RIB-BON!
YA-HOO!
GOES PER-FECTLY AROUND NARU'S WAIST!
PEKAAAN (FANFARE)
LOOK, A HAND MIRROR!
YAY! LASER BEAM!
TOO BRIGHT!
PIKAAA (GLEAM)
MIIIN (CHIRRUP)
MIN
MIN
HRMM...
NONE OF THOSE SUIT HER.
WHAT WOULD SHE LIKE...?
MIIIN
MIN
MIN
SHUT UP, CICADA!
MIIIN
MIIIN
MIN
MIN
MIIIN
AHA!

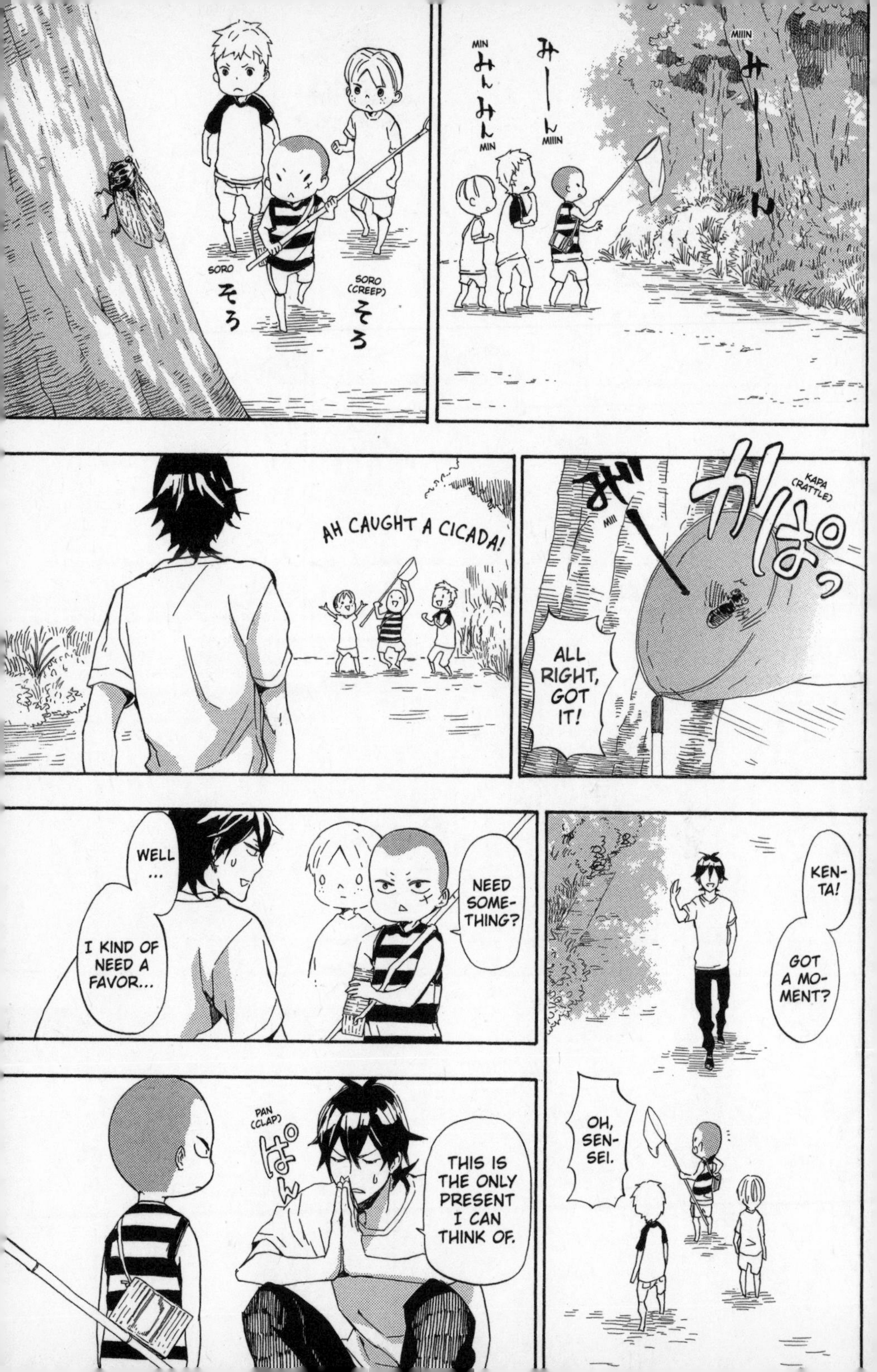
MIIIN
みーん
みーん
MIIIN
MIN
みんみん
MIN
SORO (CREEP)
そろ
SORO
そろ
KAPA (RATTLE)
かぱっ
MIII
みー
ALL RIGHT, GOT IT!
AH CAUGHT A CICADA!
KEN-TA!
GOT A MO-MENT?
OH, SEN-SEI.
NEED SOME-THING?
WELL ...
I KIND OF NEED A FAVOR...
PAN (CLAP)
ぱんっ
THIS IS THE ONLY PRESENT I CAN THINK OF.

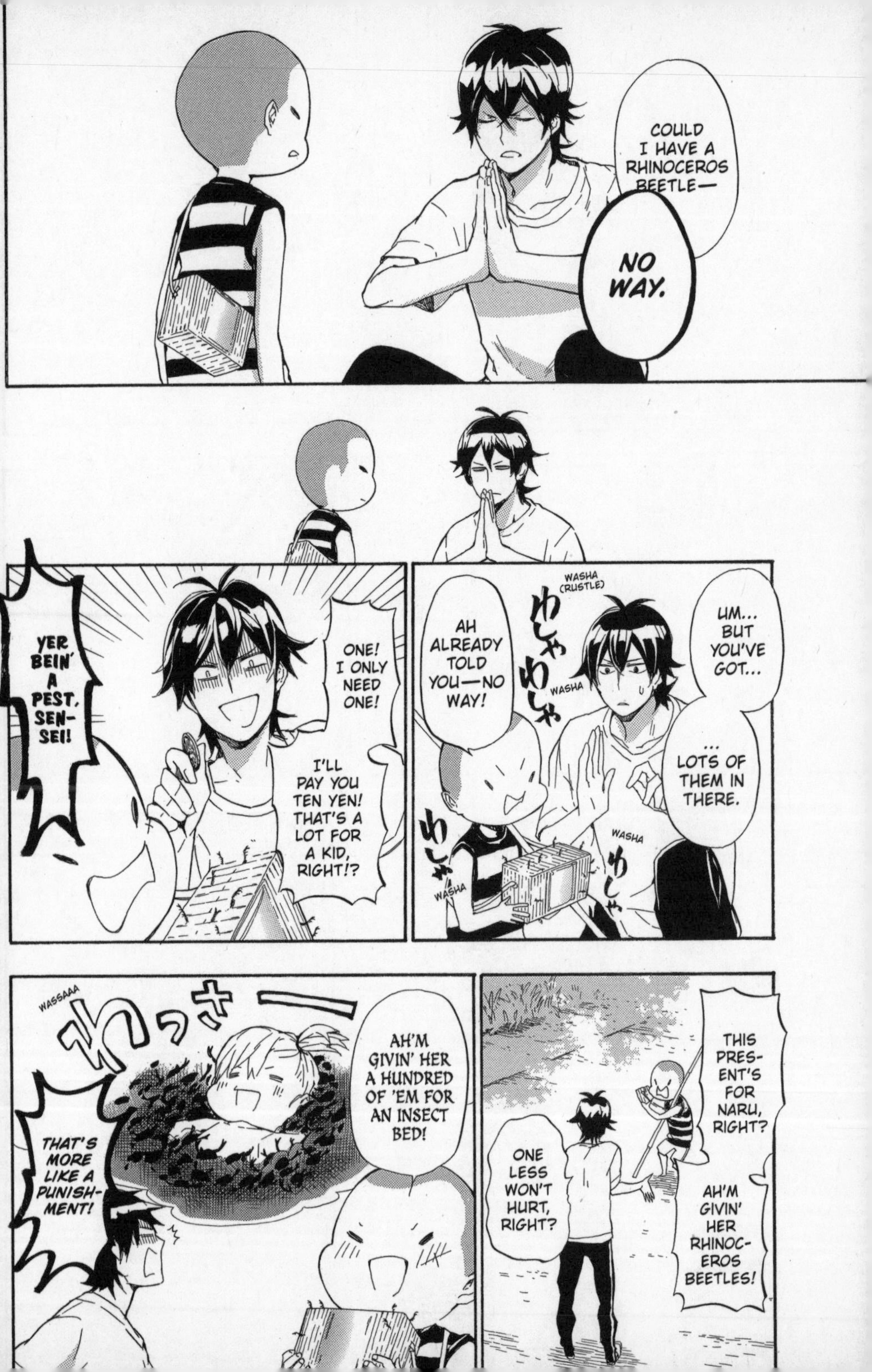
COULD I HAVE A RHINOCEROS BEETLE—
NO WAY.
WASHA (RUSTLE)
わしゃわしゃ
WASHA
UM... BUT YOU'VE GOT...
AH ALREADY TOLD YOU—NO WAY!
... LOTS OF THEM IN THERE.
WASHA
わしゃ
WASHA
わしゃ
ONE! I ONLY NEED ONE!
I'LL PAY YOU TEN YEN! THAT'S A LOT FOR A KID, RIGHT!?
YER BEIN' A PEST, SEN-SEI!
THIS PRES-ENT'S FOR NARU, RIGHT?
ONE LESS WON'T HURT, RIGHT?
AH'M GIVIN' HER RHINOC-EROS BEETLES!
WASSAAA
わっさー
AH'M GIVIN' HER A HUNDRED OF 'EM FOR AN INSECT BED!
THAT'S MORE LIKE A PUNISH-MENT!

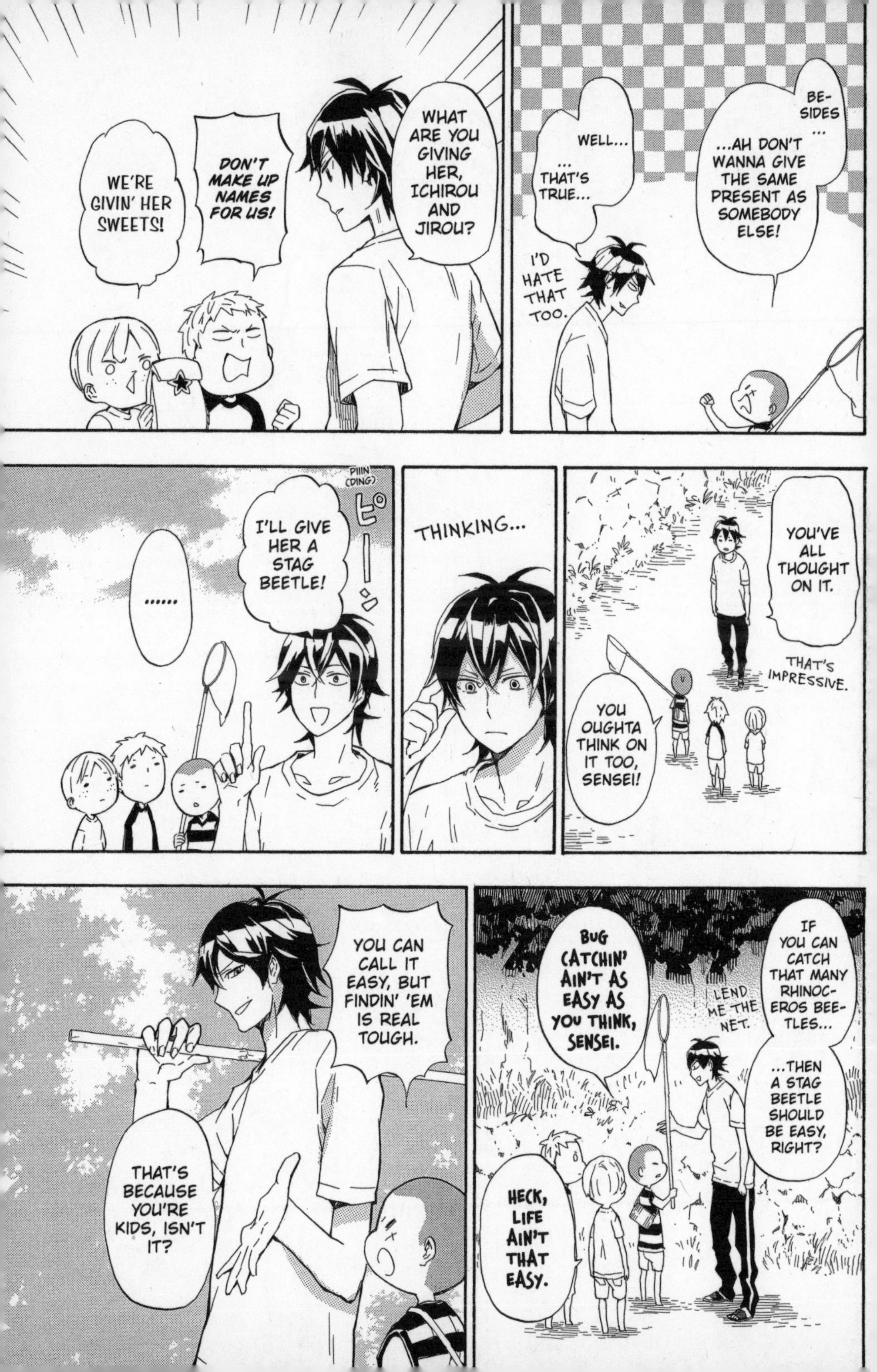
BE-SIDES...
...AH DON'T WANNA GIVE THE SAME PRESENT AS SOMEBODY ELSE!
WELL... ...THAT'S TRUE...
I'D HATE THAT TOO.
WHAT ARE YOU GIVING HER, ICHIROU AND JIROU?
DON'T MAKE UP NAMES FOR US!
WE'RE GIVIN' HER SWEETS!
YOU'VE ALL THOUGHT ON IT.
THAT'S IMPRESSIVE.
YOU OUGHTA THINK ON IT TOO, SENSEI!
THINKING...
PIIIN (DING)
I'LL GIVE HER A STAG BEETLE!
......
IF YOU CAN CATCH THAT MANY RHINOCEROS BEETLES...
LEND ME THE NET.
BUG CATCHIN' AIN'T AS EASY AS YOU THINK, SENSEI.
...THEN A STAG BEETLE SHOULD BE EASY, RIGHT?
HECK, LIFE AIN'T THAT EASY.
YOU CAN CALL IT EASY, BUT FINDIN' 'EM IS REAL TOUGH.
THAT'S BECAUSE YOU'RE KIDS, ISN'T IT?

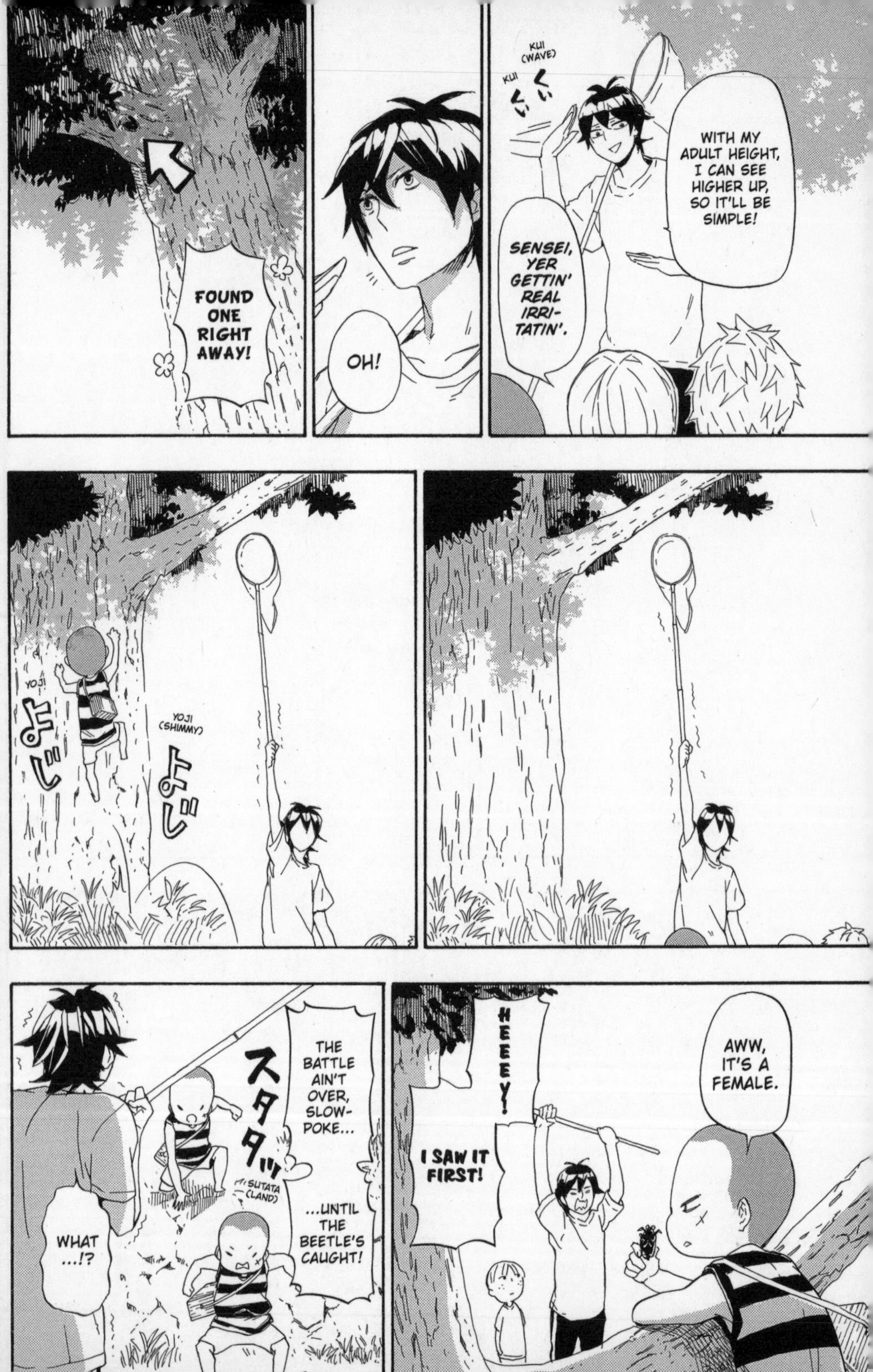
KUI (WAVE)
KUI
くい くい
WITH MY ADULT HEIGHT, I CAN SEE HIGHER UP, SO IT'LL BE SIMPLE!
SENSEI, YER GETTIN' REAL IRRI-TATIN'.
OH!
FOUND ONE RIGHT AWAY!
YOJI
よじ
YOJI (SHIMMY)
よじ
AWW, IT'S A FEMALE.
HEEEEY!
I SAW IT FIRST!
THE BATTLE AIN'T OVER, SLOW-POKE...
スタタッ
SUTATA (LAND)
...UNTIL THE BEETLE'S CAUGHT!
WHAT ...!?

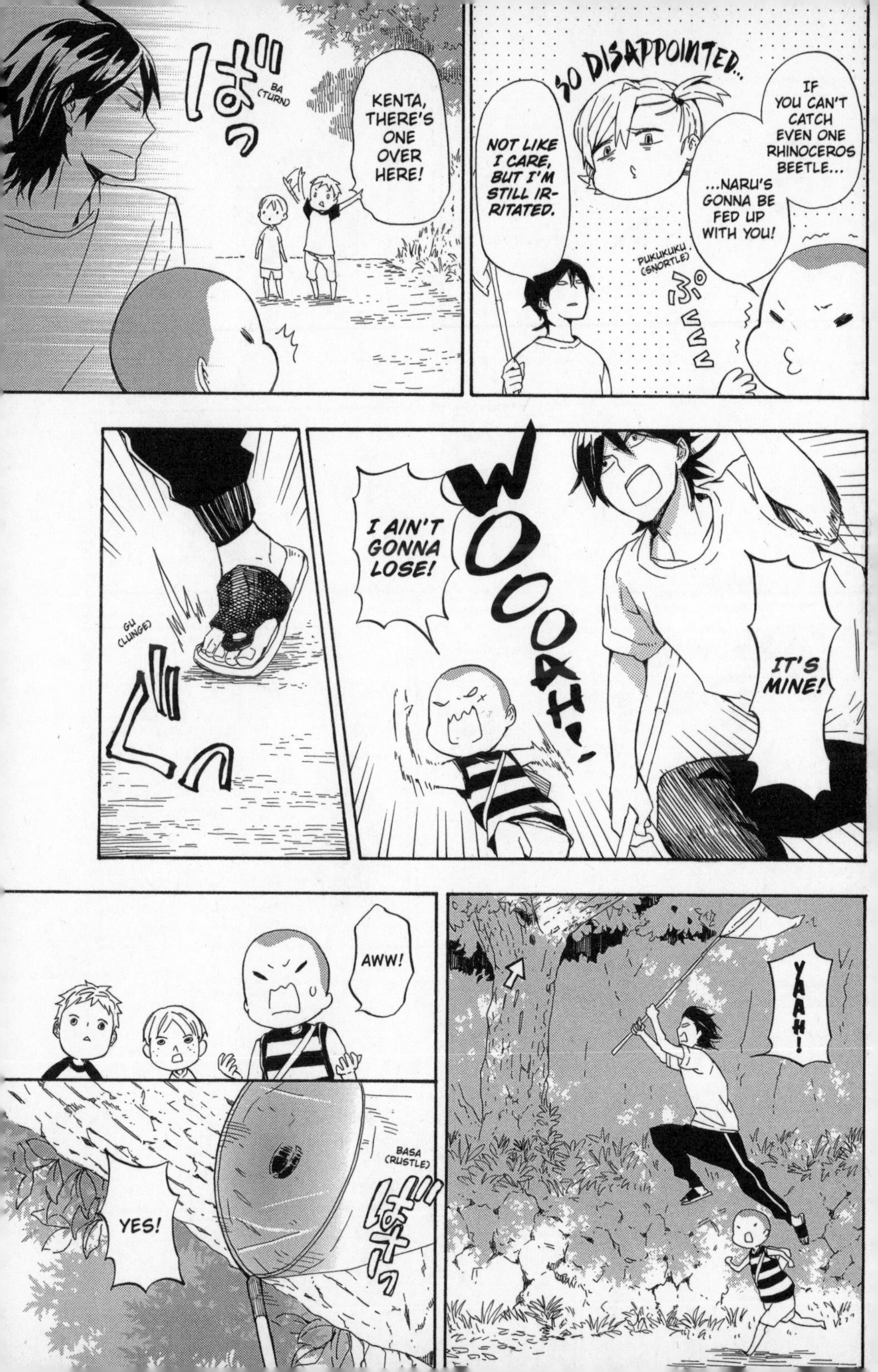
SO DISAPPOINTED...
IF YOU CAN'T CATCH EVEN ONE RHINOCEROS BEETLE...
...NARU'S GONNA BE FED UP WITH YOU!
PUKUKUKU (SNORTLE)
NOT LIKE I CARE, BUT I'M STILL IR-RITATED.
BA (TURN)
KENTA, THERE'S ONE OVER HERE!
IT'S MINE!
WOOOOAH!
I AIN'T GONNA LOSE!
GU (LUNGE)
YAAH!
AWW!
BASA (RUSTLE)
YES!

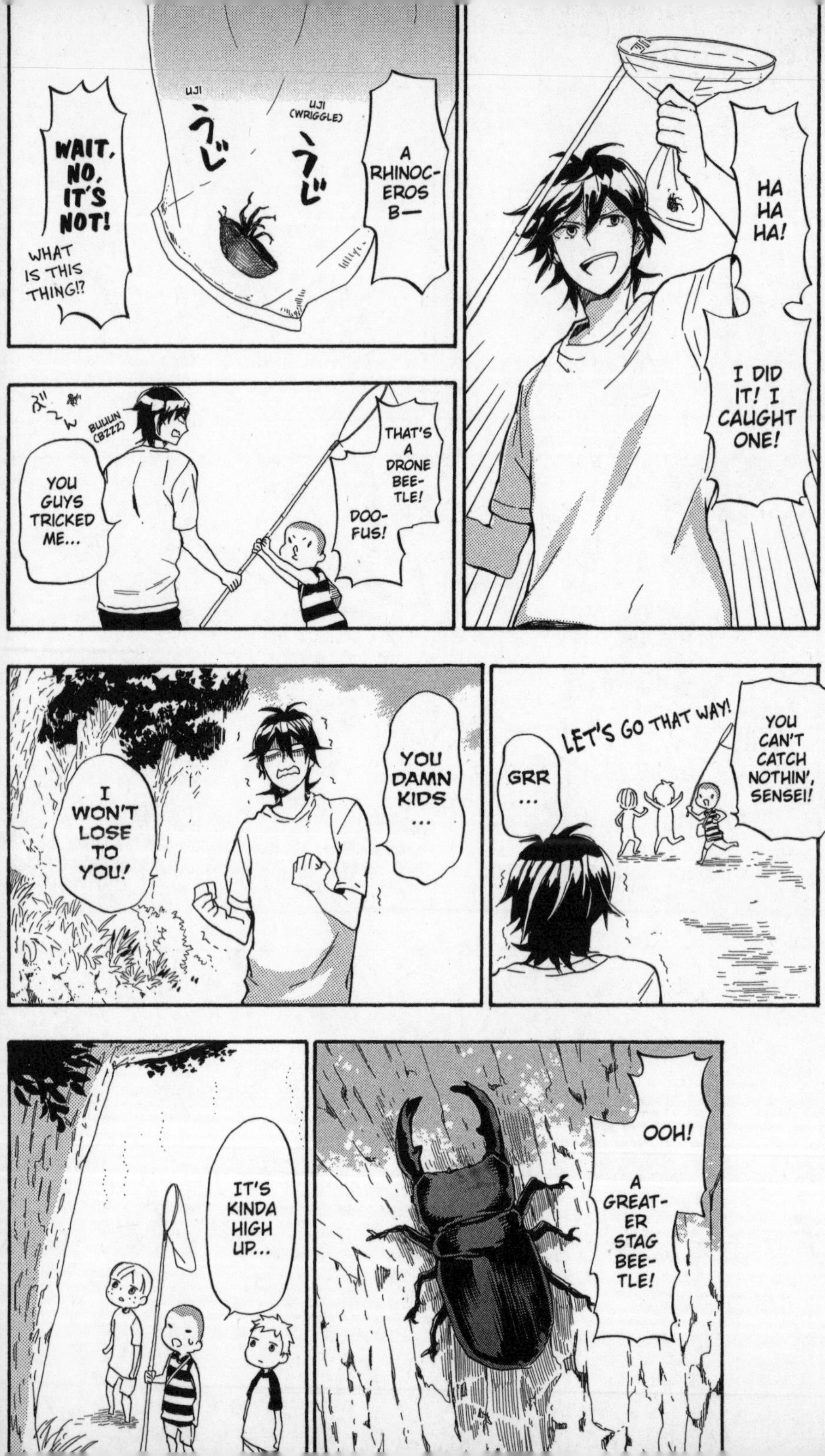
HA HA HA!
I DID IT! I CAUGHT ONE!
A RHINOCEROS B—
UJI (WRIGGLE)
うじ
UJI
うじ
WAIT, NO, IT'S NOT!
WHAT IS THIS THING!?
THAT'S A DRONE BEETLE!
DOOFUS!
BUUUN (BZZZ)
YOU GUYS TRICKED ME...
YOU CAN'T CATCH NOTHIN', SENSEI!
LET'S GO THAT WAY!
GRR...
YOU DAMN KIDS...
I WON'T LOSE TO YOU!
OOH!
A GREATER STAG BEETLE!
IT'S KINDA HIGH UP...

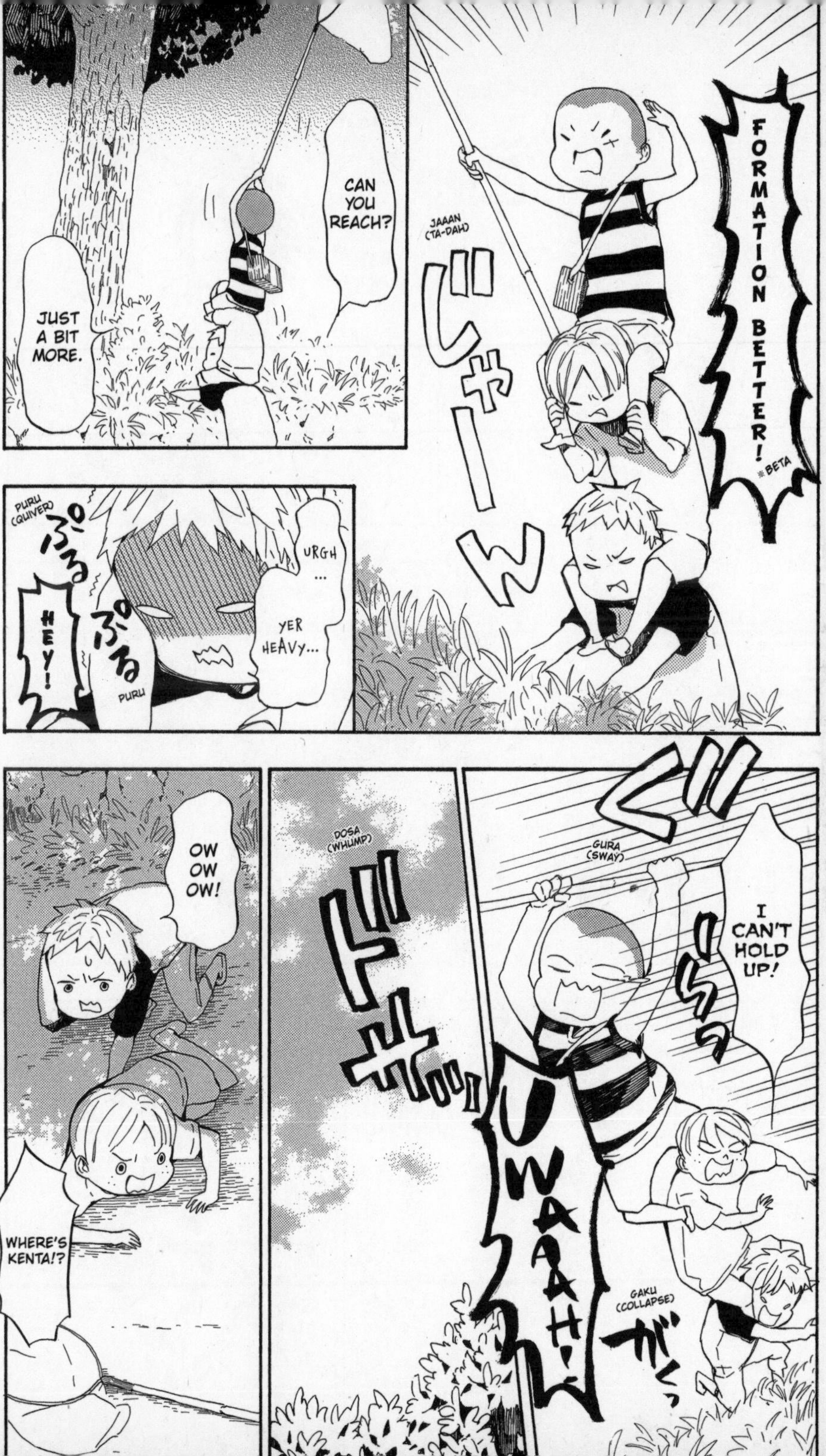

FORMATION BETTER!
※BETA
JAAAN (TA-DAH)
じゃーん
CAN YOU REACH?
JUST A BIT MORE.
URGH... YER HEAVY...
PURU (QUIVER)
ぷる
HEY!
ぷる
PURU
ぐい
GURA (SWAY)
I CAN'T HOLD UP!
ぐらっ
UWAAAH!
GAKU (COLLAPSE)
がくっ
DOSA (WHUMP)
ドサッ
OW OW OW!
WHERE'S KENTA!?

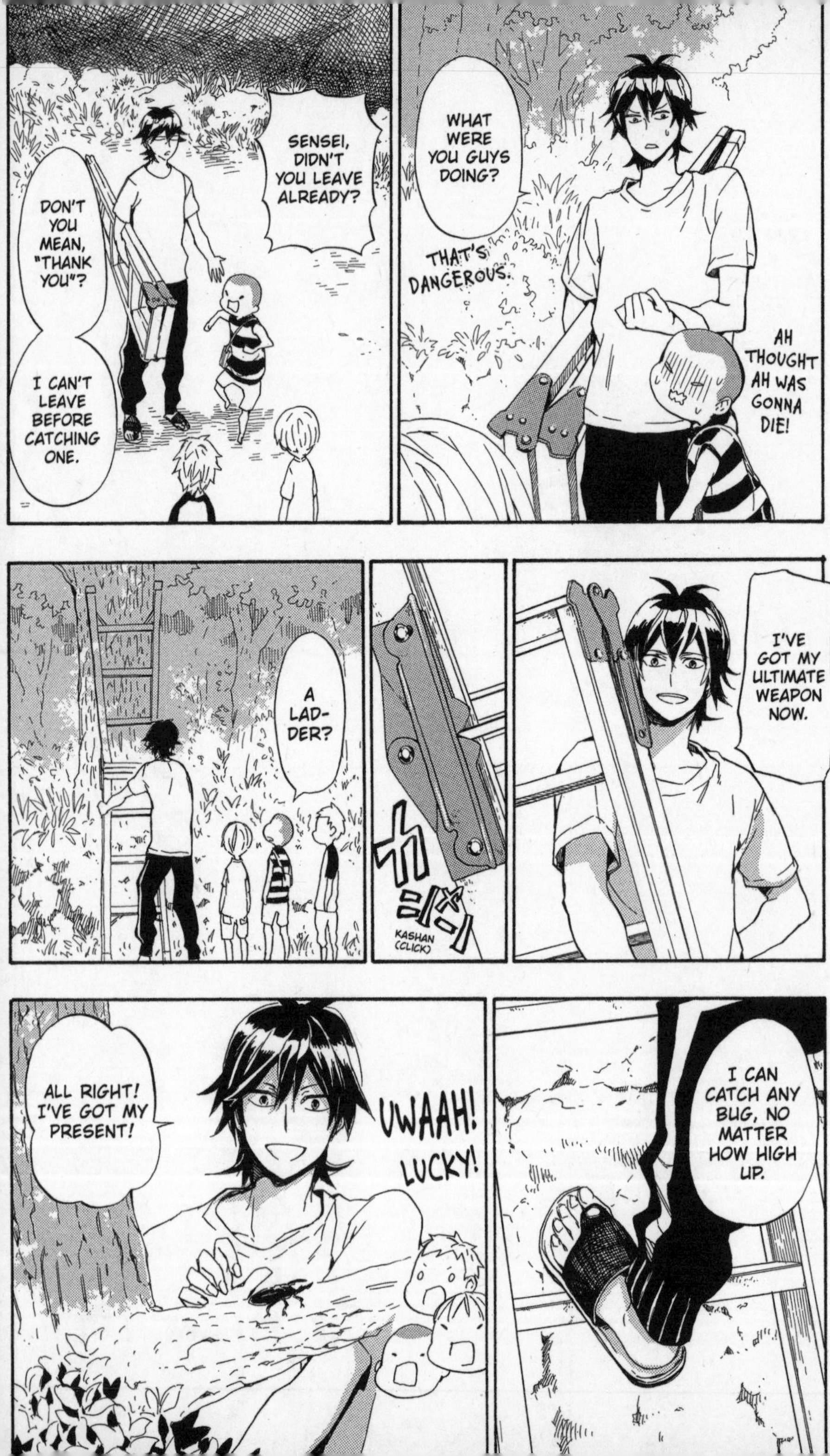
WHAT WERE YOU GUYS DOING?
THAT'S DANGEROUS.
AH THOUGHT AH WAS GONNA DIE!
SENSEI, DIDN'T YOU LEAVE ALREADY?
DON'T YOU MEAN, "THANK YOU"?
I CAN'T LEAVE BEFORE CATCHING ONE.
I'VE GOT MY ULTIMATE WEAPON NOW.
KASHAN (CLICK)
A LAD-DER?
I CAN CATCH ANY BUG, NO MATTER HOW HIGH UP.
UWAAH! LUCKY!
ALL RIGHT! I'VE GOT MY PRESENT!

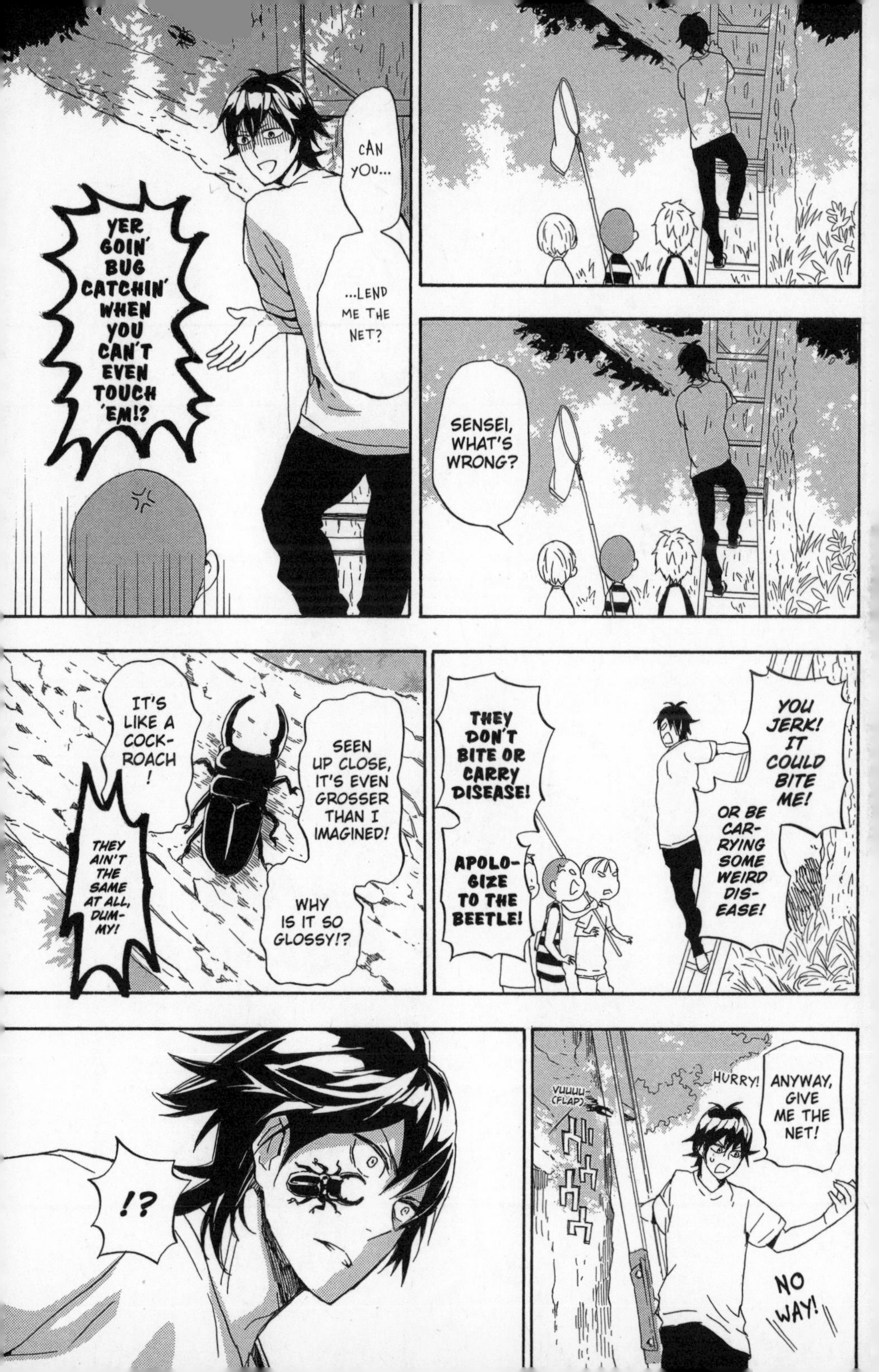
SENSEI, WHAT'S WRONG?
CAN YOU...
...LEND ME THE NET?
YER GOIN' BUG CATCHIN' WHEN YOU CAN'T EVEN TOUCH 'EM!?
YOU JERK! IT COULD BITE ME!
OR BE CARRYING SOME WEIRD DISEASE!
THEY DON'T BITE OR CARRY DISEASE!
APOLOGIZE TO THE BEETLE!
SEEN UP CLOSE, IT'S EVEN GROSSER THAN I IMAGINED!
WHY IS IT SO GLOSSY!?
IT'S LIKE A COCKROACH!
THEY AIN'T THE SAME AT ALL, DUMMY!
ANYWAY, GIVE ME THE NET!
HURRY!
VUUUU (FLAP)
NO WAY!
!?

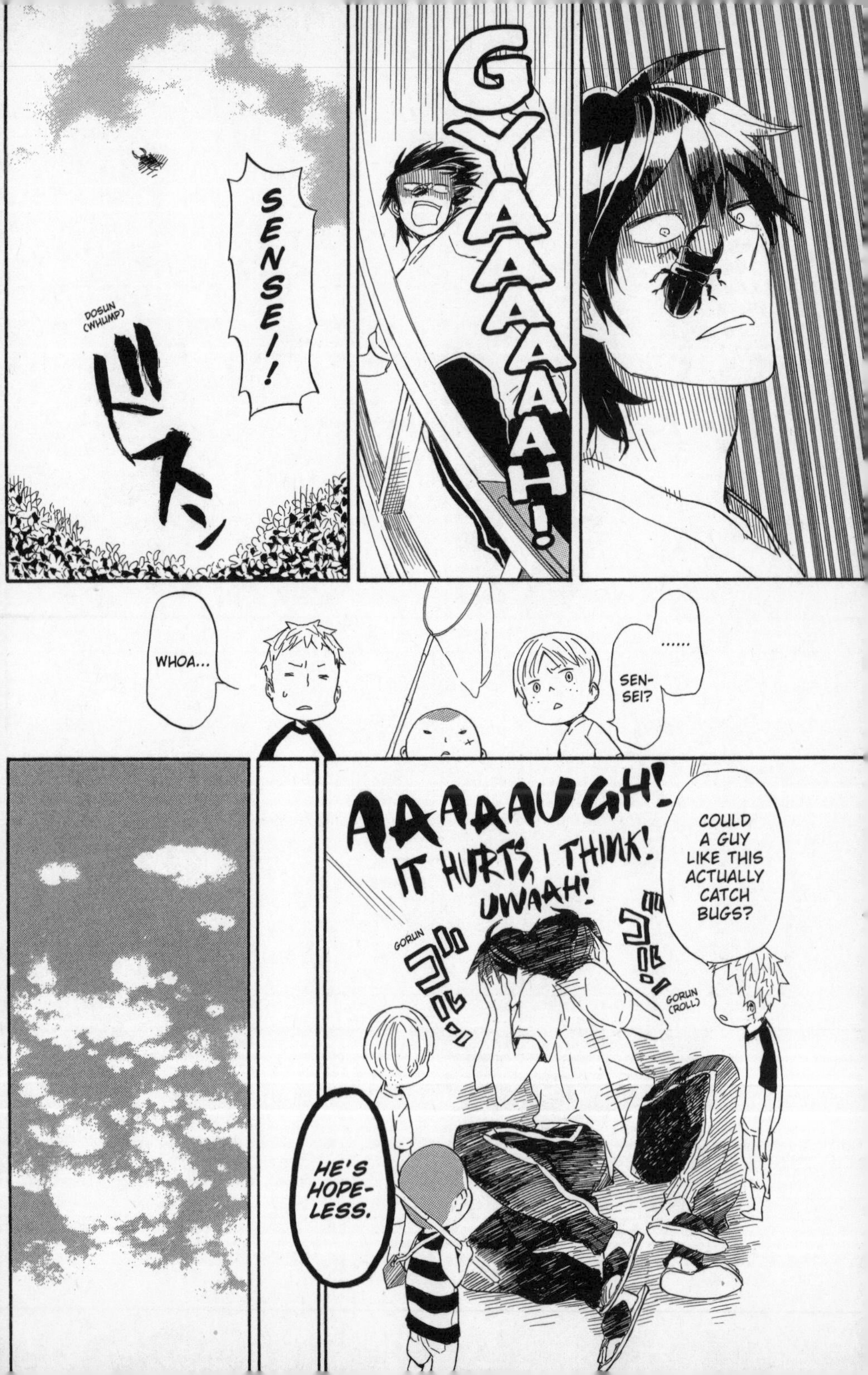
GYAAAAAAH!
SENSE!!
DOSUN (WHUMP)
ドスン
......
SEN-SEI?
WHOA...
COULD A GUY LIKE THIS ACTUALLY CATCH BUGS?
AAAAAUGH! IT HURTS, I THINK! UWAAH!
GORUN (ROLL)
GORUN
HE'S HOPE-LESS.

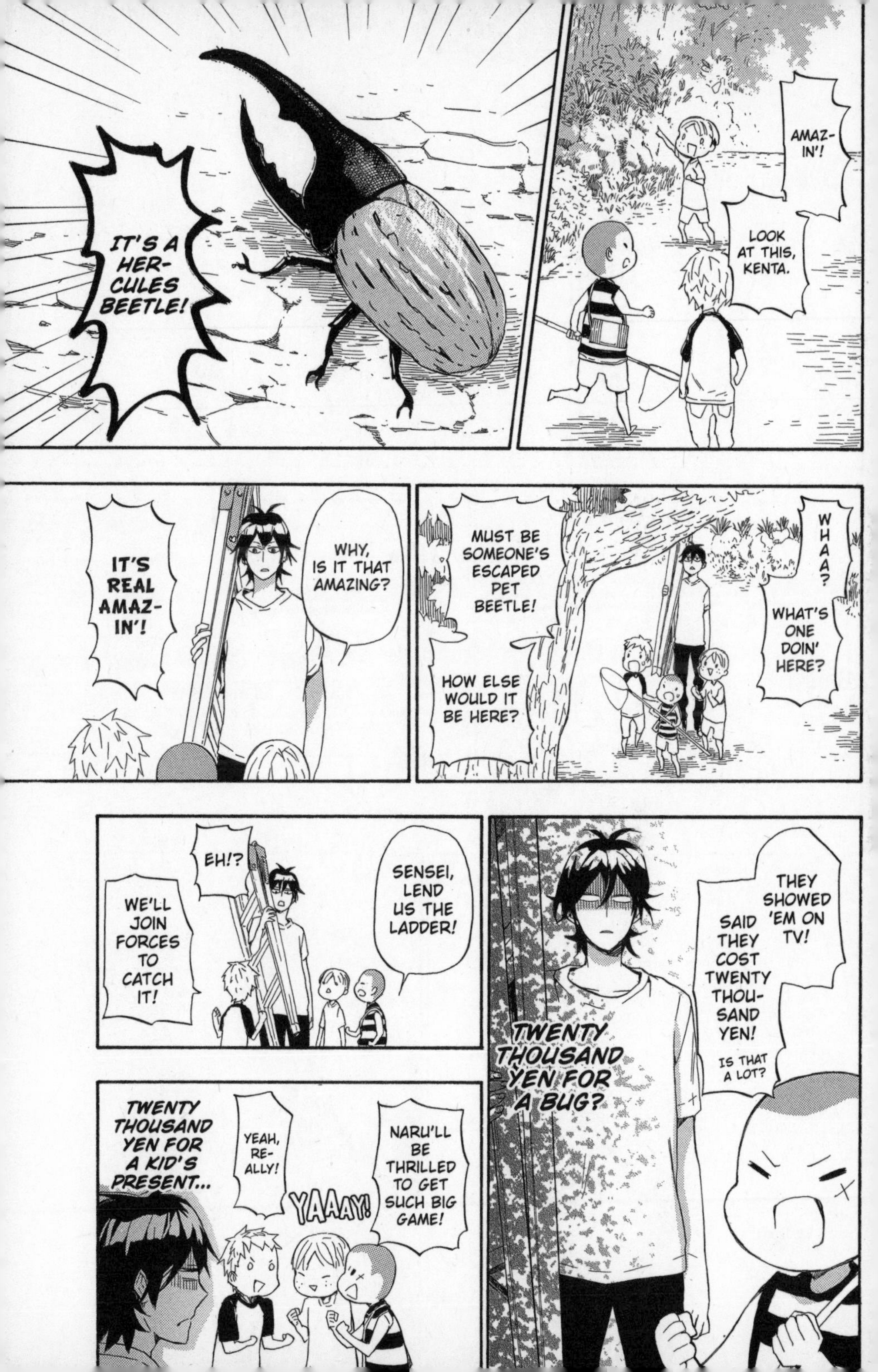
AMAZ-IN'!
LOOK AT THIS, KENTA.
IT'S A HER-CULES BEETLE!
WHAA? WHAT'S ONE DOIN' HERE?
MUST BE SOMEONE'S ESCAPED PET BEETLE!
HOW ELSE WOULD IT BE HERE?
WHY, IS IT THAT AMAZING?
IT'S REAL AMAZ-IN'!
THEY SHOWED 'EM ON TV!
SAID THEY COST TWENTY THOU-SAND YEN!
IS THAT A LOT?
TWENTY THOUSAND YEN FOR A BUG?
SENSEI, LEND US THE LADDER!
EH!?
WE'LL JOIN FORCES TO CATCH IT!
NARU'LL BE THRILLED TO GET SUCH BIG GAME!
YEAH, RE-ALLY!
YAAAY!
TWENTY THOUSAND YEN FOR A KID'S PRESENT...

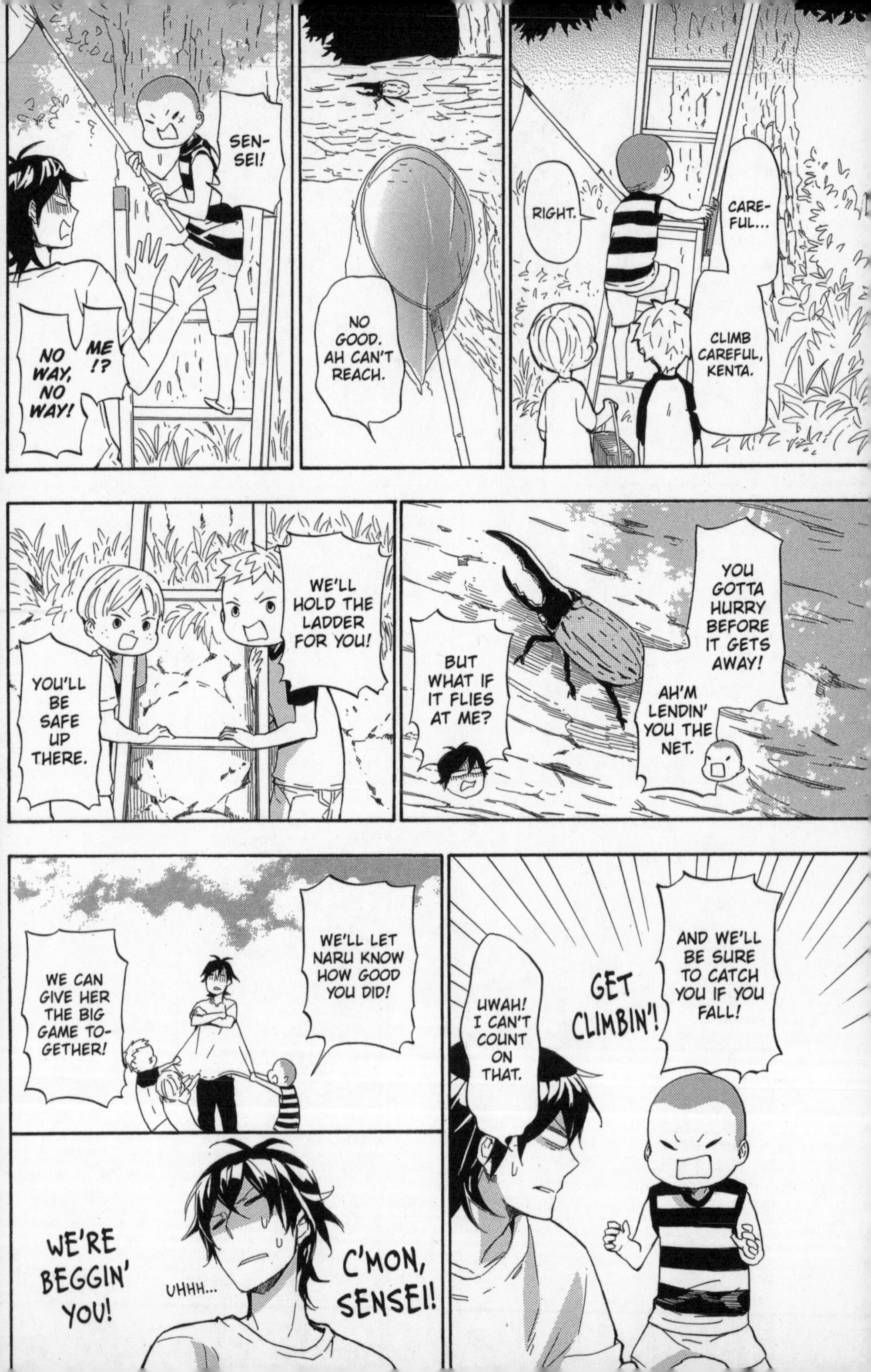
CARE-FUL...
RIGHT.
CLIMB CAREFUL, KENTA.
NO GOOD. AH CAN'T REACH.
SEN-SEI!
ME!?
NO WAY, NO WAY!
YOU GOTTA HURRY BEFORE IT GETS AWAY!
AH'M LENDIN' YOU THE NET.
BUT WHAT IF IT FLIES AT ME?
WE'LL HOLD THE LADDER FOR YOU!
YOU'LL BE SAFE UP THERE.
AND WE'LL BE SURE TO CATCH YOU IF YOU FALL!
GET CLIMBIN'!
UWAH! I CAN'T COUNT ON THAT.
WE'LL LET NARU KNOW HOW GOOD YOU DID!
WE CAN GIVE HER THE BIG GAME TO-GETHER!
C'MON, SENSEI!
UHHH...
WE'RE BEGGIN' YOU!

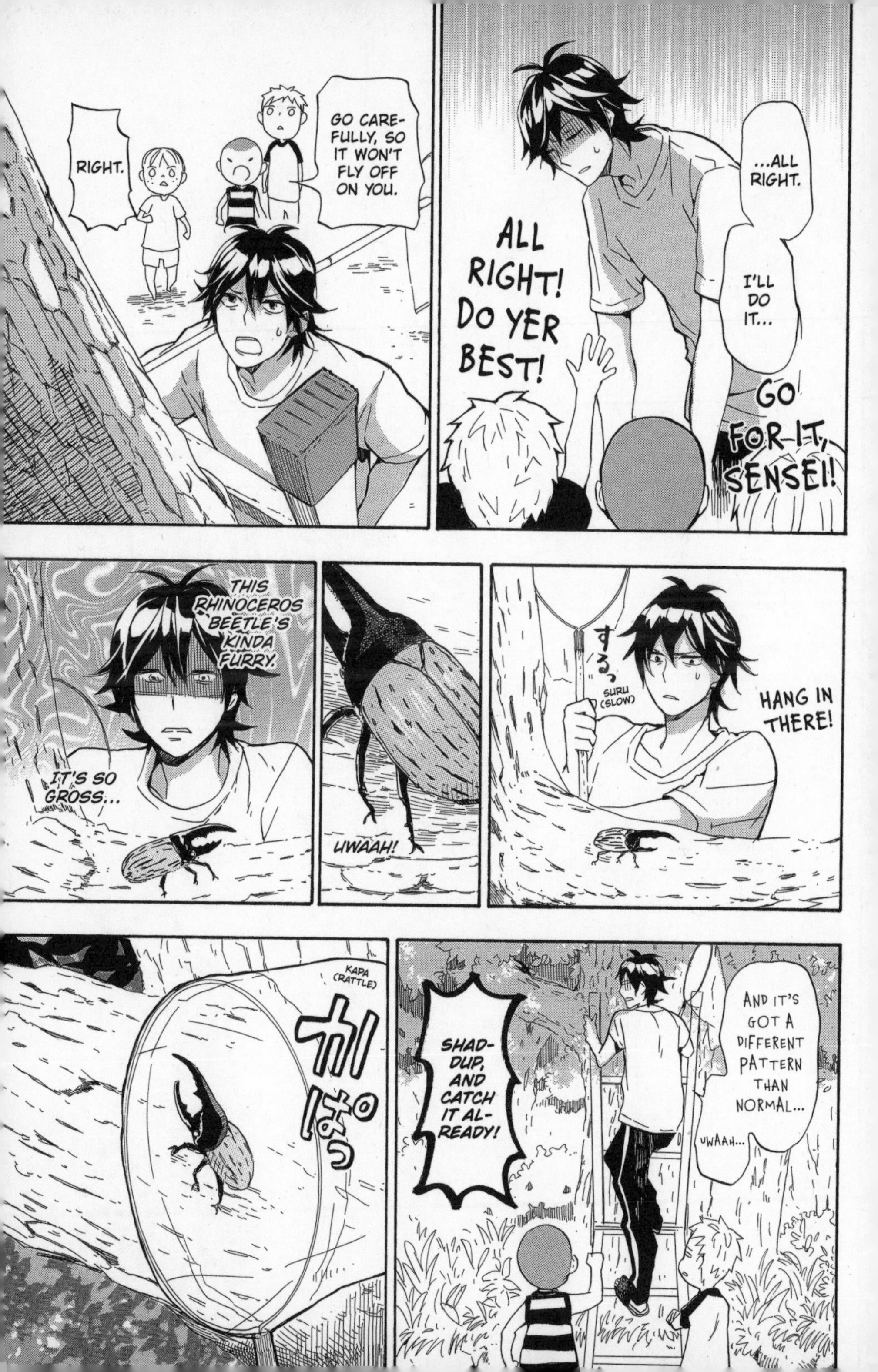
...ALL RIGHT.
I'LL DO IT...
ALL RIGHT! DO YER BEST!
GO FOR IT, SENSEI!!
GO CARE-FULLY, SO IT WON'T FLY OFF ON YOU.
RIGHT.
HANG IN THERE!
するっ
SURU (SLOW)
UWAAH!
THIS RHINOCEROS BEETLE'S KINDA FURRY.
IT'S SO GROSS...
AND IT'S GOT A DIFFERENT PATTERN THAN NORMAL...
UWAAH...
SHAD-DUP, AND CATCH IT AL-READY!
KAPA (RATTLE)
カパっ

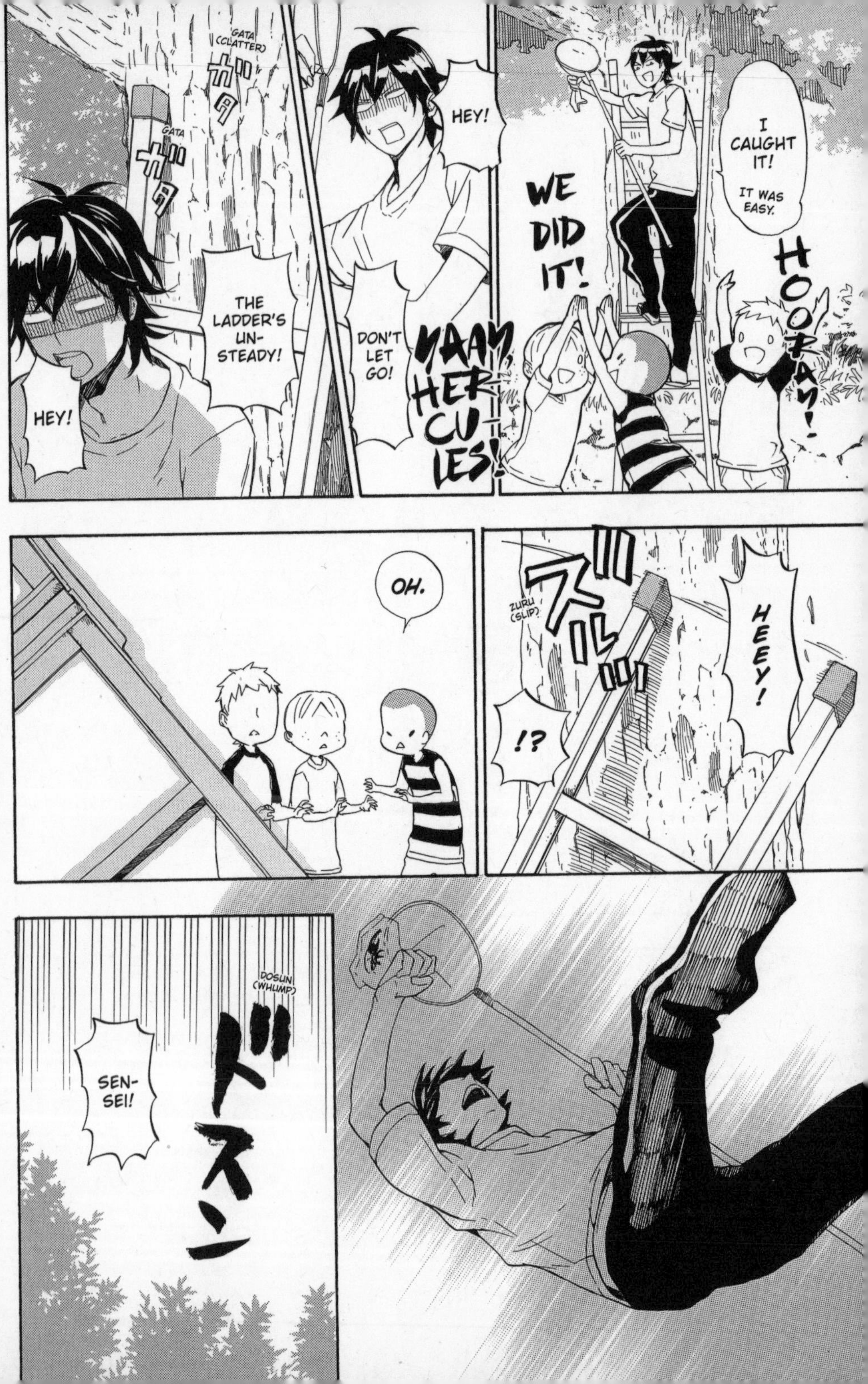
I CAUGHT IT!
IT WAS EASY.
HOORAY!
WE DID IT!
YAAY, HERCULES!
HEY!
DON'T LET GO!
GATA (CLATTER)
GATA
THE LADDER'S UN-STEADY!
HEY!
HEEY!
ZURU (SLIP)
!?
OH.
DOSUN (WHUMP)
SEN-SEI!

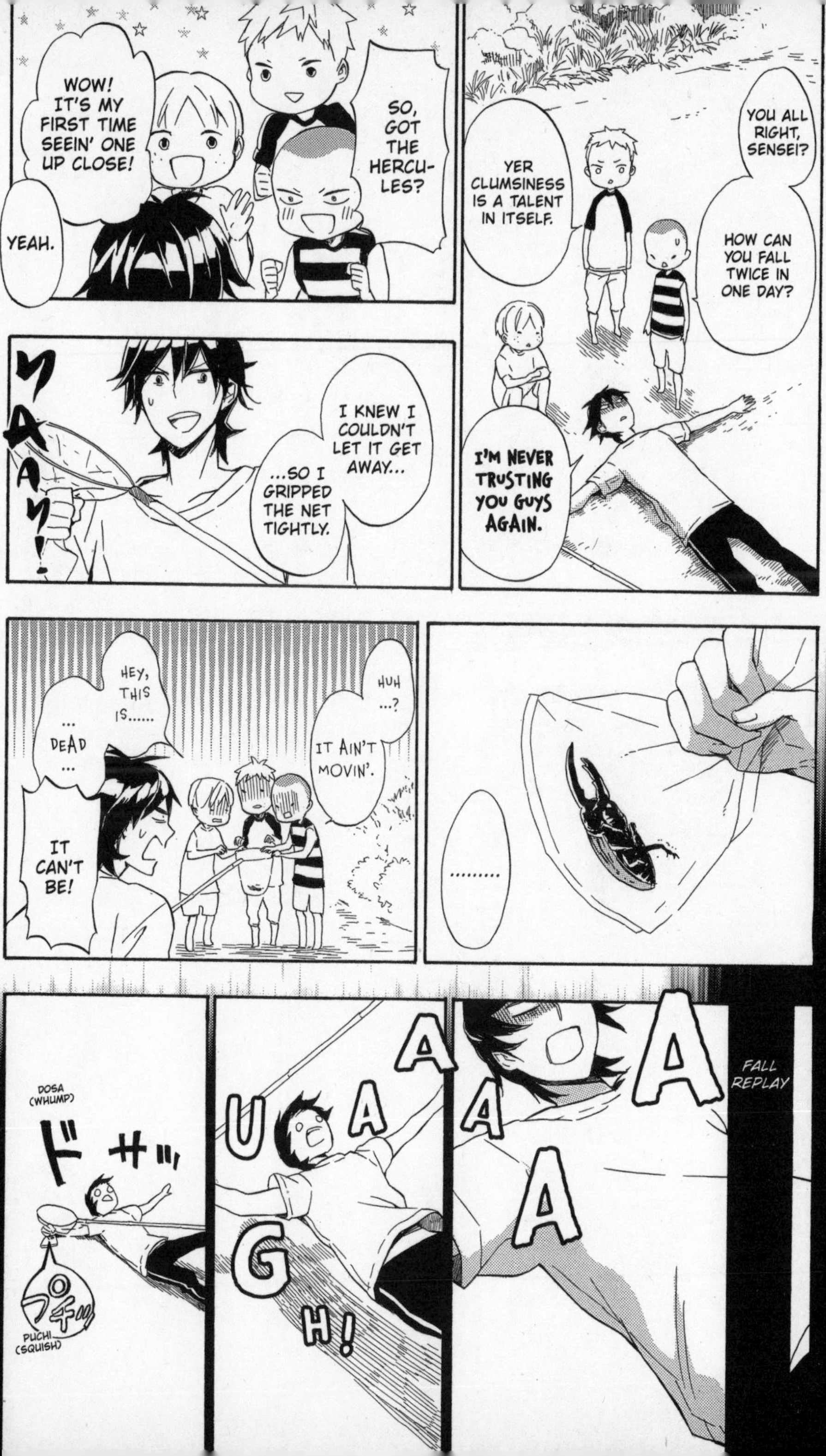
YOU ALL RIGHT, SENSEI?
HOW CAN YOU FALL TWICE IN ONE DAY?
YER CLUMSINESS IS A TALENT IN ITSELF.
I'M NEVER TRUSTING YOU GUYS AGAIN.
SO, GOT THE HERCU-LES?
WOW! IT'S MY FIRST TIME SEEIN' ONE UP CLOSE!
YEAH.
I KNEW I COULDN'T LET IT GET AWAY...
...SO I GRIPPED THE NET TIGHTLY.
....
HUH ...?
IT AIN'T MOVIN'.
HEY, THIS IS......
... DEAD ...
IT CAN'T BE!
FALL REPLAY
A A A A A
U A G H!
DOSA (WHUMP)
ドサッ
プチッ
PUCHI (SQUISH)

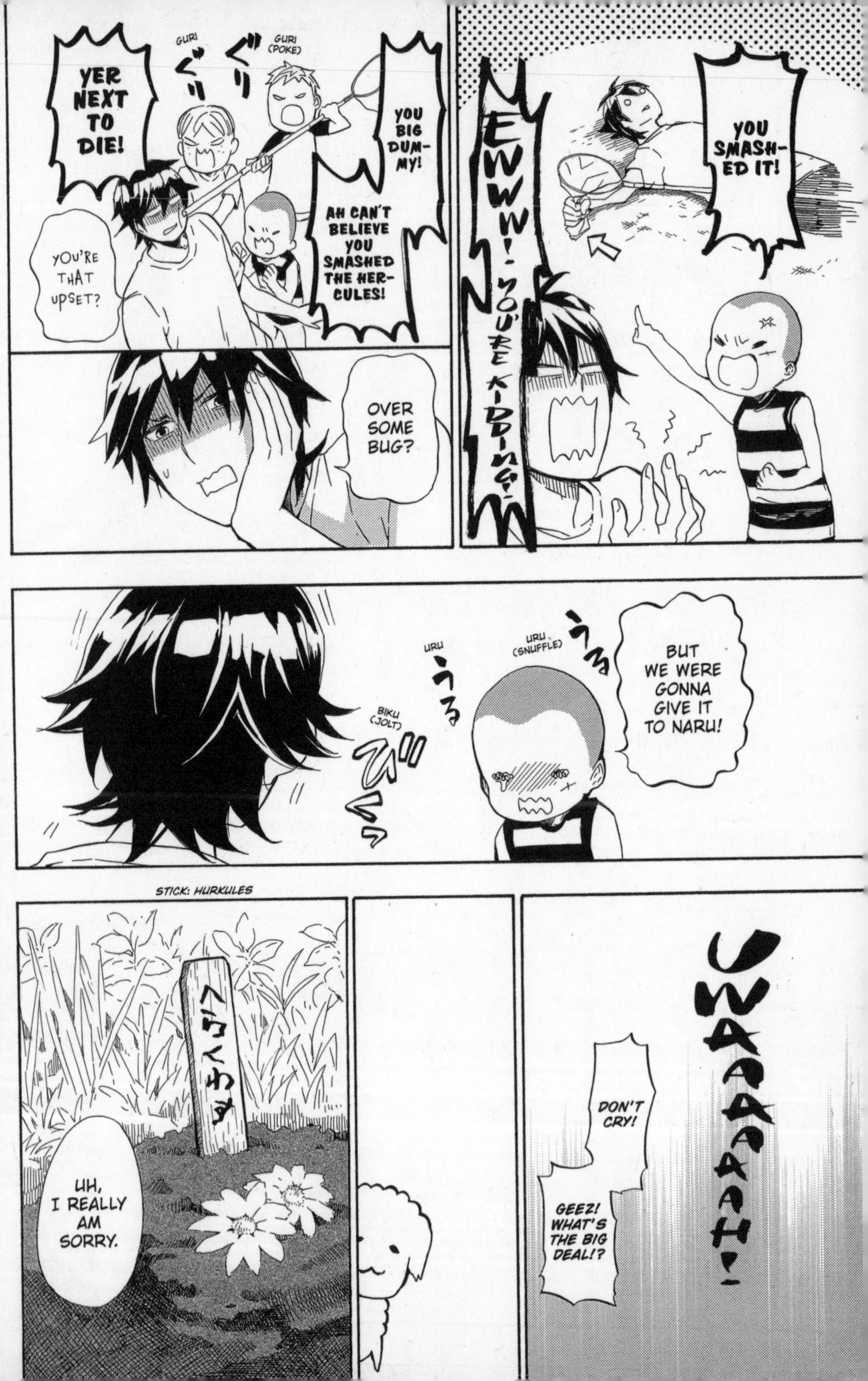
YOU SMASHED IT!
EWWWW! YOU'RE KIDDING!
GURI (POKE)
ぐり
GURI
ぐり
YOU BIG DUMMY!
AH CAN'T BELIEVE YOU SMASHED THE HERCULES!
YER NEXT TO DIE!
YOU'RE THAT UPSET?
OVER SOME BUG?
BUT WE WERE GONNA GIVE IT TO NARU!
URU (SNUFFLE)
うる
URU
うる
BIKU (JOLT)
びくっ
UWAAAAAAH!
DON'T CRY!
GEEZ! WHAT'S THE BIG DEAL!?
STICK: HURKULES
へらくれす
UH, I REALLY AM SORRY.

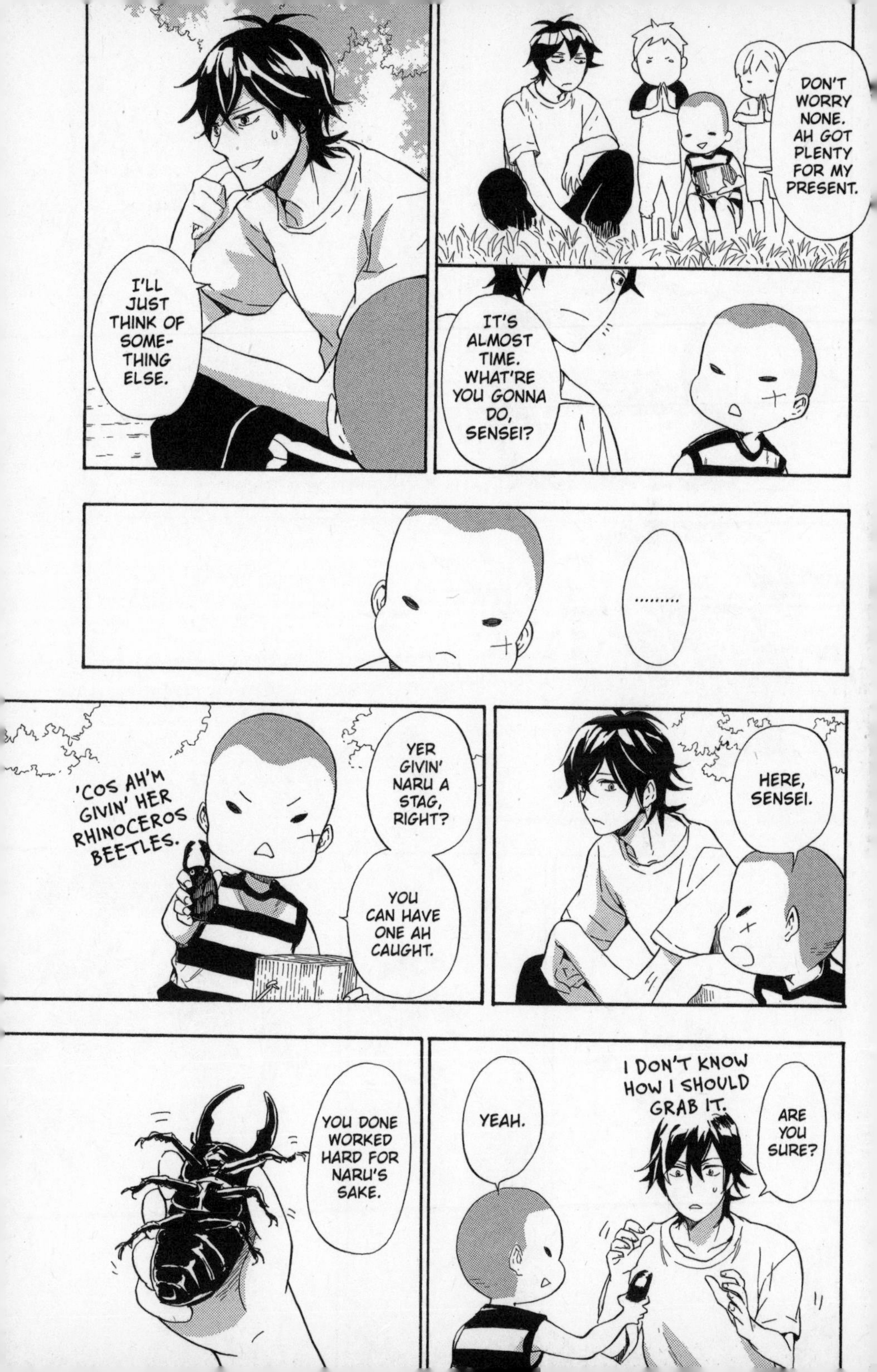
DON'T WORRY NONE. AH GOT PLENTY FOR MY PRESENT.
IT'S ALMOST TIME. WHAT'RE YOU GONNA DO, SENSEI?
I'LL JUST THINK OF SOME-THING ELSE.
....
HERE, SENSEI.
YER GIVIN' NARU A STAG, RIGHT?
YOU CAN HAVE ONE AH CAUGHT.
'COS AH'M GIVIN' HER RHINOCEROS BEETLES.
ARE YOU SURE?
I DON'T KNOW HOW I SHOULD GRAB IT.
YEAH.
YOU DONE WORKED HARD FOR NARU'S SAKE.

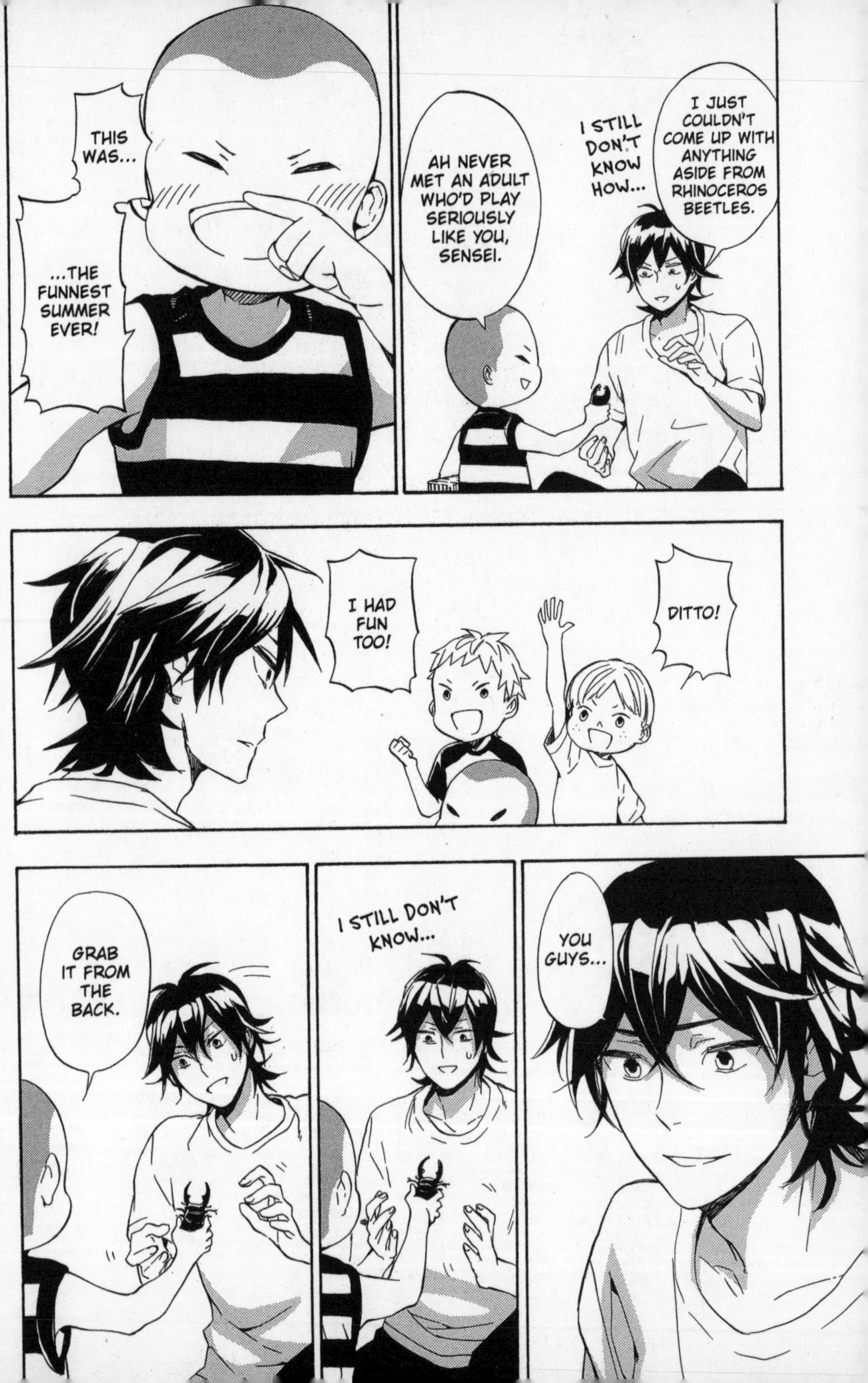
I JUST COULDN'T COME UP WITH ANYTHING ASIDE FROM RHINOCEROS BEETLES.
I STILL DON'T KNOW HOW...
AH NEVER MET AN ADULT WHO'D PLAY SERIOUSLY LIKE YOU, SENSEI.
THIS WAS...
...THE FUNNEST SUMMER EVER!
DITTO!
I HAD FUN TOO!
YOU GUYS...
I STILL DON'T KNOW...
GRAB IT FROM THE BACK.

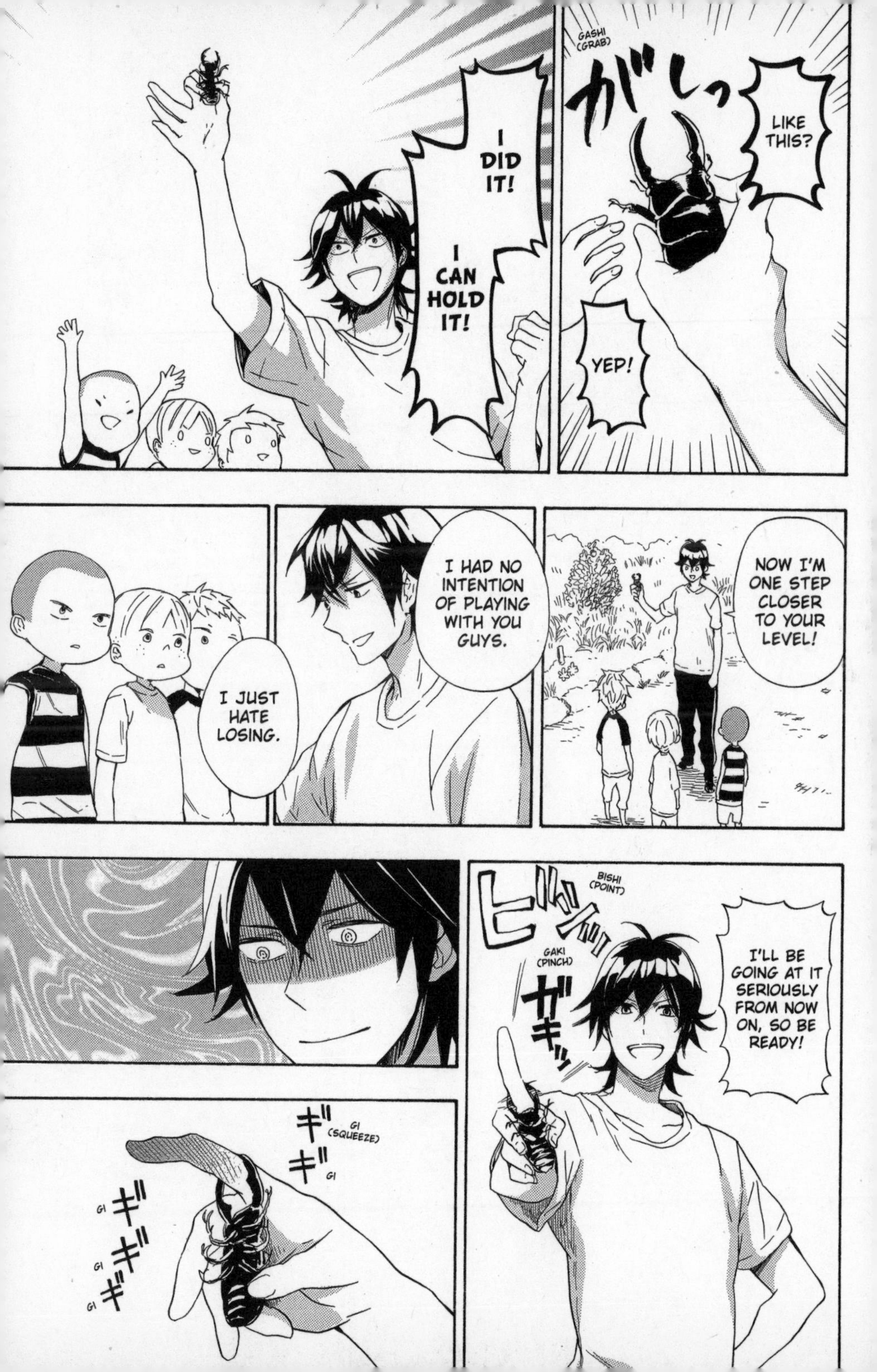
GASHI (GRAB)
がしっ
LIKE THIS?
YEP!
I DID IT!
I CAN HOLD IT!
NOW I'M ONE STEP CLOSER TO YOUR LEVEL!
I HAD NO INTENTION OF PLAYING WITH YOU GUYS.
I JUST HATE LOSING.
BISHI (POINT)
ビシッ
GAKI (PINCH)
ガキッ
I'LL BE GOING AT IT SERIOUSLY FROM NOW ON, SO BE READY!
ギ GI (SQUEEZE)
ギ GI
GI ギ
GI ギ
GI ギ

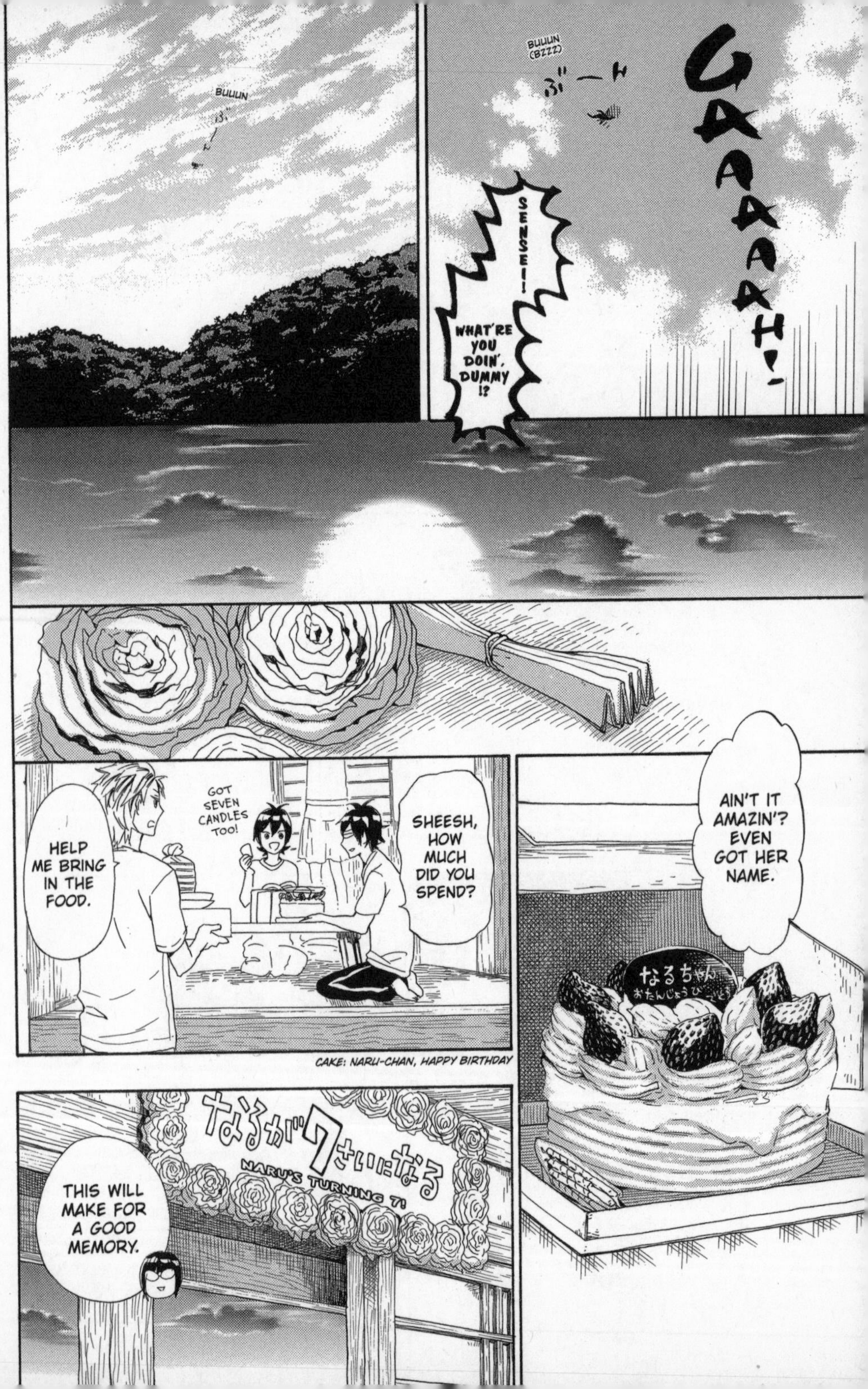
UAAAAAH!
BUUUN (BZZZ)
SENSEI!! WHAT'RE YOU DOIN', DUMMY!?
BUUUN
AIN'T IT AMAZIN'? EVEN GOT HER NAME.
なるちゃん
CAKE: NARU-CHAN, HAPPY BIRTHDAY
SHEESH, HOW MUCH DID YOU SPEND?
GOT SEVEN CANDLES TOO!
HELP ME BRING IN THE FOOD.
なるが7さいになる
NARU'S TURNING 7!
THIS WILL MAKE FOR A GOOD MEMORY.

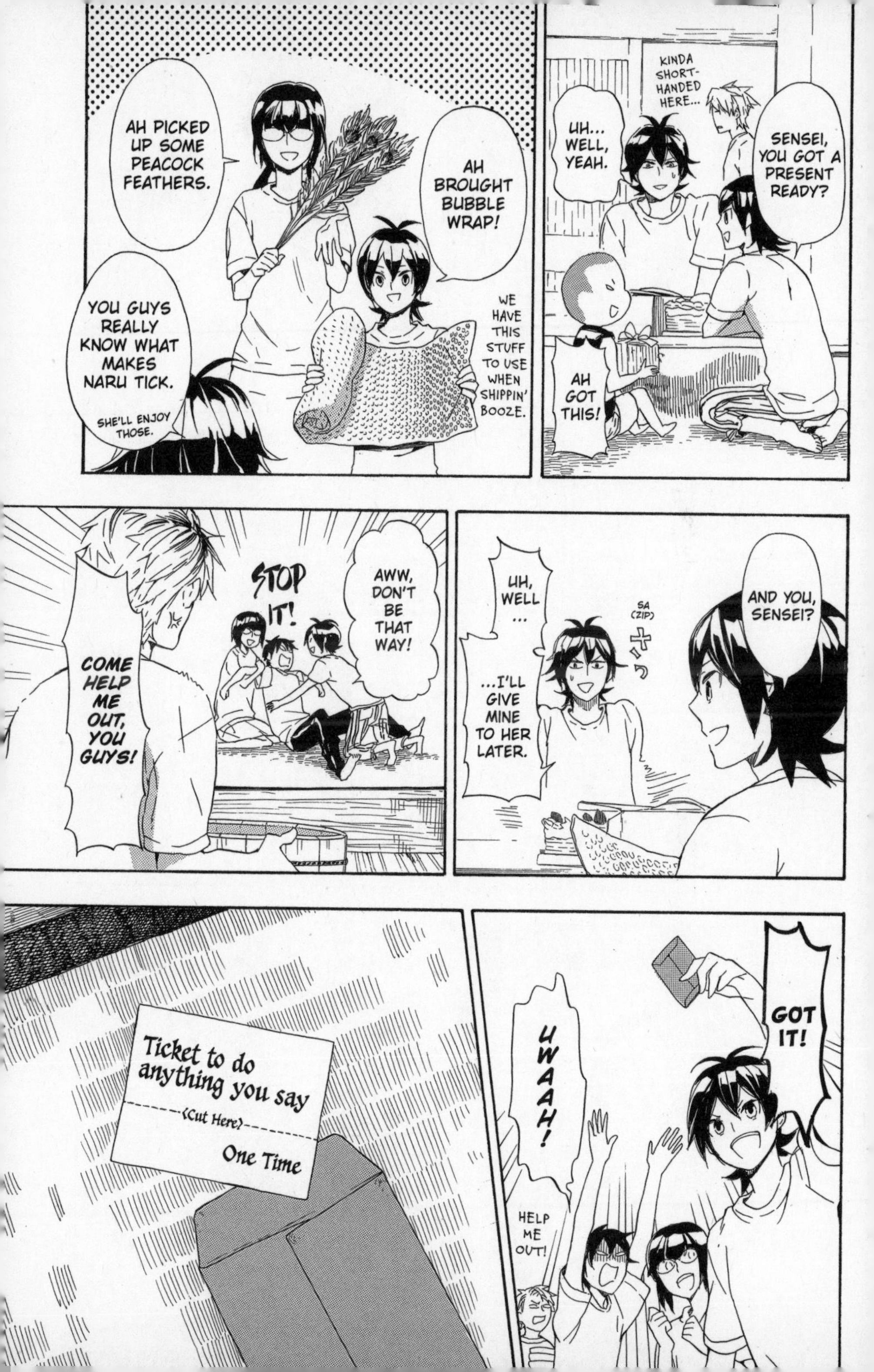
KINDA SHORT-HANDED HERE...
SENSEI, YOU GOT A PRESENT READY?
UH... WELL, YEAH.
AH GOT THIS!
AH BROUGHT BUBBLE WRAP!
AH PICKED UP SOME PEACOCK FEATHERS.
WE HAVE THIS STUFF TO USE WHEN SHIPPIN' BOOZE.
YOU GUYS REALLY KNOW WHAT MAKES NARU TICK.
SHE'LL ENJOY THOSE.
AND YOU, SENSEI?
SA (ZIP)
UH, WELL ...
...I'LL GIVE MINE TO HER LATER.
AWW, DON'T BE THAT WAY!
STOP IT!
COME HELP ME OUT, YOU GUYS!
GOT IT!
UWAAAH!
HELP ME OUT!
Ticket to do anything you say
(Cut Here)
One Time

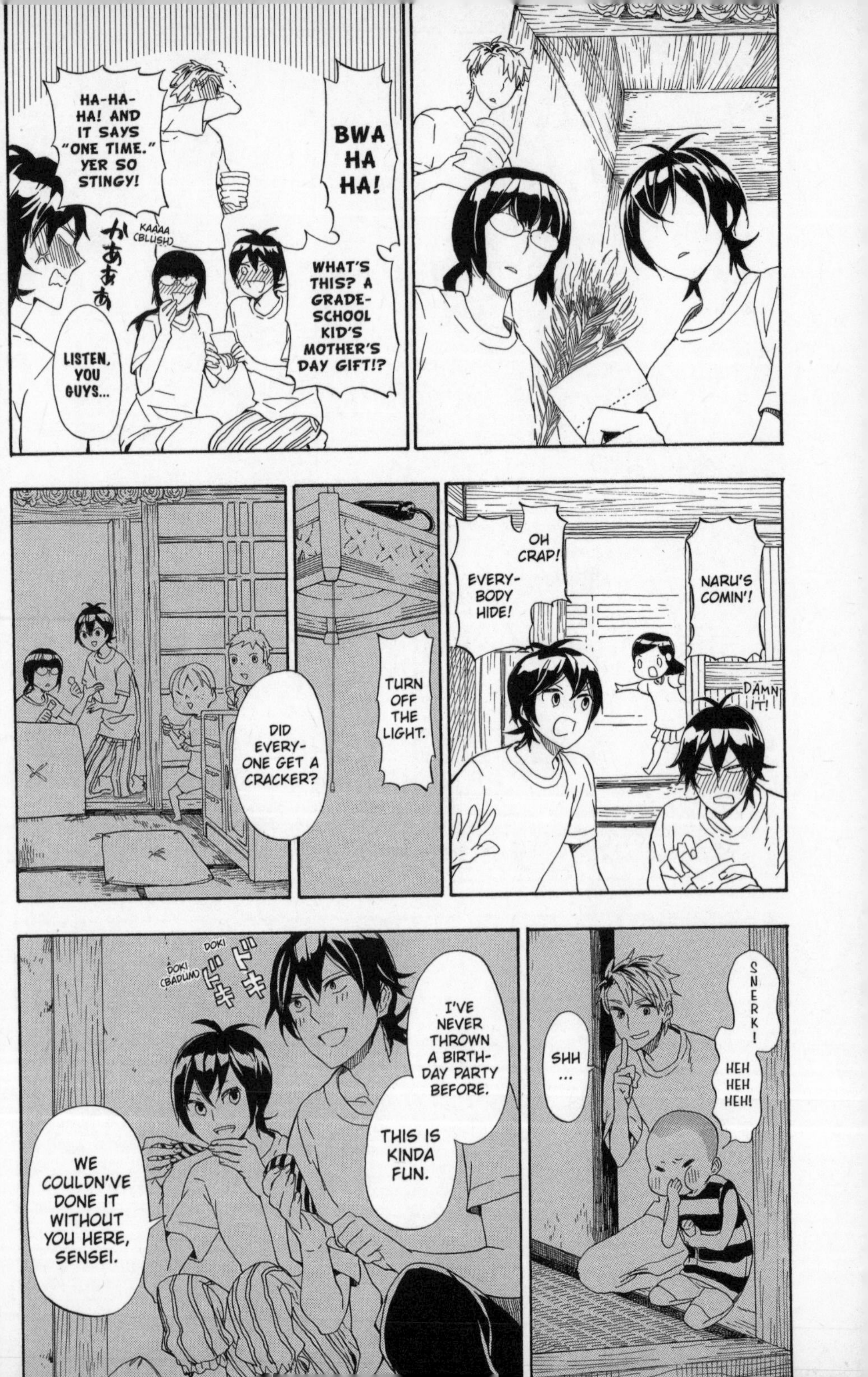
BWA HA HA!
HA-HA-HA! AND IT SAYS "ONE TIME." YER SO STINGY!
WHAT'S THIS? A GRADE-SCHOOL KID'S MOTHER'S DAY GIFT!?
KAAAA (BLUSH)
かあああ
LISTEN, YOU GUYS...
NARU'S COMIN'!
OH CRAP! EVERYBODY HIDE!
DAMN IT!
TURN OFF THE LIGHT.
DID EVERYONE GET A CRACKER?
SNERK! HEH HEH HEH!
SHH...
DOKI DOKI (BADUM)
ドキドキ
I'VE NEVER THROWN A BIRTHDAY PARTY BEFORE.
THIS IS KINDA FUN.
WE COULDN'VE DONE IT WITHOUT YOU HERE, SENSEI.

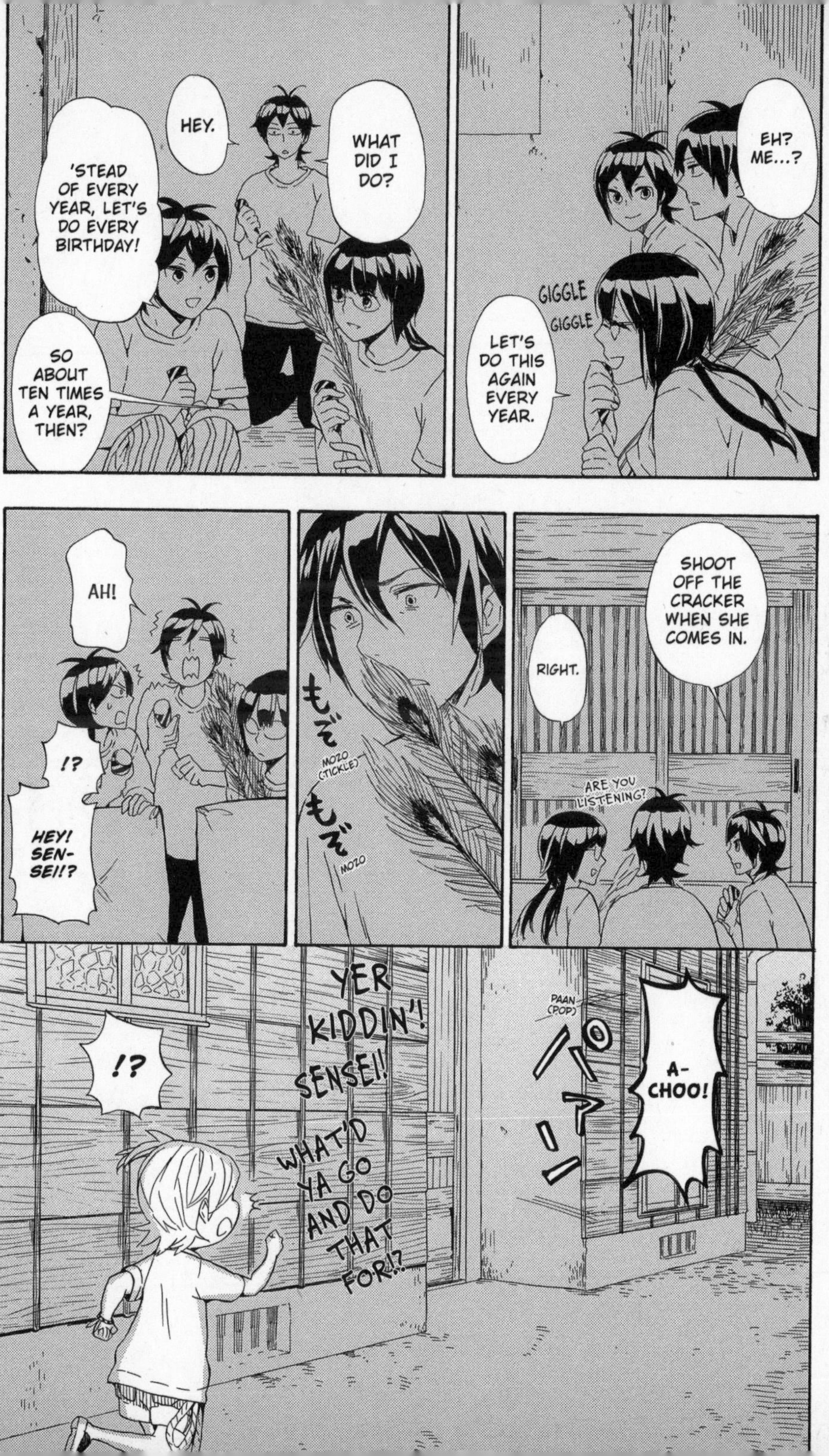

EH? ME...?
GIGGLE
GIGGLE
LET'S DO THIS AGAIN EVERY YEAR.
WHAT DID I DO?
HEY.
'STEAD OF EVERY YEAR, LET'S DO EVERY BIRTHDAY!
SO ABOUT TEN TIMES A YEAR, THEN?
SHOOT OFF THE CRACKER WHEN SHE COMES IN.
RIGHT.
ARE YOU LISTENING?
もぞ
MOZO (TICKLE)
もぞ
MOZO
AH!
!?
HEY! SEN-SEI!?
A-CHOO!
パァーン
PAAN (POP)
YER KIDDIN'!
SENSEI!
WHAT'D YA GO AND DO THAT FOR!?
!?

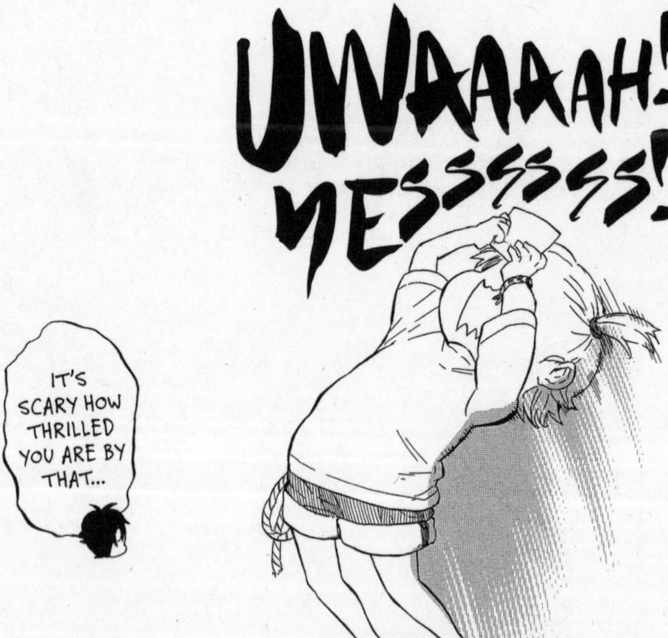
UWAAAAH!
YESSSSSS!
IT'S SCARY HOW THRILLED YOU ARE BY THAT...

ACT.43
ISHIKODZUN
(Translation: Piling Stones)

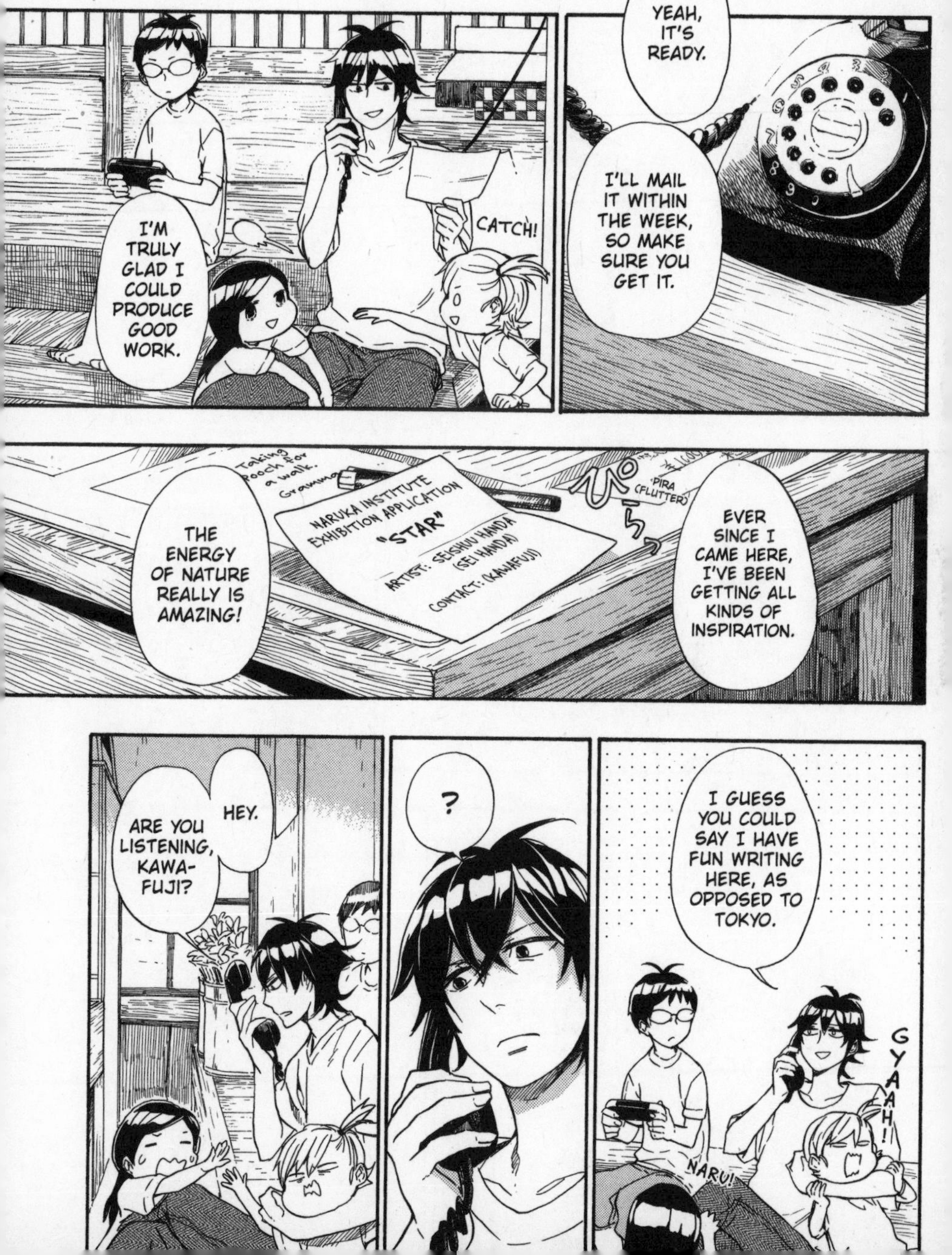

YEAH, IT'S READY.
I'LL MAIL IT WITHIN THE WEEK, SO MAKE SURE YOU GET IT.
CATCH!
I'M TRULY GLAD I COULD PRODUCE GOOD WORK.
EVER SINCE I CAME HERE, I'VE BEEN GETTING ALL KINDS OF INSPIRATION.
PIRA (FLUTTER)
NARUKA INSTITUTE EXHIBITION APPLICATION
"STAR"
ARTIST: SEISHUU HANDA (SEI HANDA)
CONTACT: (KAWAFUJI)
Taking Rooch for a walk. Gramma
THE ENERGY OF NATURE REALLY IS AMAZING!
I GUESS YOU COULD SAY I HAVE FUN WRITING HERE, AS OPPOSED TO TOKYO.
GYAAH!
NARU!
?
HEY.
ARE YOU LISTENING, KAWAFUJI?

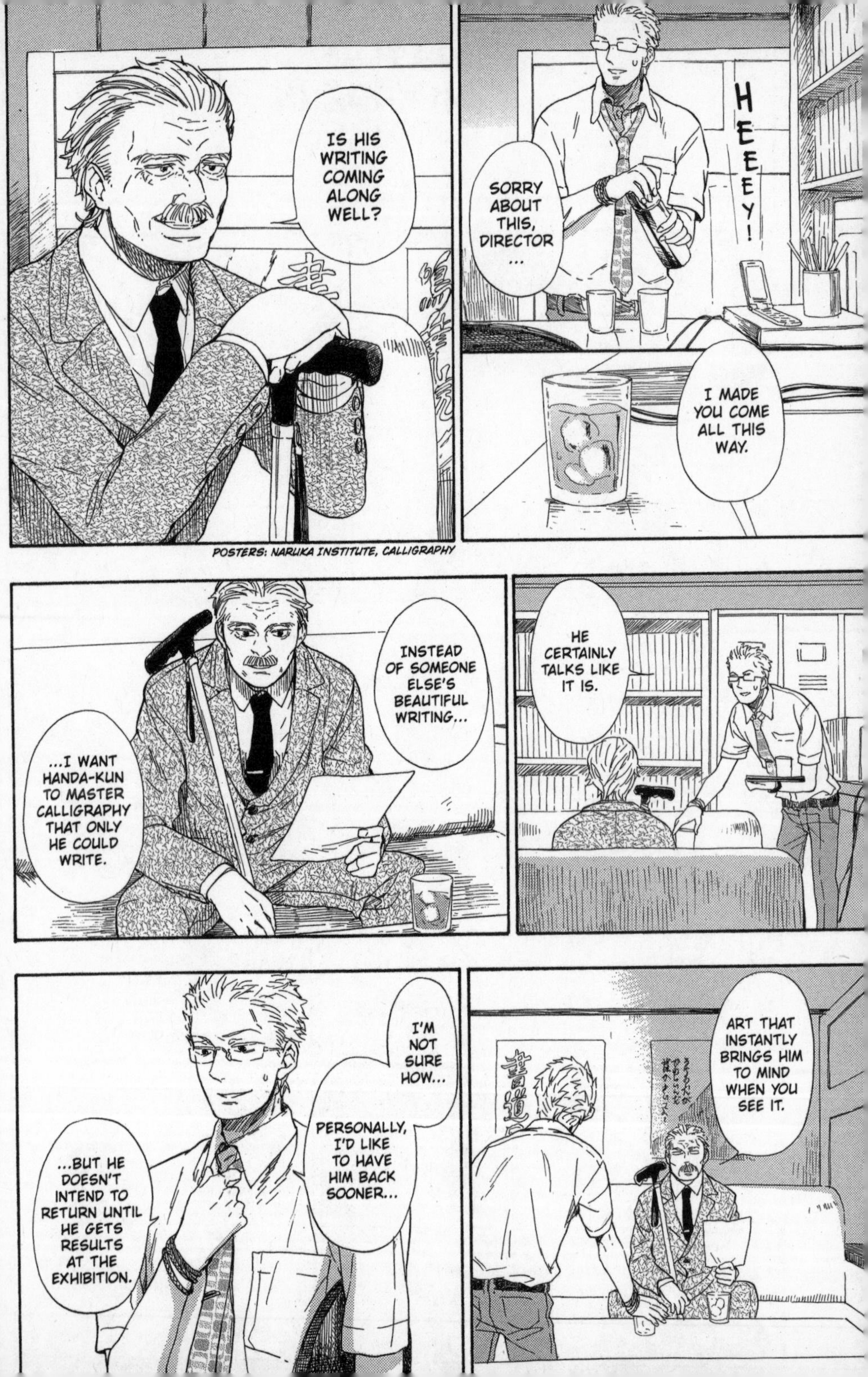
HEEEY!
SORRY ABOUT THIS, DIRECTOR ...
I MADE YOU COME ALL THIS WAY.
IS HIS WRITING COMING ALONG WELL?
POSTERS: NARUKA INSTITUTE, CALLIGRAPHY
HE CERTAINLY TALKS LIKE IT IS.
INSTEAD OF SOMEONE ELSE'S BEAUTIFUL WRITING...
...I WANT HANDA-KUN TO MASTER CALLIGRAPHY THAT ONLY HE COULD WRITE.
ART THAT INSTANTLY BRINGS HIM TO MIND WHEN YOU SEE IT.
I'M NOT SURE HOW...
PERSONALLY, I'D LIKE TO HAVE HIM BACK SOONER...
...BUT HE DOESN'T INTEND TO RETURN UNTIL HE GETS RESULTS AT THE EXHIBITION.

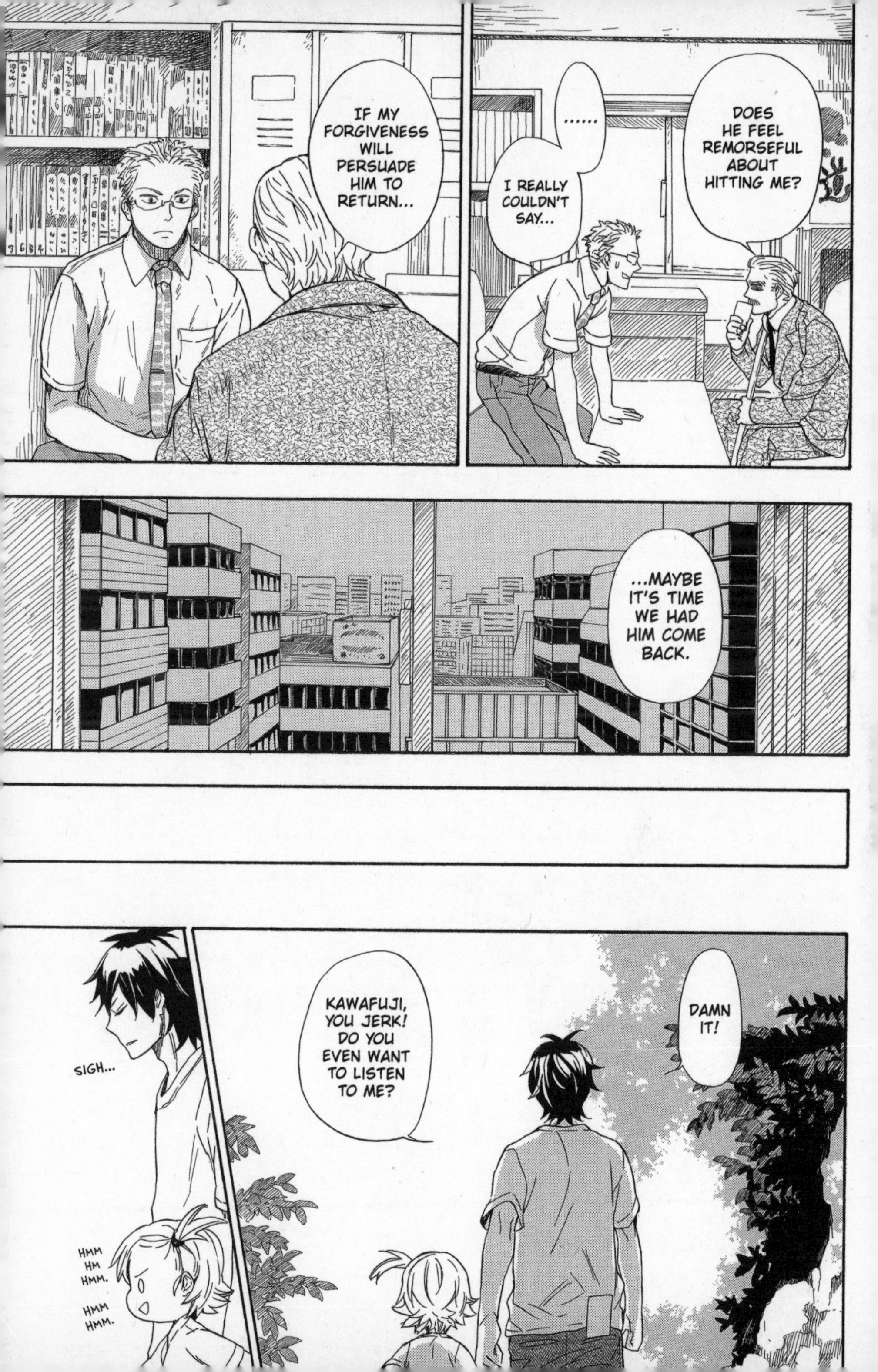
DOES HE FEEL REMORSEFUL ABOUT HITTING ME?
......
I REALLY COULDN'T SAY...
IF MY FORGIVENESS WILL PERSUADE HIM TO RETURN...
...MAYBE IT'S TIME WE HAD HIM COME BACK.
DAMN IT!
KAWAFUJI, YOU JERK! DO YOU EVEN WANT TO LISTEN TO ME?
SIGH...
HMM HM HMM.
HMM HMM.

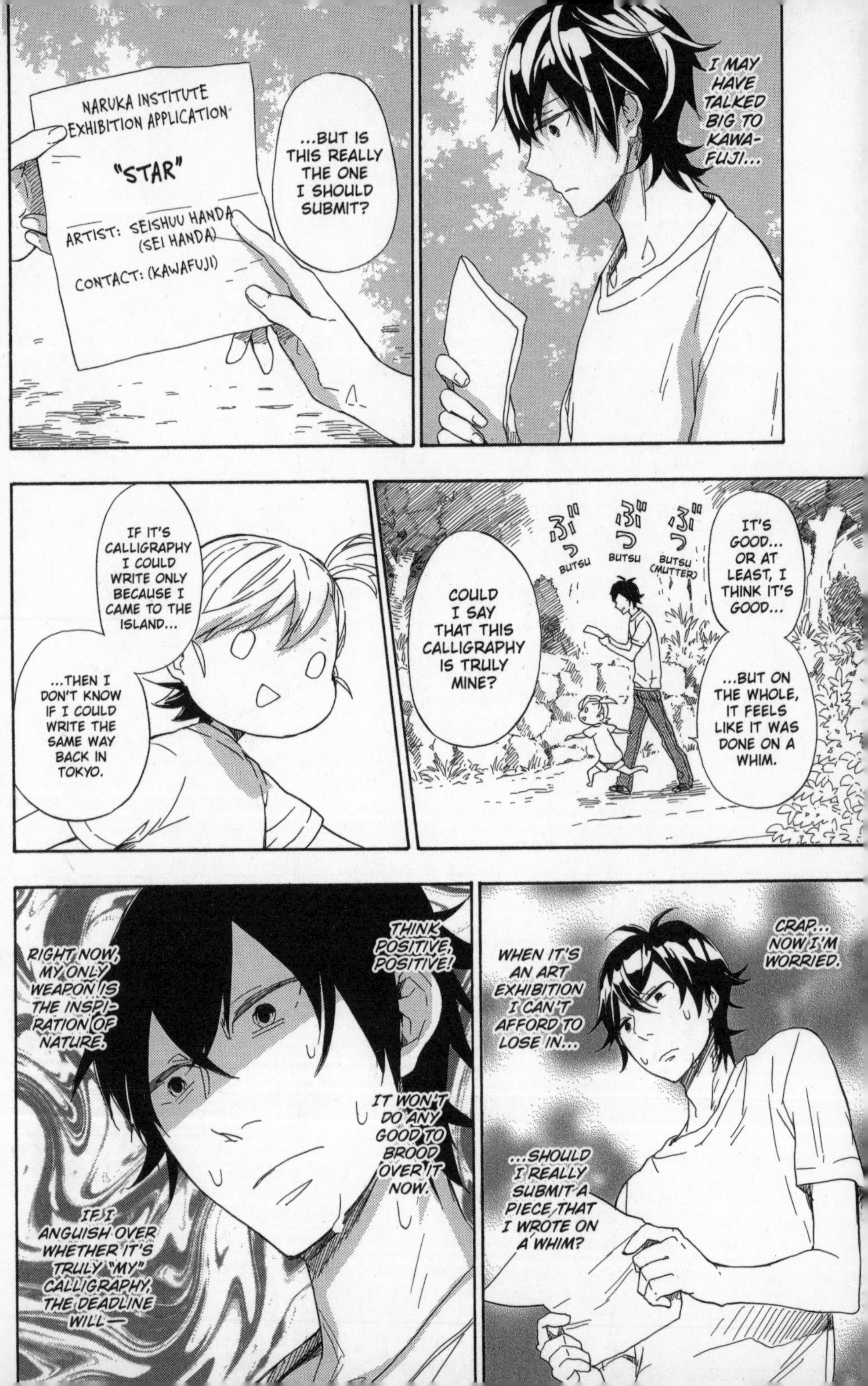
I MAY HAVE TALKED BIG TO KAWAFUJI...
NARUKA INSTITUTE EXHIBITION APPLICATION
"STAR"
ARTIST: SEISHUU HANDA (SEI HANDA)
CONTACT: (KAWAFUJI)
...BUT IS THIS REALLY THE ONE I SHOULD SUBMIT?
IT'S GOOD... OR AT LEAST, I THINK IT'S GOOD...
...BUT ON THE WHOLE, IT FEELS LIKE IT WAS DONE ON A WHIM.
ぶつ BUTSU (MUTTER)
ぶつ BUTSU
ぶつ BUTSU
COULD I SAY THAT THIS CALLIGRAPHY IS TRULY MINE?
IF IT'S CALLIGRAPHY I COULD WRITE ONLY BECAUSE I CAME TO THE ISLAND...
...THEN I DON'T KNOW IF I COULD WRITE THE SAME WAY BACK IN TOKYO.
CRAP... NOW I'M WORRIED.
WHEN IT'S AN ART EXHIBITION I CAN'T AFFORD TO LOSE IN...
...SHOULD I REALLY SUBMIT A PIECE THAT I WROTE ON A WHIM?
THINK POSITIVE, POSITIVE!
RIGHT NOW, MY ONLY WEAPON IS THE INSPIRATION OF NATURE.
IT WON'T DO ANY GOOD TO BROOD OVER IT NOW.
IF I ANGUISH OVER WHETHER IT'S TRULY "MY" CALLIGRAPHY, THE DEADLINE WILL—

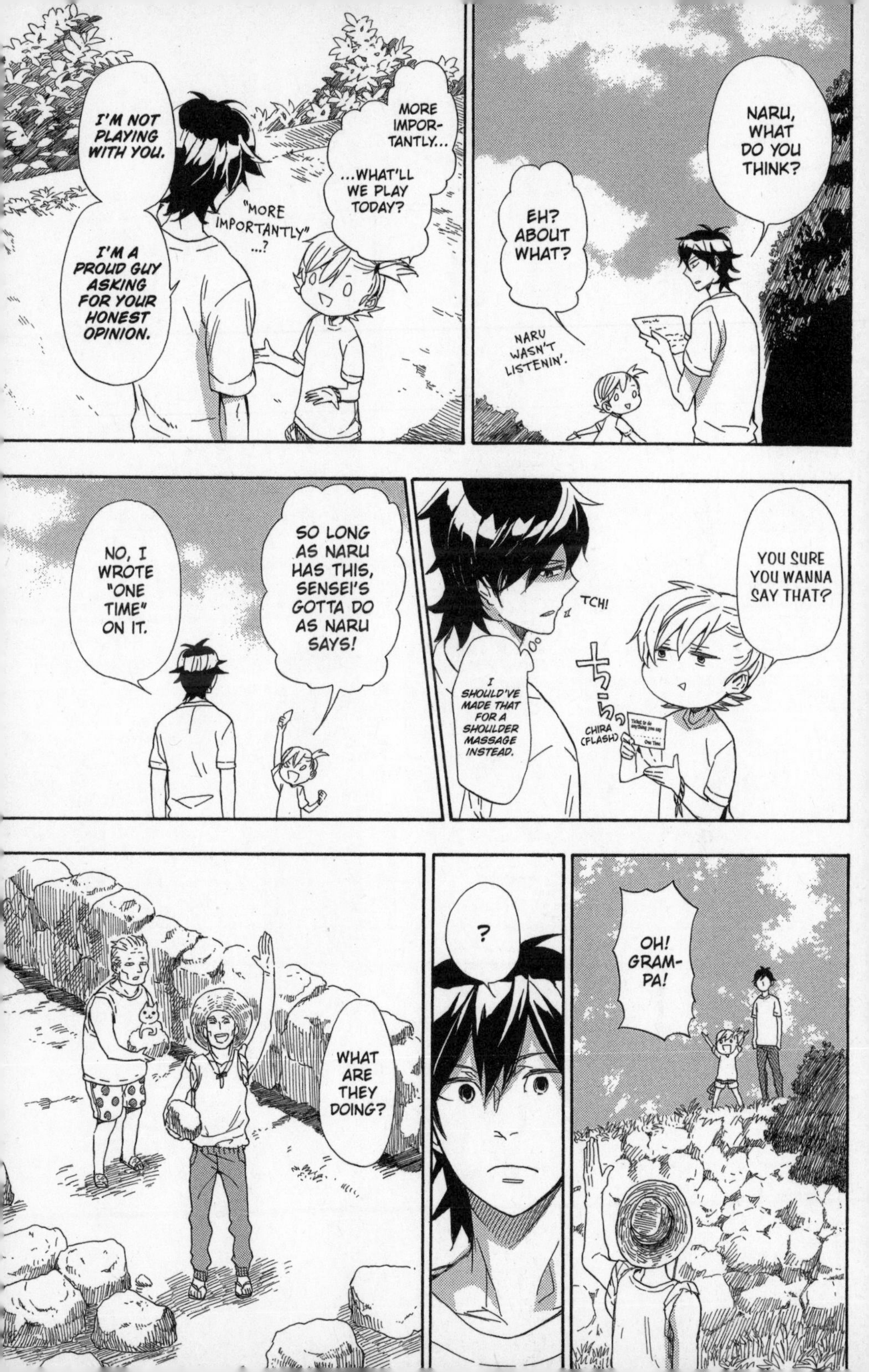
NARU, WHAT DO YOU THINK?
EH? ABOUT WHAT?
NARU WASN'T LISTENIN'.
MORE IMPOR-TANTLY...
...WHAT'LL WE PLAY TODAY?
"MORE IMPORTANTLY" ...?
I'M NOT PLAYING WITH YOU.
I'M A PROUD GUY ASKING FOR YOUR HONEST OPINION.
YOU SURE YOU WANNA SAY THAT?
TCH!
ちら
CHIRA (FLASH)
I SHOULD'VE MADE THAT FOR A SHOULDER MASSAGE INSTEAD.
SO LONG AS NARU HAS THIS, SENSEI'S GOTTA DO AS NARU SAYS!
NO, I WROTE "ONE TIME" ON IT.
OH! GRAM-PA!
?
WHAT ARE THEY DOING?

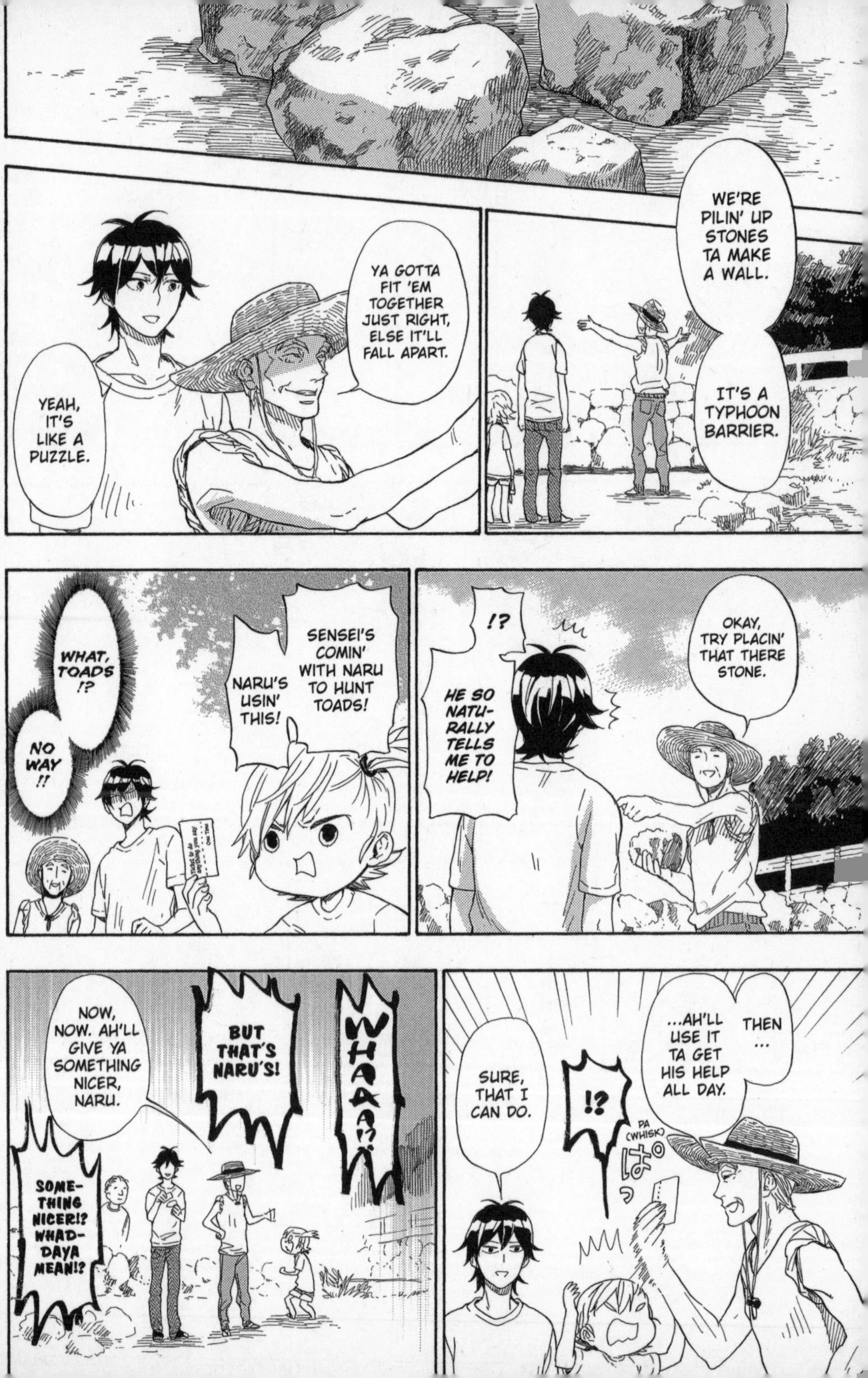
WE'RE PILIN' UP STONES TA MAKE A WALL.
IT'S A TYPHOON BARRIER.
YA GOTTA FIT 'EM TOGETHER JUST RIGHT, ELSE IT'LL FALL APART.
YEAH, IT'S LIKE A PUZZLE.
OKAY, TRY PLACIN' THAT THERE STONE.
!?
HE SO NATU-RALLY TELLS ME TO HELP!
SENSEI'S COMIN' WITH NARU TO HUNT TOADS!
NARU'S USIN' THIS!
Ticket to do anything you say
One Time
WHAT, TOADS!?
NO WAY!!
THEN ...
...AH'LL USE IT TA GET HIS HELP ALL DAY.
PA (WHISK)
ぱっ
SURE, THAT I CAN DO.
!?
WHAAA!?
BUT THAT'S NARU'S!
NOW, NOW. AH'LL GIVE YA SOMETHING NICER, NARU.
SOME-THING NICER!? WHAD-DAYA MEAN!?

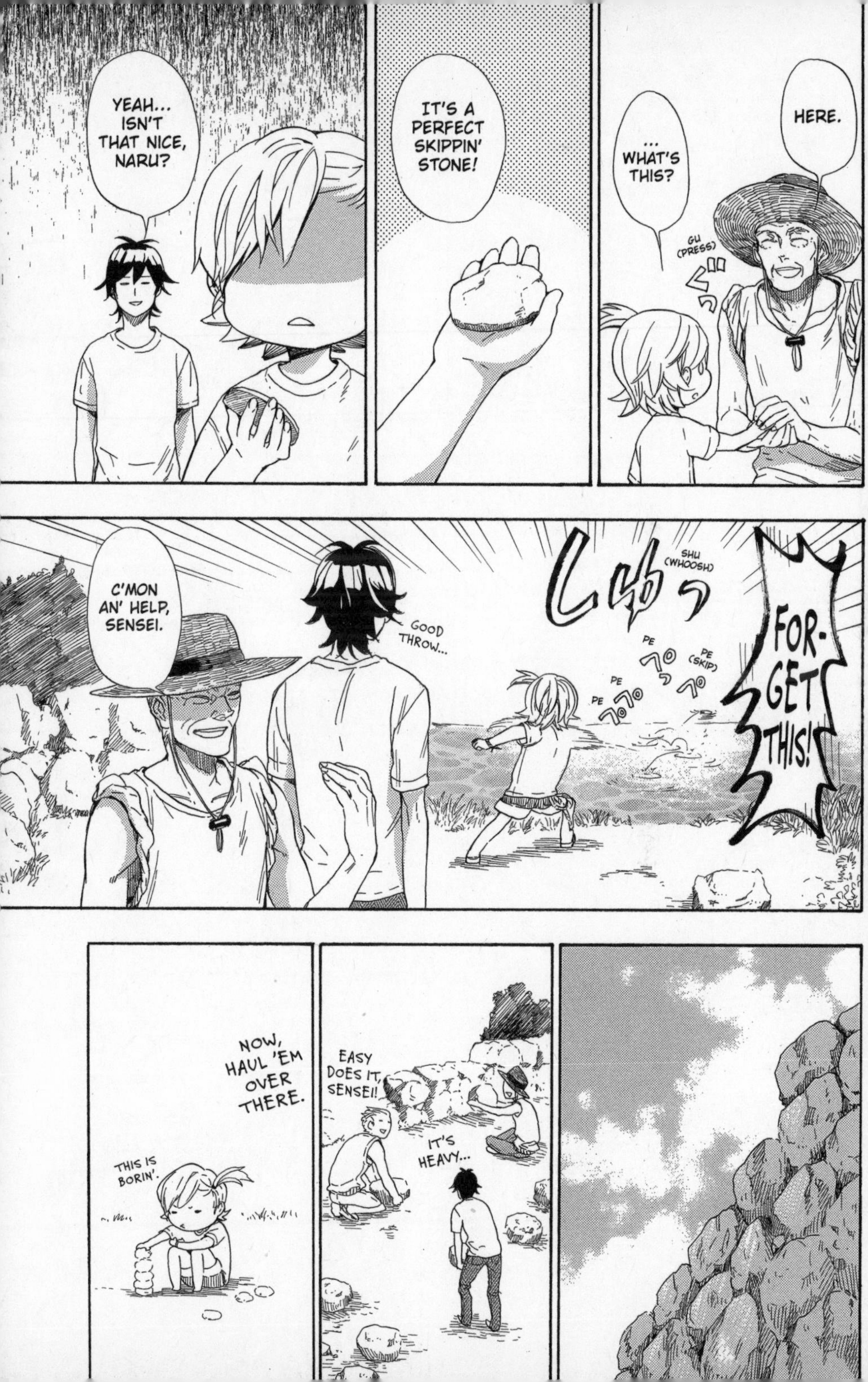
HERE.
... WHAT'S THIS?
GU (PRESS)
IT'S A PERFECT SKIPPIN' STONE!
YEAH... ISN'T THAT NICE, NARU?
FOR-GET THIS!
SHU (WHOOSH)
PE (SKIP)
PE
PE
PE
GOOD THROW...
C'MON AN' HELP, SENSEI.
EASY DOES IT, SENSEI!
IT'S HEAVY...
NOW, HAUL 'EM OVER THERE.
THIS IS BORIN'.

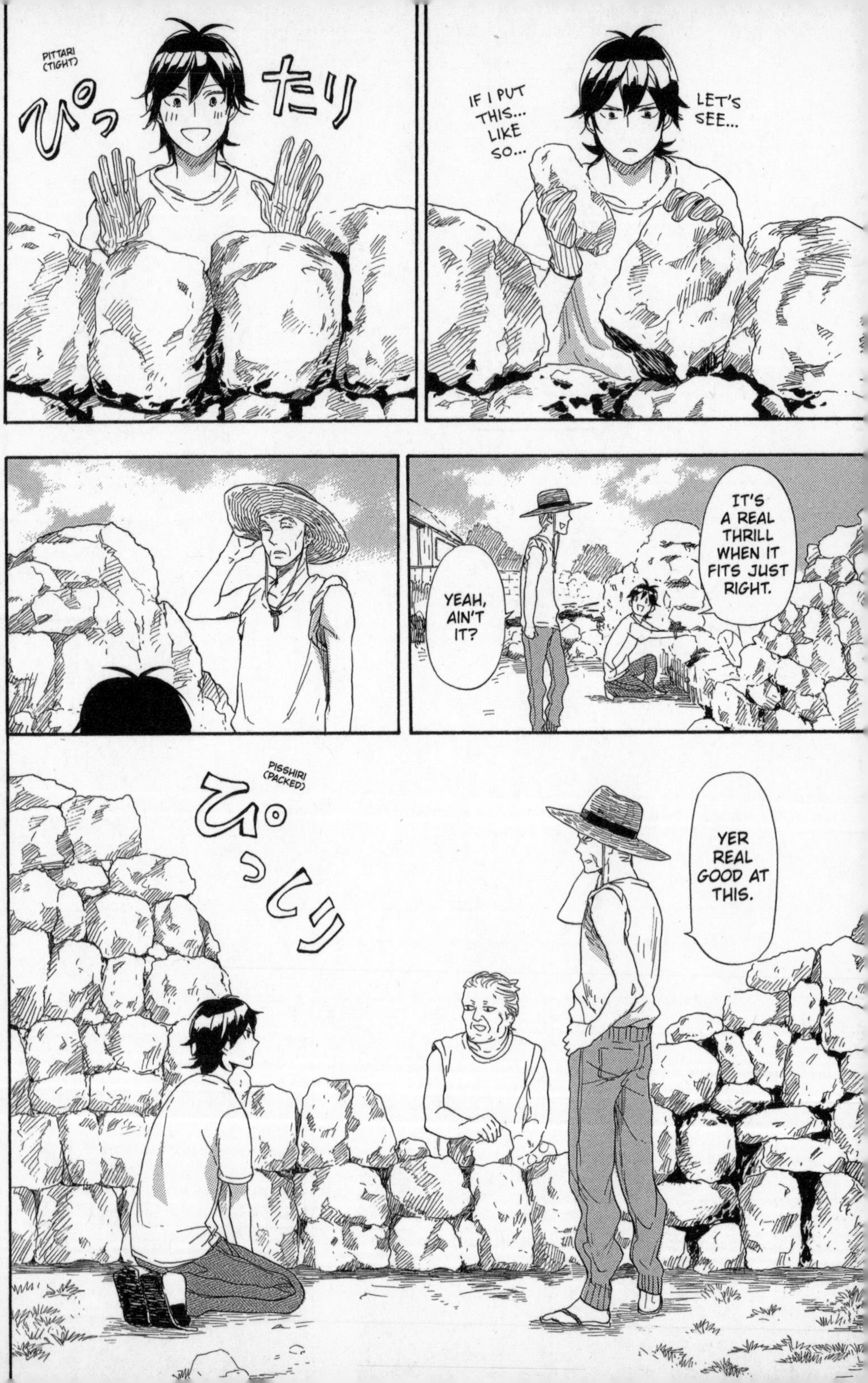
LET'S SEE...
IF I PUT THIS... LIKE SO...
PITTARI (TIGHT)
ぴったり
IT'S A REAL THRILL WHEN IT FITS JUST RIGHT.
YEAH, AIN'T IT?
YER REAL GOOD AT THIS.
PISSHIRI (PACKED)
ぴっしり

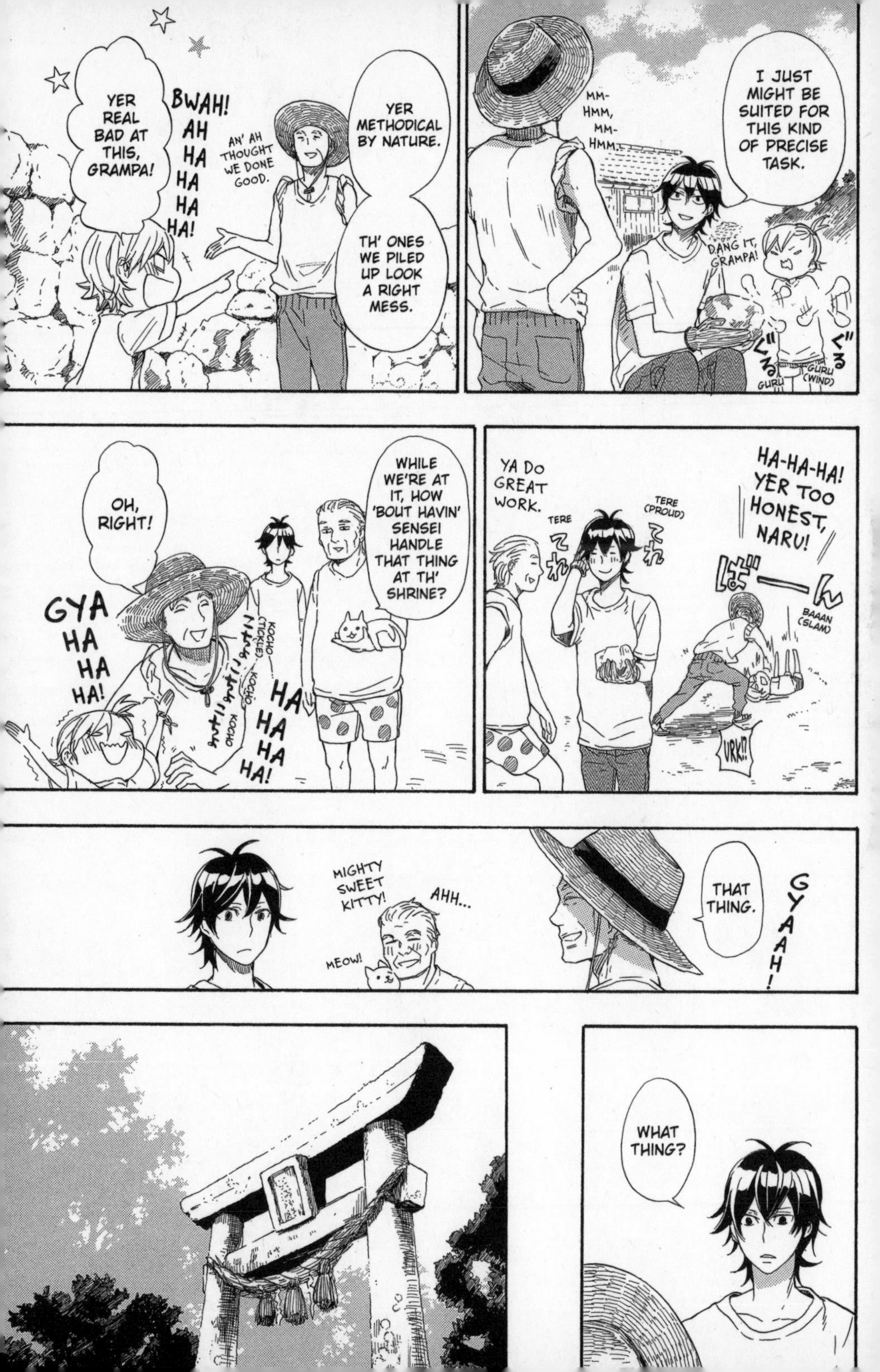
I JUST MIGHT BE SUITED FOR THIS KIND OF PRECISE TASK.
MM-HMM, MM-HMM.
DANG IT, GRAMPA!
ぐる GURU
ぐる GURU (WIND)
YER METHODICAL BY NATURE.
TH' ONES WE PILED UP LOOK A RIGHT MESS.
AN' AH THOUGHT WE DONE GOOD.
BWAH! AH HA HA HA HA!
YER REAL BAD AT THIS, GRAMPA!
HA-HA-HA! YER TOO HONEST, NARU!
ばーん BAAAN (SLAM)
てれ TERE (PROUD)
TERE
YA DO GREAT WORK.
URK!?
WHILE WE'RE AT IT, HOW 'BOUT HAVIN' SENSEI HANDLE THAT THING AT TH' SHRINE?
HA HA HA HA HA!
KOCHO (TICKLE) KOCHO KOCHO
OH, RIGHT!
GYA HA HA HA!
GYAAAH!
THAT THING.
AHH...
MIGHTY SWEET KITTY!
MEOW!
WHAT THING?

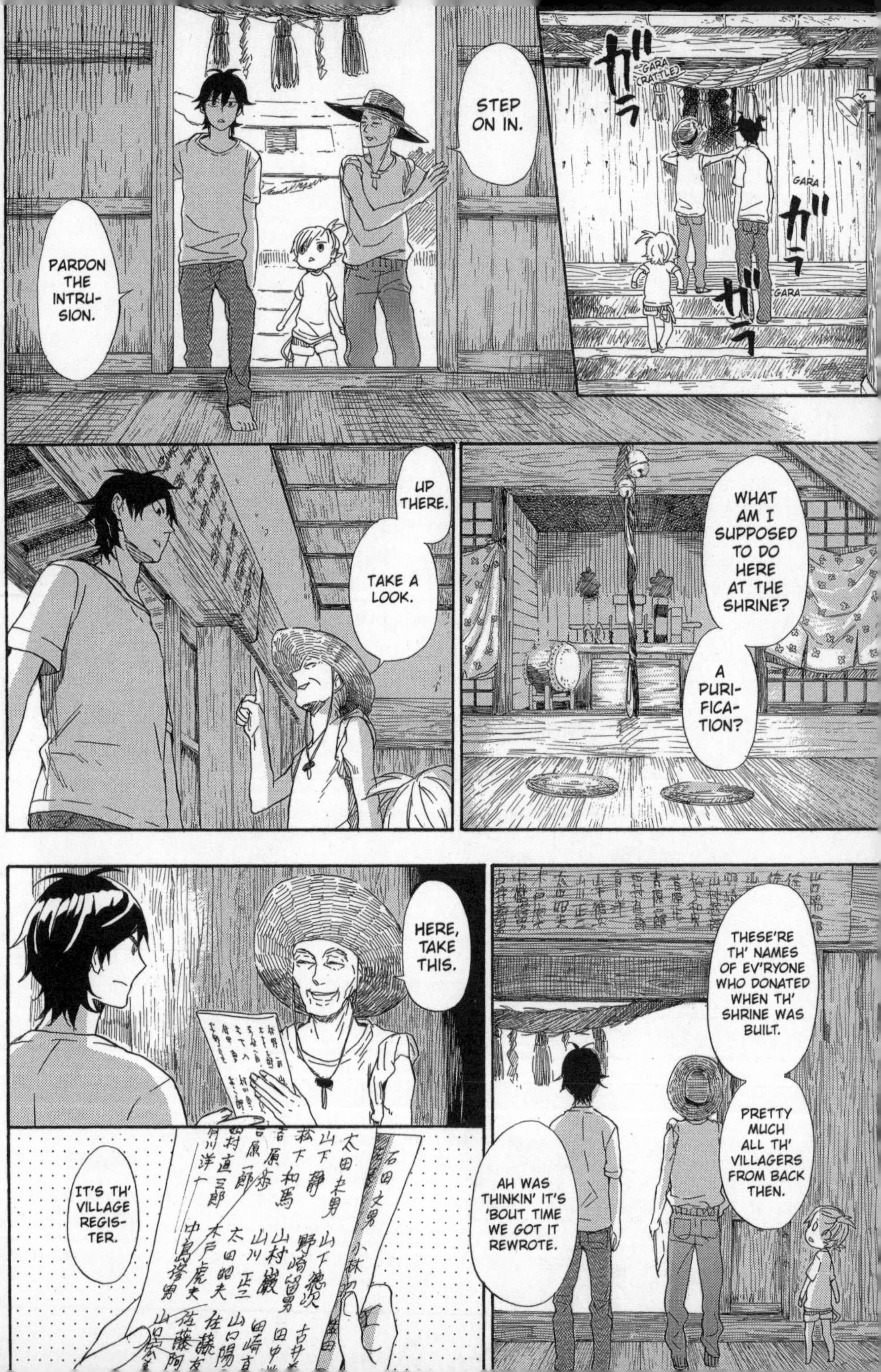
ガラ
GARA (RATTLE)
GARA
ガラ
GARA
ガラ
STEP ON IN.
PARDON THE INTRUSION.
WHAT AM I SUPPOSED TO DO HERE AT THE SHRINE?
A PURIFICATION?
UP THERE.
TAKE A LOOK.
THESE'RE TH' NAMES OF EV'RYONE WHO DONATED WHEN TH' SHRINE WAS BUILT.
PRETTY MUCH ALL TH' VILLAGERS FROM BACK THEN.
AH WAS THINKIN' IT'S 'BOUT TIME WE GOT IT REWROTE.
HERE, TAKE THIS.
IT'S TH' VILLAGE REGISTER.

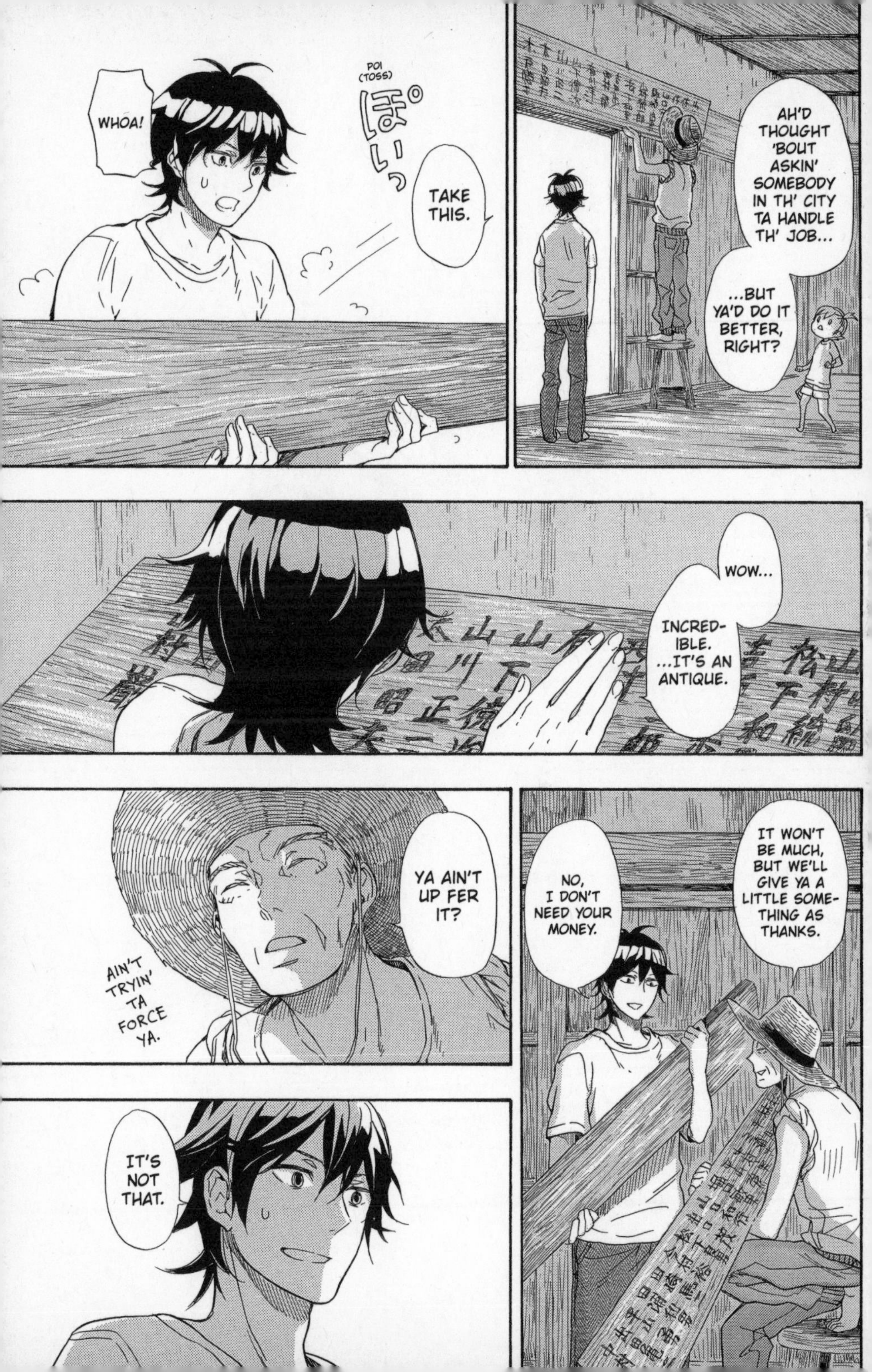
AH'D THOUGHT 'BOUT ASKIN' SOMEBODY IN TH' CITY TA HANDLE TH' JOB...
...BUT YA'D DO IT BETTER, RIGHT?
TAKE THIS.
POI (TOSS)
ぽいっ
WHOA!
WOW...
INCRED-IBLE. ...IT'S AN ANTIQUE.
IT WON'T BE MUCH, BUT WE'LL GIVE YA A LITTLE SOME-THING AS THANKS.
NO, I DON'T NEED YOUR MONEY.
YA AIN'T UP FER IT?
AIN'T TRYIN' TA FORCE YA.
IT'S NOT THAT.

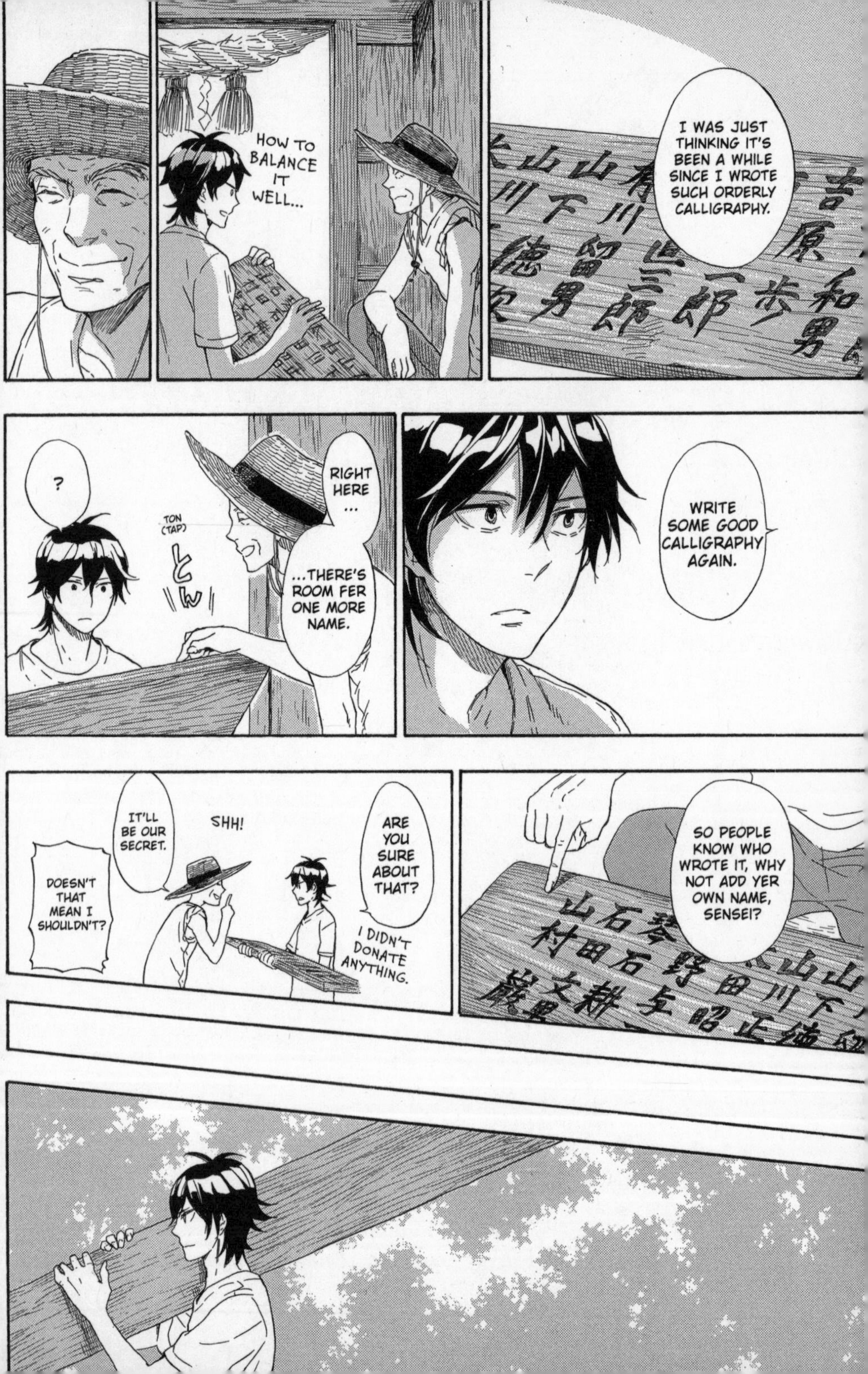
I WAS JUST THINKING IT'S BEEN A WHILE SINCE I WROTE SUCH ORDERLY CALLIGRAPHY.
HOW TO BALANCE IT WELL...
WRITE SOME GOOD CALLIGRAPHY AGAIN.
RIGHT HERE ...
...THERE'S ROOM FER ONE MORE NAME.
TON (TAP)
とん
?
SO PEOPLE KNOW WHO WROTE IT, WHY NOT ADD YER OWN NAME, SENSEI?
ARE YOU SURE ABOUT THAT?
I DIDN'T DONATE ANYTHING.
SHH!
IT'LL BE OUR SECRET.
DOESN'T THAT MEAN I SHOULDN'T?

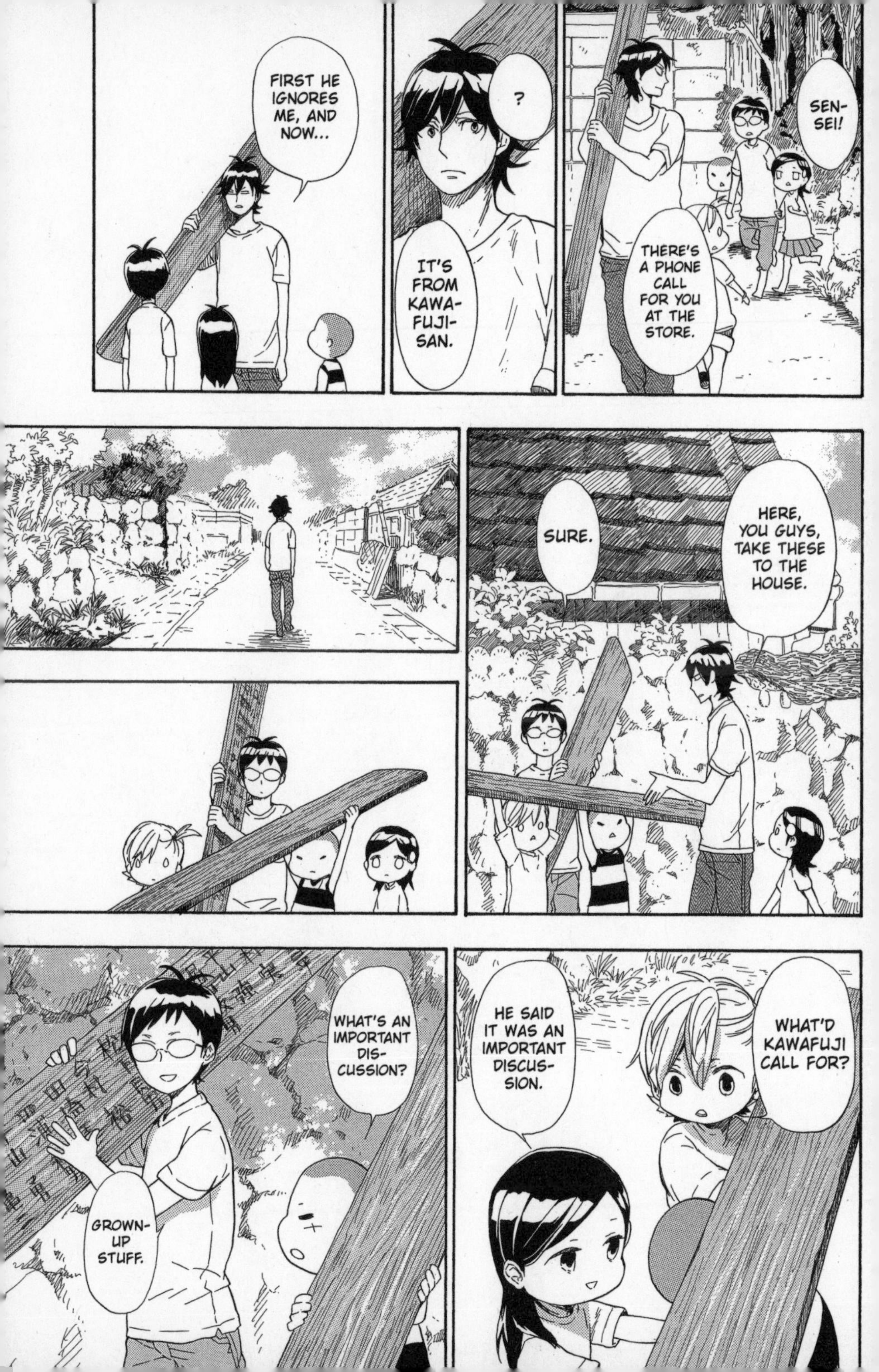
SEN-SEI!
THERE'S A PHONE CALL FOR YOU AT THE STORE.
?
IT'S FROM KAWAFUJI-SAN.
FIRST HE IGNORES ME, AND NOW...
HERE, YOU GUYS, TAKE THESE TO THE HOUSE.
SURE.
WHAT'D KAWAFUJI CALL FOR?
HE SAID IT WAS AN IMPORTANT DISCUSSION.
WHAT'S AN IMPORTANT DISCUSSION?
GROWN-UP STUFF.

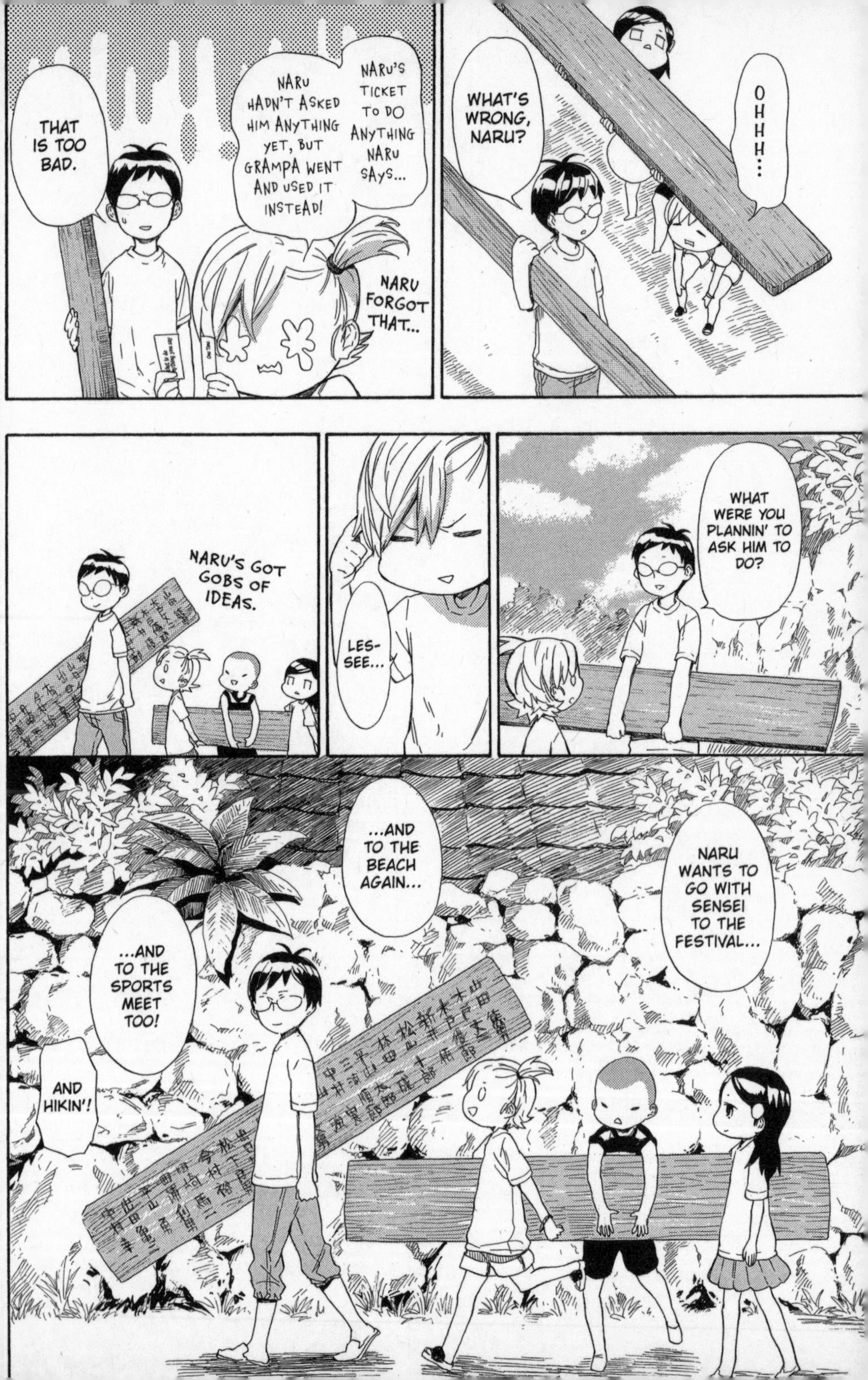
OHHH...
WHAT'S WRONG, NARU?
NARU'S TICKET TO DO ANYTHING NARU SAYS...
NARU HADN'T ASKED HIM ANYTHING YET, BUT GRAMPA WENT AND USED IT INSTEAD!
NARU FORGOT THAT...
THAT IS TOO BAD.
WHAT WERE YOU PLANNIN' TO ASK HIM TO DO?
LES-SEE...
NARU'S GOT GOBS OF IDEAS.
NARU WANTS TO GO WITH SENSEI TO THE FESTIVAL...
...AND TO THE BEACH AGAIN...
...AND TO THE SPORTS MEET TOO!
AND HIKIN'!

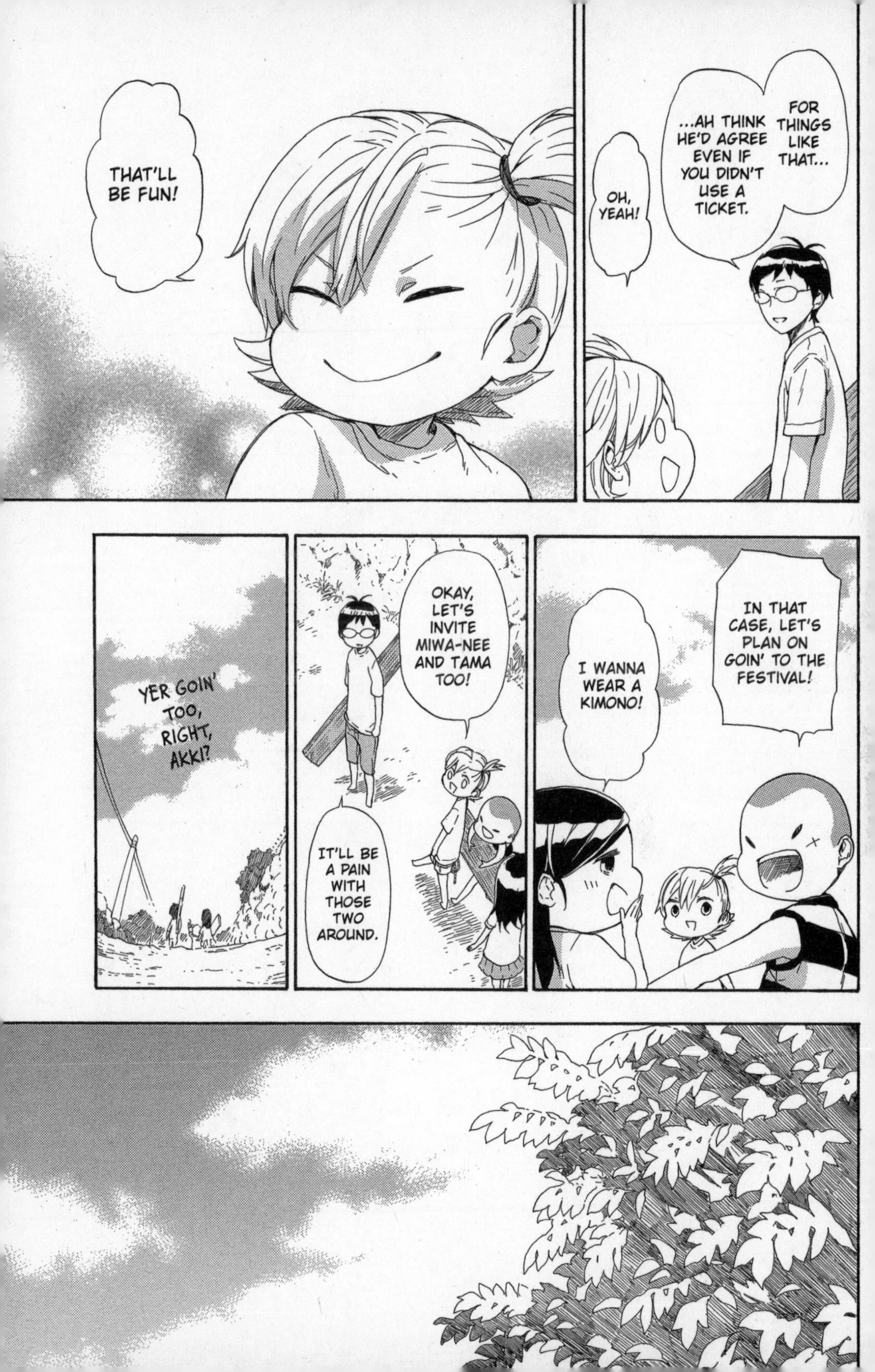
FOR THINGS LIKE THAT...
...AH THINK HE'D AGREE EVEN IF YOU DIDN'T USE A TICKET.
OH, YEAH!
THAT'LL BE FUN!
IN THAT CASE, LET'S PLAN ON GOIN' TO THE FESTIVAL!
I WANNA WEAR A KIMONO!
OKAY, LET'S INVITE MIWA-NEE AND TAMA TOO!
IT'LL BE A PAIN WITH THOSE TWO AROUND.
YER GOIN' TOO, RIGHT, AKKI?

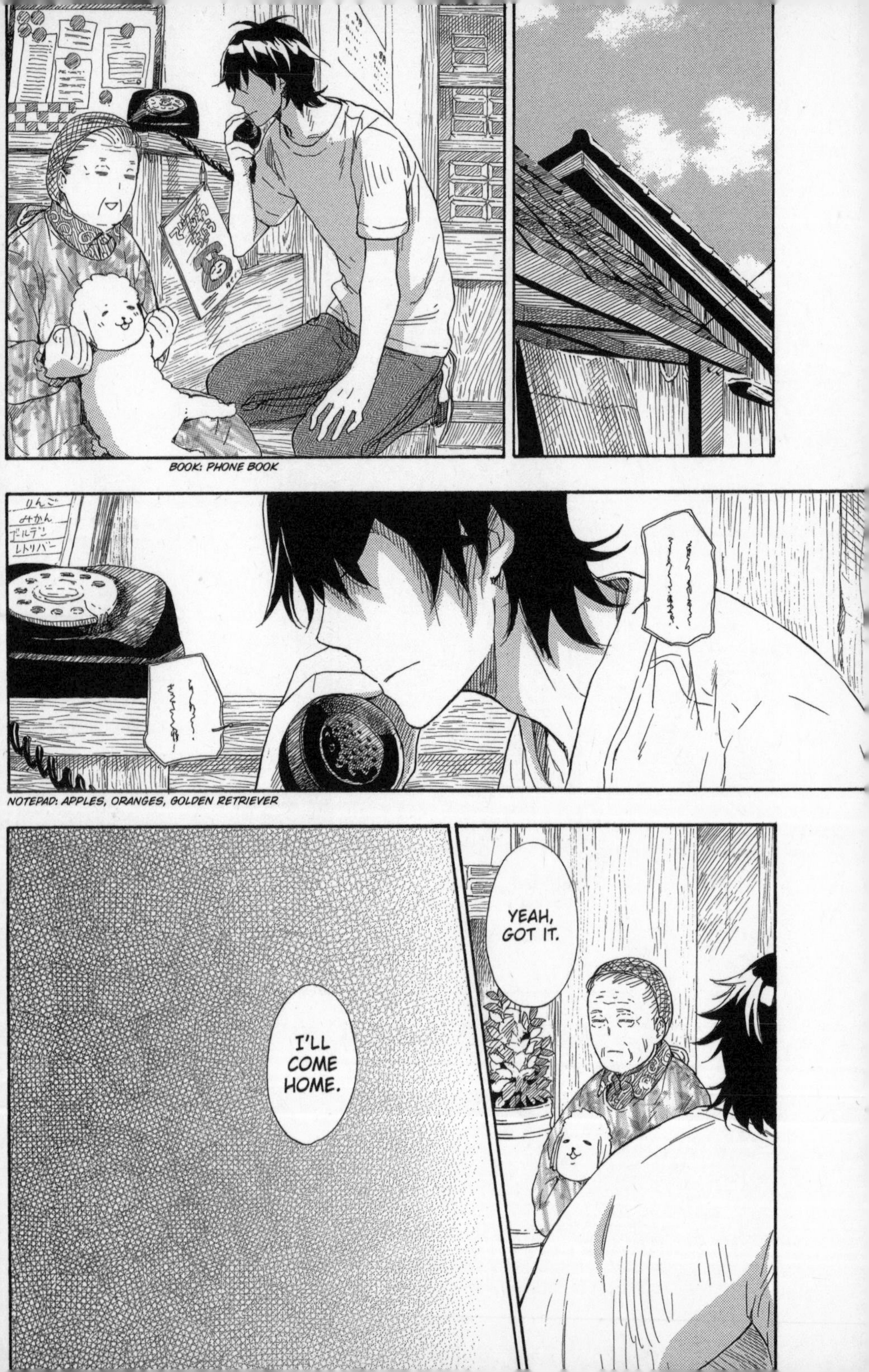
BOOK: PHONE BOOK
りんご
みかん
ゴールデン
レトリバー
NOTEPAD: APPLES, ORANGES, GOLDEN RETRIEVER
YEAH, GOT IT.
I'LL COME HOME.

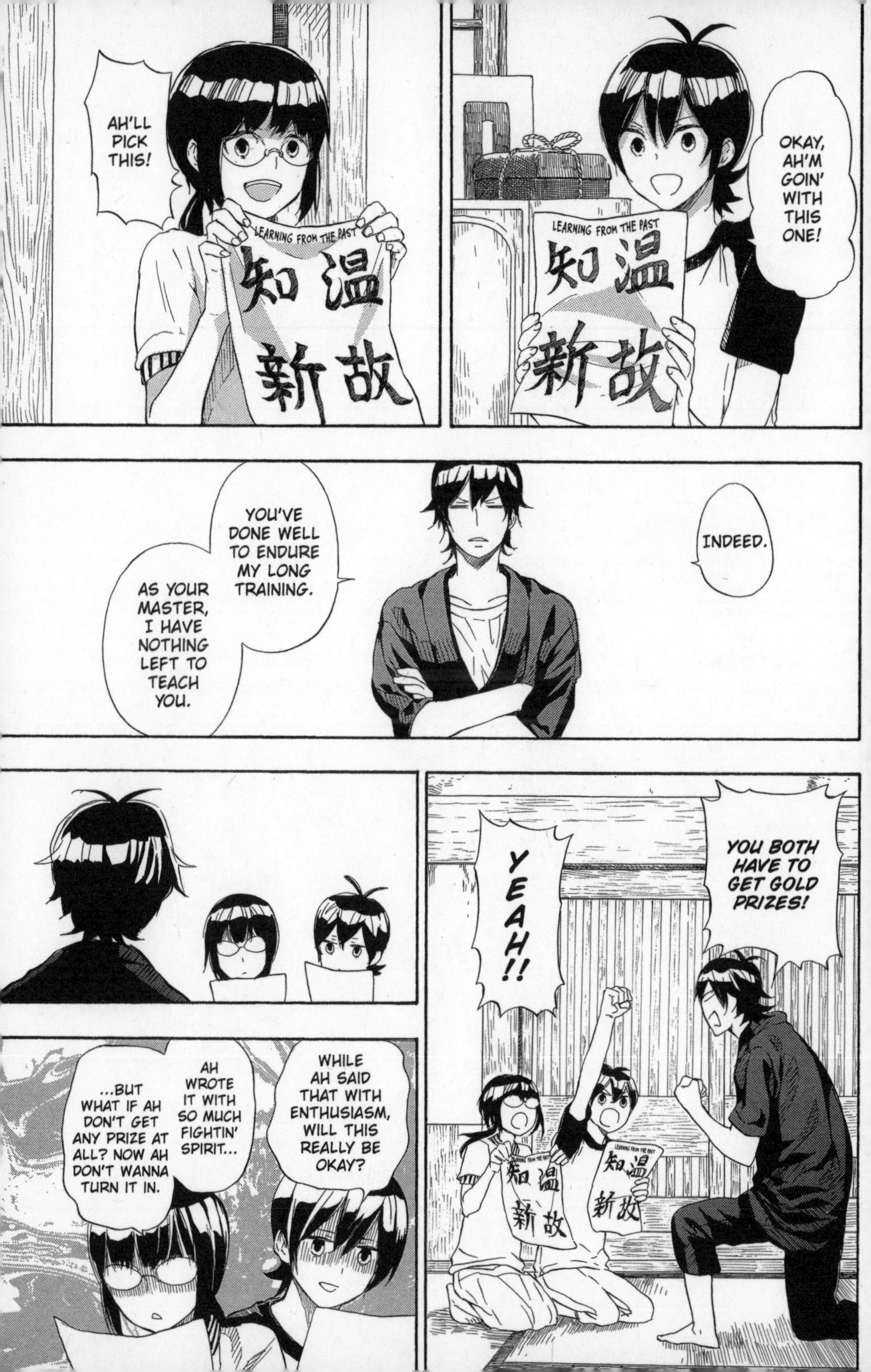
OKAY, AH'M GOIN' WITH THIS ONE!
LEARNING FROM THE PAST
温故知新
AH'LL PICK THIS!
LEARNING FROM THE PAST
温故知新
INDEED.
YOU'VE DONE WELL TO ENDURE MY LONG TRAINING.
AS YOUR MASTER, I HAVE NOTHING LEFT TO TEACH YOU.
YOU BOTH HAVE TO GET GOLD PRIZES!
YEAH!!
LEARNING FROM THE PAST
温故知新
温故知新
WHILE AH SAID THAT WITH ENTHUSIASM, WILL THIS REALLY BE OKAY?
AH WROTE IT WITH SO MUCH FIGHTIN' SPIRIT...
...BUT WHAT IF AH DON'T GET ANY PRIZE AT ALL? NOW AH DON'T WANNA TURN IT IN.

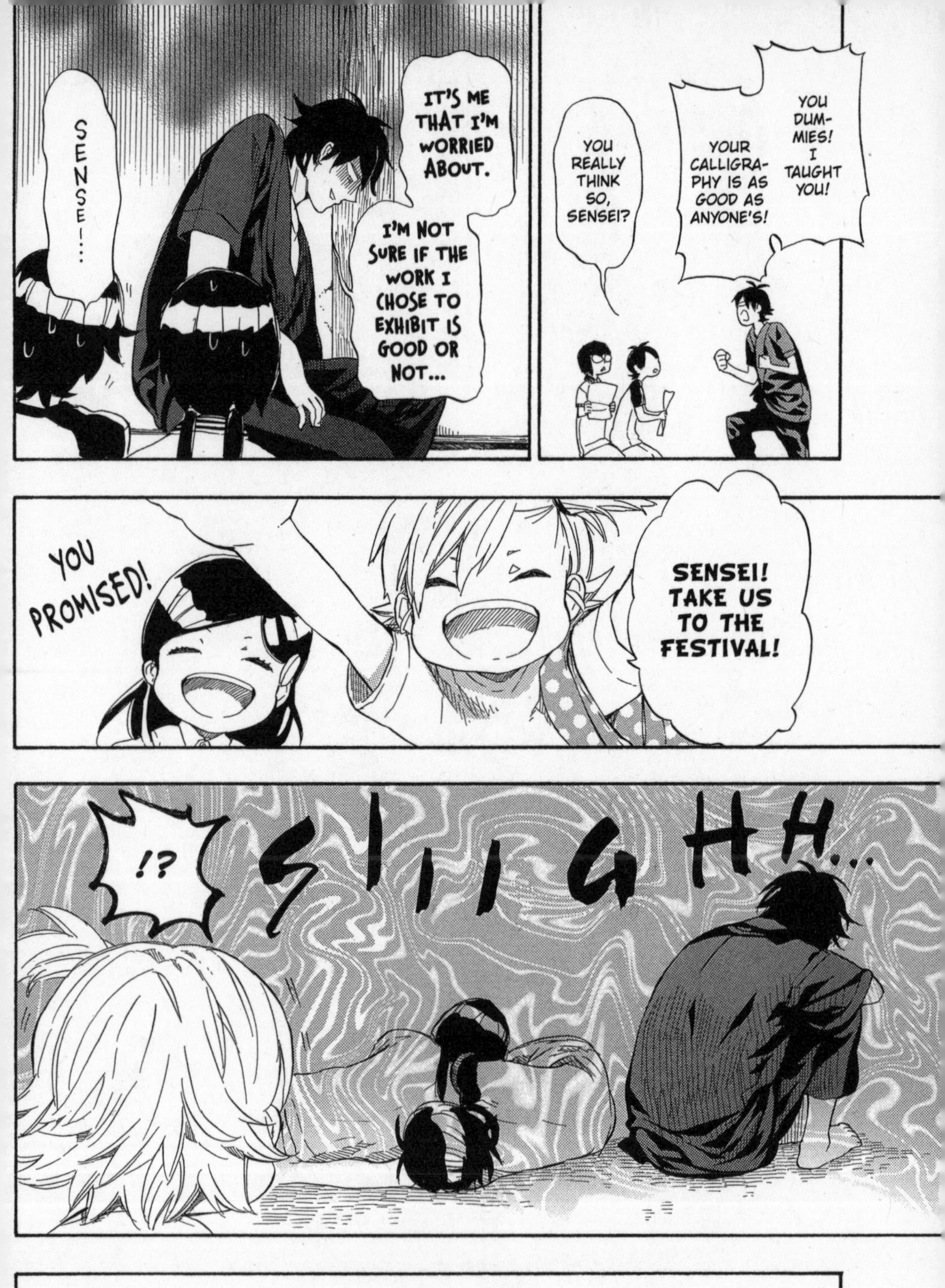
YOU DUM-MIES! I TAUGHT YOU!
YOUR CALLIGRA-PHY IS AS GOOD AS ANYONE'S!
YOU REALLY THINK SO, SENSEI?
IT'S ME THAT I'M WORRIED ABOUT.
I'M NOT SURE IF THE WORK I CHOSE TO EXHIBIT IS GOOD OR NOT...
SENSEI!...
SENSEI! TAKE US TO THE FESTIVAL!
YOU PROMISED!
SIIIGHH...
!?

ACT.44
DACCHI IKODE
(Translation: Let's All Go Together)

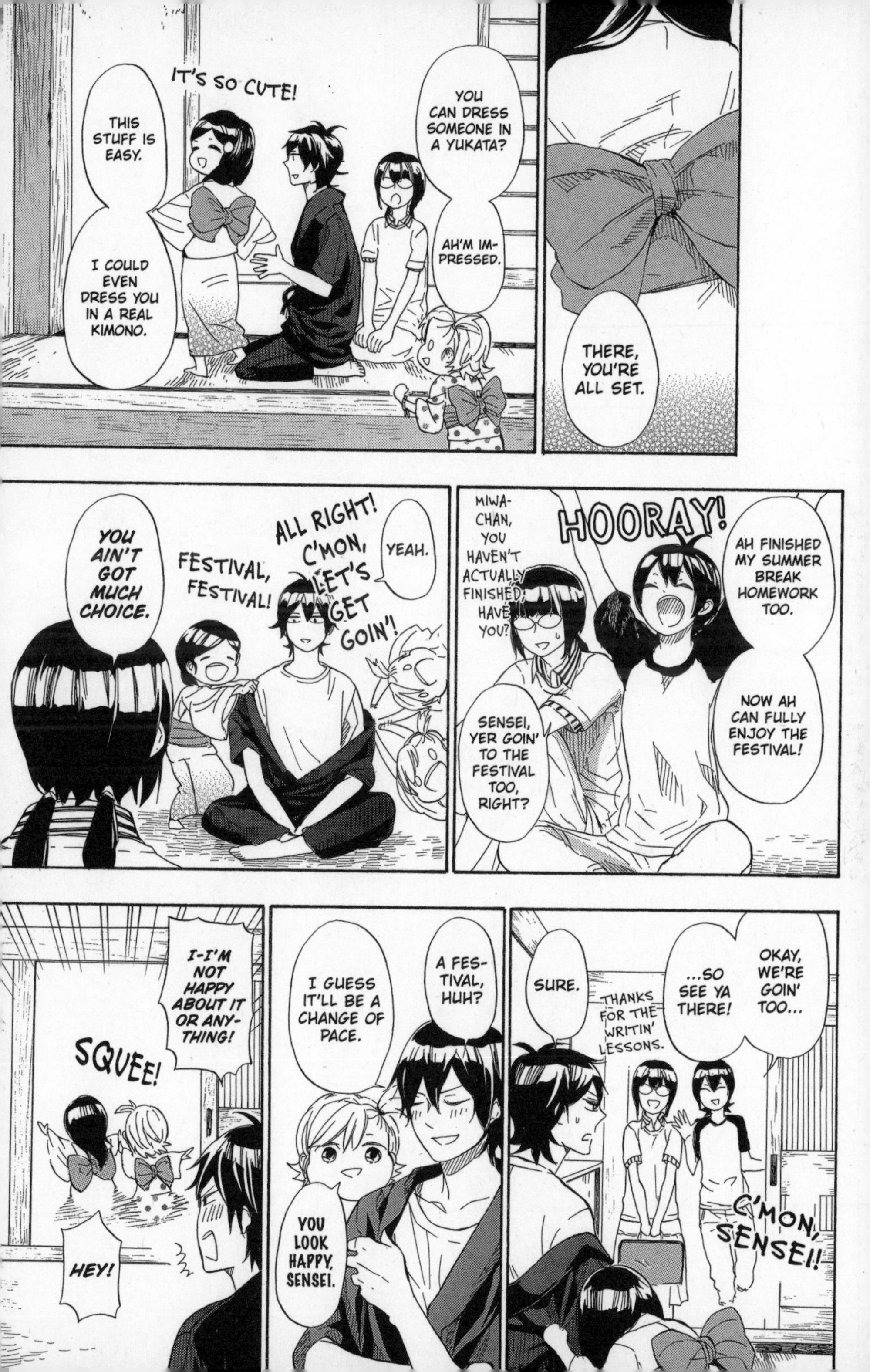
THERE, YOU'RE ALL SET.
YOU CAN DRESS SOMEONE IN A YUKATA?
AH'M IM-PRESSED.
IT'S SO CUTE!
THIS STUFF IS EASY.
I COULD EVEN DRESS YOU IN A REAL KIMONO.
AH FINISHED MY SUMMER BREAK HOMEWORK TOO.
HOORAY!
MIWA-CHAN, YOU HAVEN'T ACTUALLY FINISHED, HAVE YOU?
NOW AH CAN FULLY ENJOY THE FESTIVAL!
SENSEI, YER GOIN' TO THE FESTIVAL TOO, RIGHT?
YEAH.
ALL RIGHT! C'MON, LET'S GET GOIN'!
FESTIVAL, FESTIVAL!
YOU AIN'T GOT MUCH CHOICE.
OKAY, WE'RE GOIN' TOO...
...SO SEE YA THERE!
THANKS FOR THE WRITIN' LESSONS.
SURE.
C'MON, SENSEI!
A FES-TIVAL, HUH?
I GUESS IT'LL BE A CHANGE OF PACE.
YOU LOOK HAPPY, SENSEI.
I-I'M NOT HAPPY ABOUT IT OR ANY-THING!
SQUEE!
HEY!

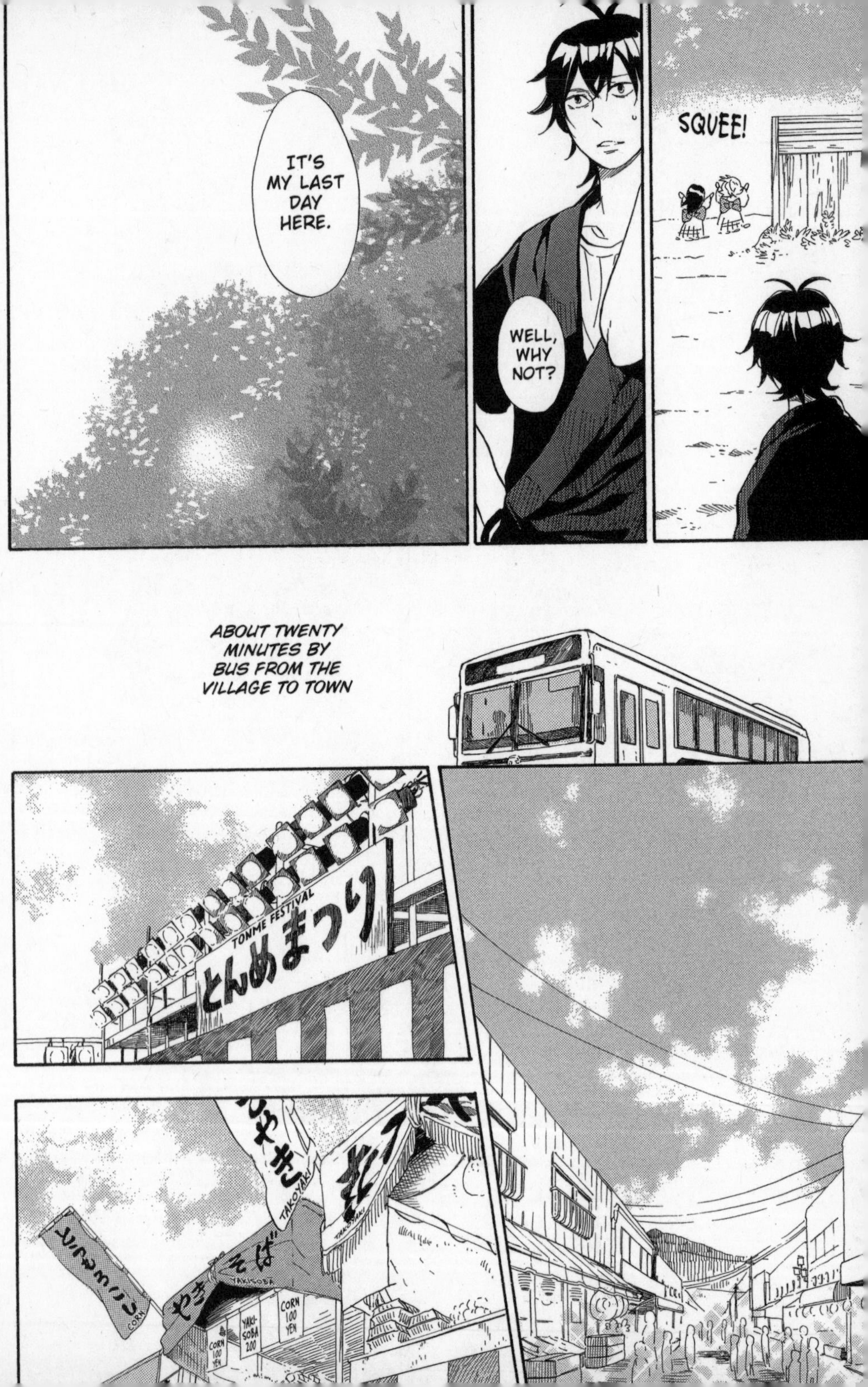
SQUEE!
WELL, WHY NOT?
IT'S MY LAST DAY HERE.
ABOUT TWENTY MINUTES BY BUS FROM THE VILLAGE TO TOWN
TONME FESTIVAL
とんめまつり
TAKOYAKI
TAKOYAKI
やきそば
YAKISOBA
CORN 100 YEN
YAKI-SOBA 200
CORN 100 YEN
CORN

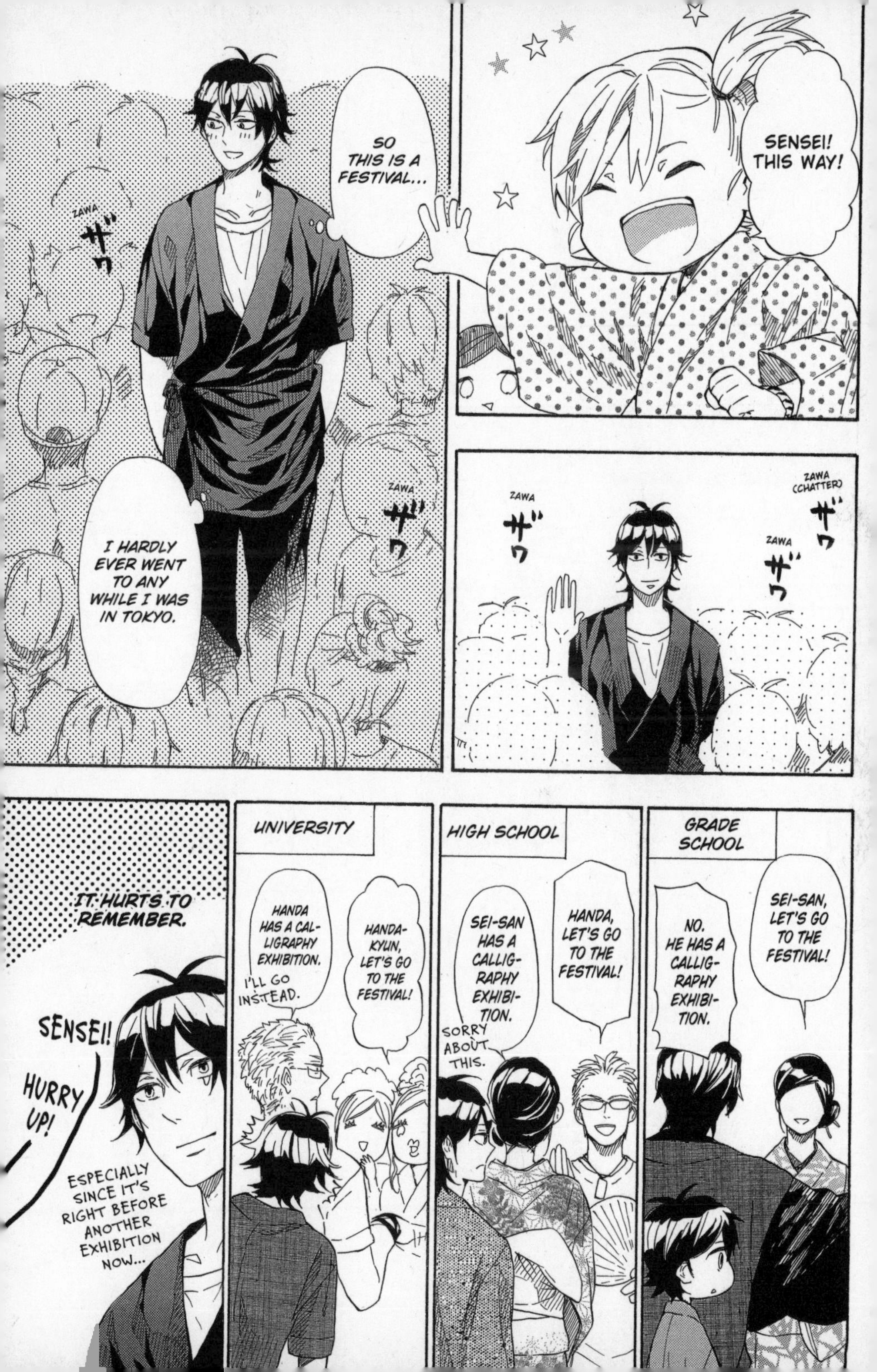
SENSEI! THIS WAY!
ZAWA
ザワ
ZAWA (CHATTER)
ザワ
ZAWA
ザワ
SO THIS IS A FESTIVAL...
ZAWA
ザワ
ZAWA
ザワ
I HARDLY EVER WENT TO ANY WHILE I WAS IN TOKYO.
GRADE SCHOOL
SEI-SAN, LET'S GO TO THE FESTIVAL!
NO. HE HAS A CALLIG-RAPHY EXHIBI-TION.
HIGH SCHOOL
HANDA, LET'S GO TO THE FESTIVAL!
SEI-SAN HAS A CALLIG-RAPHY EXHIBI-TION.
SORRY ABOUT THIS.
UNIVERSITY
HANDA-KYUN, LET'S GO TO THE FESTIVAL!
HANDA HAS A CAL-LIGRAPHY EXHIBITION.
I'LL GO INSTEAD.
IT HURTS TO REMEMBER.
SENSEI!
HURRY UP!
ESPECIALLY SINCE IT'S RIGHT BEFORE ANOTHER EXHIBITION NOW...

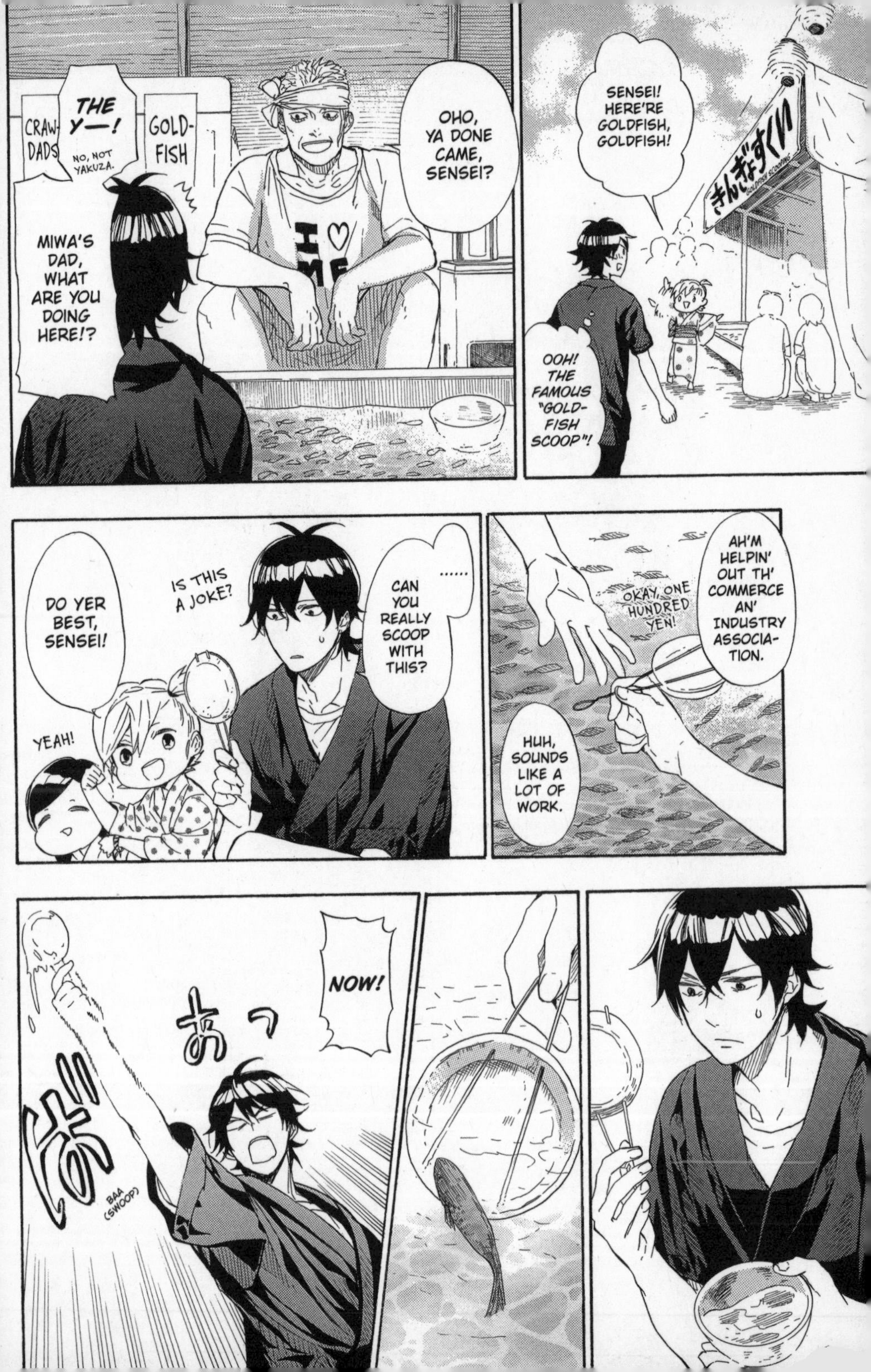
SENSEI! HERE'RE GOLDFISH, GOLDFISH!
きんぎょすくい
GOLDFISH SCOOPING
OOH! THE FAMOUS "GOLDFISH SCOOP"!
OHO, YA DONE CAME, SENSEI?
GOLD-FISH
THE Y—!
NO, NOT YAKUZA.
CRAW-DADS
MIWA'S DAD, WHAT ARE YOU DOING HERE!?
AH'M HELPIN' OUT TH' COMMERCE AN' INDUSTRY ASSOCIATION.
OKAY, ONE HUNDRED YEN!
HUH, SOUNDS LIKE A LOT OF WORK.
......
CAN YOU REALLY SCOOP WITH THIS?
IS THIS A JOKE?
DO YER BEST, SENSEI!
YEAH!
NOW!
あっ
BAA (SWOOP)

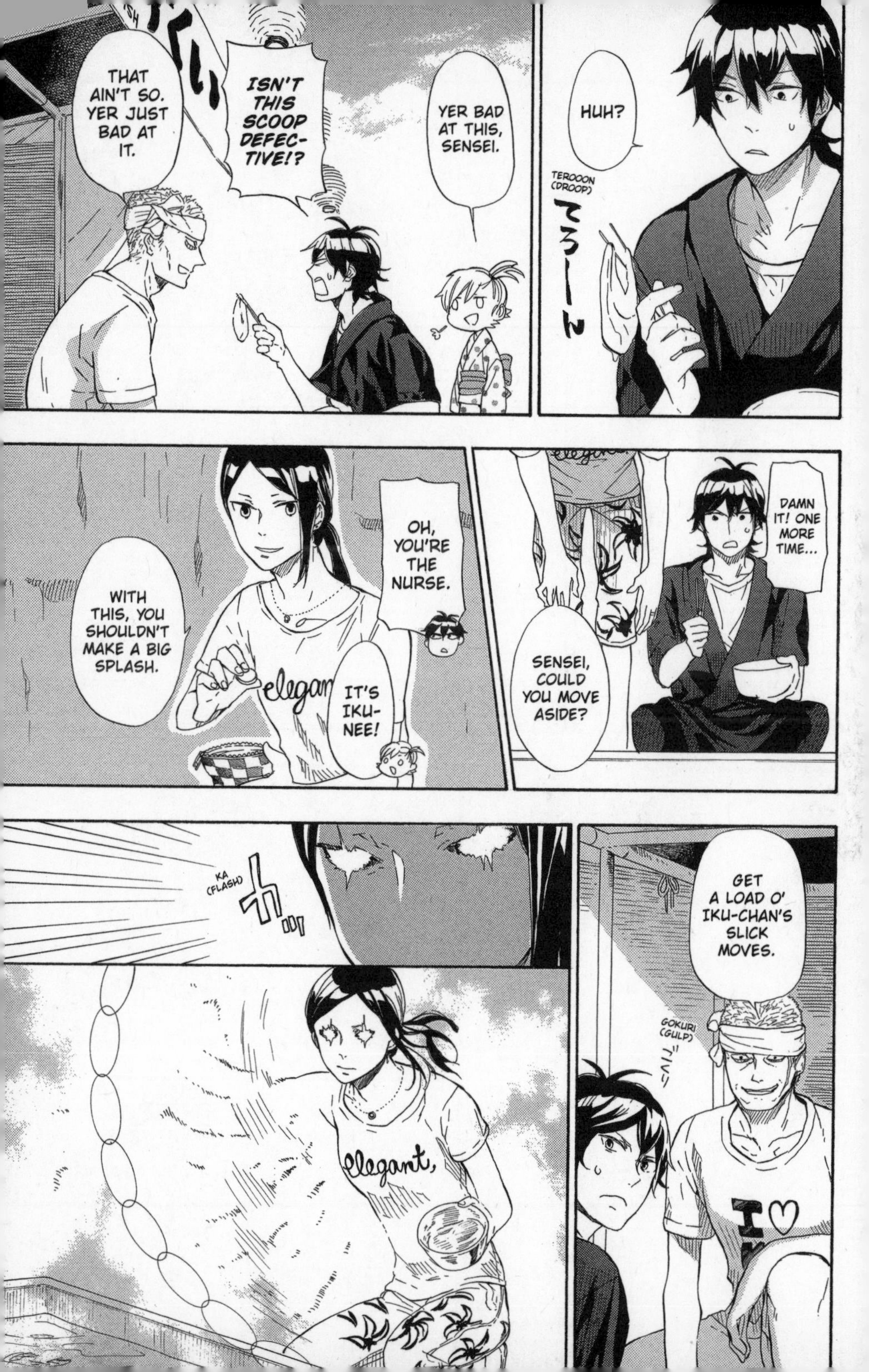
HUH?
TEROOON (DROOP)
てろーん
YER BAD AT THIS, SENSEI.
ISN'T THIS SCOOP DEFECTIVE!?
THAT AIN'T SO. YER JUST BAD AT IT.
DAMN IT! ONE MORE TIME...
SENSEI, COULD YOU MOVE ASIDE?
OH, YOU'RE THE NURSE.
IT'S IKU-NEE!
WITH THIS, YOU SHOULDN'T MAKE A BIG SPLASH.
GET A LOAD O' IKU-CHAN'S SLICK MOVES.
GOKURI (GULP)
KA (FLASH)
カッ

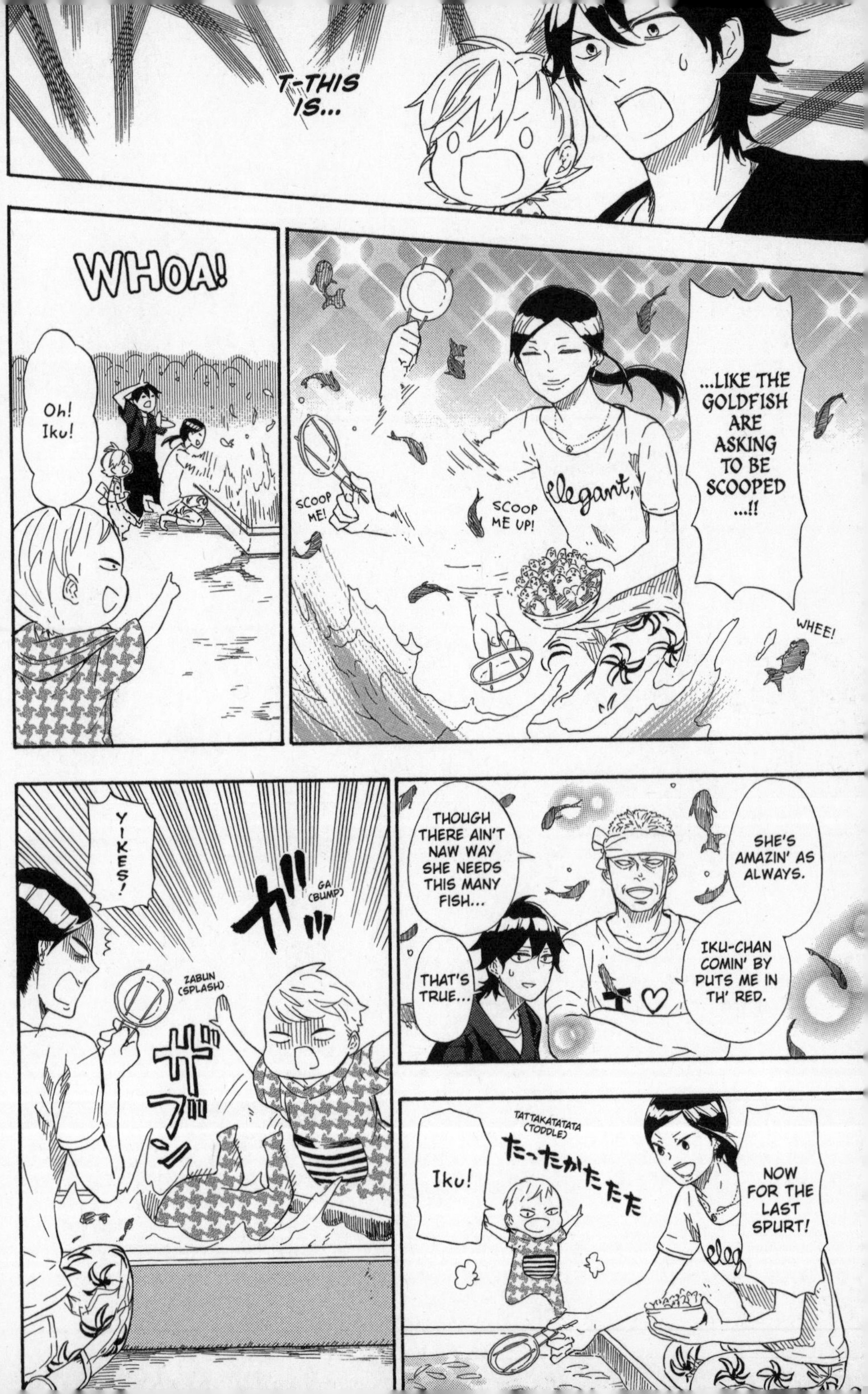
T-THIS IS...
...LIKE THE GOLDFISH ARE ASKING TO BE SCOOPED ...!!
SCOOP ME UP!
SCOOP ME!
WHEE!
WHOA!
Oh! Iku!
SHE'S AMAZIN' AS ALWAYS.
THOUGH THERE AIN'T NAW WAY SHE NEEDS THIS MANY FISH...
IKU-CHAN COMIN' BY PUTS ME IN TH' RED.
THAT'S TRUE...
NOW FOR THE LAST SPURT!
TATTAKATATATA (TODDLE)
たったかたたた
Iku!
Y!KES!
GA (BUMP)
ガッ
ZABUN (SPLASH)
ザブン

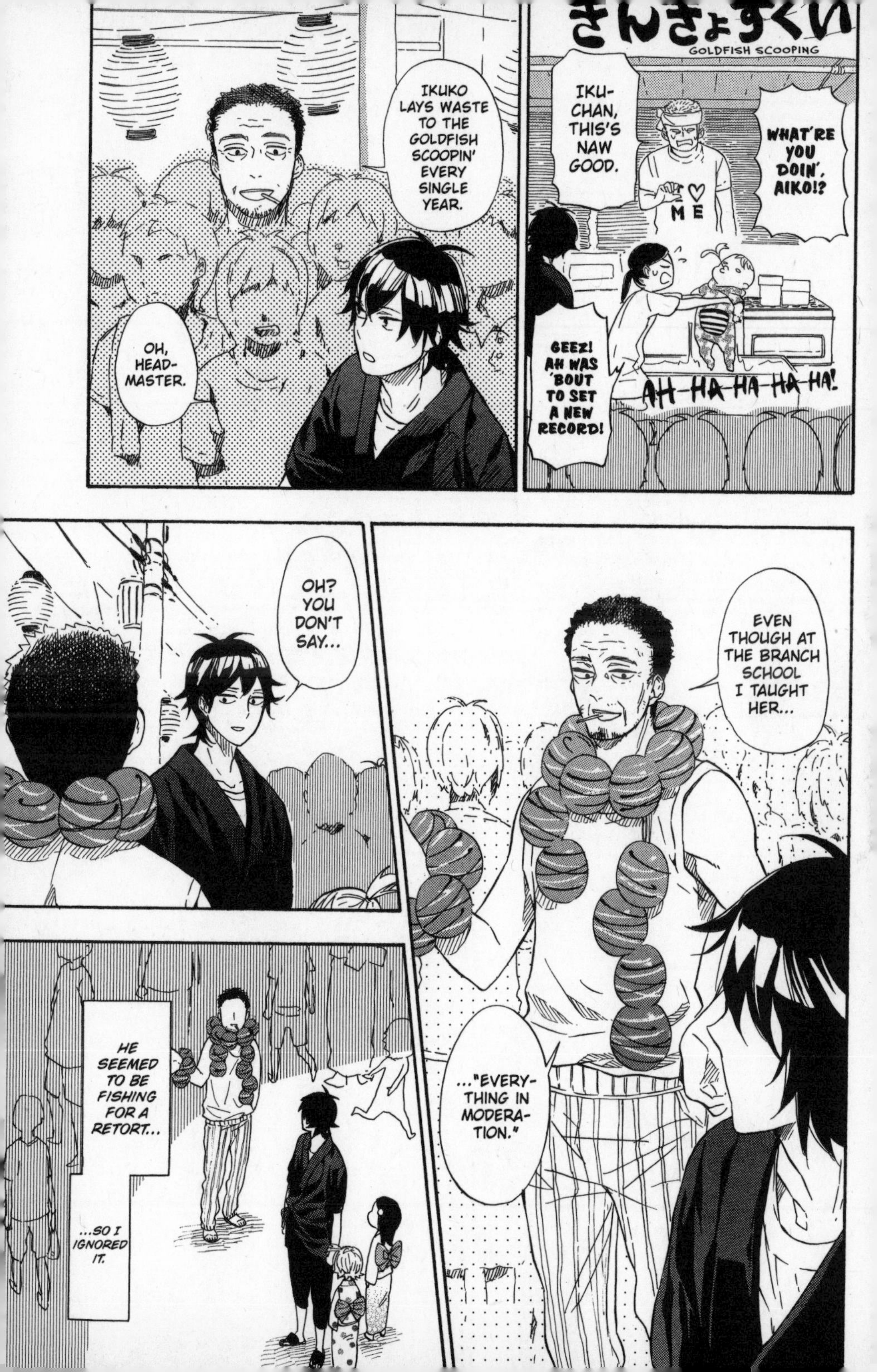
きんさょすくい
GOLDFISH SCOOPING
IKU-CHAN, THIS'S NAW GOOD.
WHAT'RE YOU DOIN', AIKO!?
GEEZ! AH WAS 'BOUT TO SET A NEW RECORD!
AH-HA-HA-HA-HA!
IKUKO LAYS WASTE TO THE GOLDFISH SCOOPIN' EVERY SINGLE YEAR.
OH, HEAD-MASTER.
EVEN THOUGH AT THE BRANCH SCHOOL I TAUGHT HER...
..."EVERY-THING IN MODERA-TION."
OH? YOU DON'T SAY...
HE SEEMED TO BE FISHING FOR A RETORT...
...SO I IGNORED IT.

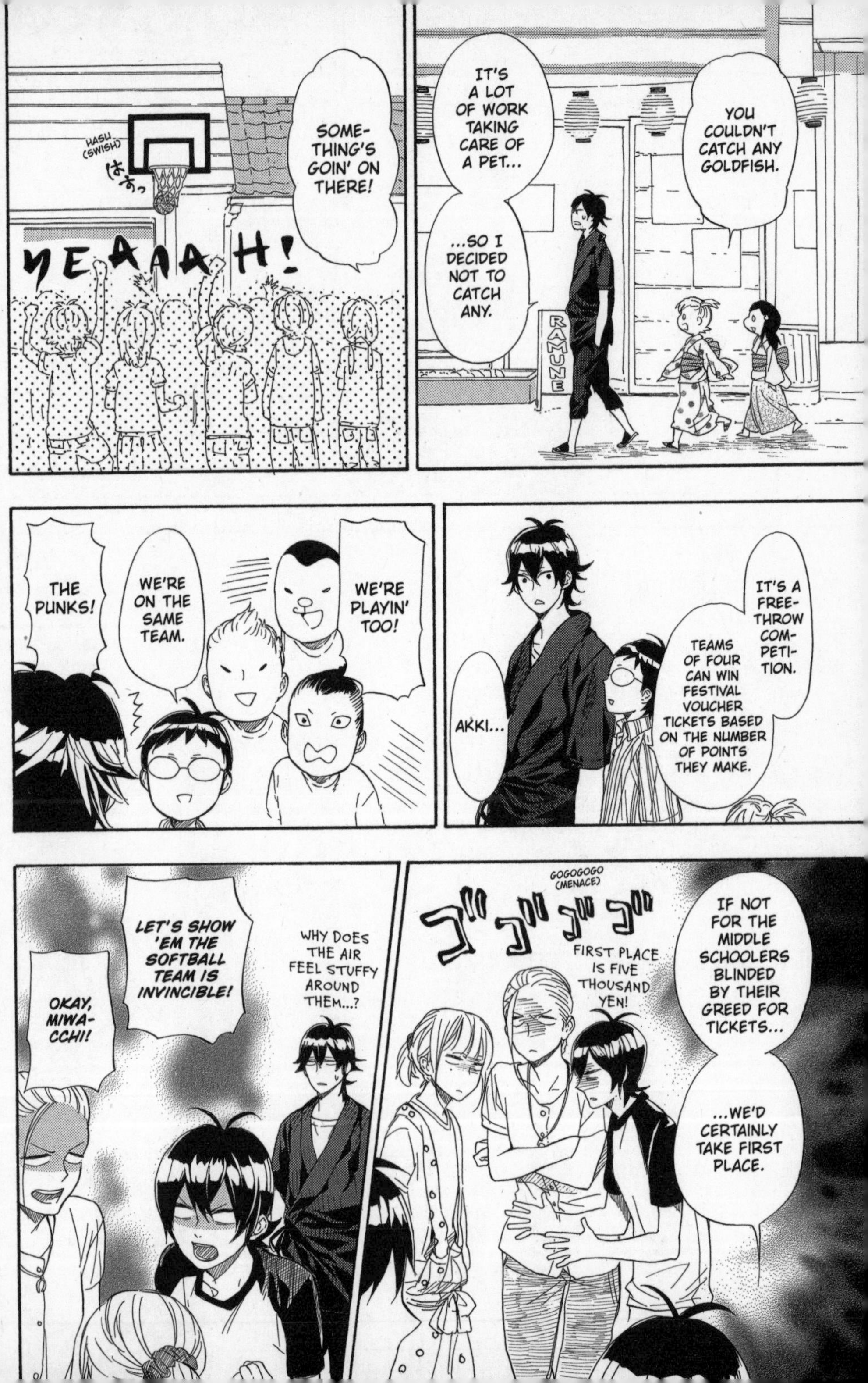

YOU COULDN'T CATCH ANY GOLDFISH.
IT'S A LOT OF WORK TAKING CARE OF A PET...
...SO I DECIDED NOT TO CATCH ANY.
RAMUNE
HASU (SWISH)
はすっ
SOME-THING'S GOIN' ON THERE!
YEAAAH!
IT'S A FREE-THROW COM-PETI-TION.
TEAMS OF FOUR CAN WIN FESTIVAL VOUCHER TICKETS BASED ON THE NUMBER OF POINTS THEY MAKE.
AKKI...
WE'RE PLAYIN' TOO!
WE'RE ON THE SAME TEAM.
THE PUNKS!
GOGOGOGO (MENACE)
ゴゴゴゴ
IF NOT FOR THE MIDDLE SCHOOLERS BLINDED BY THEIR GREED FOR TICKETS...
...WE'D CERTAINLY TAKE FIRST PLACE.
FIRST PLACE IS FIVE THOUSAND YEN!
WHY DOES THE AIR FEEL STUFFY AROUND THEM...?
LET'S SHOW 'EM THE SOFTBALL TEAM IS INVINCIBLE!
OKAY, MIWA-CCHI!

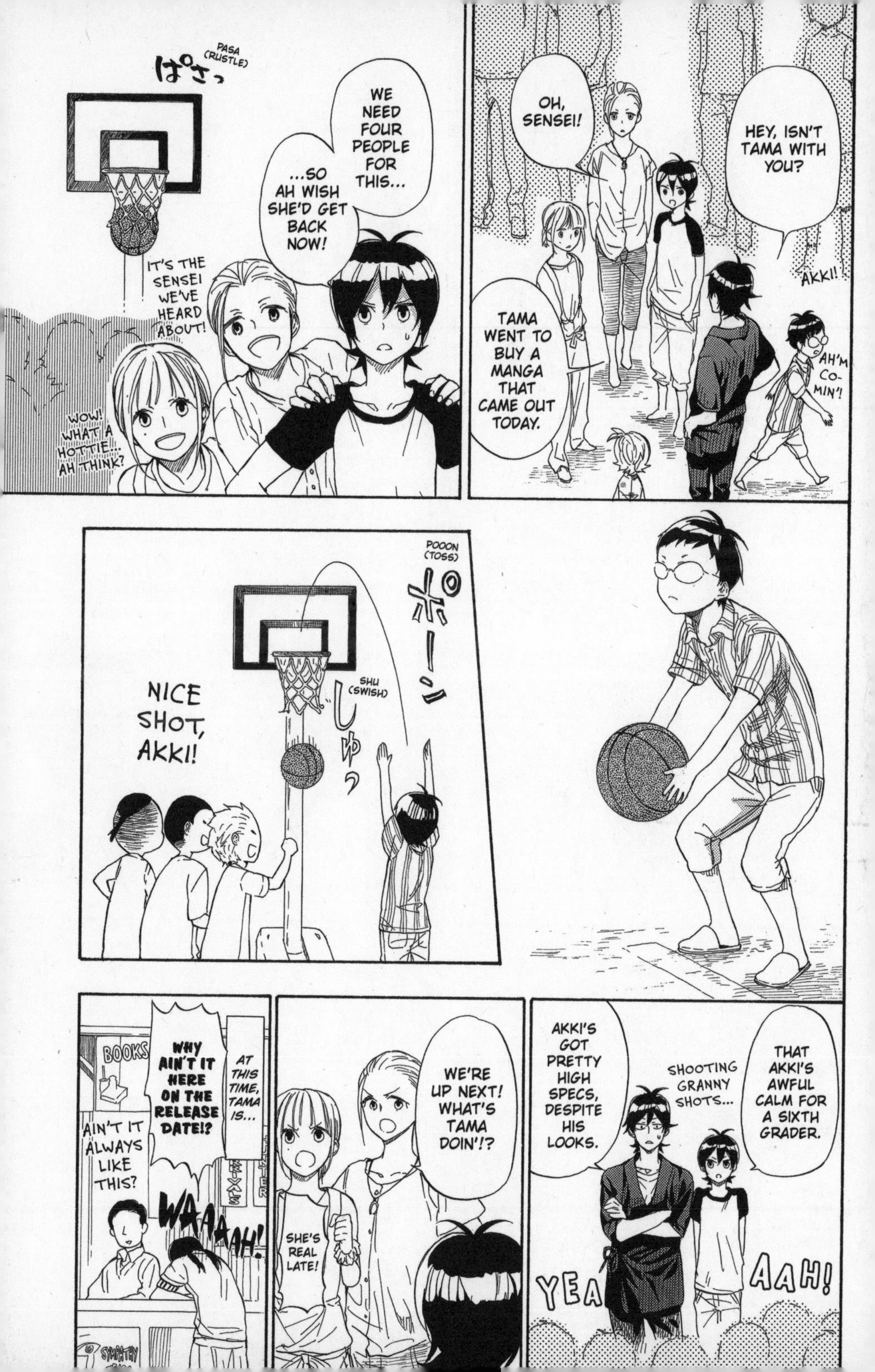

HEY, ISN'T TAMA WITH YOU?
OH, SENSEI!
AKKI!
TAMA WENT TO BUY A MANGA THAT CAME OUT TODAY.
AH'M CO-MIN'!
PASA (RUSTLE)
ぱさっ
WE NEED FOUR PEOPLE FOR THIS...
...SO AH WISH SHE'D GET BACK NOW!
IT'S THE SENSEI WE'VE HEARD ABOUT!
WOW! WHAT A HOTTIE AH THINK?
POOON (TOSS)
ポーン
SHU (SWISH)
しゅっ
NICE SHOT, AKKI!
THAT AKKI'S AWFUL CALM FOR A SIXTH GRADER.
SHOOTING GRANNY SHOTS...
AKKI'S GOT PRETTY HIGH SPECS, DESPITE HIS LOOKS.
YEA AAH!
WE'RE UP NEXT! WHAT'S TAMA DOIN'!?
SHE'S REAL LATE!
AT THIS TIME, TAMA IS...
BOOKS
WHY AIN'T IT HERE ON THE RELEASE DATE!?
AIN'T IT ALWAYS LIKE THIS?
WAAAAH!
SYMPATHY

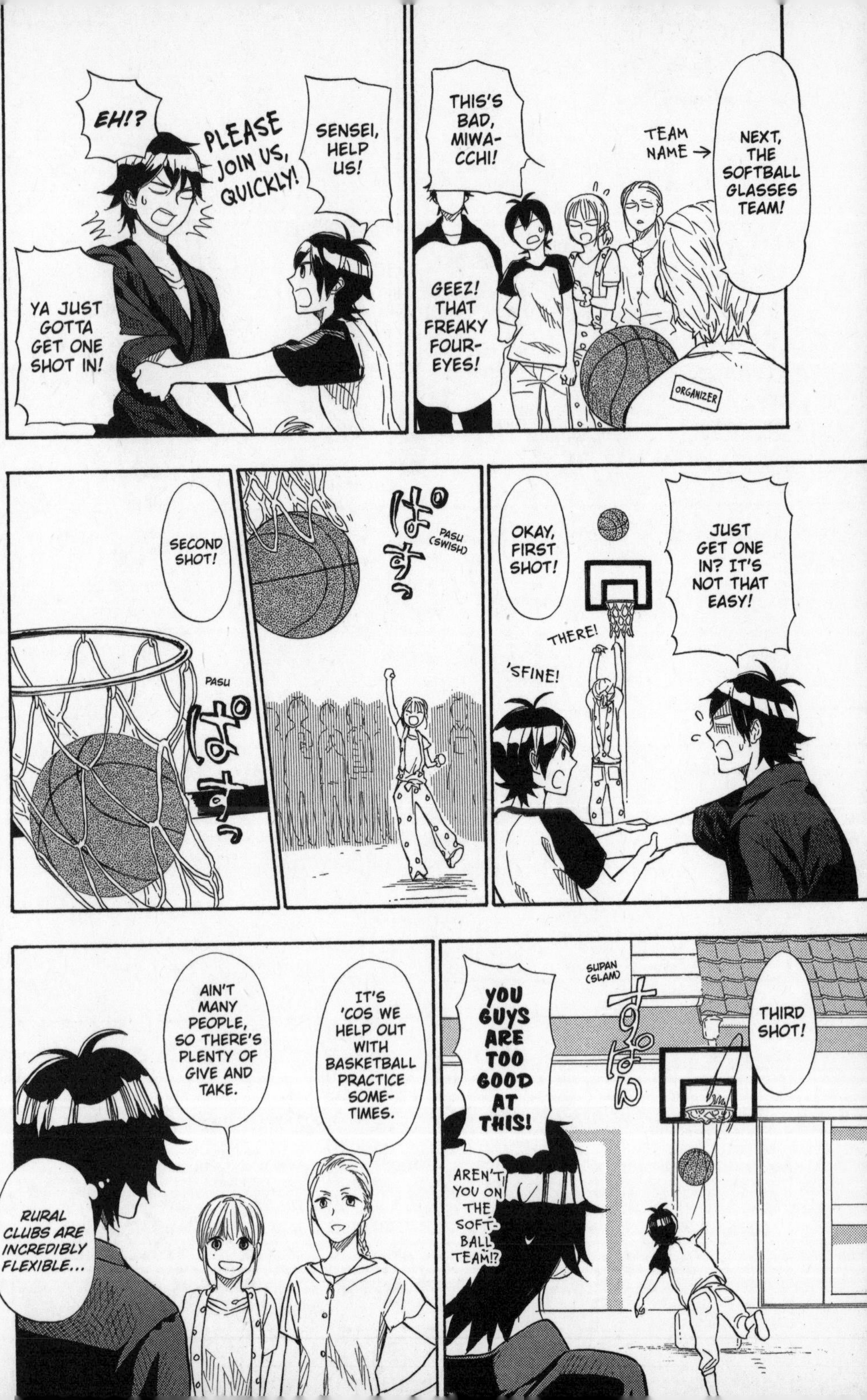
TEAM NAME →
NEXT, THE SOFTBALL GLASSES TEAM!
THIS'S BAD, MIWACCHI!
GEEZ! THAT FREAKY FOUR-EYES!
ORGANIZER
SENSEI, HELP US!
PLEASE JOIN US, QUICKLY!
EH!?
YA JUST GOTTA GET ONE SHOT IN!
JUST GET ONE IN? IT'S NOT THAT EASY!
OKAY, FIRST SHOT!
THERE!
'SFINE!
ぱすっ
PASU (SWISH)
SECOND SHOT!
ぱすっ
PASU
THIRD SHOT!
すぱん
SUPAN (SLAM)
YOU GUYS ARE TOO GOOD AT THIS!
AREN'T YOU ON THE SOFTBALL TEAM!?
IT'S 'COS WE HELP OUT WITH BASKETBALL PRACTICE SOMETIMES.
AIN'T MANY PEOPLE, SO THERE'S PLENTY OF GIVE AND TAKE.
RURAL CLUBS ARE INCREDIBLY FLEXIBLE...

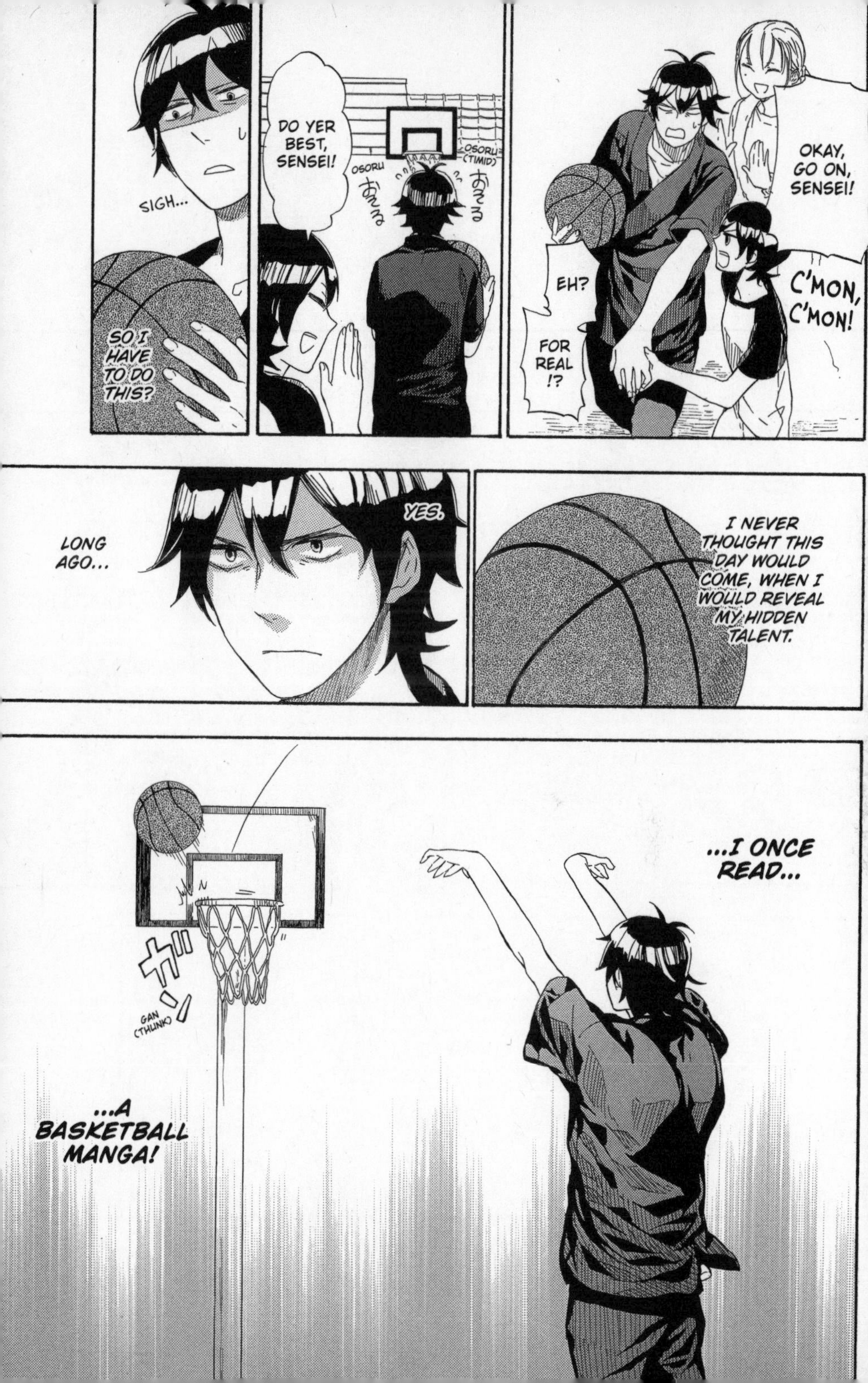

OKAY, GO ON, SENSEI!
C'MON, C'MON!
EH?
FOR REAL!?
DO YER BEST, SENSEI!
OSORU (TIMID)
おそる
OSORU
おそる
SIGH...
SO I HAVE TO DO THIS?
I NEVER THOUGHT THIS DAY WOULD COME, WHEN I WOULD REVEAL MY HIDDEN TALENT.
YES.
LONG AGO...
...I ONCE READ...
GAN (THUNK)
...A BASKETBALL MANGA!

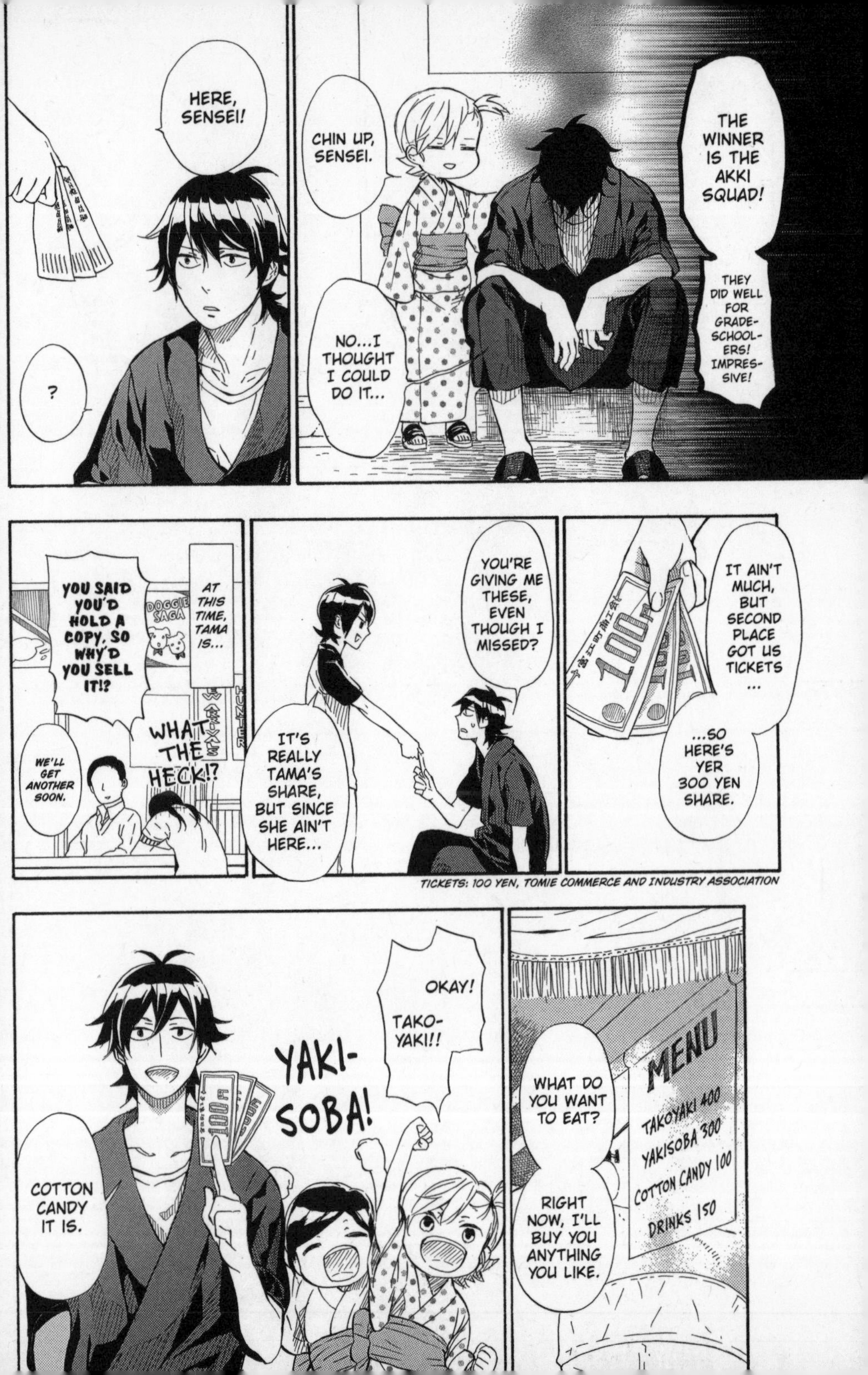
THE WINNER IS THE AKKI SQUAD!
THEY DID WELL FOR GRADE-SCHOOLERS! IMPRESSIVE!
CHIN UP, SENSEI.
NO...I THOUGHT I COULD DO IT...
HERE, SENSEI!
?
IT AIN'T MUCH, BUT SECOND PLACE GOT US TICKETS...
...SO HERE'S YER 300 YEN SHARE.
YOU'RE GIVING ME THESE, EVEN THOUGH I MISSED?
IT'S REALLY TAMA'S SHARE, BUT SINCE SHE AIN'T HERE...
AT THIS TIME, TAMA IS...
DOGGIE SAGA
HUNTER
YOU SAID YOU'D HOLD A COPY, SO WHY'D YOU SELL IT!?
WHAT THE HECK!?
WE'LL GET ANOTHER SOON.
MENU
TAKOYAKI 400
YAKISOBA 300
COTTON CANDY 100
DRINKS 150
WHAT DO YOU WANT TO EAT?
RIGHT NOW, I'LL BUY YOU ANYTHING YOU LIKE.
OKAY!
TAKOYAKI!!
YAKISOBA!
COTTON CANDY IT IS.
TICKETS: 100 YEN, TOMIE COMMERCE AND INDUSTRY ASSOCIATION

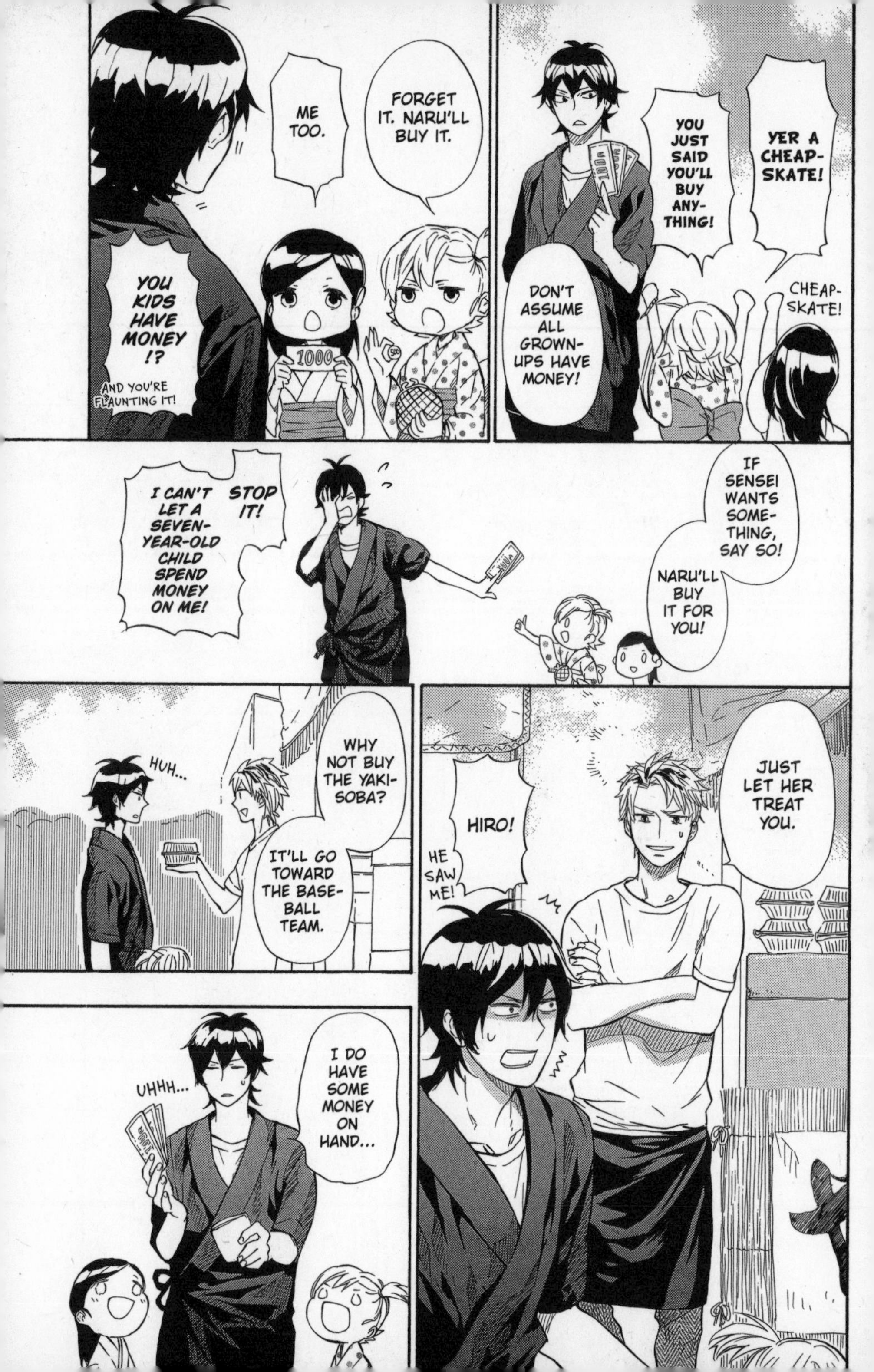
YER A CHEAP-SKATE!
YOU JUST SAID YOU'LL BUY ANY-THING!
CHEAP-SKATE!
DON'T ASSUME ALL GROWN-UPS HAVE MONEY!
FORGET IT. NARU'LL BUY IT.
ME TOO.
1000
YOU KIDS HAVE MONEY !?
AND YOU'RE FLAUNTING IT!
IF SENSEI WANTS SOME-THING, SAY SO!
NARU'LL BUY IT FOR YOU!
STOP IT!
I CAN'T LET A SEVEN-YEAR-OLD CHILD SPEND MONEY ON ME!
JUST LET HER TREAT YOU.
HIRO!
HE SAW ME!
WHY NOT BUY THE YAKI-SOBA?
IT'LL GO TOWARD THE BASE-BALL TEAM.
HUH...
I DO HAVE SOME MONEY ON HAND...
UHHH...

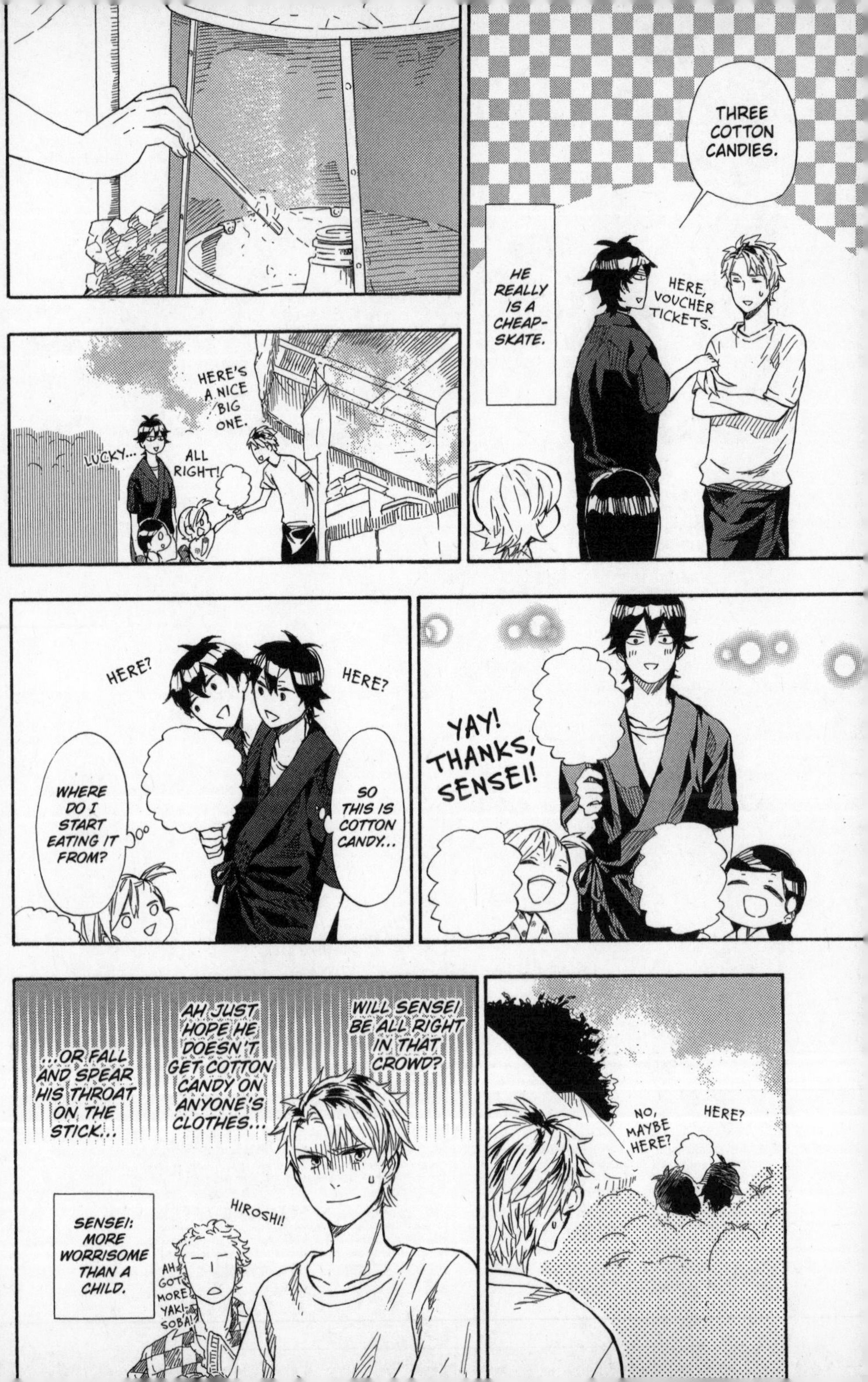
THREE COTTON CANDIES.
HERE, VOUCHER TICKETS.
HE REALLY IS A CHEAPSKATE.
HERE'S A NICE BIG ONE.
ALL RIGHT!
LUCKY...
YAY! THANKS, SENSEI!
HERE?
HERE?
SO THIS IS COTTON CANDY...
WHERE DO I START EATING IT FROM?
HERE?
NO, MAYBE HERE?
WILL SENSEI BE ALL RIGHT IN THAT CROWD?
AH JUST HOPE HE DOESN'T GET COTTON CANDY ON ANYONE'S CLOTHES...
...OR FALL AND SPEAR HIS THROAT ON THE STICK...
HIROSHI!
SENSEI: MORE WORRISOME THAN A CHILD.
AH GOT MORE YAKI-SOBA!

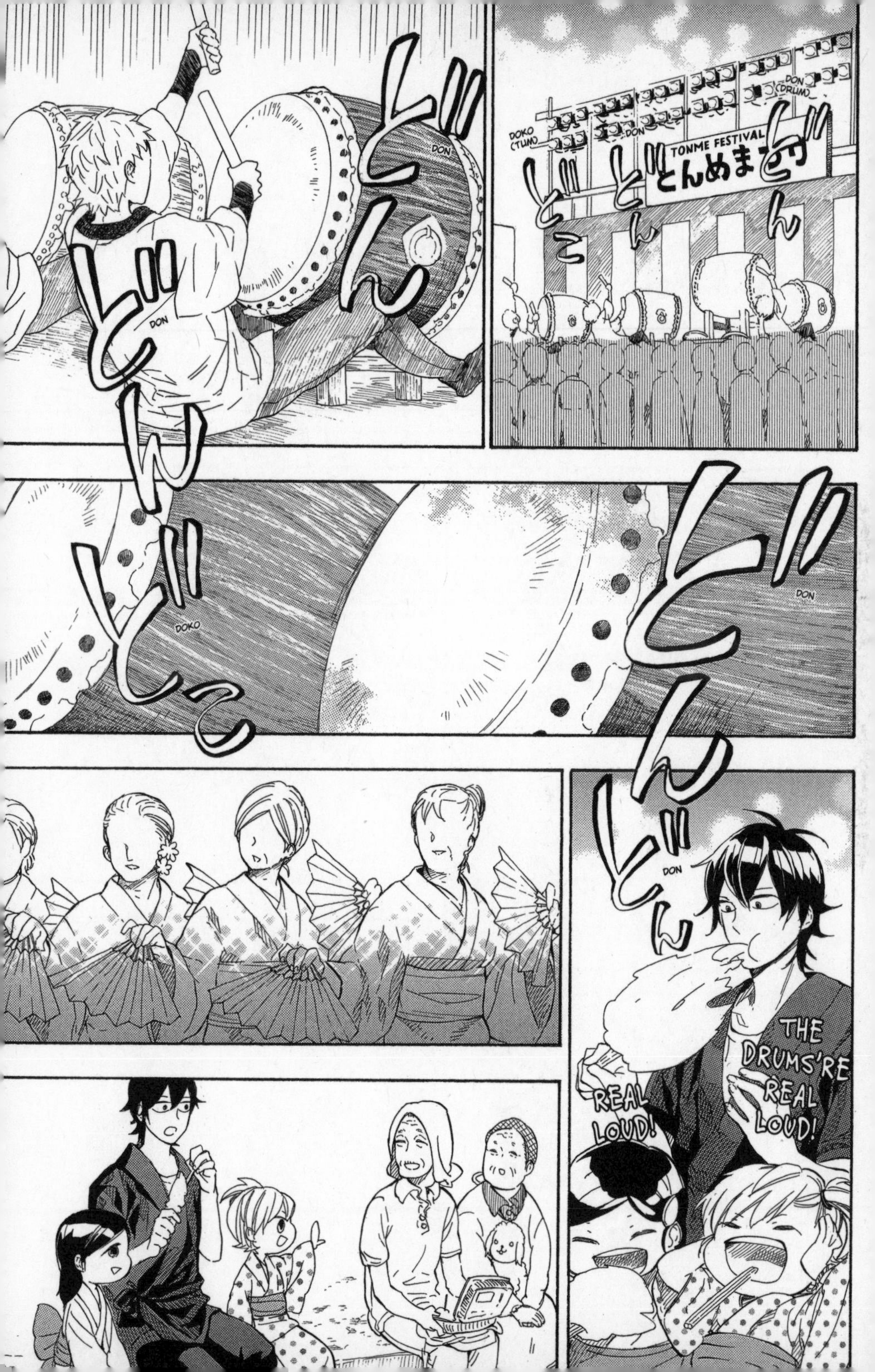
DON (DRUM)
TONME FESTIVAL
とんめまつり
DOKO (TUM)
DON
DON
DON
DON
DOKO
DON
THE DRUMS'RE REAL LOUD!
REAL LOUD!

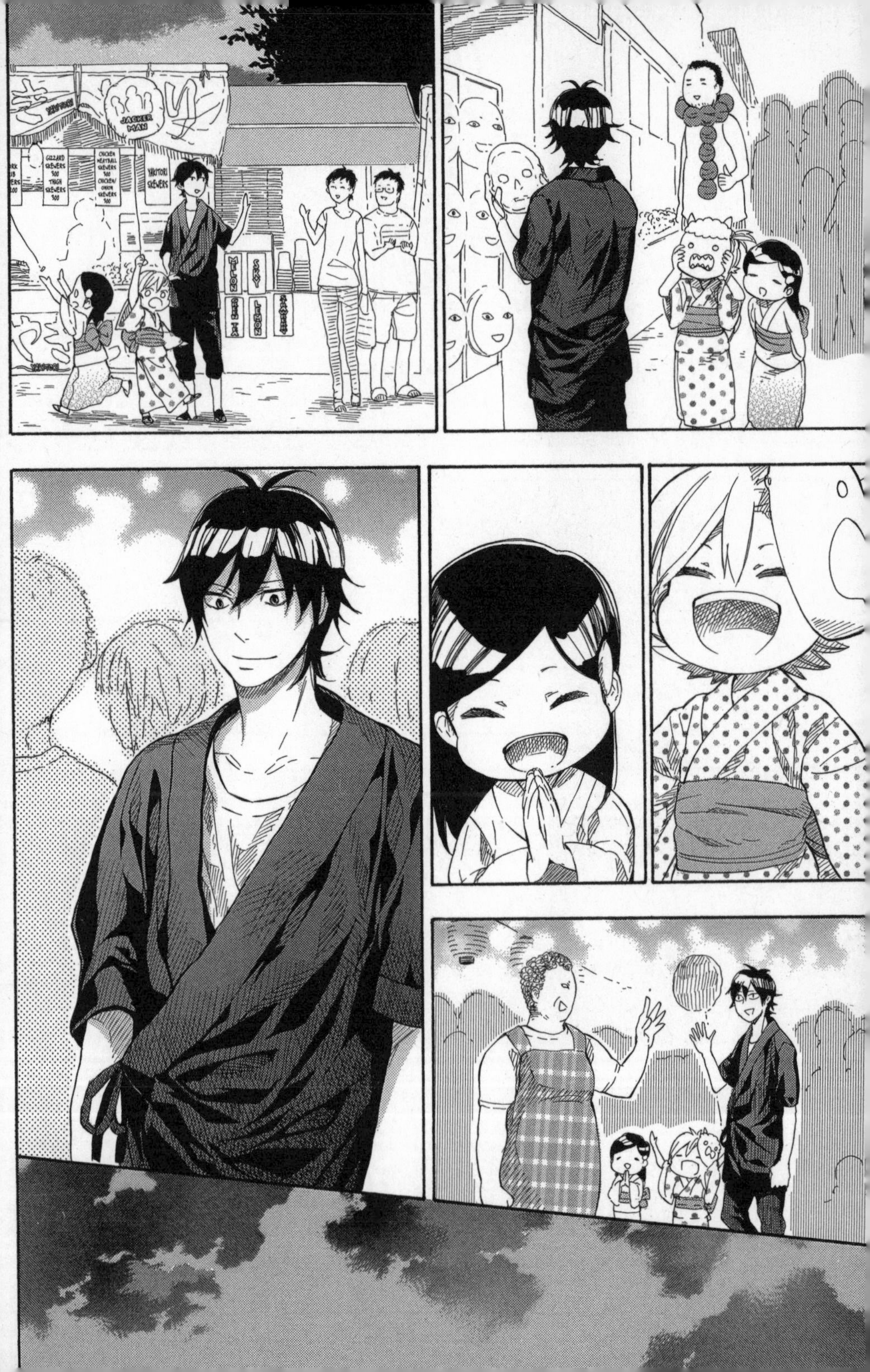
YAKITORI
JACKER MAN
GIZZARD SKEWERS 300 THIGH SKEWERS 300
CHICKEN MEATBALL SKEWERS 300 CHICKEN/ONION SKEWERS 300
YAKITORI SKEWERS
MELON
SKY
LEMON
YAKITORI

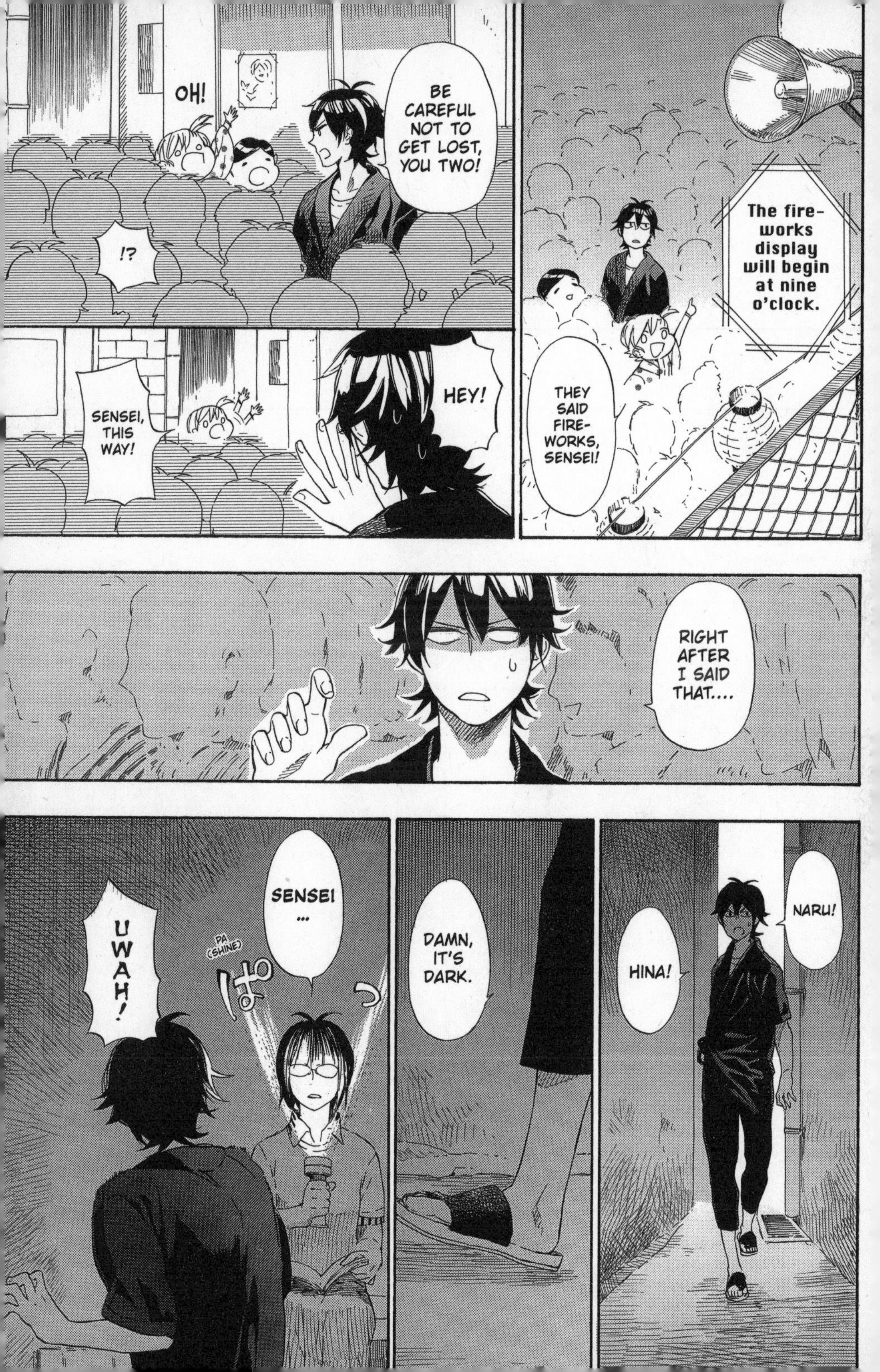
The fire-works display will begin at nine o'clock.
THEY SAID FIRE-WORKS, SENSEI!
BE CAREFUL NOT TO GET LOST, YOU TWO!
OH!
!?
HEY!
SENSEI, THIS WAY!
RIGHT AFTER I SAID THAT....
NARU!
HINA!
DAMN, IT'S DARK.
SENSEI ...
PA (SHINE)
ぱっ
UWAH!

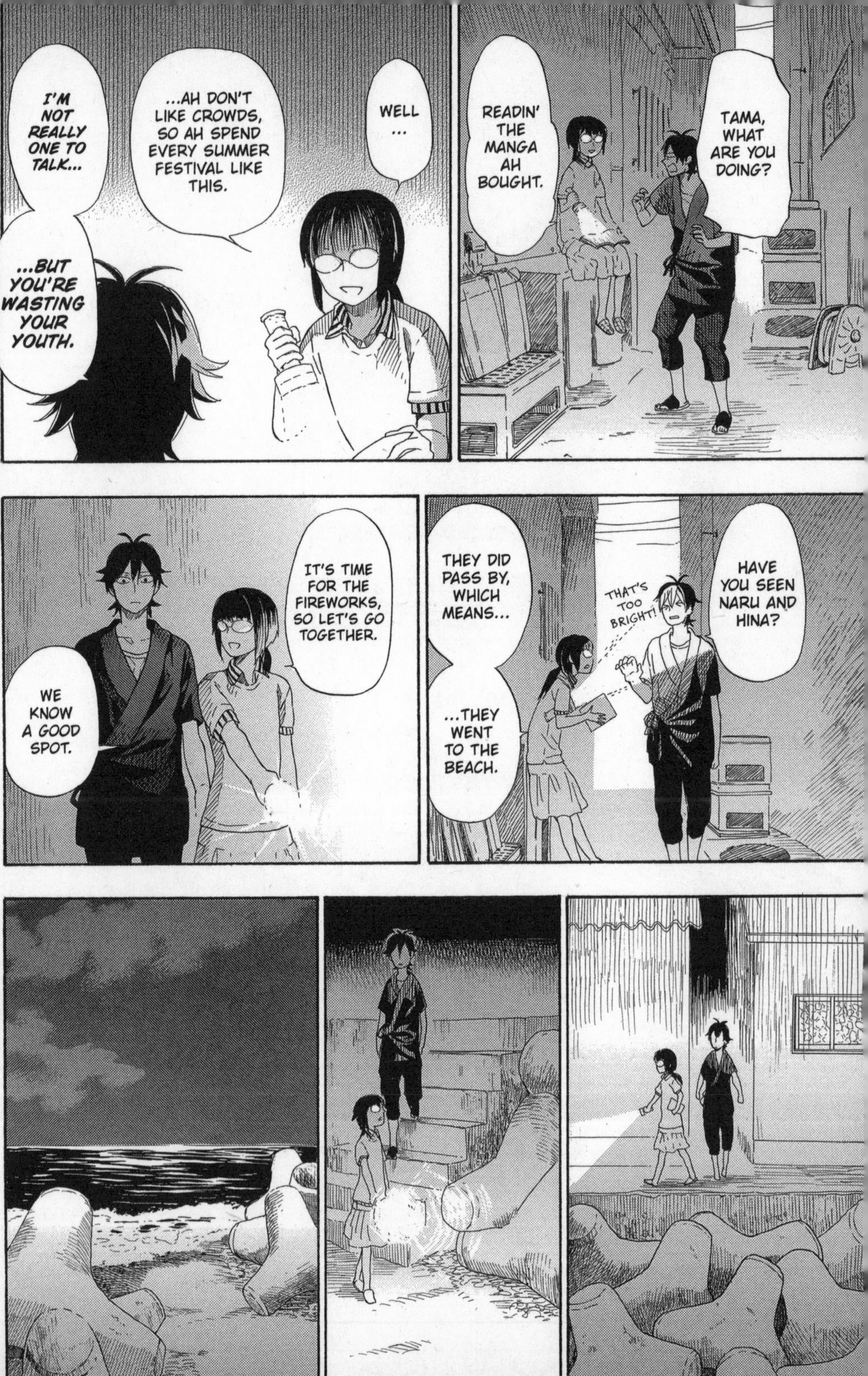
TAMA, WHAT ARE YOU DOING?
READIN' THE MANGA AH BOUGHT.
WELL ...
...AH DON'T LIKE CROWDS, SO AH SPEND EVERY SUMMER FESTIVAL LIKE THIS.
I'M NOT REALLY ONE TO TALK...
...BUT YOU'RE WASTING YOUR YOUTH.
HAVE YOU SEEN NARU AND HINA?
THAT'S TOO BRIGHT!
THEY DID PASS BY, WHICH MEANS...
...THEY WENT TO THE BEACH.
IT'S TIME FOR THE FIREWORKS, SO LET'S GO TOGETHER.
WE KNOW A GOOD SPOT.

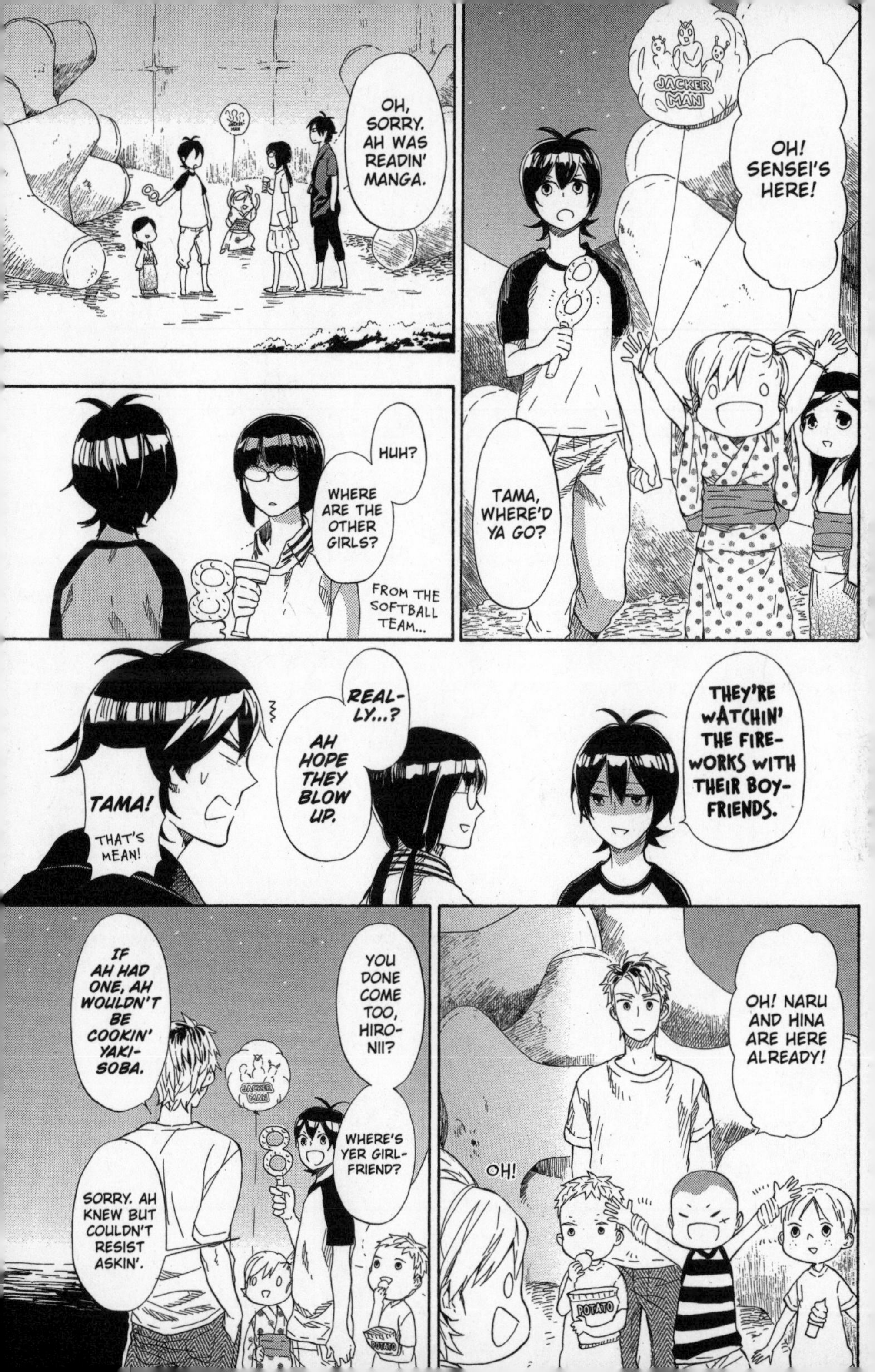
JACKER MAN
OH! SENSEI'S HERE!
TAMA, WHERE'D YA GO?
OH, SORRY. AH WAS READIN' MANGA.
HUH?
WHERE ARE THE OTHER GIRLS?
FROM THE SOFTBALL TEAM...
THEY'RE WATCHIN' THE FIRE-WORKS WITH THEIR BOY-FRIENDS.
REAL-LY...?
AH HOPE THEY BLOW UP.
TAMA!
THAT'S MEAN!
OH! NARU AND HINA ARE HERE ALREADY!
OH!
POTATO
YOU DONE COME TOO, HIRO-NII?
WHERE'S YER GIRL-FRIEND?
IF AH HAD ONE, AH WOULDN'T BE COOKIN' YAKI-SOBA.
JACKER MAN
SORRY. AH KNEW BUT COULDN'T RESIST ASKIN'.
POTATO

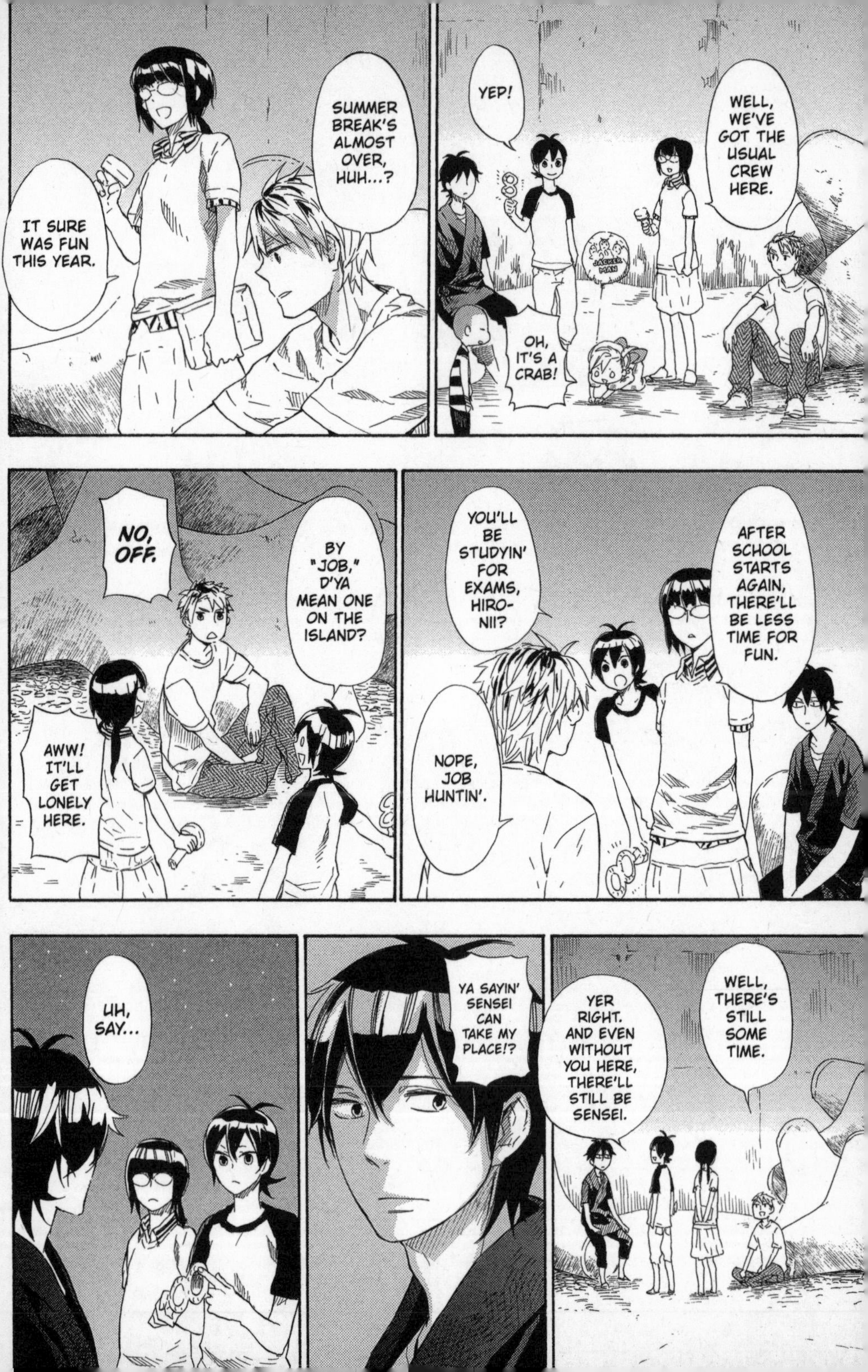
WELL, WE'VE GOT THE USUAL CREW HERE.
YEP!
JACKER MAN
OH, IT'S A CRAB!
SUMMER BREAK'S ALMOST OVER, HUH...?
IT SURE WAS FUN THIS YEAR.
AFTER SCHOOL STARTS AGAIN, THERE'LL BE LESS TIME FOR FUN.
YOU'LL BE STUDYIN' FOR EXAMS, HIRO-NII?
NOPE, JOB HUNTIN'.
BY "JOB," D'YA MEAN ONE ON THE ISLAND?
NO, OFF.
AWW! IT'LL GET LONELY HERE.
WELL, THERE'S STILL SOME TIME.
YER RIGHT. AND EVEN WITHOUT YOU HERE, THERE'LL STILL BE SENSEI.
YA SAYIN' SENSEI CAN TAKE MY PLACE!?
UH, SAY...

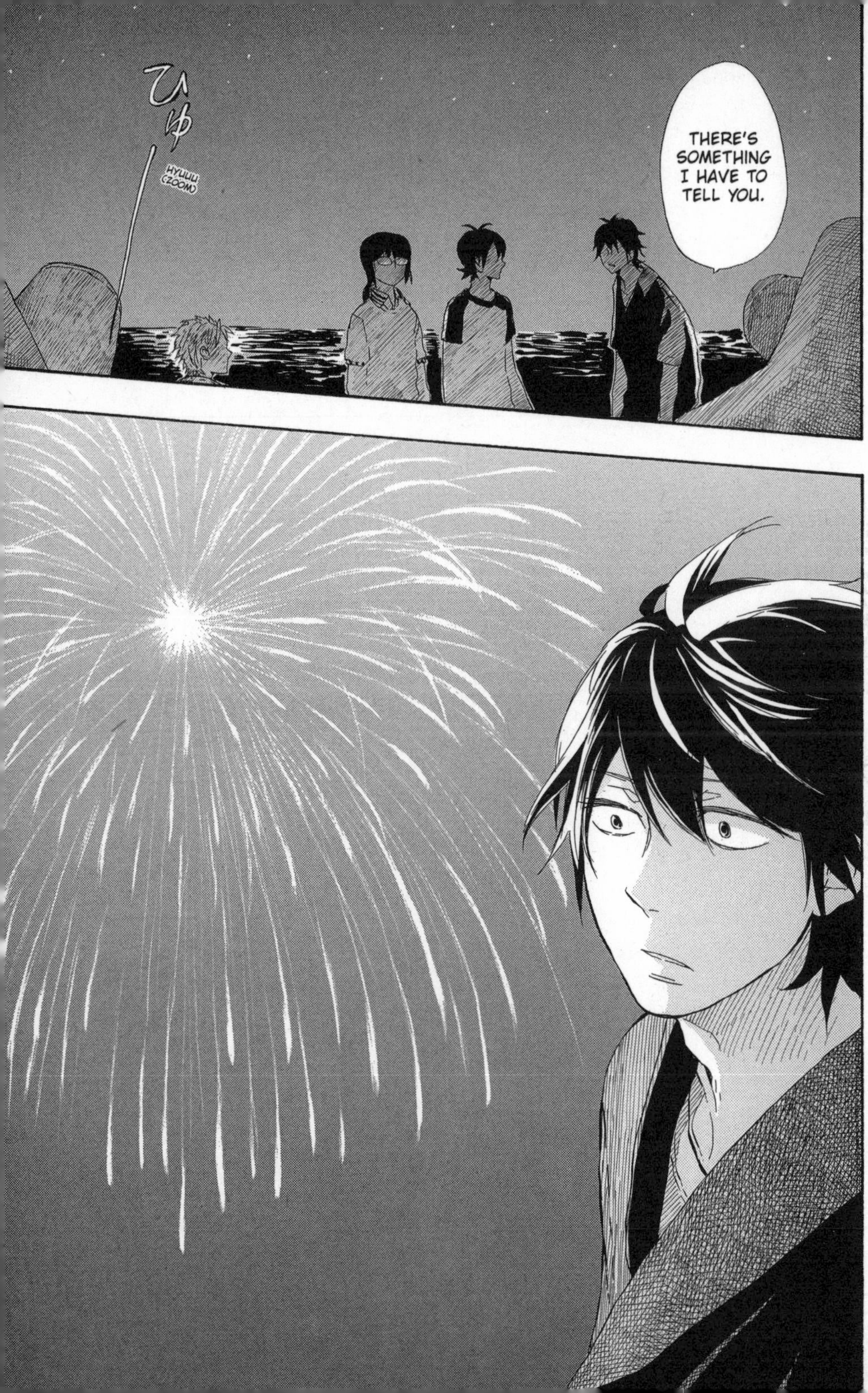
THERE'S SOMETHING I HAVE TO TELL YOU.
ひゅ
HYUUU (ZOOM)

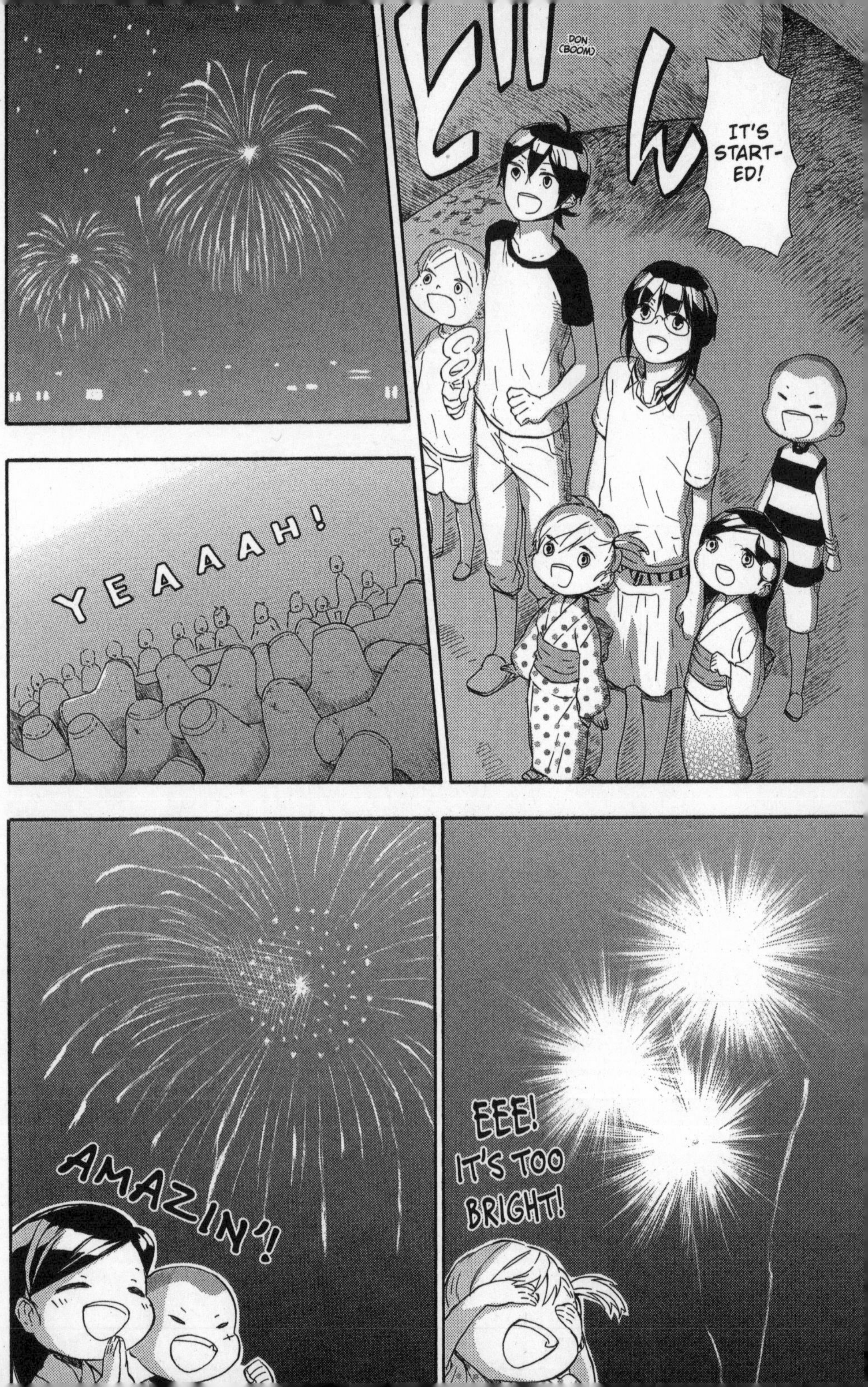
DON (BOOM)
IT'S START-ED!
YEAAAAH!
EEE! IT'S TOO BRIGHT!
AMAZIN'!

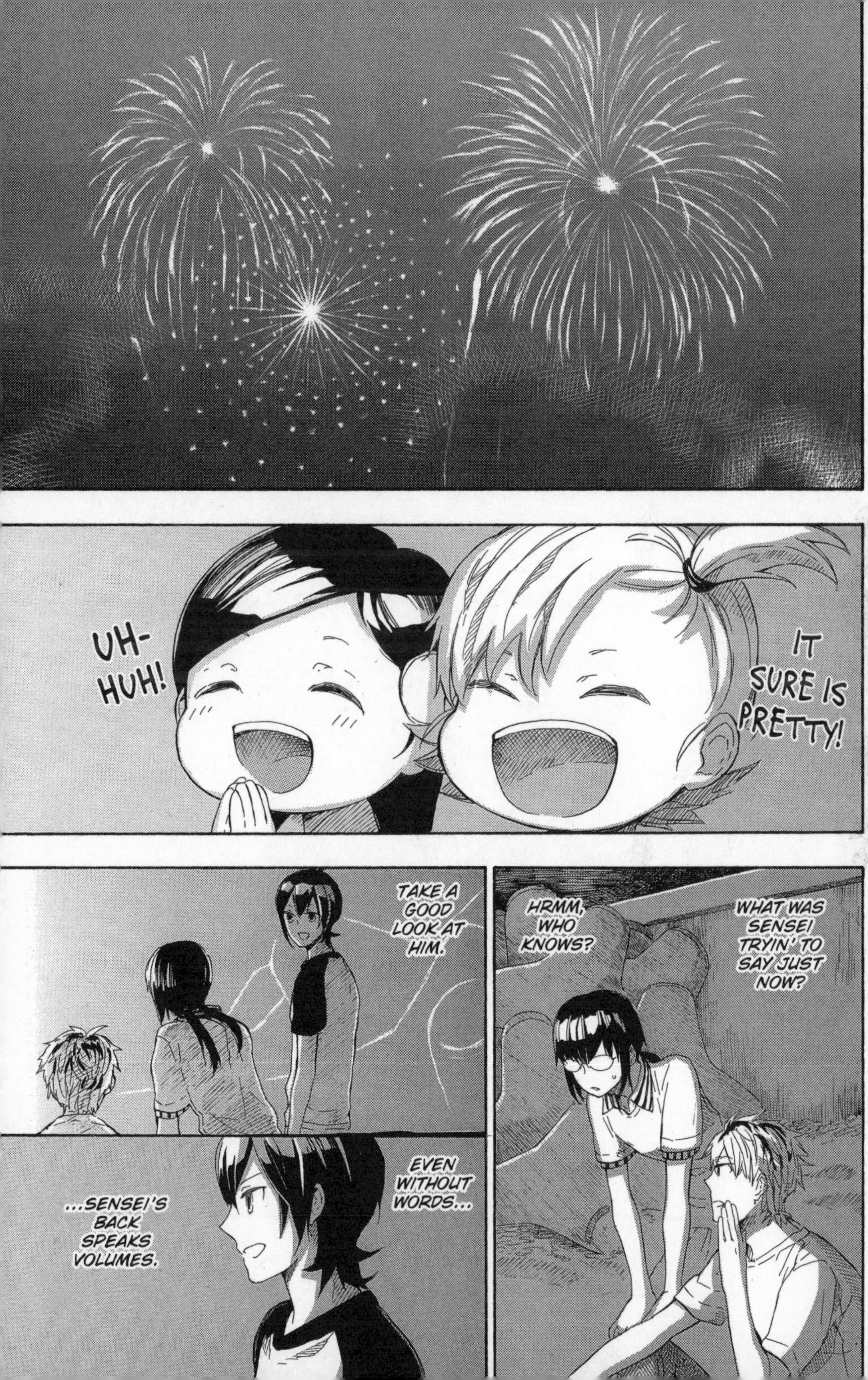
IT SURE IS PRETTY!
UH-HUH!
WHAT WAS SENSEI TRYIN' TO SAY JUST NOW?
HRMM, WHO KNOWS?
TAKE A GOOD LOOK AT HIM.
EVEN WITHOUT WORDS...
...SENSEI'S BACK SPEAKS VOLUMES.

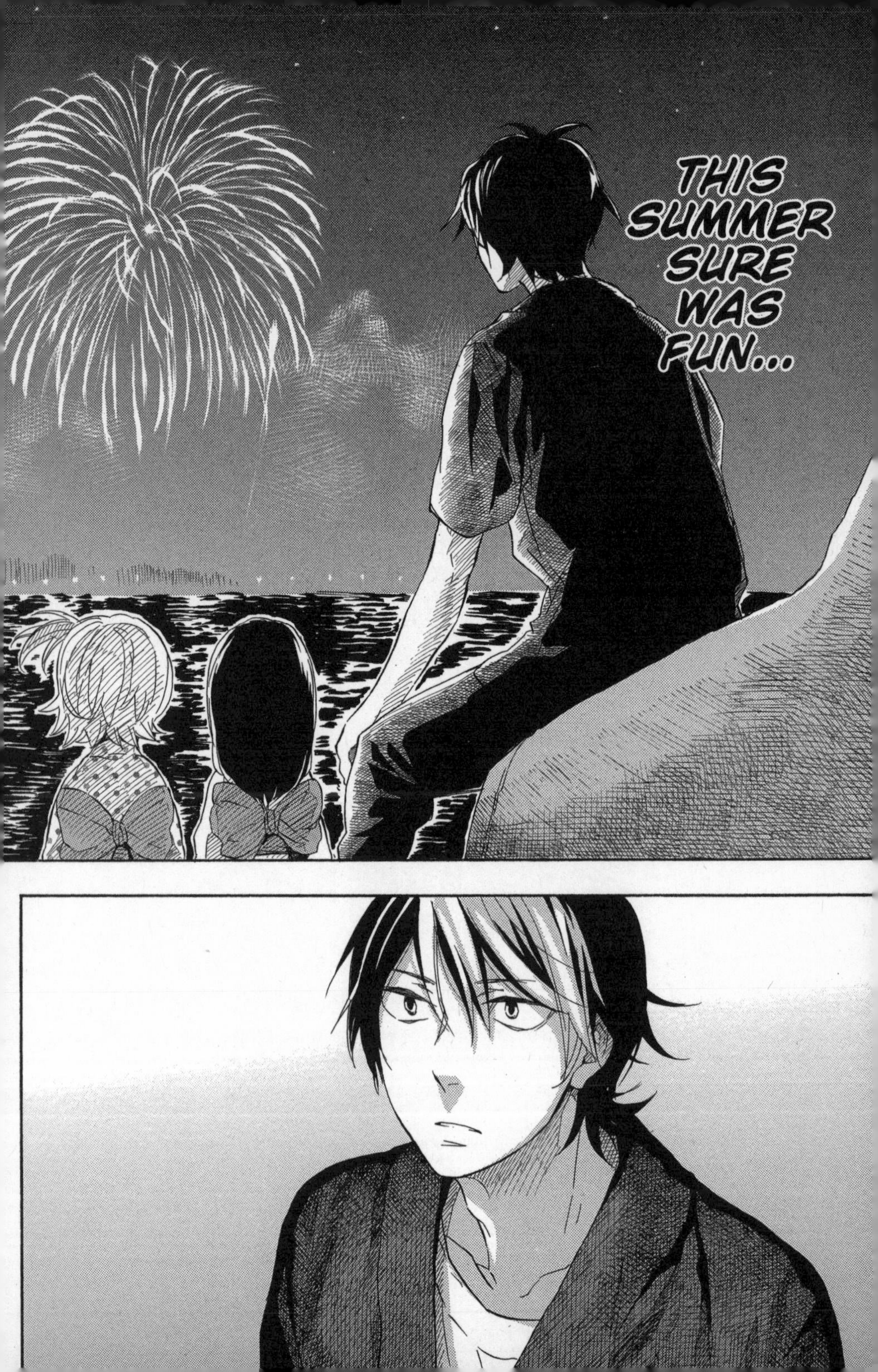
THIS SUMMER SURE WAS FUN...

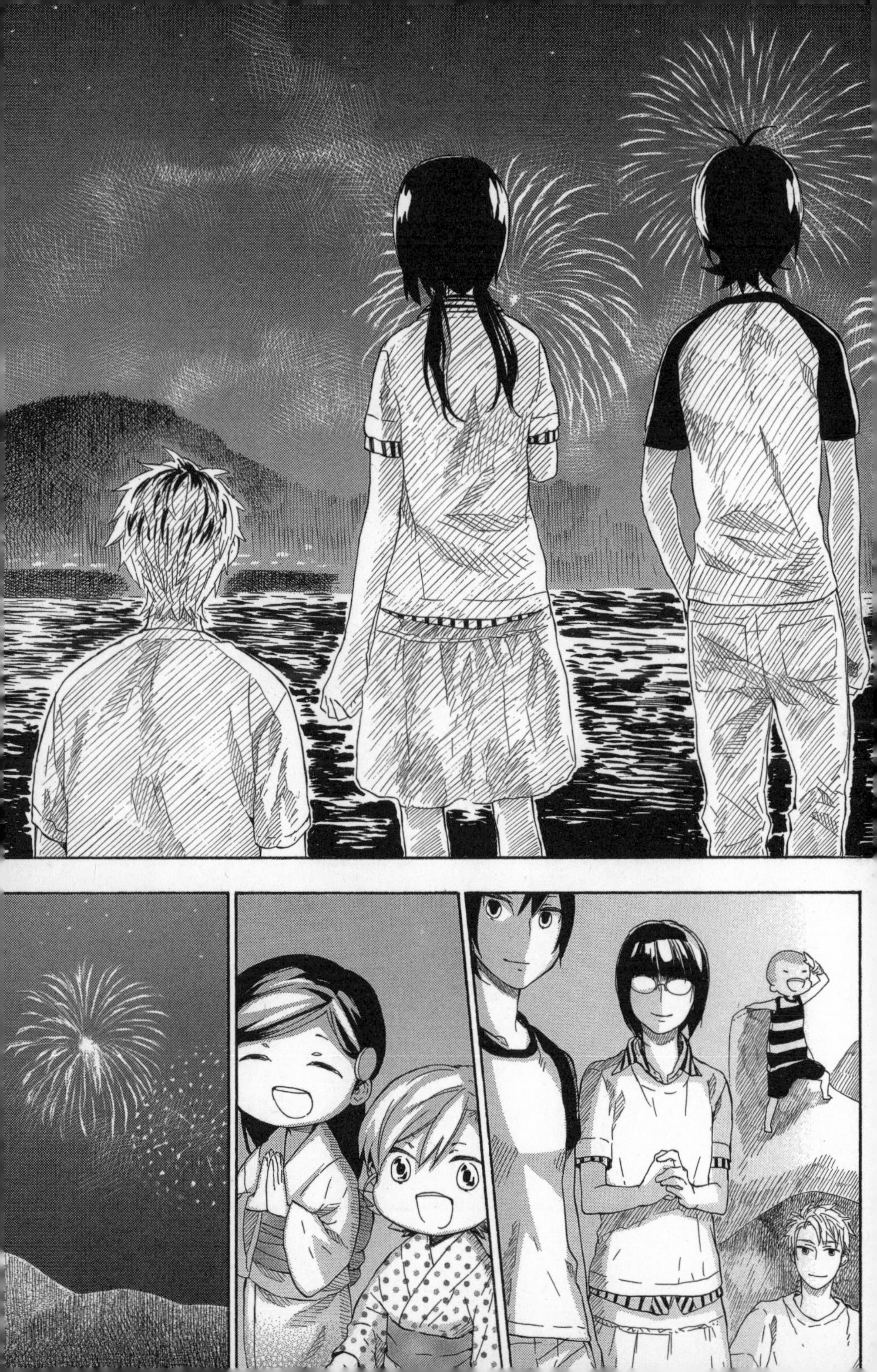

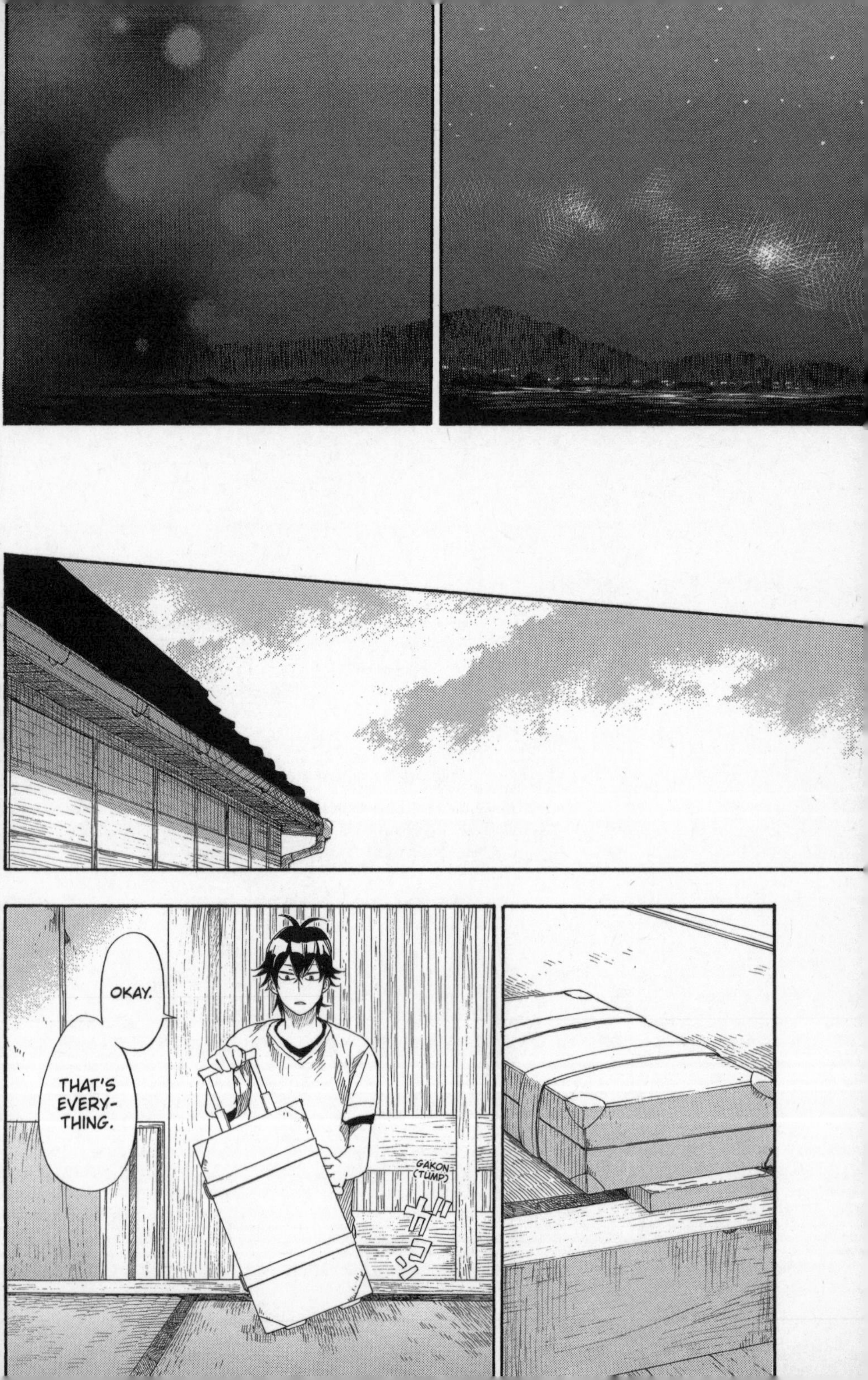
OKAY.
THAT'S EVERY-THING.
GAKON (TUMP)

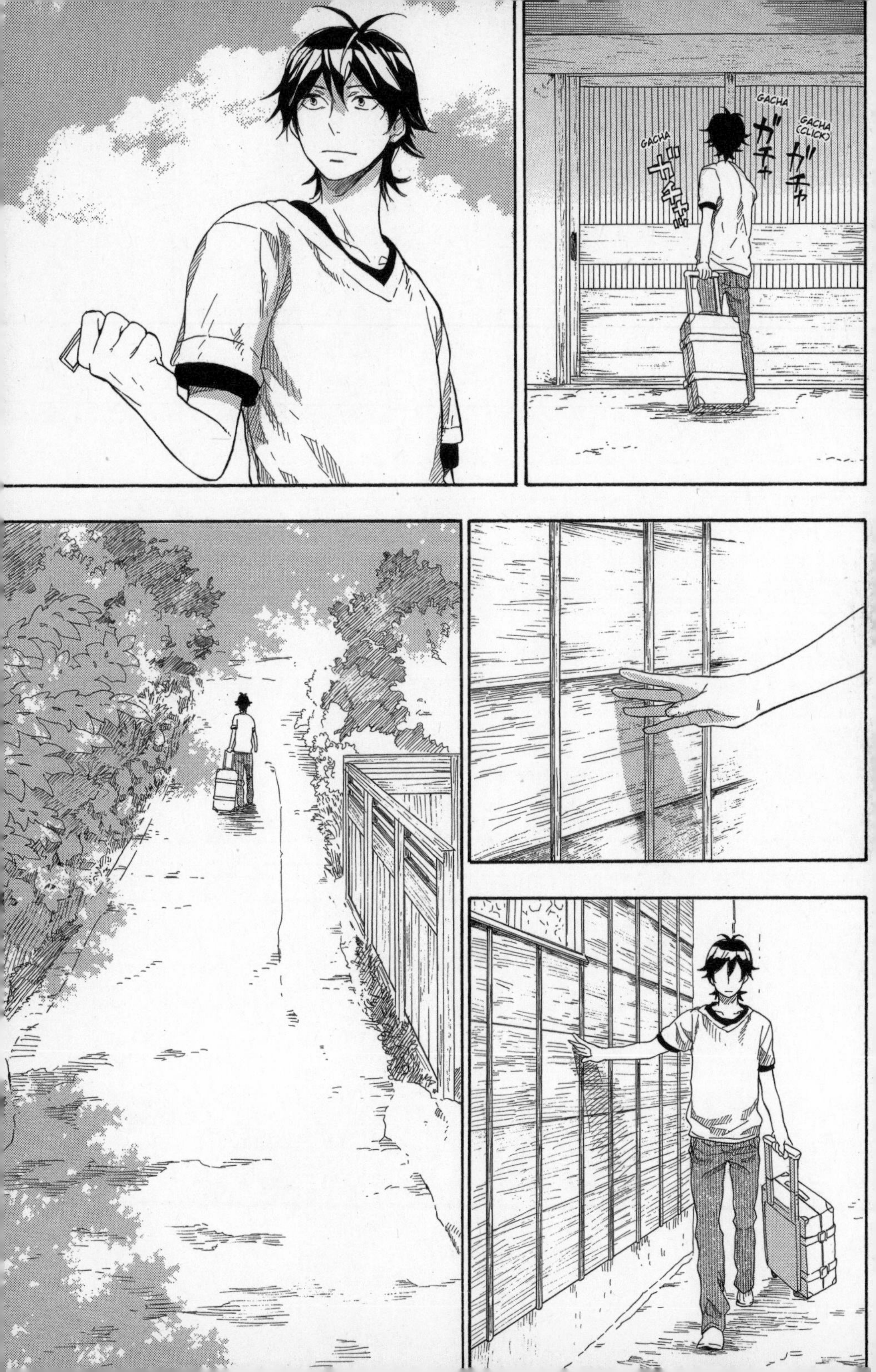
GACHA (CLICK)
ガチャ
GACHA
ガチャ
GACHA

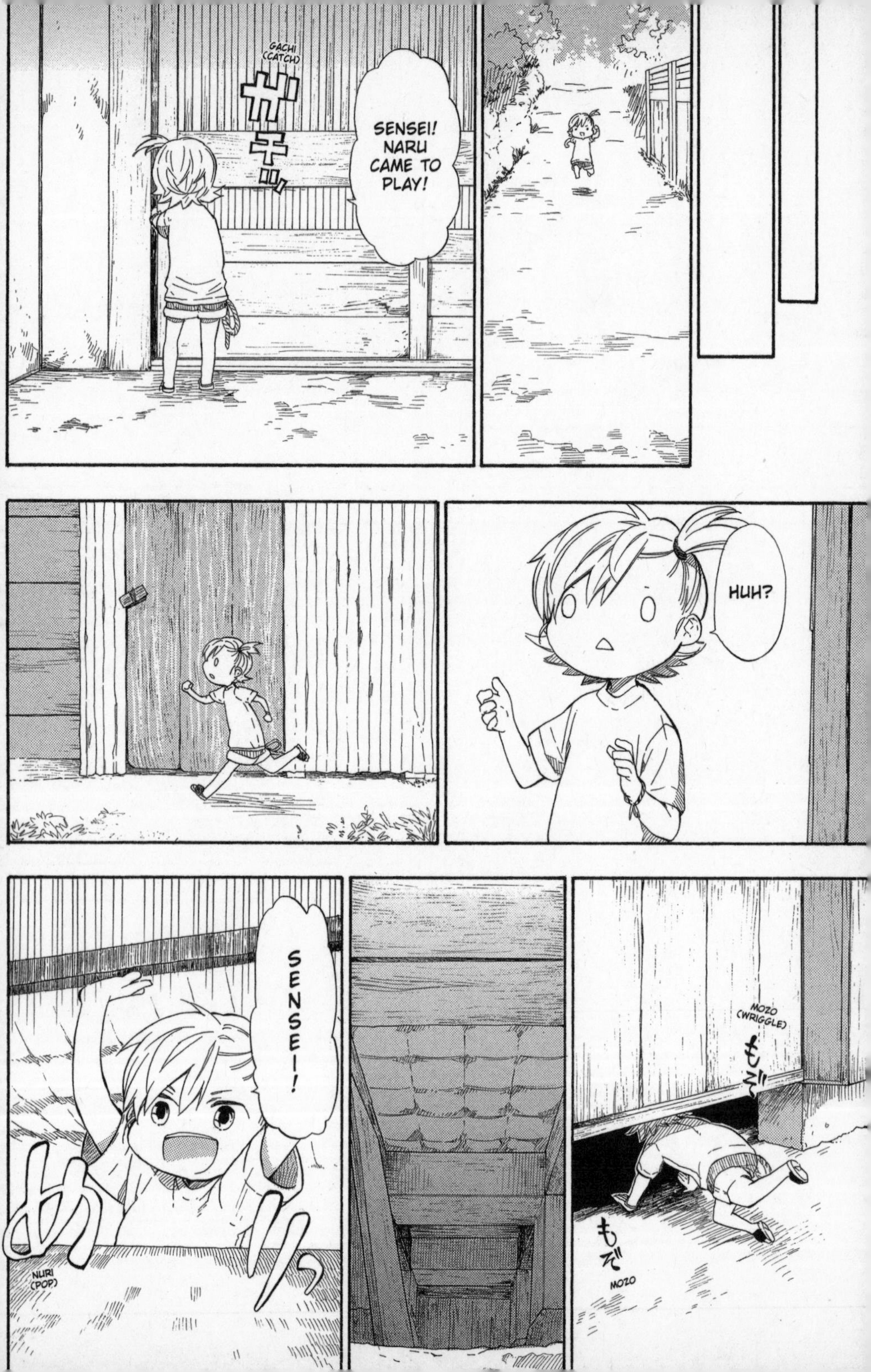
SENSEI! NARU CAME TO PLAY!
GACHI (CATCH)
HUH?
MOZO (WRIGGLE)
もぞ
もぞ
MOZO
SENSEI!
NURI (POP)

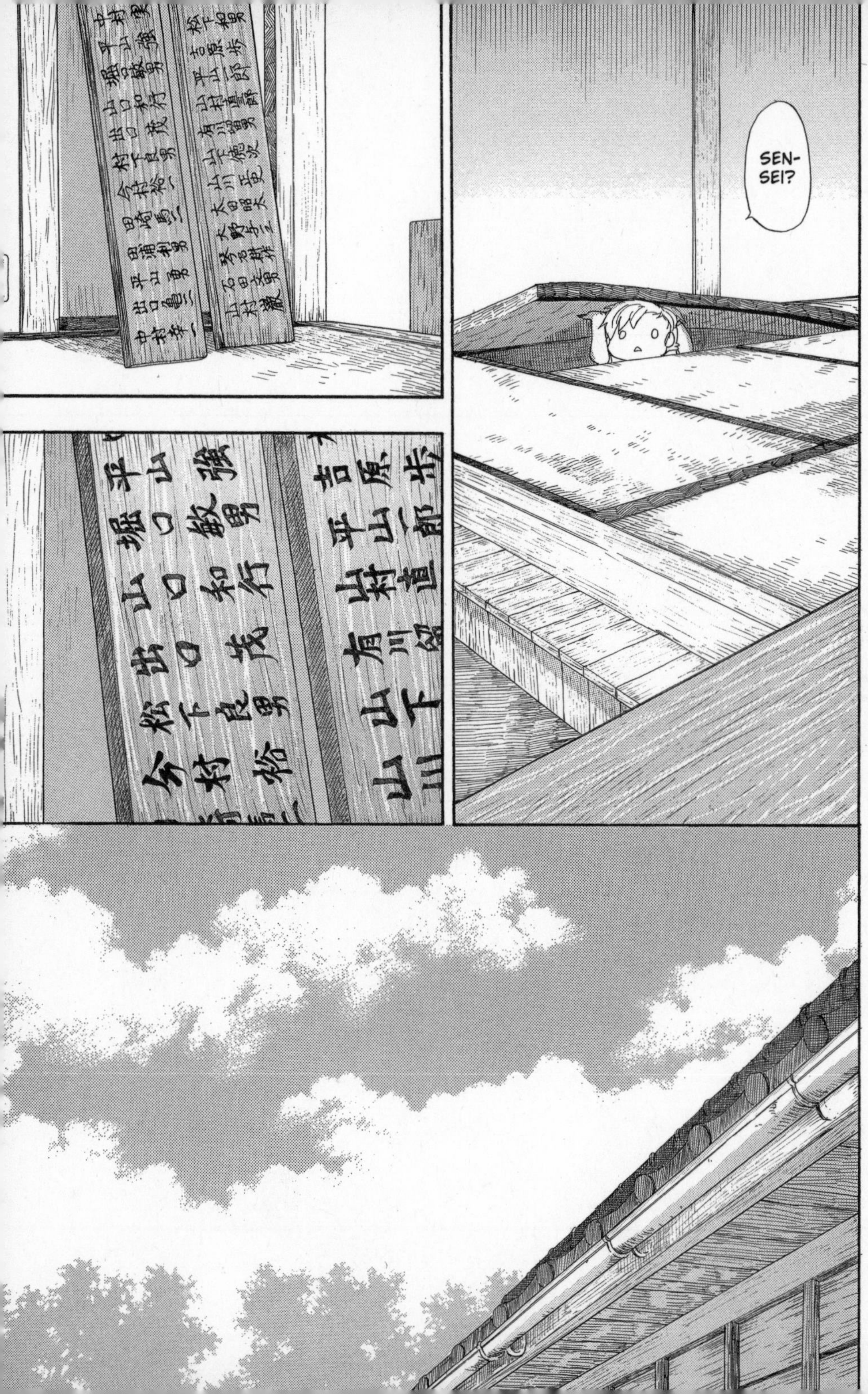
SEN-SEI?

BONUS: DANPO THE 5TH

(Translation: Pond)

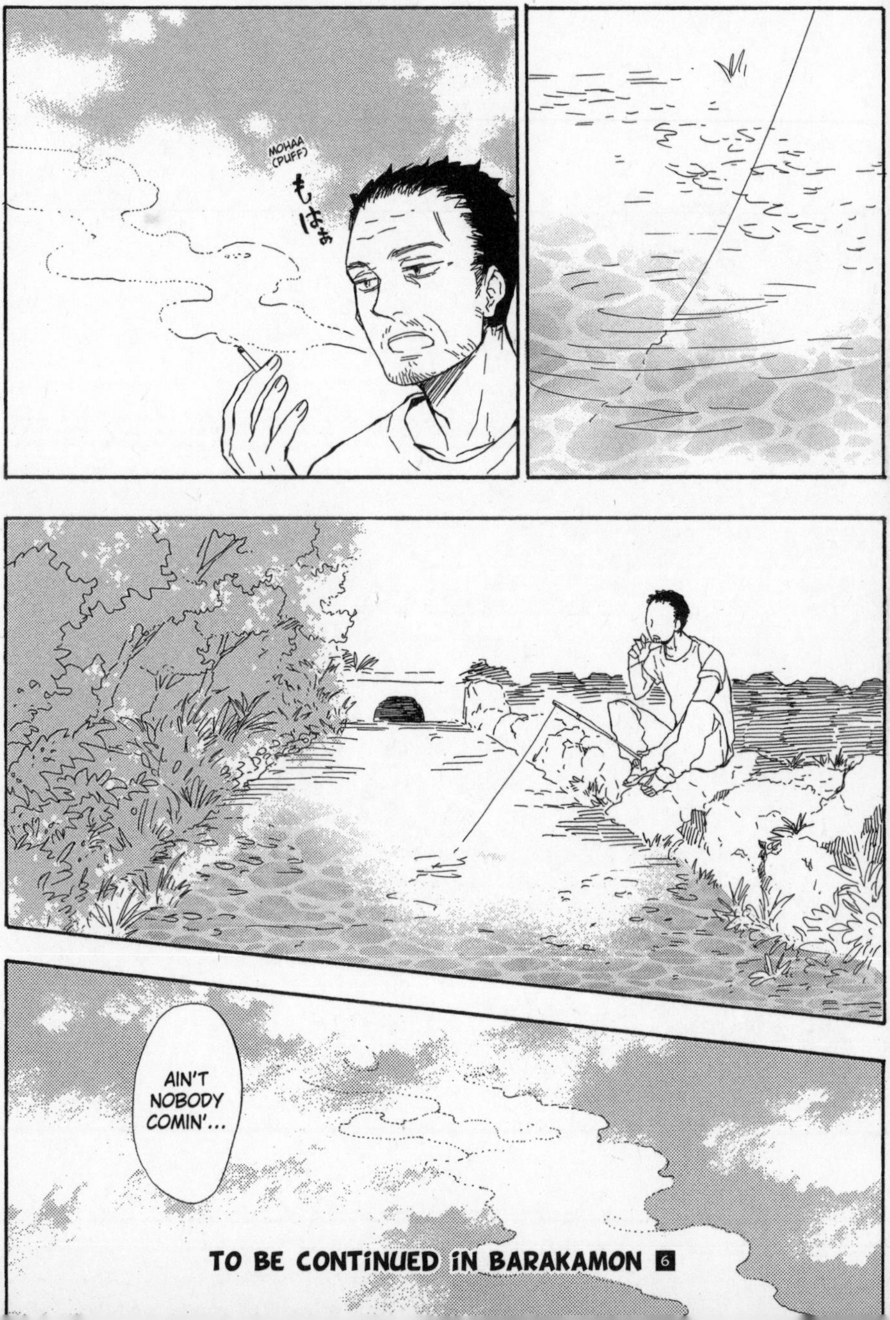
MOHAA (PUFF)
もはぁ
AIN'T NOBODY COMIN'...
TO BE CONTINUED IN BARAKAMON 6

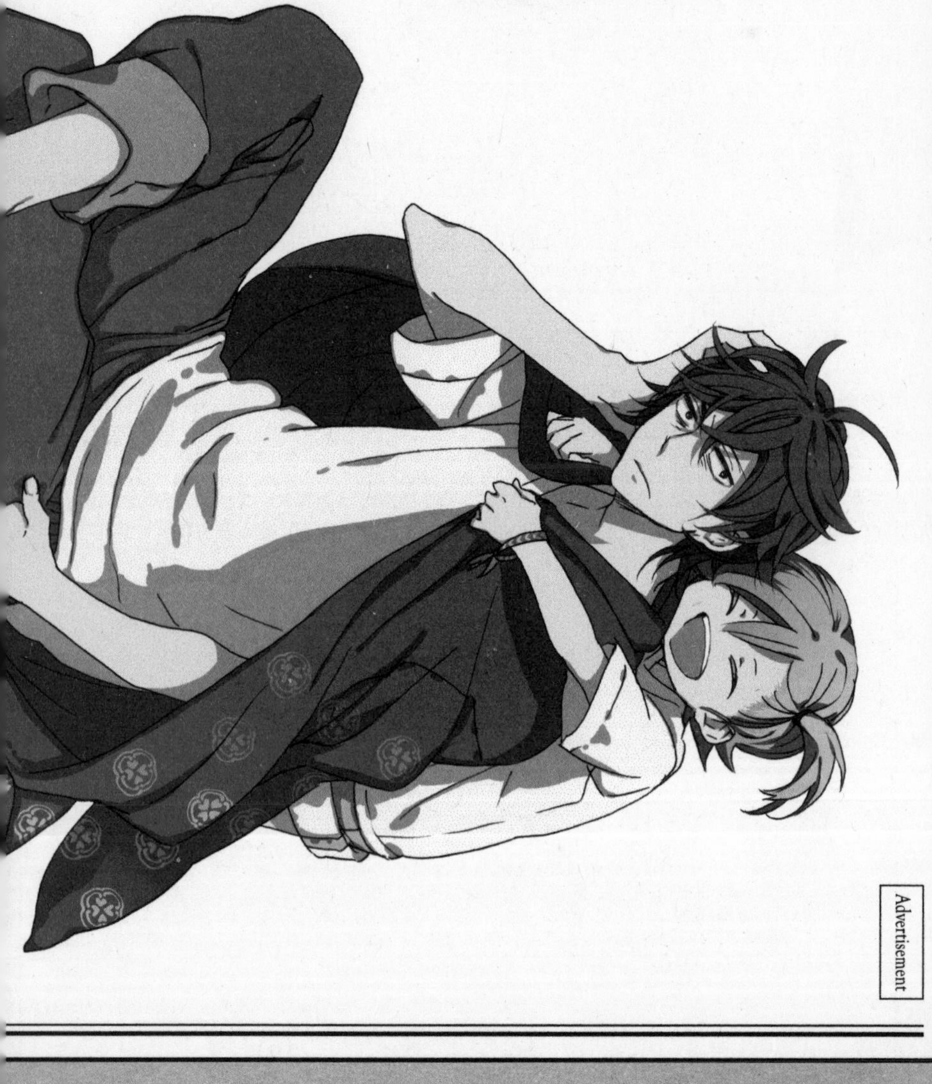
When
here, it's
annoying.
When away,
something's
missing.
Advertisement

Over One Million Sold!

BARAKAMON

Satsuki Yoshino

Volume 6

On sale August 2015!

Thank you very much for buying Volume 5 of *Barakamon*. I sincerely hope to see you all again in the next volume.

COMMON HONORIFICS

no honorific: Indicates familiarity or closeness; if used without permission or reason, addressing someone in this manner would constitute an insult.

-san: The Japanese equivalent of Mr./Mrs./Miss. If a situation calls for politeness, this is the fail-safe honorific.

-sama: Conveys great respect; may also indicate that the social status of the speaker is lower than that of the addressee.

-kun: Used most often when referring to boys, this indicates affection or familiarity. Occasionally used by older men among their peers, but it may also be used by anyone referring to a person of lower standing.

-chan: An affectionate honorific indicating familiarity used mostly in reference to girls; also used in reference to cute persons or animals of either gender.

-sensei: A Japanese term of respect commonly used for teachers, but can also refer to doctors, writers, and artists. Hence, Village Chief is not implying that Handa is a teacher when he calls him "sensei."

Calligraphy: Japanese calligraphy has a long history and tradition, with roots stemming from ancient China. One of the traditions carried over was the Chinese expression of the "Four Treasures," which refers to the brush, ink, paper, and inkstone used in calligraphy. Traditionally, an inkstick — solidified ink — is ground against an inkstone filled with water in order to produce ink with which to write. This time-consuming process helped to teach patience, which is important in the art of calligraphy. However, modern advances have developed a bottled liquid ink, commonly used by beginners and within the Japanese school system.

Gotou Dialect: Many of the villagers, especially the elderly ones, are actually speaking the local Gotou dialect in the original Japanese. This dialect is reflected in the English translation with some of the grammar elements of older Southern American English to give it a more rustic, rural coastal feel without making it too hard to read (it's not meant to replicate any particular American accent exactly). This approach is similar to how dialect is made accessible in Japanese media, including *Barakamon*, because a complete dialect with all of its different vocabulary would be practically incomprehensible to most Tokyo residents.

PAGE 5
burr-bugs, tontsuko: Tontsuko is likely a dialect word for "burrs." The tricky thing is that Hina uses the standard Japanese term for this category of seed pods, *kuttsukimushi*, which includes the word for "bug" even though they're plants.

PAGE 7
Kombu: Befitting her often savory and old-fashioned tastes, Naru is carrying around candy made from *kombu* kelp, which is a real snack in Japan.

PAGE 11
braided updo: The original Japanese term is *amikomi*, which Naru mishears as "amekome," hence her saying "braid up-two."

PAGE 13
ameme: Seems to be the variety of flower, possibly the dialect word for them; it might be a type of bug instead. In any case, the word appears to make Naru think she's found what she needs for Hina's "amekome."

PAGE 34
no full nudity: It's illegal to show adult genitalia uncensored in any media in Japan; this includes not just drawn illustrations, but actual live-action pornography.

PAGE 35
"He's a lobster!": The original had "He's Goemon Ishikawa," a reference to a robber who was boiled to death in his bath.

PAGE 38
amanatsu: A light-orange grapefruit-sized sweet citrus fruit native to Japan.

PAGE 60
croakers: In Japanese, Naru uses the word *donku*, which is Gotou dialect for "frog." You may recognize this from *Barakamon* Act.3 "Donkudon."

PAGE 67
Life's Ups & Downs: Handa's keychain says a proverb which literally means "Fall Seven Times, Get Up Eight Times." Rather fitting in this situation...

PAGE 75
Miwa's T-shirt: *Mijoka*, a Gotou specialty mentioned in the notes for Volume 3, is a small castella wheat cake with a fruit paste filling. The name literally means "pretty woman cake."

PAGE 77
ohagi: A Japanese sweet made by coating balls of sweet rice with sweet bean jam. They can look a bit like mud balls.

PAGE 93
dyed blond hair: A stereotypical look for delinquents in Japan, hence why the three bad boys seem tense when commenting on Hiroshi's hair.

PAGE 94
snot-nosed punk: The original term Hiroshi used for the kid was a dialect word for bad kid, "innowasso."

PAGE 95
white noodles: The Japanese term was *shiro soumen*, a very thin type of white wheat noodle.

PAGE 108
wasshoi!: Exclamation made by the ones hefting a portable shrine in a festival parade — all hail Akki!

PAGE 112
"like the Heian era": The Heian era of Japan was roughly a thousand years ago, from 794–1185, and is considered the peak of the imperial court. He could be referring either to the twelve-layer robe that court ladies of the time wore, or to the mostly-opaque screens and blinds that noblewomen would sit behind when in audience with men.

PAGE 119
Ichirou and Jirou: Literally meaning "First Son" and "Second Son," these are about as generic as you can get with Japanese boys' names.

PAGE 124
ultimate weapon: The Japanese saying Handa used is "oni ni kanebou" (metal rod for a demon), which is amusingly close to literal for a metal ladder.

PAGE 127
Hercules beetle: The largest of the rhinoceros beetle family. Native to Central and South America, it's definitely not a local bug. Incidentally, twenty thousand yen is roughly two hundred dollars, depending on the current exchange rate. That's a lot for a bug, but not unusual for an exotic pet!

PAGE 132
Hurkules: In Japanese, Kenta miswrote the "re" in *herakuresu* as "wa," which is an easy mistake for a beginner to make.

PAGE 136
Naru's turning 7!: The original Japanese, "Naru ga nanasai ni naru," was also a pun on Naru's name being the same as the verb for "to become."

PAGE 138
cracker: The crackers here, also called "party poppers," are cone-shaped party favors. You pull the end of the cone to make it pop out confetti.

chicken gizzards (*suna/sunagimo*), chicken thigh meat (*momo*), and pork riblets (*bara*).

PAGE 150
Villagers' names on donation boards:
Board 1
(right to left) Youichirou Yamaguchi, Tomoichi Satou, A Satou, Hiromi Yamaguchi, Tomeo Nozaki, Touichirou Yamamura, Kazuo Matsushita, Ayumu Yoshihara, Ichirou Yoshihara, Naosaburou Nishimura, Youichi Arikawa, Tokuji Yamashita, Shouji Yamakawa, Akio Ohta, Torao Kido, Nobuo Nakajima, Yoshio Furui, Yozou Ohno, Kousaku Kotoishi, Fumio Ishida, Iwao Yamamura
Board 2
(right to left) Norio Yamada, Bunji Kido, Yuuichirou Kido, Satoru Arai, Juurou Matsuyama, Issei Hayashida, Tarou Hirayama, Jun'ichirou Miura, Minoru Nakamura, Tsuyoshi Hirayama, Toshio Horiguchi, Kazuyuki Yamaguchi, Shigeru Deguchi, Yoshio Matsushita, Yuu Imamura, Baji Tasaki, Toshio Taura, Isamu Hirayama, Kameji Ideta, Kouichi Nakamura

Village Register: (left to right) Youichi Arikawa, Naosaburou Nishimura, Ichirou Yoshihara, Ayumu Yoshihara, Kazuo Matsushita, Shizuka Yamashita, Matsuo Ohta, Nobuo Nakajima, Torao Kido, Akio Ohta, Shouji Yamakawa, Iwao Yamamura, Tomeo Nozaki, Tokuji Yamashita, Hiromi Yamaguchi, A Satou, Tomoichi Satou, Youichirou Yamaguchi, Shinji Tasaki, Hotaru Tanaka, Yoshio Furui
(second page) Fumio Ishida, Aki Kobayashi, Furuta

PAGE 161
yukata vs. kimono: *Yukata* are traditional Japanese cotton garments, most often worn for summer festivals or on hot spring visits nowadays. Kimono are traditional Japanese silk garments similar to yukata but usually involving more and warmer layers of clothing. Many modern-day Japanese don't learn how to dress in either *yukata* or kimono, and kimono especially can take a lot of effort to put on with their many pieces, so kimono dresser is a viable profession.

PAGE 162
Japanese summer festival foods: Handa gets to see pretty much all of the common traditional Japanese summer festival foods, on what may well be his first festival visit ever. Here are the ones seen on this page:
takoyaki: Soft savory wheat dumplings made from seasoned batter grilled in a special pan with round indentations, with a piece of octopus (*tako*) inside and topped with light mayonnaise, a brown takoyaki sauce, and shaved dried bonito fish.
yakisoba: Noodles stir-fried with thin-sliced pork, cabbage, onion, and carrot in a savory sauce. Despite the name including the word *soba*, meaning "buckwheat," the noodles used in this dish are actually regular wheat.
corn: Good old corn on the cob, originally imported from North America.

PAGE 164
Goldfish Scooping: A traditional festival stall game. The net part of the scoop is made of tissue paper, so it's very hard to scoop up a fish with it.

PAGE 167
Headmaster's getup: He clearly did at the Balloon Scooping game what Iku did at the Goldfish Scooping game, so let's not comment on his talk of "moderation." Incidentally, Balloon Scooping can use a tissue-paper scoop net similar to with the goldfish, or fragile hooked lines to catch small loops tied to the balloons for even greater difficulty.

PAGE 168
ramune: A sweet soda that comes in a variety of flavors, sold in glass bottles sealed with a marble that rattles in the top part of the bottle after opening, to provide entertainment as well as sustenance.

PAGE 176
fruit flavors: The flavors listed are for syrup added to shaved ice (*kakigoori*). Yes, green tea (*uji/ujicha*) is a common flavor for sweets in Japan. Unclear if the flavor *sukai* (sky) is short for Sky-Blue, a variation of the tropical Blue Hawaii flavor, or a misspelling of *suika* (watermelon).

yakitori: Though essentially pieces of chicken grilled on skewers, there are additional common skewer variations offered at this yakitori stall, including chicken meatballs (*tsukune*), chicken pieces alternating with onion (*negima*),

BARAKAMON

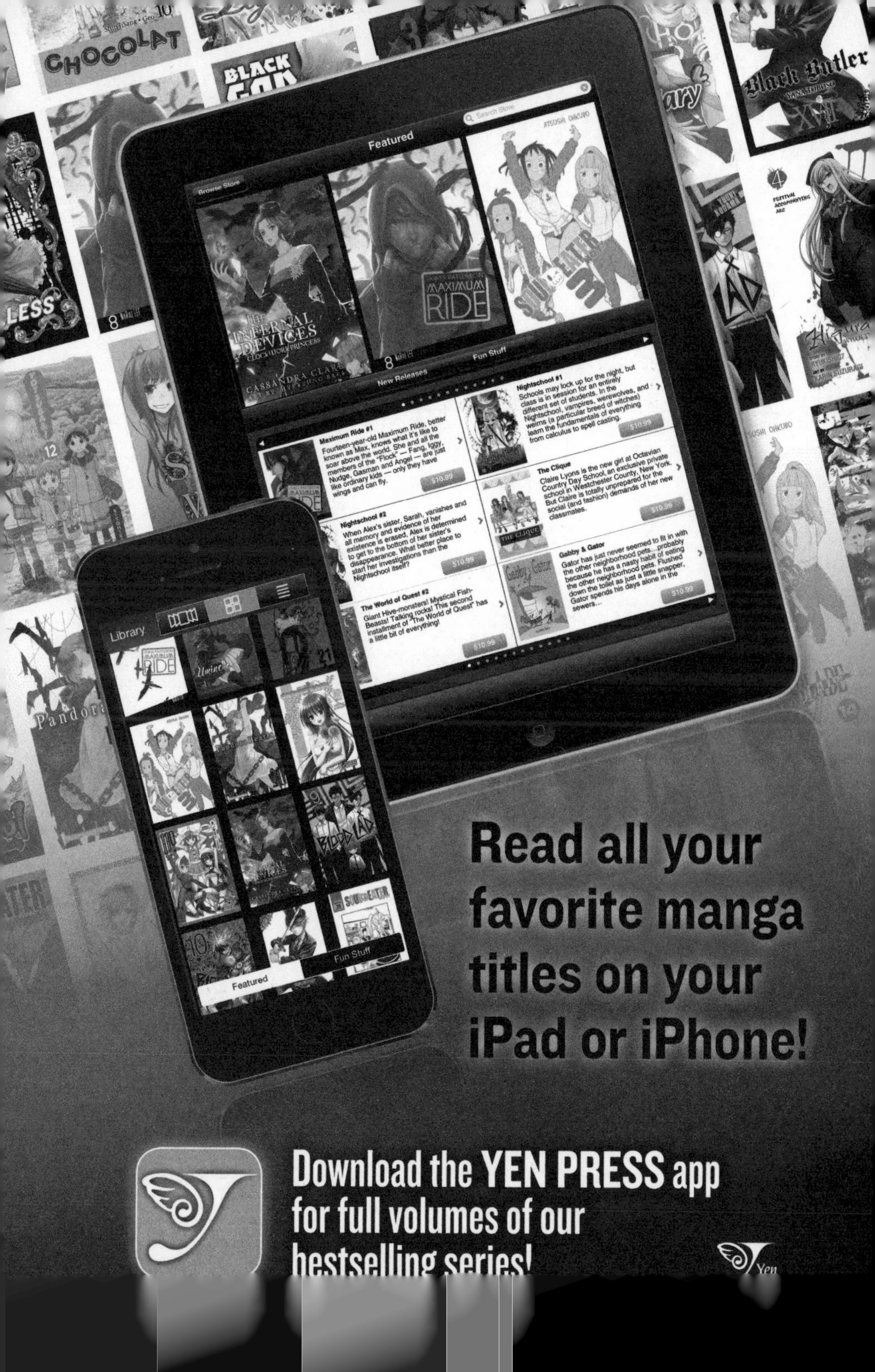
Read all your favorite manga titles on your iPad or iPhone!
Download the YEN PRESS app for full volumes of our bestselling series!
Yen

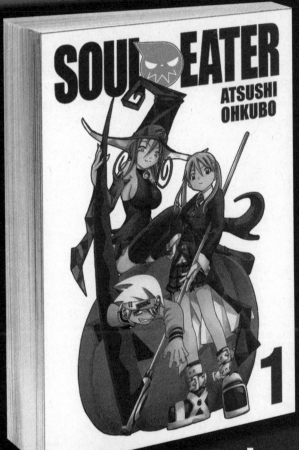

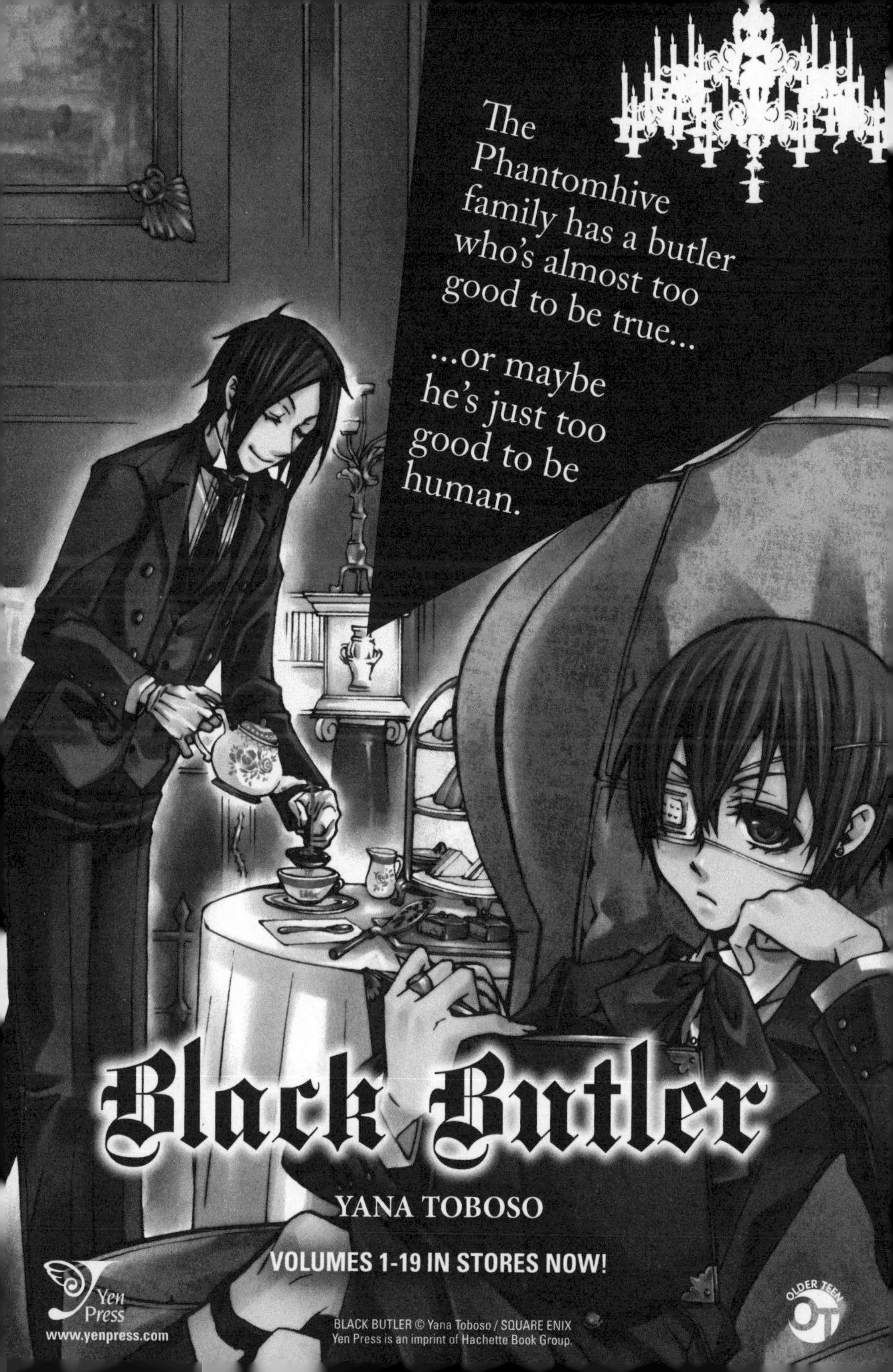
The Phantomhive family has a butler who's almost too good to be true...
...or maybe he's just too good to be human.
Black Butler
YANA TOBOSO
VOLUMES 1-19 IN STORES NOW!
Yen Press
www.yenpress.com
BLACK BUTLER © Yana Toboso / SQUARE ENIX
Yen Press is an imprint of Hachette Book Group.
OLDER TEEN
OT

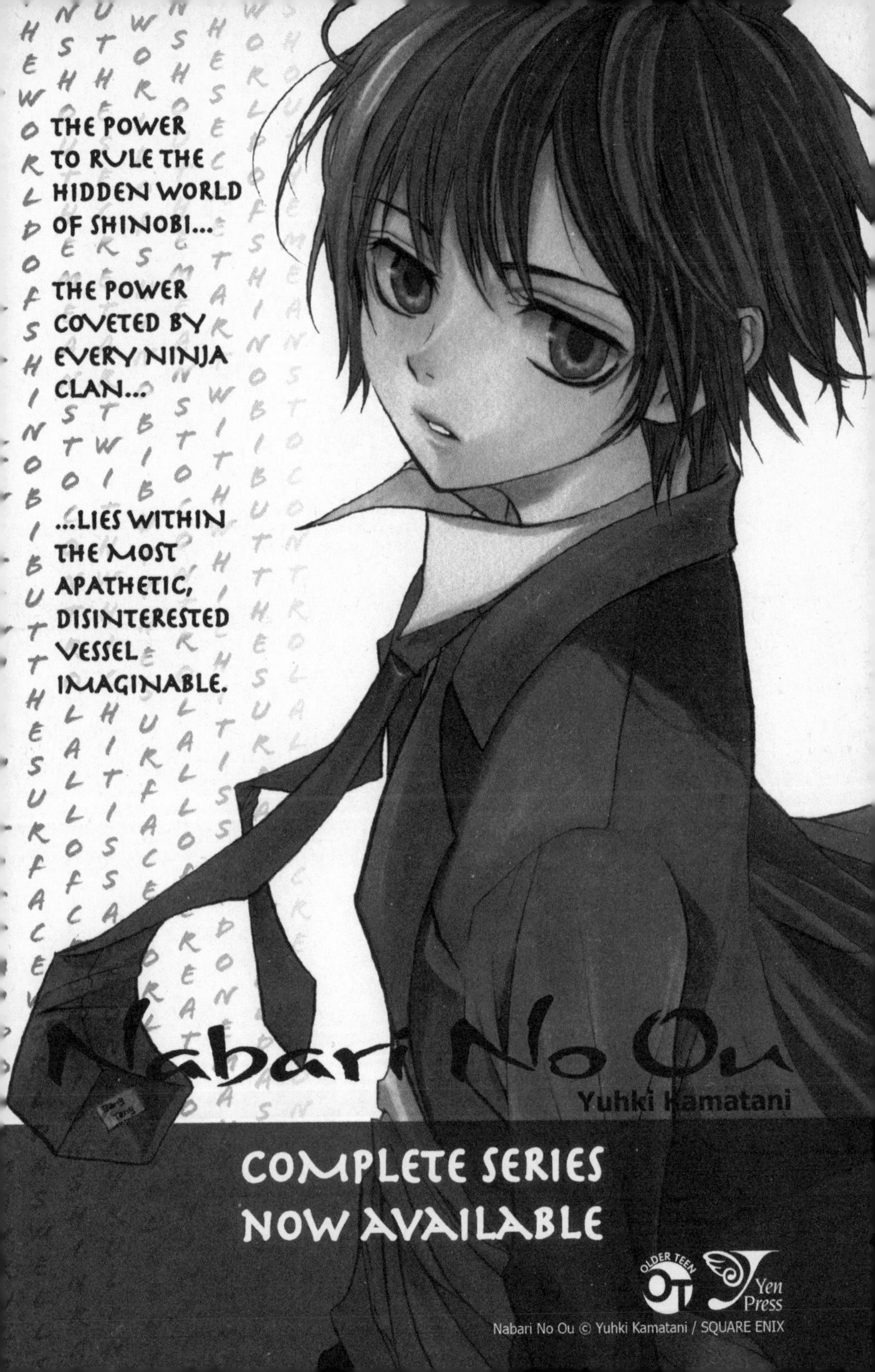
THE POWER TO RULE THE HIDDEN WORLD OF SHINOBI...
THE POWER COVETED BY EVERY NINJA CLAN...
...LIES WITHIN THE MOST APATHETIC, DISINTERESTED VESSEL IMAGINABLE.
Nabari No Ou
Yuhki Kamatani
COMPLETE SERIES NOW AVAILABLE
OLDER TEEN OT
Yen Press
Nabari No Ou © Yuhki Kamatani / SQUARE ENIX

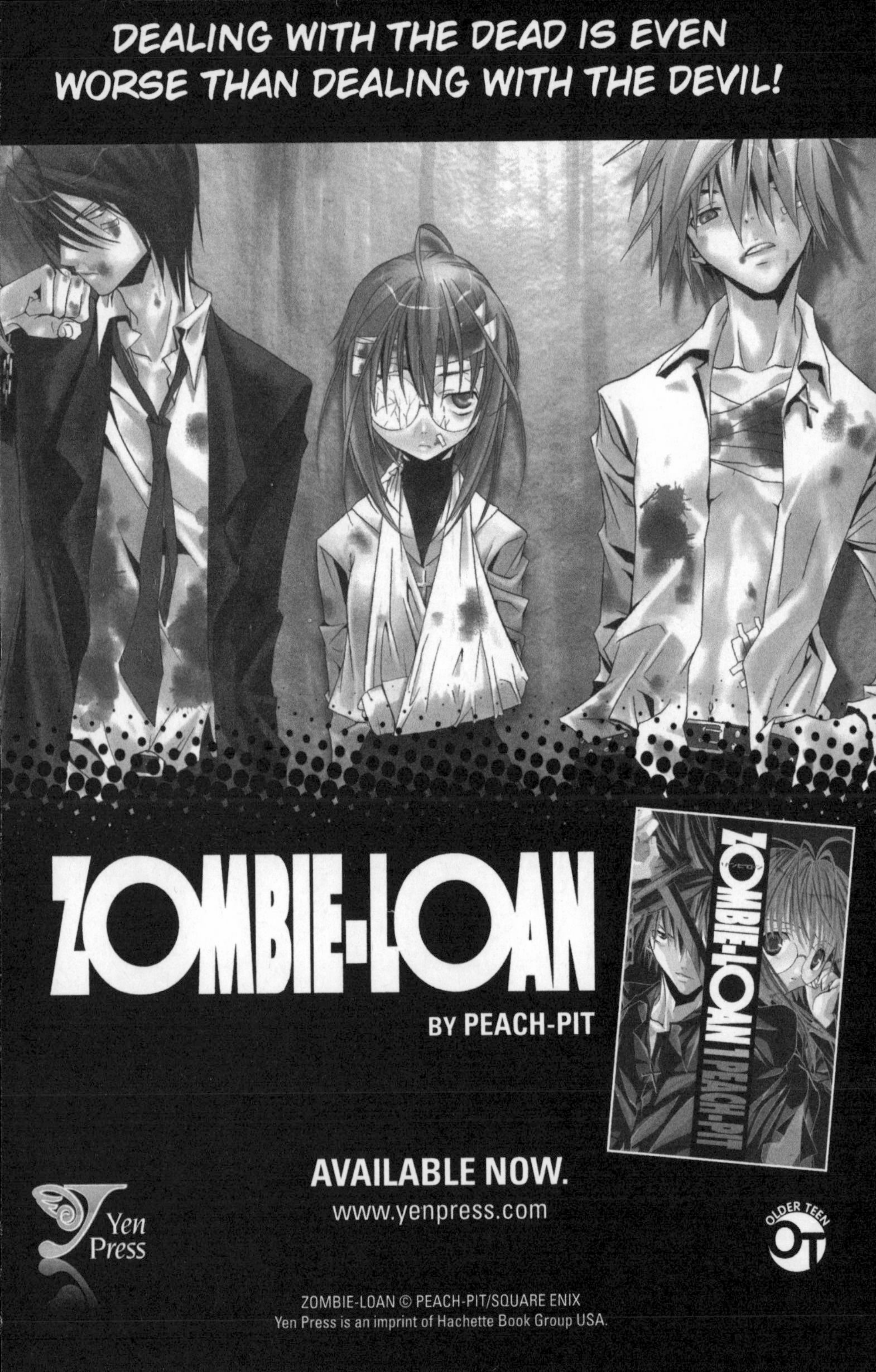
DEALING WITH THE DEAD IS EVEN WORSE THAN DEALING WITH THE DEVIL!
ZOMBIE-LOAN
BY PEACH-PIT
ZOMBIE-LOAN 1 PEACH-PIT
AVAILABLE NOW.
www.yenpress.com
Yen Press
OLDER TEEN
OT
ZOMBIE-LOAN © PEACH-PIT/SQUARE ENIX
Yen Press is an imprint of Hachette Book Group USA.

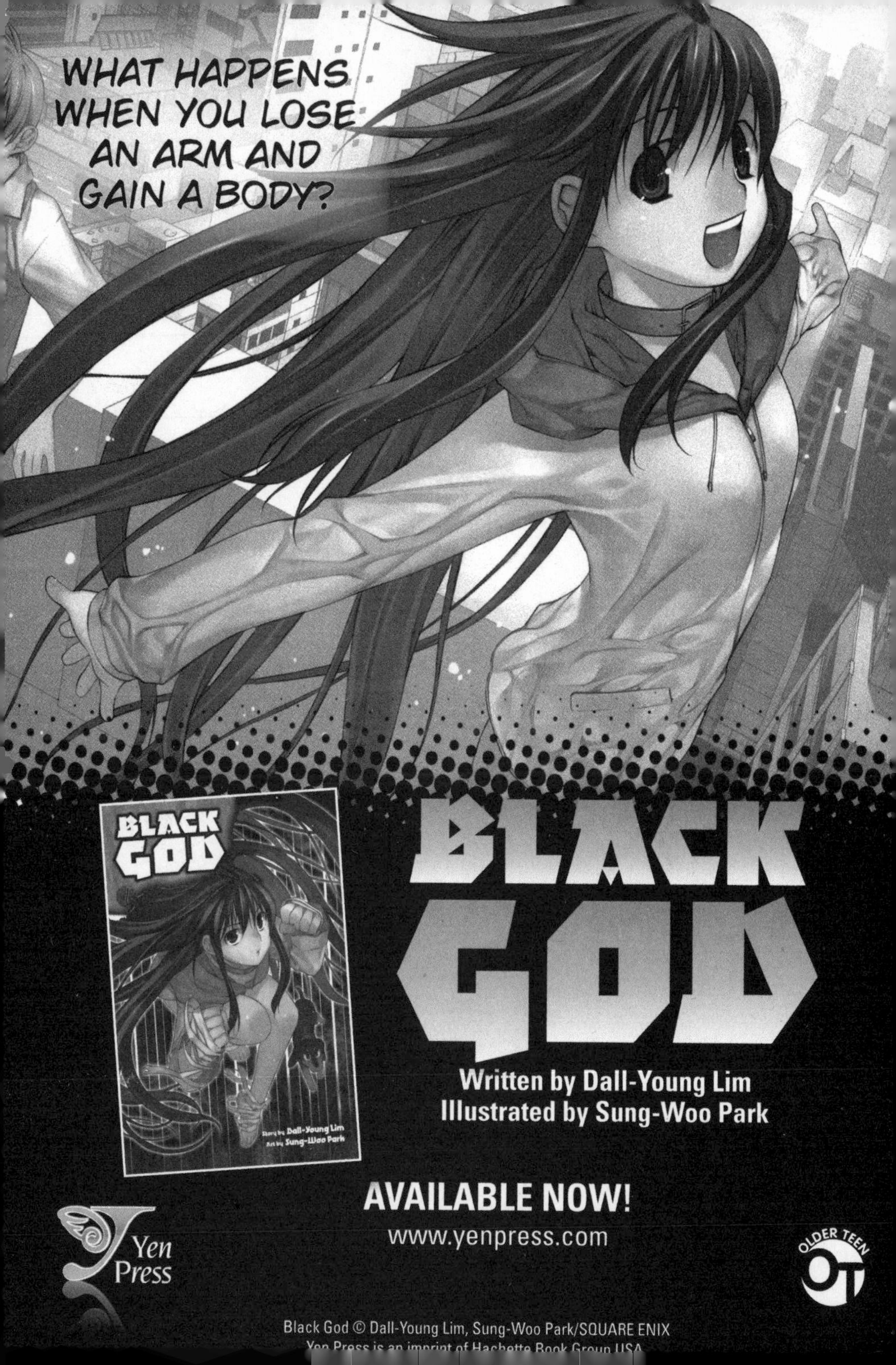
WHAT HAPPENS WHEN YOU LOSE AN ARM AND GAIN A BODY?
BLACK GOD
Story by Dall-Young Lim
Art by Sung-Woo Park
BLACK GOD
Written by Dall-Young Lim
Illustrated by Sung-Woo Park
AVAILABLE NOW!
www.yenpress.com
Yen Press
OLDER TEEN
OT
Black God © Dall-Young Lim, Sung-Woo Park/SQUARE ENIX
Yen Press is an imprint of Hachette Book Group USA

Hello! This is YOTSUBA!

Guess what? Guess what?
Yotsuba and Daddy just moved here
from waaaay over there!

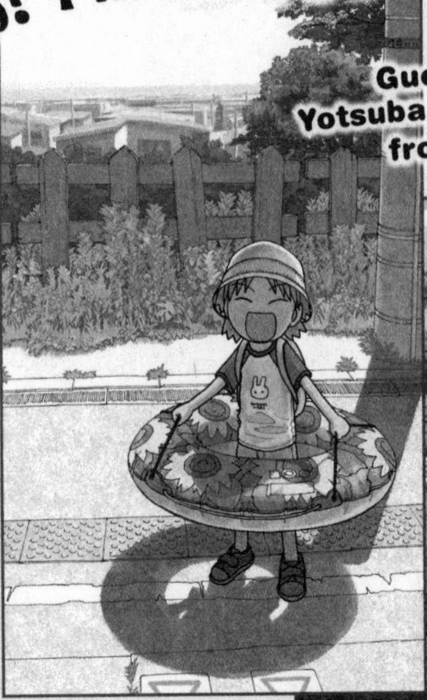

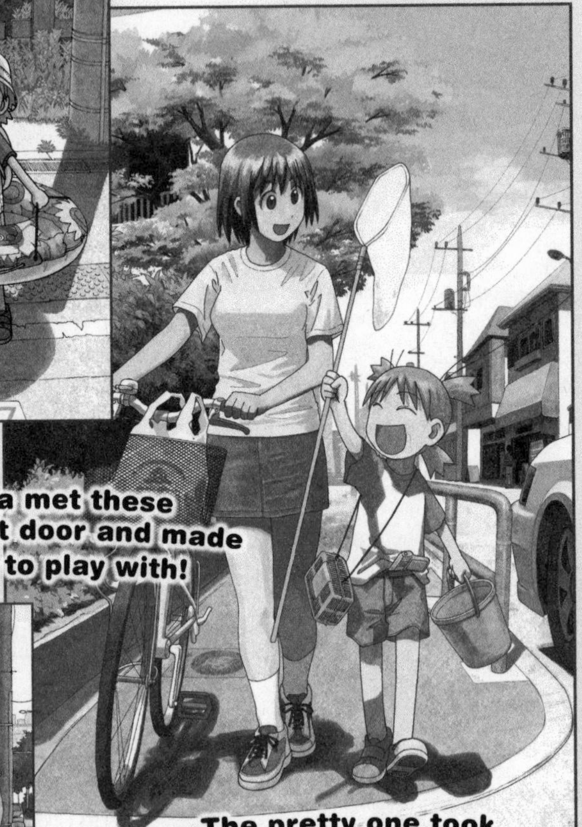

And Yotsuba met these
nice people next door and made
new friends to play with!

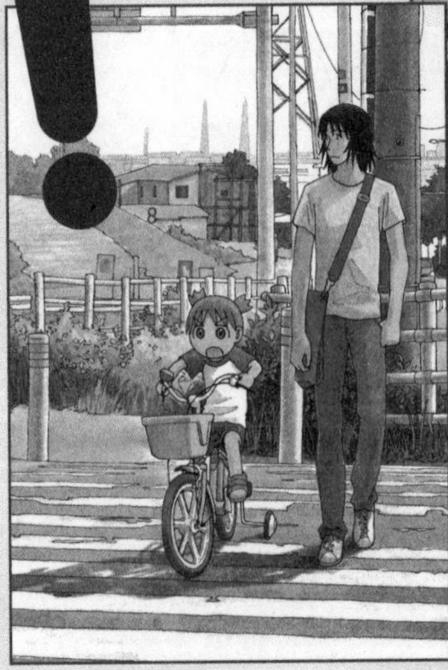

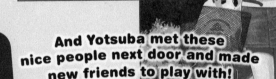

The pretty one took
Yotsuba on a bike ride!
(Whoooa! There was a big hill!)

And Ena's a good drawer!
(Almost as good as Yotsuba!)

And their mom always
gives Yotsuba ice cream!
(Yummy!)

And...
And...
OHHHH!

THE NEW YORK TIMES BESTSELLING SERIES

Nightschool

WHERE DO DEMONS GET THEIR DIPLOMAS?

Schools may lock up for the night, but class is in session for an entirely different set of students. In the Nightschool, vampires, werewolves, and weirns (a particular breed of witches) learn the fundamentals of everything from calculus to spell casting. Alex is a young weirn whose education has always been handled through homeschooling, but circumstances seem to be drawing her closer to the nightschool. Will Alex manage to weather the dark forces gathering?

VOLUMES 1-4 AVAILABLE NOW

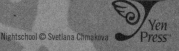

Yen Press

Nightschool © Svetlana Chmakova

SATSUKI YOSHINO

Translation/Adaptation: Krista Shipley, Karie Shipley
Lettering: Lys Blakeslee

This book is a work of fiction. Names, characters, places, and incidents are the product of the author's imagination or are used fictitiously. Any resemblance to actual events, locales, or persons, living or dead, is coincidental.

Barakamon vol. 5 © 2011 Satsuki Yoshino / SQUARE ENIX CO., LTD. First published in Japan in 2011 by SQUARE ENIX CO., LTD. English translation rights arranged with SQUARE ENIX CO., LTD. and Hachette Book Group through Tuttle-Mori Agency, Inc.

Translation © 2015 by SQUARE ENIX CO., LTD.

Yen Press
Hachette Book Group
1290 Avenue of the Americas
New York, NY 10104

www.HachetteBookGroup.com
www.YenPress.com

Yen Press is an imprint of Hachette Book Group, Inc.
The Yen Press name and logo are trademarks of Hachette Book Group, Inc.

The publisher is not responsible for websites (or their content) that are not owned by the publisher.

First Yen Press Edition: June 2015

ISBN: 978-0-316-34031-1

10 9 8 7 6 5 4 3 2 1

BVG

Printed in the United States of America